MW00629787

Latinos and the
Voting Rights Act

Latinos and the Voting Rights Act

The Search for Racial Purpose

Henry Flores

LEXINGTON BOOKS
Lanham • Boulder • New York • London

Published by Lexington Books
An imprint of The Rowman & Littlefield Publishing Group, Inc.
4501 Forbes Boulevard, Suite 200, Lanham, Maryland 20706
www.rowman.com

Unit A, Whitacre Mews, 26-34 Stannary Street, London SE11 4AB

British Library Cataloguing in Publication Information Available

Library of Congress Cataloging-in-Publication Data

Flores, Henry, author.
  Latinos and the Voting Rights Act : the search for racial purpose / Henry Flores.
      pages cm
  Includes bibliographical references and index.
  ISBN 978-0-7391-9045-6 (cloth) — ISBN 978-0-7391-9046-3 (electronic) 1.
Apportionment (Election law)—Texas. 2. Hispanic Americans—Legal status, laws,
etc.—Texas. 3. United States. Voting Rights Act of 1965. 4. United States. Congress.
House—Election districts. 5. Voter registration—United States. 6. Minorities—
Suffrage—United States. 7. Election districts—Texas. I. Title.
  KFT1620.85.A6F56 2015
  342.764'072—dc23
                                                                                      2015000317

∞™ The paper used in this publication meets the minimum requirements of
American National Standard for Information Sciences—Permanence of Paper
for Printed Library Materials, ANSI/NISO Z39.48-1992.

Printed in the United States of America

To Gwen

Contents

Acknowledgments

It goes without saying that any writing project, although a solitary journey for the author, is not possible without the support of others. Had Ms. Nina Perales, Vice-President of Litigation for the Mexican American Legal Defense and Educational Fund, not offered me the opportunity to serve as the "racial purpose or intent" expert in both the Texas Redistricting and Voter Identification Card trials I would not have had a front-row seat for the goings and comings of the trial nor would I have had access to the many documents required to substantiate many of my observations. Also, I would like to thank Mr. Earnest Herrera, MALDEF Staff Attorney and assistant to Ms. Perales, for assisting me with some of the graphics used in various chapters throughout this volume. Additionally, I wish to acknowledge the advice and counsel I received from my wife and colleague, Dr. Gwendolyn Díaz, who endured my oral readings of various chapters. This work is much better because of her observations and comments. Finally, I wish to thank St. Mary's University for the support they provided in allowing me the time to conduct the research required to produce the papers that gave birth to this book and for the sabbatical that gave me the time to finish the manuscript in a timely fashion.

Introduction

After more than thirty years of civil rights activism at various levels and almost thirty years as a litigation expert witness in voting rights cases I have reached several conclusions concerning why American culture and politics cannot leave behind the ugly mantle of racism. One conclusion I reached is that racism, a product of socialization and historical relations among the population of any given jurisdiction, masks the struggle for political control over that jurisdiction. Simultaneously, the political struggle obscures racism within those same communities. The most recent iteration of the question arose in the aftermath of my experiences as an expert witness in the 2011–2014 Texas Congressional and House Redistricting[1] and the 2012 Texas Voter Identification lawsuits. The redistricting trial was a challenge by the Texas Latino Redistricting Task Force and others to the manner in which the state legislature conducted the redistricting of both chambers during the 2011 session. The second trial was over a constitutional challenge by the State of Texas to the denial of preclearance, under Section 5 of the Voting Rights Act of 1965, to the Voter Identification Law or Senate Bill 14 passed by the state assembly and signed by the governor in 2011.

I was asked by the attorney of record to serve on both trial teams as a Section 5 witness.[2] I had always been a Section 2[3] witness testifying to the racially polarized nature of elections in redistricting cases. The lawyer I worked with specifically requested that I serve as the witness regarding "the racially discriminatory purpose" behind the passage of both the redistricting plans and the Voter ID law. I responded that I had never conducted research of this nature before; consequently I wasn't sure where to begin. She directed me to consult the United States Supreme Court (SCOTUS) decision issued in 1977 *Village of Arlington Heights v. Metropolitan Housing Development Corp (429 US 252)*.

In *Arlington Heights*[4] the Supreme Court ruled that a government's action will not be ruled discriminatory simply because "it results in a racially disproportionate impact." If the plaintiffs wished to have the court rule a governmental action discriminatory, they were required to show that the government acted with "racially discriminatory intent or purpose." Then the court presented a road map that a plaintiff could pursue to show that the government had acted with a racially discriminatory purpose but pointed out that since the plaintiffs had not presented such evidence, it could not rule in their favor. The directions SCOTUS gave in *Arlington Heights* provided the only clue I had available to prepare for trial.

Nevertheless, as I began preparation for both trials, it became evident that the issue of why race was fundamental to the cases was compounded by an interesting pattern I saw unfolding in the evidence I was organizing. During the preparation for the first trial, redistricting, e-mail communications obtained through a subpoena during the Sec. 5 preclearance hearing uncovered direct evidence of racial intent. As I searched records of Texas House and Senate journals, depositions, memos, e-mail, and all documents pertinent to the Voter ID case a different picture emerged. The documentary evidence in the latter case found a complete lack of discussion concerning race. The Texas assembly had passed Voter ID by consciously avoiding any reference to race, even when pressed by minority members of their body. Some of the discussions and attempts at debating the issue of whether the Voter ID law was racially discriminatory or violated federal laws, particularly the Voting Rights Act of 1965, were amusing but sad. The debates were amusing because the day in question was filled with legislative debate that appeared more like amateurish theatrics. At the same time the debate was sad because it revealed the extent of racial hatred that existed in the hearts and minds of many state legislators. Additionally, the substance of the debate demonstrated a concerted effort to unravel the constitutional protections guaranteeing the voting rights of millions of Latinos and African Americans. All attempts at pointing out avoidance tactics were either ignored by the legislative leadership and the issue was tabled or brusquely denied and parliamentary rules used to end debate.[5] In every instance I document these attempts at legislative obfuscation at the appropriate place within this volume.

After a matter of time I realized that not only was I beginning a type of research effort in both cases I had never before attempted, but it also appeared that I might have to create an entire new methodological technique to perform my research. I was confronted by a difficult and complex problem in one case: I concluded that "race" was the principal variable used by the legislature to compose and pass the Voter ID law yet legislators never referred to race in their arguments. So, the research question became "how does one prove that race is the principal variable in a decisional process where race is not mentioned or intentionally avoided or hidden?" Essentially, I was confronted with two questions. The first: Why is race such a vital element in the writing and structuring of the Voter ID Law in Texas? The second: What methodological approach is appropriate for investigating a research question where an important variable is missing? I attempt to answer both questions in this book.

The search for the answers to both questions is pursued by comparing and contrasting the manner in which the proof for racial purpose was sought in both cases. The most important contrast between both cases was that a "smoking gun" e-mail was discovered in the redistricting case revealing the intent of the redistricters to manipulate Latino voters in such a way as to make it appear that the requirements of the VRA were not violated while at the same time ensuring the creation of congressional districts that would return Republican incumbents to office. There was no "smoking gun" uncovered in the voter identification lawsuit because the method of presenting evidence differed from that used during redistricting. In the voter identification case the methodology focused on how the language describing the goals of the law changed historically. The rhetoric began by seeking to create a voter identification law to prevent "illegal immigrants" from casting a vote and evolved into one where the goal was to "protect the integrity and security of the ballot." Although the rhetoric changed, the actual law's structure did not.

THE RACIAL ISSUE

The beginning of the explanation as to why race is so deeply embedded in the American public policy process varies depending on the perception of the person or group. The relationship between race and the American political system, however, appears to predate the founding of this country. It is a story of unknown origins, but it appears to have been born whenever the institution of slavery began. The institutionalization of slavery gave birth to the development of a rationale for seeing and treating some humans as lesser than others.[6] Nevertheless, slavery was and is not a uniquely American institution; it most likely predates written history. Regardless, slavery was imported to America by the Spaniards, Portuguese, and English and designed as a colonial weapon to enrich some and dominate others.

I don't wish to delve into ancient history because I am not a historian, but I do wish to point out that with slavery came racism as a rationale for that institution.[7] I have tried to trace the historical origins of racism and have come to the conclusion that it is a social construct. This I do in chapter 3. All attempts at defining racism biologically are efforts at lending scientific legitimation to a subjectively constructed concept. Racism gave dominators the rationale to dominate. Racism gave those in power more power. Essentially, racism was a socially constructed excuse used by some to subordinate others for political and economic gain.

Essentially racism, as a socially constructed concept, is used as an excuse for taking an action or making a specific social decision. From the sixteenth through the nineteenth centuries racism was used as a *raison d'être* for the maintenance of a slavery system in the United States. African Americans could be kept in servitude because they were considered to be less than whites because of their race. Slavery produced a cheap and plentiful labor supply that formed the core of the agricultural economy in America at the dawn of the industrial revolution. Defining African Americans as "less than" whites also required whites to be defined as superior. According to some scholars the concept of "whiteness" did not appear in American social history until some-time within the seventeenth century.[8] The British and Germans developed and propagated the notion that "white" was good, superior, and "black" was the opposite.[9] These perceptions, when applied to the social definition of a group of people, provided the rationale as to why one group could enslave another, why one group could pass laws controlling another, and why one group could write laws condoning crude domination.

Racism, in the American tradition, found its way into the worlds of science, religion, and education, and eventually into the public policy arena.[10] Various historians have pointed out that racism tinged the constitution as well as local laws in many realms of public life. Race has been and is at the center of many of our laws governing public education, political representation, voting, public health, land use, and so forth. At the beginning of the republic, race was used explicitly to make laws. As laws and customs became institutionalized and regularized, the explicitness of race disappeared or, at least, took on a different color or tenor. In the current historical era, race is *implied* (rather than openly stated) when the law is discussed or debated and other language, a different rhetoric, is used to hide racism from the public policy realm. Presently, people of color, who have been the traditional victims of racism, are referred to in a veiled manner rather than in the traditional sense. Instead of overtly racial terms such as "black," "Mexican," "Indian," or "Oriental," other labels are used such as "immigrants," "illegal aliens," or "non-English speakers." Racial rhetoric has changed, in the public policy arena, from the overt to the less than explicit since the early nineteenth century to avoid any charges of racism being leveled at decision makers. The "new" racial rhetoric is now held up partially substantiating the false notion that the United States has become a "color-blind" society and we have evolved into a "post-racial" era.

It is not a unique observation that attitudes, perceptions, opinions, and behaviors are institutionalized into a political system as well as the structure that upholds that system. A plethora of literature abounds demonstrating this phenomenon. Conceptually, racism is an essential thread in America's political and cultural tapestry. It is just one of the many value-laden concepts that have become institutionalized within the American cultural superstructure. Other examples of these concepts include "equality," "fair play," "fudging," and so forth. A complete list would be endless; regardless, these concepts, in their totality, make up the American ideological framework. This framework allows all societal members, whether elected officials, citizens, all individuals residing within the cultural parameters of America, to see a social, economic, or political reality and interpret it a certain way. This interpretation passes from one generation to another through society's normal socialization mechanisms.[11] Eventually, those who become lawmakers take their biases with them, bringing them to bear in the public policy process. The biases assist lawmakers in identifying and interpreting problems and issues and are at the core of how and why a lawmaker proposes solutions to any given problem.[12]

Racism, however, is more complex. It is not simply an attitude or opinion about a group of people; it defines a power relationship between groups and individuals in control of the state apparatus and those subject to and not in control of the same apparatus. The use of race as a justification of why a law or policy must be written or worded or defined a particular way is one manner, and a most important and powerful one, in which political power can be manipulated in a political system.[13]

At a certain point in the evolution of the state racism is used explicitly to control access to the political system, for instance, when African Americans were denied the franchise at the founding of the United States. This general attitude toward African Americans was transferred to other groups as they became incorporated into the American cultural and political landscape, including Native Americans, Asians, and Latinos. In each of these cases, however, racism defined the relationship between dominators and the dominated, assigning them different political values. The values were determined by the manner in which each group was incorporated into American society whether by conquest, treaty, or specific immigration law. The definition of a relationship of domination changes from one historical era to another, and this is manifested primarily through the use of signifiers utilized by the dominators when presenting their rationale for a particular public policy decision. For instance, in the current development of voter identification laws throughout the United States, those proposing the laws sometimes justify their position by stating that the laws are to deter fraudulent voting on the part of illegal immigrants. Unpacking this statement allows one to uncover both the presuppositions and intent of the statement.

The presuppositions, assumptions if you will, of voter fraud allegations simply are that there is a great deal of fraudulent voting occurring, and it is perpetrated by illegal immigrants. The Texas legislature determined that the way to control fraudulent voting was to write a law specifically targeting illegal immigrants rather than a law specifically oriented to restrict potential acts of fraudulent voting. The Brennan Center for Justice at New York University School of Law has concluded that in-person voter fraud barely exists in the United States and does not pose any threat to the integrity of the election system.[14] Fundamentally, the fallacy in the state's rationale for supporting the Voter ID law is obvious: individuals who are not authorized to be in the United States cannot vote. More importantly, one should ask the question as to why would anyone living in the United States illegally risk jail or deportation just to cast a vote in any election? A person without documentation generally would be denied the ballot; however, if allowed to vote provisionally, the vote would be cast out when that individual did not or could not produce appropriate identification when required. In the event that an individual were to submit illegal documentation, it would be caught almost immediately because the information on the provisional ballot would not match the information in the registration database. In the end, it violates logic that someone not legally authorized to be inside the United States would risk family, work, and their way of life simply to cast a vote in an election they may or may not care about, understand, or have little interest in. Frankly, undocumented immigrants follow all laws meticulously; otherwise they risk imprisonment, deportation, or both. Subsequent research indicates that undocumented immigrant communities have lower crime rates than other social groups. Additionally, there is no evidence that undocumented immigrants take undue advantage of the social service networks in the United States. Finally, the courts have long since ruled that undocumented communities pay taxes of all categories including property, sales, and income.[15] In short, undocumented immigrants do everything possible to remain undetected on a daily basis.

The claims by those supporting Voter ID laws, as a deterrent against voter fraud perpetrated by undocumented individuals, speak to the fearmongering and xenophobic rantings that "nativists" have used throughout the history of the United States to garner support for their political agendas. The fear that illegal immigrants will enter this country and cast enough ballots to threaten the very way of life and culture in the United States resonates with those sharing racist sympathies or who are ignorant of the truth. The term *illegal immigrants* and the even more derogatory *illegal aliens* carry additional weight within American political culture. Behind these terms is the imagery of waves of Latin American, Spanish-speaking, and dark-skinned people invading the United States and dramatically dismantling or changing the mythical American Dream. The same racial fear that drove Americans to pass laws governing the political access of African Americans in the nineteenth and twentieth centuries is the political accelerant behind the passage of laws preventing Latinos from political participation in the twentieth and twenty-first centuries.

The political reality, however, is that nativist apologists are simply diluting the voting power of those who will not vote for the candidates that support nativist legislation. When the voter identification laws are said to prevent votes cast by individuals who are in the United States without appropriate documentation, in reality the dominators are using this rhetoric as a racial shield to mask their real motive: to deny the vote to Latinos. Racism, then, plays a dual role. It allows policy makers to maintain social control over groups defined as "less" while simultaneously maintaining control over the political apparatus. As I indicated at the beginning of this discussion, one of the main reasons for this book is to point out that "race" is an essential, if not the main, element in the construction of the Texas Voter ID law and the Congressional and state house redistricting plans passed in the 2011 state legislative session. In the redistricting lawsuit the redistricters insisted that race was not a variable considered in drawing the lines for Congressional Districts 23 and 27. This refusal however was handicapped by the revelation of e-mail communications between and among redistricters indicating that Latino voters were to be manipulated in such a manner as to give the appearance that the districts remained majority Latino keeping in the spirit of the VRA. Simultaneously, the majority Latino districts were to be reconfigured so that the Latino voters included in the new districts were low-performing voters thus allowing themselves to be overwhelmed at the ballot box by the Anglo minority. This situation would guarantee the reelection of Republican incumbents. Although the State of Texas and various political actors who participated in the composition of the law deny that there was any racial purpose behind the law, I contend they were being less than forthright.

THE METHODOLOGICAL ISSUE

The second question raised in this work is "What methodological approach is appropriate for investigating a research question where an important variable is missing?" Ideally, when one attempts to conduct any traditional research effort, one lays out the design at the beginning of the project identifying the rationale for the research, the variables in question, and then proceeds with the different stages of operationalization, data gathering, and so forth.

Of course, hypothesis construction and testing can play a role here as well, depending on the type of data and research. When doing historical research, whether on a topic many centuries old or on a situation that occurred in the recent past, identifying all of the appropriate variables may prove difficult. As a matter of course, uncovering the missing variable is generally what historians do because the fact that an important variable is missing from the analysis may not be evident until after the first complete set of preliminary findings are produced or the project is replicated many years later. This is especially true at the initial stages of primary, foundational, or experimental research where one pursues discovery of new variables.

In the Voter ID case one rationale for assuming that race was an important consideration was the extent to which legislators attempted to avoid discussion of race or racism during their deliberations. These avoidance efforts were most evident in the March 23, 2011 House Journal.[16] Nevertheless, to ensure that this research possesses a good and stringent design, the assumption that racism or racial purpose was present throughout the deliberations can act as a guiding research hypothesis that can in turn be tested with my findings. How to substantiate the observation or suspicion becomes the next question.

PLAN OF THE BOOK

The initial chapter, "Uncovering Racial Purpose in Voting Rights Politics," discusses the importance of this research to the academy, the legal community, and the public. The chapter sets the stage both politically and, to a certain extent, legally for the passage and continuing approval of the Voting Rights Act of 1965 and its subsequent amendments. The chapter begins with a presentation of what Sections 2, 3, 4, and 5 of the VRA say, why they are written the way they are, under what circumstances they are applied, and a general history of their approval. The narrative moves then to a discussion of the constitutional history of Section 5 and its current status. Here, a close look is taken at *Shelby County, AL v. Eric Holder, et al., 570 US ___ (2013)* where SCOTUS found the Section 4 (b) provisions of the VRA unconstitutional. The result was that the VRA was left with the Section 5 "preclearance" provision but lacked the standards under which a jurisdiction would come under the provision. This opinion generally gutted the enforcement powers of the VRA.

This volume focuses on the concept of "racially discriminatory purpose," which has never been the subject of a SCOTUS decision or any federal court to date. The legal roots of racial purpose are traced from their inception by looking at the historical relationship between the concepts of "states' rights" and the Supreme Court's position on the Tenth Amendment to the Constitution. This discussion is essential to an understanding of the State of Texas's argument in the redistricting lawsuit because a crucial element in the state's appellate brief was that the federal court's intervention in the redistricting process was an overly intrusive federal action into a state's privileged and constitutionally protected function. This Tenth Amendment claim was parroted by nine other states who submitted *amicus* briefs. However, a textual analysis of the briefs raises the question of just "What is it that the states are really appealing?" Tracing the historical relation between racial purpose and intent and "states' rights," "states' sovereignty," "equal sovereignty of all states," and "traditional Federalism," reveals the answer to all Section 5 challenges historically and against the VRA generally. Here the concept of a "racial shield" is first introduced because using the Tenth Amendment or any reference to "states' rights" clearly is a shield concealing acting with racial intent or purpose. All Section 5 cases, and there are very few, turn entirely on the effect prong, which is relatively easy to test. Generally, the preclearance process, which will also be discussed in this chapter, looks primarily at the effect standard when the Department of Justice (DOJ) or the United States District Court of the District of Columbia (DCDC) are deliberating Section 5 submissions. Racially discriminatory purpose is easy to show if there is direct evidence of its existence in the form of clear statements by policy makers or written documentation such as in the redistricting case. The lack of clear statements, however, is usually the current norm. Most policy makers do not and will not make racially discriminatory statements publicly due to their awareness of possible litigation. As a result, "racially discriminatory purpose" is usually veiled in "racial code words" or "shields" to insulate against civil rights litigation. A brief history of the number of times any jurisdiction in Texas has been sued under the VRA and why the suspicion arose that behind Texas Voter ID lurked a "racially discriminatory purpose" forms the core of the discussion in this chapter.

The second chapter, "In Search of Racism," presents the research questions, both primary and subsidiary, and discusses the *Arlington Heights* Factors.[17] Principal to this discussion is the identification of what the research design looks like and what variables are included in the model. Complementing this presentation is a discussion of how the variables are operationalized and the quantity and quality of the information required substantiating each variable.

Here a methodological note is in order. As the discussion in this chapter unfolds, it will become abundantly clear that some of the major research categories containing the model's variables overlap substantively and require the utilization of a combination of methods to gather and organize data. Truth be told, the nature of the basic research question requires the application of various methodological techniques taken from both quantitative and qualitative worlds. Although there has been criticism of a *mixed-methods* approach, which will be addressed in this chapter as well, the one utilized here is designed narratively without placing more weight on either empirical or normative methods incorporating each where appropriate. Regardless of the criticism of mixed-methods approaches, the model presented here is designed as a narrative because it is designed to tell a story, "paint a picture," if you will, of how racial purpose becomes institutionalized to the extent that it does not need to be mentioned explicitly to affect the substance of public policy. Here a discussion of the "political layers" within which a decision maker functions is set forth. These layers act as "selective mechanisms" that either exclude or include information or data for use in the creation of the specific policy at hand. As a result, the design utilized here places equal weight on quantitative as well as qualitative methods. Essentially, the technique appropriate for each research phase, following the Court's guidance in *Arlington Heights*, is applied and used sometimes in combination, sometimes solely. SCOTUS has provided guidance in its opinion in the *Arlington Heights* case that will be presented here as well as my interpretation of what data fit the Court's wishes. The data and narrative that follow in the subsequent chapters are designed to follow the SCOTUS road map set forth in *Arlington Heights*.

The exploration of racism is the subject of the third chapter, entitled "Racism, the *Arlington Heights* Factors, and Latinos." The discussion here will begin with identifying the origins of racism generally, how it found its way to the United States of America, and then how it became a thread in the tapestry of Texan culture. Research contributing to this chapter is drawn from the worlds of cultural and historical anthropology, including the works of Thomas F. Gossett, Ashley Montagu, George M. Fredrickson, Kenan Malik, Stefan Kühl, K. Anthony Appiah, Amy Gutmann, Michel Wieviorka, Joel Olson, Mab Segrest, and Pat Shipman. This chapter speaks to racism as an ideology allowing those who are racists to define the social and political place of groups within their society. In the political arena, using race when writing public policy is important because it allows those anchored in racism to maintain the cultural and political status quo. This chapter also introduces the reader to the concepts of "negative and positive discrimination." One excludes individuals because of who they are with no rationale; the other is selectively inclusive because the individuals have been excluded historically from participation. Essential to this discussion is the rise of scientific racism and how it became a tool in the rationalization for negatively discriminating against African Americans and Latinos. This discussion leads the reader into that of the next chapter.

Chapter 4 speaks to the notion that race has been at the forefront of Texas political history since the founding of the Texas Republic. This chapter,

"Latino Identity, Whiteness and Dual-Race Theory," reflects the essence of racism in the state's history. The history set forth in this chapter is not comprehensive or primary but based upon research that has already been conducted by scholars such as David Montejano, Mario Garcia, Alfredo Mirandé, Andres Tijerina, and Rudy Acuña, to mention but a few.[18] The discussion in this chapter lends emphasis to the fact that racism against Latinos has been an essential element in the structural relations between Anglos and Latinos since they first encountered each other in the early nineteenth century. The discussion in this chapter is designed to demonstrate that race is an important and defining element in the cultural chemistry of the state. This is especially true in the area of election law where the state government has historically passed laws or modifications to laws designed to disenfranchise minority voters generally and Latinos specifically. In the final analysis, that the Texas legislature had a racial purpose for writing the Texas Voter ID Law and constructing its congressional and state house plans is not surprising but in keeping with long-standing cultural and political traditions. Simply stated, when it comes to election law, Texas lawmakers are anchored in the history and culture of racism.

The racial structure in the United States has always been considered biracial, African Americans and whites. A biracial analytical structure is not appropriate for understanding the racial and political situation of Latinos generally or in Texas. One must begin with the issue of our legal and political identity. The two principal factors here are that of our national origin and identity and the historical era during which our particular group was incorporated into the United States. Complicating the issue of our identity are the rapidly changing demographics in the latter half of the twentieth century and the beginning of the twenty-first, resulting in Latinos becoming the largest numerical minority group in the United States. The residential patterns of Latinos at the beginning of the twenty-first century complicate the Electoral College process in Presidential election years, making the Latino vote potentially the most important block in the nation with the prospect of controlling access to the White House.

Traditionally, Latino identity is based on data generated by surveys where individuals select their identity from an array of choices, including national origin, race, ethnicity, and so forth. These data form the core of information used during every redistricting effort at all governmental levels. Nevertheless, these self-identification efforts attempt to tap into how individuals perceive their social essentiality. The choice for the individual represents much more than a simple choice from a list constructed by instrument designers because individuals are limited to the list provided by the Census Bureau. Oftentimes, this leads to confusion and results in responses indicating that a person is of mixed race, or, sometimes the person refuses to answer the question because of the confusing array of choices.[19]

So this is our identity, an identity chosen and crafted by others and only speaking to superficial categories. This level of identity, because that's what it is, only one level of identity, misses our essentiality. Our real identity is political and legal in nature because this level of identity guarantees us political participation and protection under the constitution. Political and legal identity separates full citizenship from partial citizenship. Full citizenship allows one to exercise the franchise almost completely free from manipulation by the state or political actors seeking to maintain control of the state through means beyond the election process. In Texas, Latinos who are citizens have historically had to overcome many political barriers, for instance poll taxes, "white" primaries, gerrymandering, and, now, voter identification, in order to reach the same level of citizenship that "fully white" voters have. Although a Latino may self-identify as "white" according to the choices offered by the Bureau of the Census, Latinos are not "fully white," they are "less than white," and not full citizens because their political and civil rights are constantly under attack and limited by the Texas State government (Olson, 2004). The substance of this chapter, then, draws a distinction and differentiates between the cultural and social identity of Latinos and their political and legal identity.

There are great differences between how Latinos of Mexican origin are treated as opposed to Cuban or Puerto Rican or any other Latinos. On one level, we are defined as Latinos or Hispanics[20] by society in general; on another level we are spoken of as persons of a certain national origin, for instance, Mexican, Puerto Rican, and so forth. Finally we are identified as immigrants regardless of how many generations we have been in the United States. These are all identifiers that we are submitted to, not that we have given ourselves. Self-identity is personal and is made more complex by how society and the state create identifiers for us.

As the identity of Latinos has become clearer, it is apparent that we require constitutional protection in the same social areas as African Americans because both our private and public treatment have been governed by racial preferences. As a famed civil rights attorney made clear to SCOTUS in *Hernandez v. Texas (1954),*[21] we were different because we had been treated differently since the days of and prior to incorporation. Although we were classified as "whites" by the state of Texas, we were treated differently and "less than" whites. I make the argument here that "white" as a social construct is beyond the reach of Latinos until they obtain full political and legal status with other persons in American society classified as "white." The importance of the discussion in chapter 4 is that a historical legacy of the racial treatment of Latinos as different has been evident and part of the traditional legislative decisional process to such an extent that the protections of the VRA were extended to this group in 1974.

Since the 1990 census and reapportionment, however, a great deal of the congressional and state level redistricting has been driven by fear of the potential political power possessed by the Latino community throughout Texas. As depositions, expert reports, and trial transcripts have revealed throughout, all redistricting efforts since *White v. Regester* have been driven by a conscious effort to minimize Latino representation, both substantively and literally, in congressional and state level assembly chambers. The evidence presented in this chapter suggests that although redistricting is a political matter protected by law, the way in which the State of Texas pursues it is racially motivated. Fundamentally, there is a "racial purpose" behind the redistricting process in order to achieve a political gain by those in charge of the process. The manner in which redistricting is decided, written, and implemented in Texas is designed to allow the maintenance of the political status quo and to prevent Latinos from increasing their electoral and subsequent political power in the state.

Two case studies constructed out of the trial transcripts of the redistricting and voter identification trials form the core of chapter 5. The title of this chapter is "Do Citizens Select Legislators or Do Legislators Select Their Constituents?" The title, a rhetorical question muttered by one of the trial judges during the redistricting deliberations, reflected his frustration at both sides given the paradox of the redistricting process. The central contradiction of the process is that the districts are designed to group together individuals to be represented by an elected official. Each district must be relatively equal in population depending on the chamber. The contradiction is that in almost all states, including Texas, the responsibility for redistricting rests in the hands of legislators who will do almost anything to ensure their reelection and control of an elected body by their party. The discussion centers on the trial arguments for both plaintiffs and defendants as seen through the direct and cross-examinations of the attorneys and the testimonies of the expert witnesses. The focus of the discussion in this chapter is to sift through the arguments and evidence presented at trial highlighting the search for racial purpose. Representatives of racial minority groups argue and present evidence of racial purpose and representatives of the State of Texas focus on the adequacy of the evidence and argue that any dilutive effects are circumstantial and unintended. In the end the courts rule that racial purpose was at the heart of the redistricting arguments but avoid the issue completely in the Voter ID decision. In both instances, however, the court rules in favor of the Latino and African American communities. In the voter identification case the court also sided with young, senior, women and low-income voters and against the State of Texas.

Chapter 6, entitled "There is a Method to This Madness," is an evaluation of the methodology, based upon the Supreme Court's guidance in *Arlington Heights*, as an appropriately acceptable research device. The *Arlington Heights* Factors are refined, making data gathering more efficient, and hypotheses are constructed. The racial purpose methodology is evaluated using the traditionally accepted norms of the scientific method. What is clear is that the methodology fits the standards created historically by the academy and is appropriate for application in the search for racial purpose.

Chapter 7, "Strategic Racism Uncovered," serves as the conclusion of this volume and reviews all of the findings. Most importantly, the discussion centers on what has been learned from all of the evidence and testimonies that comprise the empirical substance in *Searching for Racial Purpose.* The chapter speaks to the contributions that the volume makes to jurisprudence, social science methodology, and race theories. The findings speak to what may be helpful to the courts when evaluating evidence produced by experts through the methodology developed in this book when confronted by claims of racial purpose. Most importantly, the chapter's discussion offers a response to the question raised by one of the judges that lies at the heart of why it is so difficult to reach a decision on racial purpose. The judge asked whether when people vote they are casting a racial or political vote and whether the redistricters were acting as partisans or were they acting with racial purpose? This question, this "Gordian Knot," is addressed in this chapter.

The complexity of the problem identifying racial purpose in the deliberative process is caused because of the use of "racial shields" by decision makers. These shields make a decision appear political when in reality it is racial; the decision has a racial purpose hidden by the racial shield. The book's contribution to social science is simply the reorganization of the *Arlington Heights* factors into a structure that meets the strictures of the Scientific Method. Finally, the theoretical contributions are really refinements on the original work of Joel Olson. Nevertheless, the book presents definitions for "racial shields or shielding," how the shielding is an essential element in how the state reaches decisions allowing some individuals to participate in the electoral processes more than others, and how racial purpose is important to the maintenance of political control of the state.

Essentially, the concluding chapter brings together the theoretical arguments with the case studies, presents some conclusions, and makes observations as to why it is still necessary to include Texas under coverage of all provisions of the VRA. The VRA in itself has ensured political access for covered groups, yet it is still considered a temporary measure periodically reviewed. What is required, given the persistence of racial purpose and the continuing efforts at disenfranchising voters for political gain throughout the nation, is a national and permanent Voting Rights law overseeing all election processes and systems throughout the United States. Each state should still be allowed to design and construct their respective election systems. Nevertheless, certain practices that predominate where racial purpose and racism have become institutionalized must be outlawed and overseen at the national level by a federal agency free of political manipulation. These proposals are not new or revolutionary but have been proposed in the past. What is new is the proposal that these recommendations grow into enforceable statutes, permanently safeguarding the franchise for all citizens, not just in Texas, but throughout the nation.

NOTES

1. The 2014 lawsuit also cited as *Perez v. Perry* is referenced throughout this volume because it was subsequent to the legislature's decision to accept the court imposed districts as the final redistricting plans in 2012. The plaintiffs felt that their dissatisfaction with the court-imposed plan was a strategic moment to launch a Section 3(c) challenge seeking to force the court to declare that Texas had acted with "racial purpose," thus requiring the state to be placed under permanent Section 5 coverage. Plaintiffs felt this was their only recourse given the *Shelby* decision. Nevertheless, the 2014 case will not be thoroughly discussed in this volume except in sections deemed relevant.

2. Ms. Nina Perales, Vice-President for Litigation, MALDEF.

3. Section 2 Voting Rights expert witnesses provide statistical analyses of racially polarized voting as well as the efficacy of drawing viably efficacious minority electoral districts.

4. This case will be referred to as *Arlington Heights* or *Village of Arlington Heights* throughout the remainder of this work.

5. *Texas House Journal*, March 23, 2011. http://www.journals.house.state.tx.us/hjrnl/82r/82RDAY40FINAL.PDF#page=74.

6. Gossett, Thomas F. 1997. *Race: The History of an Idea in America.* New York: Oxford University Press. Segrest, Mab. 1994. *Memoir of a Race Traitor.* Boston, MA: South End Press.

7. Olson, Joel. 2006. *Abolition of White Democracy.* Minneapolis, MN: University of Minnesota Press.

8. Gossett, 1997; Segrest, 1994; and, Olson, 2006.

9. Segrest, 1994, pp. 188–95.

10. Gossett, 1997; Olson, 2006.

11. Typical socialization mechanisms are the family and its structure, educational system and specific school, religion, denomination, size, location, peer groups of various sorts, profession, media, and so forth.

12. Offe, Claus. 1974. *Structural Problems of the Capitalist State: Class Rule and the Political System, on the Selectiveness of Political Institutions.* London: Sage Publications, Inc.; Flores, Henry. 2003. *The Evolution of the Liberal Democratic State with a Case Study of Latinos in San Antonio, Texas.* Lewiston, NY: The Edwin Mellon Press.

13. Foucault, Michel. 1979. *Discipline and Punish: The Birth of the Prison.* Translated by Alan Sheridan. NY: Vintage Books.

14. "Voting Laws Roundup," 2007. New York: New York University School of Law.

15. *Rodriguez v. San Antonio Independent School District, et al., 411 US 1(1973); Plyler, et al. v. Doe, et al., 457 US 202 (1982).*

16. *Texas House Journal*, March 23, 2011. http://www.journals.house.state.tx.us/hjrnl/82r/pdf/82RDAY40FINAL.PDF#page=74.

17. These were set forth by the court's majority in *Village of Arlington Heights, et al. v. Metropolitan Housing Development Corporation, et al.*, 429 US 252 (1977).

18. Representative of some of this scholarship are Montejano's *Anglos and Mexicans in the Making of Texas, 1836–1986*, (Austin, TX: University of Texas, 1987); Gonzales, Manuel G., *Mexicanos: A History of Mexicans in the United States* (Bloomington, IN: Indiana University Press, 2000); and Reynaldo Valencia, Sonia R. Garcia, Henry Flores, and José Roberto Juárez. *Mexican Americans and the Law* (Tucson: The University of Arizona Press, 2007).

19. Kenneth Prewitt, *What is Your Race? The Census and Our Flawed Efforts to Classify Americans* (Princeton, NJ: Princeton University Press, 2013).

20. I will use these terms interchangeably at various places throughout this work, but I prefer the term Latino.

21. Mr. Gus Garcia made the arguments before the court and was part of a legal team comprised of Judge Carlos Cadena and John J. Herrera.

Chapter One

Uncovering Racial Purpose in Voting Rights Politics

The search for the proof of racial purpose or intent in voting rights litigation research must begin with a historical discussion of several concepts including "states' rights," "states' sovereignty," "equal sovereignty of all states," and "traditional Federalism." The reference to "racial purpose" and "intent" found in Section 3(c) of the Voting Rights Act of 1965 (VRA)[1] are essential elements of the VRA that is the implementing legislation for the Fifteenth Amendment to the Constitution of the United States passed by congress in 1869 and the states in 1870. The Amendment was an explicit statement granting the right to vote to all citizens without regard to "race, color, or previous condition of servitude." Why it took so long for the country to write an implementation law speaks volumes about the determination of political forces in the United States to inhibit African Americans from voting. Regardless, Section 3(c) of the VRA stipulates that while the Department of Justice (DOJ) is in the process of enforcing the provisions of the Fifteenth Amendment and it is found that a "test" or "device" having a racial purpose or intent is found it should be eliminated and the jurisdiction placed under the pre-clearance provisions of Section 5.

The Supreme Court of the United States once declared that only direct proof of racial purpose or intent would be allowed in a redistricting lawsuit *Mobile v. Bolden.*[2] In the 1982 revision of the VRA, Congress changed the language to read "purpose or with the effect of denying or abridging the right to vote on account of race." As a result, from a legal perspective courts no longer require explicit proof of intent to discriminate but may base their decision on the effect the change has on a covered population. This position is slowly devolving back to the Court's position in *Bolden* particularly since the Roberts' majority struck down Section 4 (b) of the VRA in *Shelby County.* The elimination of 4 (b) left plaintiffs no alternative but to bring suit under

Section 3 (c) of the VRA, which requires proof of racial purpose or intent. The problematic simply stated, in light of the *Shelby County, AL v. Eric Holder, et al.*[3] is how does one generate and produce explicit proof of racial purpose or intent in voting rights cases when direct evidence is lacking? This question bears strategic importance because the *Shelby County* decision appears to mark the Court's intention to narrow the protective scope of voting rights protections in the future.

A close reading of *Shelby County* reveals that the search for a methodology that clearly identifies racial purpose or intent is of paramount importance to future congressional deliberations when considering renewal and updating of the VRA, the consideration of a more comprehensive Voter Rights Law, and for judicial interpretations of these laws. There also appears to be a direct link between the Supreme Court's decisional rationale for overturning Section 4(b) and the concepts of "states' rights," "states' sovereignty," "equal sovereignty of all states," and "traditional Federalism." This linkage will be discussed in a later section of this chapter, but these concepts appear to be a recurring theme in recent Section 5 challenges and judicial opinions nationally and used to camouflage racial purpose in the two cases at the heart of this book.

The states' rights, states' sovereignty, and Federalism issues are clearly discussed from the states' point of view in both cases as well as in the *amicus curiae* briefs filed by the states of Alabama, Virginia, Florida, South Carolina, Arizona, Georgia, Michigan, and Louisiana before the Supreme Court in *Perry v. Perez.*[4] Each of the *amicus* states were covered in whole or part by Section 5 of the VRA at that time. The district court found that the redistricting process had been tainted by racial intent and the state was ordered to redo its process. Not satisfied with the district court's decision, the Texas Attorney General, Mr. Greg Abbott, appealed to the Supreme Court which upheld the district court's opinion. In the Texas state brief it appeals to the Supreme Court to require the Western District Court, of Texas to use the congressional redistricting plan in their final deliberations pointing out that "common sense" dictated that the court simply modify an existing plan to make any needed adjustments. The *amicus* briefs also pointed out that the court did not have the human or technological resources to draw a map from scratch, so relying on the already existing plan was easier, timelier, and resource efficient. The brief then went on to say that the district court's intervention was a "federal problem of a different order of magnitude"[5] and "in at least three respects, the lower court's interim Section 5 remedy threatens to 'exacerbate the 'substantial' federalism costs that the preclearance procedure already exacts, perhaps to the extent of raising concerns about §§5's . . . constitutionality."[6]

The *amicus* states saw the district court's intervention as a clear "threat" to the traditional manner in which the United States is governed and functions.

The attorneys for the states saw the imposition of a redistricting plan on Texas by the Western District of Texas' three-judge panel as intrusive and coercive, "exacerbating" the federalism costs already imposed by the very existence of Section 5's preclearance requirement. The brief leaves unanswered what the federalism costs of Section 5 may be, but it may be safe to conclude that the costs might include the complaint that Section 5 treats some states differently than others and forces state governments to structure their electoral system to conform to norms not approved by either Texas voters or the legislature. This latter argument is based on the notion that courts are appointed and do not reflect the voice of the states' citizenry as opposed to the voters themselves or their duly elected officials.

The three "respects" are then pointed out. The first is "forcing a State to adopt an entirely new practice that it never chose in the first place."[7] The *amici* are implying an overly intrusive action on the part of the national government as it forces a state to accept a new way of redistricting that "certainly infringes on State prerogatives."[8] Instead of a redistricting plan chosen by a democratically elected body, the state is being forced to accept a plan from a group of individuals, judges, who are not politically account- able to the people of the state. The second "respect" is that the district court's decision "effectively allows the federal government to dictate the substance of state law *in the first instance* (italics in original document) and comes perilously close—if it does not go all the way—to authorizing precisely the sort of 'commandeering' of state governmental processes that the Constitu- tion condemns."[9] The brief cites both *Printz v. United States*[10] and *New York v. United States*[11] as precedents for their second "respect." Both *Printz* and *New York* spoke to the structure of the federal system of government, dual sovereignty, and local authority over local laws and processes as "enshrined" in the Tenth Amendment. Yet these are the only two Supreme Court deci- sions that make this claim. The court felt in both *Printz* and *New York* that what the federal government was asking went beyond the meaning and intent of the Fifteenth Amendment's enforcement clause. Historically, the Tenth Amendment has been seen by the Supreme Court as a "truism"[12] because it states the obvious, that the power of Congress rests in the hands of the people and Congress manages its oversight responsibilities accordingly. Besides, the court added, the Supremacy Clause of the Constitution governs the relations between the national and state governments. The third "respect" discussed in the *amicus* brief is that of "our historic tradition that all the States enjoy equal sovereignty. . . . The constitutional concerns are exacerbated because the Constitution expressly 'leaves with the State's primary responsibility for apportionment' of their federal congressional districts."[13] Here *Growe v. Emison*[14] and *Chapman v. Meier*[15] are cited for justification; however, a close reading of these two decisions actually indicates the first cracks in the *amicus curiae* brief. Both *Growe* and *Chapman* do, in fact, declare that reapportionment is a state responsibility, but they also indicate that the federal court can step in if the state designs a reapportionment plan not constitutionally acceptable. Although the *amici* in *Perry v. Perez* fall back on states' rights, equal sovereignty, and federalist concerns as the principal reasons for the possibility that Section 5 is unconstitutional, they fail to state that these rights are not absolute but are subject to federal intervention.

The *amicus* brief mimics Texas' appeal in that all nine states are claiming an overly intrusive federal action into a state's privilege and constitutionally protected function, redistricting. But the question at the very core of these appeals is still "What is it that the states are really appealing?" Are they truly appealing the intrusion of the federal government or are they using the federal government's intrusion as a mask to hide the racial purpose or intent pursued in the redistricting process? It appears that they are doing both simultaneously; the conundrum is that one cannot do one without doing the other. In each of these cases, minority group populations, protected by both the constitution and the VRA, are being manipulated to achieve a political end. Achieving a political end in the redistricting process is, in and of itself, not unconstitutional, but when a jurisdiction manipulates a covered population in such a way as to deny their ability to elect a candidate of their choice, these jurisdictions are then taking racially discriminatory action against these groups (*LULAC v. Perry,* 2006).

Methodologically, this situation is tantamount to a "Gordian Knot" and speaks to the research question discussed in a subsequent chapter but deserves a brief mention here. What the complaining states are attempting to do is to say that doing something that is racially discriminatory is a separate and completely unique action from that of the redistricting effort and must be treated differently in any judicial deliberation. From the perspective of decisional theory, however, racial purpose and the redistricting process must be considered as "two sides of the same coin." This is the complexity underlying the problem of redistricting in Texas. One cannot have one without the other. The problem's complexity is compounded given the broad array of variables that are brought to bear in this instance and the manner in which the problem is conceived and stated. The court touched on the intricacy of this problem when it referred to the manner in which one could go about determining racial purpose in its *Arlington Heights*[16] decision, where it identified eleven possible areas of inquiry and countless numbers of variables requiring operationalization and quantification substantiating the proof. These *Arlington Heights* Factors will be discussed in great detail in a subsequent chapter specifically addressing their efficacy. Underlying some of the factors, however, is the need to understand the historical reasons or forces giving birth to the decision and use of racial purpose in the public policy process as a possible solution to the problematic or conundrum. As a result, an essential part of the inquiry requires delving into the history and root source of the rationale for a decision and how a decision evolves the way it does.

FROM EXPLICIT TO SHIELDED RACISM

During the nineteenth and much of the twentieth centuries in the United States one heard the use of derogatory racial terms used openly when referring to African Americans, Latinos, Native Americans, and Asians. Currently, any racially derogatory terms are either expressed behind closed doors or spoken only in informal settings away from the prying ears of the general public or media. Occasionally, politicians will make their racial or other prejudices evident in what they assume are private meetings and are surreptitiously recorded. Sometimes these recordings are made public and politicians are forced to make some public excuse for their indiscretion.[17]

Using racially derogatory language openly when describing persons of color in the United States does not occur often in this day and age, particularly in the public sector. To do so risks embarrassment and possible litigation. Most importantly, it reflects on the state of the political culture and reputation of a given public jurisdiction. No city or state likes to have a reputation for being a bastion of racist or intolerant behavior. Instead any racially charged language or stated intent to make a public decision based on racial grounds are made in the privacy of staff meetings or in places out of the sight of the public and media.

The hiding of racism and racial purpose in the public policy process lies at the heart of this volume. How one solves the problem of identifying racial bias and discriminatory purpose or intent when hidden behind closed doors is the impetus for both the theoretical and methodological issues presented here. Although this is not necessarily an old issue, it has become of paramount importance since the United States Supreme Court (SCOTUS) struck down the provisions of Section 4(b) of the Voting Rights Act of 1965[18] (VRA) in *Shelby County.*[19] SCOTUS ruled that the provisions in Section 4(b) were outdated and thus irrelevant today and directed that Congress move to update the standards. The court partially based its decision on the notion that the Jim Crow laws and voting practices in the post-Civil War South were no longer in existence. Race relations had changed and, as a result, the VRA had to change.

Prior to SCOTUS rendering an opinion in the *Shelby* matter, two other cases had been decided by lower courts that raised questions about the substance of the majority opinion in *Shelby*. Both cases originated in Texas in 2012. The first case was *Perry v. Perez*[20] the second was *Texas v. Holder.*[21] *Perry v. Perez* was the Texas congressional redistricting lawsuit that was

brought by the Mexican American Legal Defense and Educational Fund
(MALDEF) on behalf of the Latino Redistricting Task Force. The plaintiffs
in *Perry* claimed that "racially discriminatory purpose" was the primary motivating factor in the way in which Texas constructed its congressional districts
during the 2011 legislative session. The courts agreed with MALDEF; Texas
appealed and eventually was forced to accept a court-imposed plan. *Texas v.
Holder*, otherwise referred to as the Voter ID case, was heard in July 2012
by the United States District Court for the District of Columbia (DCDC).
In this case, Texas was the plaintiff suing the federal government claiming
that Section 5, the preclearance provision, of the VRA was a violation of
the Tenth Amendment of the Constitution. The federal government together
with a defendant intervener, MALDEF again, claimed that Texas had acted
with "racial purpose" in determining the substance of the Voter ID law. The
DCDC ruled the law unconstitutional because it would have a deleterious
effect on low-income persons, women, and younger and older voters but did
not rule on the racial purpose underlying the law and agreed with the federal
government ruling against Texas.

Both of the Texas cases will be discussed at great length in a subsequent
chapter. It only requires noting here that in the redistricting case direct evidence of racial purpose was uncovered, but in the Voter ID case, there was
no direct evidence. The DCDC ruled on clear evidence that the new ID law
would overburden low-income, older, and younger voters and members of
protected minority groups, thus diluting their vote. In other words, the court
ruled that the Voter ID law violated the effect standard of the VRA remaining silent on the racial purpose issue because the court held that the evidence
supporting their position on the effect prong was sufficient.

The two cases offered interesting contrasts and comparisons: for one they
originated in Texas and spoke to two pieces of legislation that had passed during the same legislative session. As a result, many politicians who acted on
one acted on the other. The most glaring contrast though was in the evidence
generated in both cases. In the redistricting case, visible evidence in the form
of personal e-mail between some of the decision makers clearly indicated
that racial purpose was behind the drawing of congressional districts. This
evidence had been subpoenaed by the federal court during the preclearance
hearing, because Texas refused to release it, claiming legislative privilege.
Once released, the evidence damned Texas' arguments. In the Voter ID lawsuit, Texas moved before trial to protect any and all e-mail communications,
so these were not available for trial. This action, of course, raised everyone's
suspicions as to why the state took such an action. On a political level, the
state's actions led some to believe that there were, in fact, racially discriminatory reasons stated in the e-mail discussing the need for a Voter ID law.

Given the racial effect of the Voter ID law that was uncovered during the trial, it is difficult to believe there was a lack of racial purpose during the private deliberations and communications leading to the bill's passage in the Texas legislature. This incongruity, together with the history of race relations between Anglos and Latinos in the state provided the inspirational spark that gave birth to this book. Simply stated, the research question became "how can one uncover a variable in a decisional matrix that has not been explicitly identified as an essential part of the decision?" Whether the variable is intentionally hidden or accidentally left out of the decisional process is important only to the extent of the implications surrounding the decision. For instance, a variable intentionally hidden to prevent a legal decision from going forward is very different from a situation where a variable is simply unknown or accidentally overlooked. From a purely academic perspective, the question is interesting because it speaks to a problem common to almost all researchers performing original or exploratory research. The question is important to litigation experts because the answer to this question helps navigating around the need to subpoena information that is being shielded by an opponent in the courtroom. From the perspective of the general public, uncovering information intentionally hidden by public decision makers expands transparency that is important to the functioning of democratic institutions.

The most important subsidiary questions arising from the previous discussion are why did the Texas decision makers in both cases hide or attempt to hide the fact that racial purpose was foundational to their decisions? Also, why race? Why did the decision makers have to use racial purpose to draw congressional district lines or construct the Texas Voter ID law the way they did? The answers to this set of questions are based in a thorough analysis of the politics underlying the legislative process in Texas and the historical race relations between Anglos and Latinos that have colored the state's history since the founding of the Texas Republic. Before delving into these realms, however, it is important to understand the forces that drove the Texas decision makers to behave the way they did. The state's history of passing laws and creating structures to inhibit and dilute the votes of African Americans and Latinos resulted in the state being covered under Sections 4 and 5 of the VRA. A good starting place—there could well be others—is then a discussion of the Voting Rights Act.

THE VOTING RIGHTS ACT

The Voting Rights Act of 1965 was the signature piece of President Lyndon Johnson's domestic agenda. It was born during the Kennedy administration but didn't reach fruition until after the famous marches in Selma, Alabama, and Washington, DC, led by Dr. Martin Luther King Jr. and other civil rights activists. A thorough history of the VRA's passage is not important here because it has been covered extensively by others.[22] The passage of this landmark legislation was based on a number of factors, but most important "findings" that were made to Congress of the history of racism throughout the nation, particularly in the southeastern part of the United States. Texas was numbered among these states for its overt attempts to inhibit African Americans from voting. The most important sections of the VRA that would allow for enforcement of the right to vote in Texas were Sections 2, 3, 4, and 5 of the act. Section 5 is the most controversial and has been the subject of attacks by those who oppose the VRA generally. Before delving into the objections surrounding Section 5, a brief discussion of the other sections is in order however.

A lawsuit can be brought under Section 2 if it is found that a "standard, practice or procedure" within the context of "the totality of circumstances" is found to deny the vote to a member of a group covered under the VRA. Covered groups include African Americans, Latinos, Asians, and Native Americans. Members of all these groups, other than African Americans, are considered protected under the language provisions of Section 203 of the act. The "totality of circumstances test" was added to Section 5 in 1982 by the Senate Judiciary Committee to lend more clarity to the provision.[23] The factors as described in Section 2 are listed below:

1. the history of official voting-related discrimination in the state or political subdivision;
2. the extent to which voting in the elections of the state or political subdivision is racially polarized;
3. the extent to which the state or political subdivision has used voting practices or procedures that tend to enhance the opportunity for discrimination against the minority group, such as unusually large election districts, majority-vote requirements, and prohibitions against bullet voting;
4. the exclusion of members of the minority group from candidate slating processes;
5. the extent to which minority group members bear the effects of discrimination in areas such as education, employment, and health, which hinder their ability to participate effectively in the political process;
6. the use of overt or subtle racial appeals in political campaigns; and
7. the extent to which members of the minority group have been elected to public office in the jurisdiction.[24]

The Judiciary Committee also noted in its report that the above factors were not all inclusive, and the court could consider other factors such as whether there is a history of a lack of responsiveness on the part of elected officials to the needs of minority communities.

Section 2 is applicable if, given the above factors, the "political processes leading to nomination or election" in the jurisdiction "are not equally open to participation by members of a class of citizens protected" by the VRA "in that its members have less opportunity than other members of the electorate to participate in the political process and elect representatives of their choice." According to the Senate report, Section 2's language was designed to allow covered members the opportunity to determine whether a violation of the VRA had occurred in order to bring a voting rights lawsuit. Subsequent litigation and scholarly research defined several of the Section 2 factors particularly that of "racially polarized voting."[25]

It should be noted that some of the VRA sections are permanent and do not require reapproval by Congress while other sections are considered temporary and must be reviewed and reapproved every so many years. Section 2 is one of the permanent sections and thus can only be modified if SCOTUS changes it through judicial interpretation or finds it unconstitutional. Section 2 can also be modified if Congress chooses to reevaluate the entire VRA. To date, Congress has only chosen to review those sections of the VRA that are defined as temporary. The only changes that the court has made to this section are to insist that only election systems can be sued under this section in *Holder v. Hall,*[26] and *Connor v. Finch.*[27] The *Holder* case tried to narrow the focus of Section 2 provisions by pointing out that the structure of an election system such as the number of members of an elective body are not subject to Section 2 provisions. SCOTUS pointed out, in a plurality decision, that only election procedures were subject to Section 2 litigation. The *Connor* decision solidified the concept that all congressional districts are required to have, as near as possible, equal populations. This section of the VRA is utilized only after some citizen feels that a violation has occurred and requires the filing of a lawsuit that may or may not go to trial. Still, a Section 2 filing requires hiring competent attorneys, academic experts, and entails a great deal of expense for the average person which may run between $250,000 for a lawsuit involving a small jurisdiction where the case may settle out of court to as high as $2.5 million or more for larger jurisdictions. In this latter situation, a trial of this type may involve the redistricting of a state, and the trial may go through an extensive and time-consuming appeals process that may end up at the Supreme Court. If a case is appealed through the various levels of the federal judiciary system, additional attorneys, experts in preparing and arguing appeals, are required. In some situations like the Texas redistrictings that occurred between 2001 and 2006 the process could go on for years. Regardless, many Section 2 trials are brought by average citizens who cannot typically afford to finance the trials themselves, requiring either *pro bono* private attorneys, or litigation teams brought together by public interest law groups such as those sponsored by the NAACP, the Mexican American Legal Defense and Educational Fund (MALDEF), or the Lawyer's Committee in Washington D.C. These groups obtain their litigation funds from endowments built through attorney's fees or foundation grants and philanthropy. In short, a private individual will find it difficult to finance a Section 2 lawsuit through their own means because of the expense and expertise required.

Section 3 (c) of the VRA states that:

> If in any proceeding instituted by the Attorney General under any statute to enforce the guarantees of the fifteenth amendment in any State or political subdivision the court finds that violations of the fifteenth amendment justifying equitable relief have occurred within the territory of such State or political subdivisions, the court in addition to such relief as it may grant, shall retain jurisdiction for such period as it may deem appropriate and during such period no voting qualification or prerequisite to voting, or standard, practice, or procedure with respect to voting different from that in force or effect at the time the proceeding was commenced shall be enforced unless and until the court finds that such qualifications, prerequisite, standard, practice, or procedure does not have the purpose and will not have the effect of denying or abridging the right to vote on account of race or color. *Provided*, That such qualification, prerequisite, standard, practice, or procedure has been submitted by the chief legal officer or other appropriate official of such State or subdivision to the Attorney General and the Attorney General has not interposed an objection within sixty days after such submission, except that neither the court's findings nor the Attorney General's failure to object shall bar a subsequent action to enjoin enforcement of such qualifications, prerequisite, standard, practice, or procedure.

This particular subsection of the VRA is intriguing because it appears to give the Attorney General of the United States more latitude to monitor the election behavior of all states, not just those covered under Sections 4 and 5. It also, unlike Section 4, does not require a specification of a prior history of discriminatory behavior on the part of any political jurisdiction, only that whatever "qualification or prerequisite to voting, or standard, practice, or procedure with respect to voting" not inhibit the ability of citizens regardless of race or color to effectively participate in that jurisdiction's election process. If the Attorney General, really the Civil Rights Division of the DOJ, finds that a political jurisdiction's actions in the election process are discriminatory, then that jurisdiction can be made to preclear any changes before implementation. This is the basis for DOJ's lawsuit against Texas over the Voter ID law subsequent to the *Shelby* decision.

Section 4(b), otherwise known as the coverage formula of the VRA, was struck down by SCOTUS in the *Shelby* decision as outdated.[28] The Supreme

Court did not rule on Section 5, the preclearance requirement, only the coverage formula. The court pointed out that it was acting under *stare decisis* (court precedent) as set forth in *Northwest Austin Municipal Utility District No. 1 v. Holder*, 557 US 193, when it warned that the coverage formula may be outdated and Congress might find it wise to update the formula. Chief Justice Roberts echoed this warning in *Shelby*, pointing out that he was forced to rule the way he did because of Congress' inaction.

The Section 4 coverage formula appears in Section 4 (b) and states:

> The provisions of subsection (a) shall apply in any State or in any political subdivision of a state which (1) the Attorney General determines maintained on November 1, 1964, any test or device, and with respect to when (2) the director of the Census determines that less than 50 per centum of the persons of voting age residing therein were registered on November 1, 1964, or that less than 50 per centum of such persons voted in the presidential election of November 1964. A determination of the Attorney General or of the Director of the Census under this section or under section 6 or section 13 shall not be reviewable in any court and shall be effective upon publication in the Federal Register.

Section 4 then goes on defining what "tests" and "devices" are, including mechanisms designed to test whether one can read, write, understand, or interpret any matter; demonstrates educational achievement of knowledge of a particular subject; possesses good moral character; or prove "his" qualification by being vouched for by other registered voters. Variations of each of the tests or devices had been used throughout the states that formed the old Confederate states to deny or inhibit the ability of African Americans to register and vote and were part of what came to be known as Jim Crow laws.[29]

In reaching its decision, SCOTUS presented selected data of African American turnout in six of the originally covered states, data that were seven years old on which to partially base their conclusion.[30] The court concluded that African Americans were participating at almost an equal rate as whites in those six states in 2004 as opposed to 1965 when the VRA was originally approved by Congress. SCOTUS also ruled that the tests and devices used to deny African Americans voting access in 1965 had long since been eliminated. Essentially, the Supreme Court stated that Section 4(b) was outdated, and Congress needed to revisit and update if they were so inclined. Regardless, Section 4(b)'s original provisions were in place when the Texas Voter ID case was heard and decided in July 2012 and established the standards for the inclusion of the state under Section 5 of the VRA.

Section 5 is the better known of the major VRA sections and is known as the "preclearance" requirement and is also a temporary provision of the act. This section requires the identified jurisdictions to have any changes to their election processes or structures "precleared" by either DOJ or a three judge panel of the United States District Court of the District of Columbia before implementation. The list of jurisdictions was originally established by Congress because the jurisdictions in question had less than 50 percent voting age population registered or participated in general elections in the presidential elections of 1964.[31] Some of the original jurisdictions covered have since "bailed out" under the provisions set forth in Section 4(a). Immediately prior to *Shelby County*, all or almost all of nine states, parts of five others, and independent townships in two other states were covered under the provisions of Sections 4(b) and 5 of the VRA. When SCOTUS overturned the provisions of Section 4(b), however, the "preclearance" provision was left with no standards for enforcement. Texas had been fully covered under the Section 4(b) provisions, so traditionally it was required to submit any and all changes including redistricting plans for "preclearance" to DOJ or the DCDC. Over the years, the state had availed itself of both preclearance venues depending upon the situation. In almost all political subdivisions of the state, submission for preclearance had become customary. It was during this process that the Texas Voter ID law was found to violate provisions of the VRA because the DCDC found that the new law would have a disparate impact on members of minority groups, young and senior voters, and the poor.

Section 5's history is very different from those of Sections 2, 3, and 4. It was first approved as part of the original VRA in 1965 for five years, extended for another five years in 1970, extended another seven years in 1975, and in 1982 was extended for another nineteen years. In 2006, Section 5 was extended for another twenty-five years. Extending Section 5 since 1965 was not easy, and this section has always had a rocky existence to say the least. It was challenged initially in 1966 in *South Carolina v. Katzenbach*,[32] as exceeding the powers of Congress and encroaching in areas reserved for state powers. SCOTUS denied this in an 8-1 decision with the only dissenter being Justice Hugo Black. This was the first states' rights challenge to Section 5, and Justice Black's comments would be echoed throughout the history of the challenges, eventually ending as the inspiration for Justice Roberts's conclusions in the *Shelby* decision. Black's dissent appeared isolated numerically but was portentous in many ways. Years later, Black's position inspired the fundamental philosophies of the conservative wing of the Roberts Court and underlay the *Shelby* ruling. Justice Black's dissent was based in his perception that Section 5 was an over-exercise of congressional powers in Section 2 of the Fifteenth Amendment. The significance of Justice Black's comments requires an extensive citation. He said that his

> second and more basic objection to 5 is that Congress has here exercised its power under 2 of the Fifteenth Amendment through the adoption of means that conflict with the most basic principles of the Constitution. As the Court says the

limitations of the power granted under 2 are the same as the limitations imposed on the exercise of any of the powers expressly granted Congress by the Constitution. . . . Section 5, by providing that some of the States cannot pass state laws or adopt state constitutional amendments without first being compelled to beg federal authorities to approve their policies, so distorts our constitutional structure of government as to render any distinction drawn in the Constitution between state and federal power almost meaningless. One of the most basic premises upon which our structure of government was founded was that the Federal Government was to have certain specific and limited powers and no others, and all other power was to be reserved either "to the States respectively, or to the people." Certainly if all the provisions of our Constitution which limit the power of the Federal Government and reserve other power to the States are to mean anything, they mean at least that the States have power to pass laws and amend their constitutions without first sending their officials hundreds of miles away to beg federal authorities to approve them. Moreover, it seems to me that 5 which gives federal officials power to veto state laws they do not like is in direct conflict with the clear command of our Constitution that "The United States shall guarantee to every State in this Union a Republican Form of Government." I cannot help but believe that the inevitable effect of any such law which forces any one of the States to entreat federal authorities in far-away places for approval of local laws before they can become effective is to create the impression that the State or States treated in this way are little more than conquered provinces.[33]

Justice Black articulated the state's rights position of those who would put forth future challenges to Section 5 of the VRA that Congress had intruded in an area constitutionally reserved to the states. Justice Black's perception is not in itself unique and has been argued in many other areas of jurisprudence, most notably in the ongoing struggles over the meaning and intent of the Commerce Clause throughout the life of this nation beginning with *McCullouch v. Maryland*,[34] through *City of Boerne v. Flores*.[35]

THE MOUNTING ATTACK ON THE VRA

The importance of Black's dissenting opinion cannot be overlooked as the beginning of the attacks on Section 5 of the VRA. Justice Black's dissent highlighted three themes that would become important throughout the long debates over Section 5 and form the heart of Justice Roberts's arguments in both the *Northwest Austin Municipal Utility District, No. 1*[36] and *Shelby County* decisions. Initially, Justice Black argues that Section 5, deriving its authority from Section 2 of the Fifteenth Amendment, conflicts with the limitations placed on the expressly granted powers of Congress under the Constitution. The limitations are based in those that would be granted due to our federal form of government, which is the second theme that federal interference in certain powers reserved to the states violates the basic tenets of Federalism. Justice Black argued that Section 5 violated federalism and imposed the power of the national government on states in areas reserved to them, organizing and structuring their election systems, an area where states have constitutionally protected sovereignty.

In subsequent litigation beginning with *City of Rome v. United States,*[37] specifically Justice Rehnquist's dissent, and culminating with the majority opinion in *Shelby,* the constitutional position inspired by Justice Black reared its head. Justice Black's concern with the protection of states' rights found its way from a solitary dissenting opinion in *Katzenbach* evolving into the heart of the majority opinion in *Shelby County.* The evolution of the states' rights concept between the two cases is interesting in itself because it reflects manipulations of both logic and language that tax the imagination. The final edition, in *Shelby County,* should strike fear in the hearts of voting rights activists because it lays the foundation for the dismantling of the VRA and future attacks on both the Fourteenth and Fifteenth Amendments to the Constitution.[38]

As Professor Hasen has pointed out, "the arrogance" of the Roberts Court can be found in the brevity of the *Shelby County* majority opinion, and it creates new law without adequate justification which limits congressional power to enforce voting rights; it willfully ignores political realities; its brevity, rather than signaling humility and minimalism, demonstrates a failure to engage with the voluminous congressional record and substantial arguments of the law's defenders and of the dissent; and the Court issued a broad decision when minimalism counseled issuing a narrow one.[39]

Professor Hasen proceeds with his analysis by pointing out that future attacks on Sections 2 and 203 of the VRA are embedded in the manner in which the majority logicized their *Shelby County* opinion.[40] If the Roberts majority has the desire to dismantle one of the most important civil rights laws in the history of the United States, it requires only a short leap in logic to suggest that it does not require much for them to narrow the protections of the Fourteenth and Fifteenth Amendments to the Constitution. Narrowing the protections of these two Civil War Amendments, passed to ensure the granting of full citizenship to freed slaves, can be accomplished by constraining the powers of congress to pass enforcing legislation such as the VRA. The Roberts Court, like the Rehnquist Court before, has been narrowing the powers of Congress in areas other than voting and elections for several decades. Congress has been unable to respond because of the partisan gridlock created when Republicans first came to power in 1994. The partisan divide, made more and more severe with the arrival of more and more extremist congressional members, has resulted in a situation where Congress has difficulty even passing a budget upon which the government can function daily.[41] Essentially, Congress's inability to pass legislation has also created a situation where it is ceding its coequal status to the Supreme Court weakening the entire principle of the balance of powers between the three branches of national government. In the end, the only concession that the liberal wing of the Supreme Court could elicit from the majority in *Shelby*, after making the observation that reviewing an act of Congress was a grave action, was declaring that Congress and the court were co-equal branches and the Fifteenth Amendment gave Congress, not the court, the right to make enforcing legislation.

BIRTH AND EVOLUTION OF STATES' RIGHTS

Regardless, the evolutionary journey of the states' rights argument is firmly founded in race relations in the United States, and the journey begins at the dawn of the Republic. States' rights were first seriously brought forward in the *Resolutions of '98*, which were the combined *Kentucky* and *Virginia Resolutions of 1788–89* penned by Thomas Jefferson and James Madison, respectively. The original basis for the resolutions was to establish a legal response to the Alien and Sedition Acts of 1798 and reflected the early legal struggles over the power of the national government in relation to that of the state governments. The original argument itself grew out of the then widespread disagreement that the federal government had been born out of necessity to deal with large issues beyond the scope of state powers. There were those, the Federalists, who felt that the fledgling country required a strong national government to survive and those who felt that the national government's powers should be limited and, instead, were grants from the states. Essentially, the non-Federalists felt that any powers, only those explicitly stated in the new Constitution, emanated from an agreement among the states. Federalists saw this argument as one that if allowed to stand would prove to be a major weakness of the young country. A later president, Andrew Jackson, even stated when he spoke on the Nullification Crisis of 1828–1832, that the nation could not stand as a nation if the states were considered to be primary to the national government. President Jackson pointed out that states' rights ran counter to the entire concept of having a nation and in the end would lead to the dissolution of the nation.[42]

Although the initial arguments for states' rights had to do with tariffs imposed by the federal government on European imports at the beginning of the nineteenth century, the argument would be used to justify the maintenance of slavery throughout the South, eventually culminating in the Civil War. The states' rights arguments in defense of slavery began appearing during the national debates surrounding the Fugitive Slave Acts of 1793 and 1850. The states' rights arguments would be made by both sides of the abolition arguments. Essentially, the abolitionists argued the rights of personal liberty in attempts to avoid following the laws, and the anti-abolitionists argued in defense of the laws allowing them to empower and pay individuals when crossing state lines to apprehend and return escaped slaves.[43] The secession of the Confederate states fulfilled President Jackson's prophecy in his famous Yale University speech. States' rights theoretically are an outgrowth of the concept of state sovereignty that proved to be the major reason the original Articles of Confederation proved unwieldy. This strain of thought has been at the center of almost all state-level challenges to the VRA since its passage and implementation. The line of argument can be easily traced, but the foremost statement was made by Justice Black in *Katzenbach* and echoed by Justice Rehnquist in *City of Rome.*

Chief Justice Roberts used the states' rights argument in writing the majority opinion in *Northwest Austin Municipal Utility District, No. 1* and refined it in *Shelby County.* In the *Northwest Austin Municipal Utility District, No. 1* decision, Judge Roberts pointed out that the government of the United States' power is limited by the Constitution, citing *United States v. Cruikshank,*[44] and that the states have primary authority over the structure of the election systems, *White v. Weiser* and *Burns v. Richardson*[45]and the states, within the limits of the Constitution, have the power to determine the qualifications of their own voters, *Oregon v. Mitchell.*[46] He then cites the Tenth Amendment of the Constitution to allude to the sovereign nature of each state in relation to the Federal government-stating, "State autonomy with respect to the machinery of self-government defines the States as sovereign entities rather than mere provincial outposts subject to every dictate of a central governing authority." Finally, citing *City of Mobile v. Bolden,*[47] stating that since states still retain "sovereign authority" over their election systems, any congressional action attempting to enforce the Fifteenth Amendment must be "closely examined to ensure that its encroachment on state authority in this area is limited to the appropriate enforcement of this ban on discrimination." The Chief Justice, and it is not clear why this was not pointed out in a concurring opinion, assumes the existence of legal or judicial precedence for states' rights, sovereignty, and autonomy. Additionally, his reliance on the Tenth Amendment of the Constitution to support his claims of state sovereignty or of what constitutes the traditional federalism structure of the United States lays the groundwork for more detailed interpretations in future suits.

RACIAL PURPOSE AND STATES' RIGHTS

Deconstructing each opinion cited by Justice Roberts in the *Shelby County* decision, however, reveals the relationship between racial purpose and the states' rights arguments embraced by those challenging voting rights laws in the United States. Justice Roberts begins his analysis by citing *Cruikshank* as his authority that there is a constitutional limitation on the powers of the national government. The *Cruikshank* opinion is an interesting one to cite for the Chief Justice because it was born out of an attempt to enforce the provisions of the Fifteenth Amendment in Colfax, Louisiana, during the era of Reconstruction. It appears that Republican Party candidates supported by the African American community had won several local county offices in the most recent election. White supremacist Democrats tried to take over the county courthouse in order to run off the Republican officeholders. The courthouse was defended by African Americans and white officeholders. The battle that ensued resulted in the deaths of as many as 150 African Americans and three white casualties; more than fifty African Americans were executed after they had surrendered. Several white persons were indicted for the murders and were found guilty of violating the First, Second, and Fifteenth Amendment rights of the deceased. On appeal to the Supreme Court, the case was reversed. SCOTUS declared that the national and state governments were distinct from each other, and their citizens had multiple and distinct allegiances to both levels of government. The Court pointed out that the powers of the national government were delegated to it by the states and delimited by the Constitution. Chief Justice Waite then paraphrased the Tenth Amendment by saying, "No rights can be acquired under the Constitution or no laws of the United States, except such as the Government of the United States have the authority to grant or secure. All that cannot be granted or secured are left under the protections of the State."[48] Although this decision was reached during the emotionally charged times of Reconstruction, the authorities, by charging the defendants with violations of various constitutional amendments, were attempting to argue the overarching importance of the newly ratified Fifteenth Amendment. The Supreme Court appeared to reflect national sentiment at the time and wished to moderate the national government's power during that historical era. Although Waite was personally opposed to slavery and in support of extending full citizenship rights to African Americans, the court felt that a moderate position on congressional powers was warranted; thus, the position that the national government only had power over national laws while individual protections were the purview of the states. Regardless, this position was driven by the racial tensions of the time causing the majority on the court to indicate that they were not willing to extend congressional power to the states in these matters unless clear evidence of racial discrimination could be put forth, which the court indicated was lacking in the original indictment. Still the notions of dual sovereignty and states' sovereignty were born into constitutional law as ways of diverting attention from racial injustice.

In citing *White v. Weiser,* Justice Roberts disingenuously chose a case where the majority opinion, written by Justice Powell, recognized that reapportionment was a function of the state. What Justice Roberts ignored or overlooked was that the *White* majority pointed out that failure of a legislature to apportion according to "federal constitutional requisites in a timely fashion" warranted federal relief. Almost as a harbinger of things to come, the *White* decision concerned a challenge to the process that the state of Texas used to reapportion its congressional districts. The majority opinion agreed with Justice Roberts's perception that apportionment was principally a state responsibility, but the federal courts could intervene, as unobtrusively as possible, if the state failed to apportion according to federal constitutional requirements.

Another decision cited by Roberts that he used to substantiate state sovereignty was *Burns v. Richardson,* but here he duplicated his *White* observation. The court in *Burns* was clear in that the state of Hawaii possessed the power to reapportion their state assembly chambers free of federal interference until the state violated federal constitutional requisites. The federal courts, again as unobtrusively as possible, could step in and direct the state to change its reapportionment plan. In *Northwest Austin Municipal Utility District, No. 1* both *White* and *Burns* are used as examples where the Supreme Court indicated the supremacy of the state and the subordination of the federal government in the area of voting rights and election systems. Both decisions had racial implications as well, as African Americans were the plaintiffs in the *White* case while native Hawaiians were plaintiffs in *Burns.* On one level, it is the nature of voting cases that racial groups have brought almost all cases; on the other hand, it has become traditional for the courts or defendants to speak in terms of states' rights, state sovereignty, or federalism when arguing a point of law in these matters rather than openly discussing the issue that racial discrimination was the foundation of each case. Essentially, the court sweeps racial purpose under the proverbial rug in every instance using the discussion of states' rights as a shield concealing the racism of the political decisions.

As in *Burns* and *White, Oregon v. Mitchell* drew the same observation by the Supreme Court concerning the relationship between the federal and state levels of government and a state's election system. In this case, the states of Oregon, Texas, and Utah challenged certain 1970 amendments to the Voting Rights Act. Specifically, the states did not wish to change their voting age

from twenty-one to eighteen, but they also challenged the amendments eliminating the use of literacy tests and other voter qualifying devices and residency
requirements. The court again reiterated its position that states were supreme
in the area of election administration and management until they violated federal laws, at which time the courts could step in with appropriate corrective
action. In this case, the Supreme Court ruled that the states needed to do away
with all literacy tests and other qualifying devices. The residency requirements
for presidential and vice-presidential elections were also deemed unconstitutional. The problem created for the states with this decision was that they were
required to manage two sets of voter registration rolls: one for state elections
and the other for national elections in order to implement the Supreme Court's
decision. SCOTUS ruled, by a narrow 5–4 majority, that states were still supreme in how they regulated state and local elections but that Congress had
the power to set laws for national level elections. So, this decision parsed the
argument and included support for both the states' rights advocates and their
opponents. Still, Justice Roberts fails to point out that in every case he cites
Congress does have a right to make all "proper and necessary" laws regulating
national elections, and federal courts may step in when a state violates federal
law in this area. It should be added that the Twenty-sixth Amendment of the
Constitution changed the voting age from twenty-one to eighteen in 1971,
rendering this part of the *Oregon* decision moot.

The last case cited by Justice Roberts is *City of Mobile v. Bolden*[49] which
was a challenge to the at-large election scheme used in Mobile, Alabama.
This suit was brought by the local African American community claiming
violations of their Fourteenth and Fifteenth Amendment rights. The Supreme
Court ruled that at-large election schemes were not unconstitutional inher-
ently or violative of the VRA unless plaintiffs could prove that the scheme
was created purposely to discriminate against black voters. Again, the court
ruled that states' authority was in deciding upon what election scheme would
govern local elections. Interference by the federal government was only warranted when there was a violation of federal law. This decision was rendered
moot when the language was changed in the VRA revision of 1982 and racial
effect was added as an option to intent.

There have been only two instances where state autonomy under the
auspices of the Tenth Amendment has been upheld by the Supreme Court.
The first was in *New York v. United States*[50] the other was *Printz v. United
States.*[51] In the first case, SCOTUS ruled that requiring states to take "title"
to and be liable for toxic waste cleanup and any externalities as a penalty for
not complying with a federal regulation was found to be "impermissibly coercive" and in violation of the Tenth Amendment. The second case involved the
Brady Handgun Prevention Act, Public Law 103-159, which was a revision

of the Gun Control Act of 1968, Public Law 90-618. SCOTUS ruled that a state could not be required to have its employees enforce a federal law. One justice likened the concept as having the states' law enforcement officers drafted into federal service. Justice Scalia pointed out in his dissent that the Framers of the Constitution meant to have the national government supervise and oversee international relations and relations between states, not policies internal to each state. Justice Scalia indicated that the Brady Law, in *Printz*, violated the concept of "dual sovereignty" that described the constitutionally mandated structure of the United States government. To force state employees to do the work of the national government was to allow the national government more power than the Constitution intended. As one can easily observe, the state sovereignty or federalism issue crosses many policy areas; however, a reading of Article 1, the Tenth and Fifteenth Amendments of the Constitution raises many questions concerning the manner in which Justices Roberts, Black, Harlan, O'Connor, and Scalia interpreted and expounded on the relations between states and the federal government. Only O'Connor in *New York* clearly drew a line between what could be considered coercive behavior by the national government and thus violative of the spirit of the Tenth Amendment. The other justices in the other opinions simply say there are violations, but don't discuss them in any great detail.

A careful reading of the Constitution leads one to a suspicion as to the constitutional place of states' rights, sovereignty, dual sovereignty, and what some of the justices call traditional Federalism principles. The suspicion is raised because the Constitution is not explicit about any of these concepts; they are implied by the justices and nothing more. Still, in every case used by Justice Roberts to justify his conclusions in *Northwest Austin Municipal Utility District, No. 1* he chooses to ignore the expressed powers of Congress to interfere where there is a violation of federal voting laws. He only chose to use the implied argument that states' rights give the states the right to do as they wish in this area of law and that the federal structure prohibits the federal government from being overly intrusive. A full reading of the case history of the cited decisions reveals that there has been movement on the court beginning with Justice Black's lone dissent in *Katzenbach* in 1966 to the majority opinion in *Shelby County*, tipping the scales of power between the court and Congress in voting rights law. The court has now taken the place of Congress in determining what the law should be in this area, and it is basing its conclusions on concepts that do not exist constitutionally. However, various justices over the last forty-five years or so have elevated mythology to legal precedent. The court has made the states' rights concept the center of its position on voting rights law, essentially setting this concept above Article 1, Section 8 and the Fourteenth and Fifteenth Amendments of the constitution.

The Roberts Court, it appears, has taken what was considered a "truism" at one point in history and turned it into foundational law.

THE SHELBY DECISION

The *Shelby County* decision is important on many levels. First and foremost, of course, is that it overturned one of the most important provisions of one of the most important federal laws in the history of United States jurisprudence. One may even consider the *Shelby County* decision on a par with the infamous *Dred Scott*[52] decision declaring that African Americans could not have citizenship and, therefore, had no standing upon which to bring a lawsuit in federal court; or, on a par with *Plessy v. Ferguson*[53] where the Supreme Court upheld segregation. Both of these nineteenth-century cases are considered by some constitutional scholars as among the worst ever decided by SCOTUS.[54] The *Dred Scott* case was overturned by the signing of the Emancipation Proclamation and the passage of the Thirteenth, Fourteenth, and Fifteenth Amendments to the Constitution. Some historians attribute the *Dred Scott* case as somewhat responsible for the War Between the States or Civil War and the bloody border-state war in Kansas. The "separate but equal" doctrine which emanated from *Plessy* was responsible for a series of segregated parallel institutions that were eventually created across the United States, including schools, recreational accommodations, religious institutions, and public transportation among others, that were not eliminated until *Brown v. Board of Education*[55] and its progeny.[56] Essentially, *Dred Scott* and *Plessy* required drastic means to overcome and also assisted in lending depth to the system of tense race relations existing in the United States post–Civil War and post-Reconstruction, respectively. The *Shelby County* decision may have the same effect as the nineteenth-century cases because it stripped the protections that had been built into federal law to overcome part of the legacy of racism that was established by *Plessy*. This suspicion may bear fruit in that immediately upon the publication of the *Shelby* decision at least twenty-three states publicized their intentions to change voter identification and registration rules and limit the number of early voting days with Texas being the first to make such a statement after having its voter identification law ruled in violation of VRA provisions earlier.

Shelby County is also important because it further elaborates the Roberts Court's reputation as being one of the most ideological and political of any Supreme Court in history, cementing the Chief Justice's legacy. The legacy of Supreme Court chief justices and that of the courts they manage are based on the jurisprudential record established during their term. For instance, the

Marshall Court was important because it set the foundation of what role the court would play in our system of government. The Warren Court was famous because of the civil rights decisions it made that broke down many of the social and civil barriers that maintained the racial segregation created by *Plessy.* The Roberts legacy, however, is for constitutional scholars to determine in years to come but appears to have begun by negating some of the most important civil rights laws of the land.

Another reason for the importance of the *Shelby County* decision is because it marks an important victory for the "white" backlash that began with the *Bakke*[57] ruling extending through the widespread attacks on the Voting Rights Act.[58] Representative of this backlash are the activities of Mr. Edward Blum, a visiting fellow at the American Enterprise Institute in Washington, DC, and the director of the Project on Equal Representation, who recruited plaintiffs to challenge a University of Texas affirmative action undergraduate admissions policy. Mr. Blum also recruited Shelby County and appropriate attorneys to challenge Section 5 of the VRA. Mr. Blum's operations, according to his website, are financed by Donors Trust, a private nonprofit 501(c) (3) private charity. Donors Trust's mission partly is "to encourage philanthropy and individual giving and responsibility as opposed to government involvement, as an answer to society's needs."[59] Mr. Blum's intent is to have affirmative action programs in education, contracting, and employment found unconstitutional as well as the Voting Rights Act.[60] His website points out that he wishes to pursue strategies "to influence jurisprudence, public policy and public activities regarding race and ethnicity in four areas: voting, education, contracting and employment."[61] The *Shelby County* decision was the first of his victories. It should be pointed out that he was not victorious in *Fisher v. The University of Texas at Austin,*[62] which was his attempt to have SCOTUS overturn the university's undergraduate affirmative action program. The Supreme Court did remand the decision and ordered the Fifth Circuit Court to review the program to see if it met the *Grutter*[63] narrowly tailored standards.

At the core of *Shelby* though is some language that makes one suspicious that the future of the VRA itself may be in jeopardy, a contention that will be addressed shortly. The disappointing aspect of this is that *Shelby*, although directed at one small county in a state with one of the worst voting rights records in this nation's history, applies to all groups in all covered areas nationally. Essentially, the Roberts majority used an example in one small suburban county having an almost all white population to make a judgment about the entire United States. This is tantamount to a social scientist making a universalizing statement about a concept based upon an inordinately small sample size. This would be considered not simply methodologically flawed by the academy but not publishable for public consumption let alone in a scholarly journal. This is disappointing because if the Supreme Court wanted their decision to apply to all groups, then they needed to discuss the voting rights conditions of all groups in all of the covered jurisdictions and beyond. One can only agree with Professor Hasen that *Shelby* should have been narrowly tailored; in other words, the decision should have been directed only at Shelby County, as opposed to all covered jurisdictions. The *Shelby County* decision may be considered by constitutional scholars in the future as "bad law" in this respect.

The importance of *Shelby County* to the theme of this book is clear. An essential part of the rationale the Roberts majority used to substantiate the overthrow of Section 4(b) of the VRA elevates to a higher level of significance the arguments used by the state of Texas in their attempts at hiding racial purpose in both the 2011 redistricting process and in the creation and passage of the Voter ID law. The *Shelby County* decision turns on the Roberts majority interpretation of the Tenth Amendment and the principle of "dual sovereignty" and the notion that "current conditions" require more "up-to-date" data upon which the court can make its decision. By choosing to base the rationale of its opinion on the "dual sovereignty" and "current data" arguments, the Roberts majority failed to address the major reason for the existence of the VRA in the first place. The Voting Rights Act of 1965, together with all of its extensions, was written and passed by Congress to address the extensive racial discrimination that existed and still does in the manner in which many politicians were and are elected to office, how voters are qualified to vote, how voters cast their ballots and those ballots are administered, and how elections are conducted. Albeit the original VRA was directed toward a unique category of state jurisdictions but for a good reason, the need to identify some obvious examples of racial discrimination in order to get the legislation passed, expediency ruled the original deliberations surrounding the passage of the VRA in 1965. The initially included jurisdictions were found in the southeastern United States where the publicity of that day, Bloody Sunday[64] and the murders of three voter registrars in Philadelphia, Mississippi,[65] highlighted and uncovered many examples of racial discrimination in their election processes.

The Roberts majority not only refused to address directly the issue of the existence of racial discrimination in the election systems generally but based its attack on the VRA on one small county in Alabama. Shelby County has been at the heart of several other voting rights cases and three objections by the Attorney General's office under Section 5 of the VRA; still it is a small county having a population of 197,936 in 2011 and is more than 89 percent white.[66] The court based its opinion on the concept of "dual sovereignty," which was not much more than an illusion prior to *Northwest Austin Municipal Utility District, No. 1,* and the court attempts to turn it into a constitutional principle implied in the Tenth Amendment and the contention that Section 4(b) was not approved appropriately by congress because they ignored "current data," instead relying on information more than forty years old.

Basing the *Shelby County* decision on the Tenth Amendment avoids the issue of racial discrimination but also makes perfect sense historically. This amendment has been used variously throughout history by courts to either curtail or expand the powers of the national government. There was concern during the Constitutional Convention that the federal government would have too much power over the states while others feared that the national government would not have enough.[67] As the Framers suspected any state assertion of sovereignty or supremacy could be and would be overruled by the Supremacy Clause in Article VI, Section 2 of the Constitution, a perusal of all the cases throughout history that SCOTUS has decided that deal with the Tenth Amendment reveals an inconsistent pattern of the majority decision weighing on either the side of the national or state government. Without an in-depth investigation of the history and politics surrounding each of the cases, it is difficult to determine what the motivation of the court was in reaching each of the decisions.

The argument that states enjoy constitutionally protected dual sovereignty is a newly minted Roberts principle that he created in the *Northwest Austin Municipal Utility District, No. 1* decision and is found nowhere in the constitution. Still because Roberts managed to crown dual sovereignty as a principle, it is, temporarily at least, a concept that must be addressed and is a concern of anyone who is granted *certiorari* by SCOTUS in future lawsuits. This principle gives states the same level of authority as the national government and places the national government on notice that states have a certain degree of autonomy within their own jurisdictions. Of course, the Roberts majority also probably has a different perception of the Supremacy Clause as well, but that too may come under their scrutiny. Although this comment may appear facetious, at least some Supreme Court observers feel that the current majority has set a course to remake various parts of the Constitution and constitutional law that have drawn the ire of conservatives and libertarians since *Brown v. Board of Education.*[68]

The Roberts majority also pointed out, in *Shelby*, that Congress had failed to incorporate "current data" when they reapproved the VRA in 2006, making the coverage formula in Section 4(b) outdated. This requirement is interesting in that regardless of what Congress does to update the coverage formula SCOTUS can always claim that the data utilized are outdated. This is simply a requirement impossible for Congress to fill without developing and utilizing a dynamic formula, one that is flexible enough so that the Department of Justice or any three judge panel of the District Court in Washington, DC, those responsible for performing the Section 5 review, will have a fluid baseline from which to make their determination. Dynamism and fluidity in population estimates are necessary to ensuring timeliness because of the naturally constantly changing patterns of demographics. Still, this leaves the reviewing authorities an impossible task and one that, superficially at least, appears to make preclearance impossible for the moment.

Regardless, the *Shelby County* majority's perception that "current data" were not used by Congress when it made its decision to reauthorize the preclearance formula and Sections 4(b) and 5 of the VRA flies in the face of the facts. As Justice Ginsberg pointed out in her dissent[69] and as substantiated by DOJ databases, "the record before Congress was huge."[70] Justice Ginsberg, citing reports submitted during the 2006 VRA congressional reauthorization hearings, noted that "there were more DOJ objections (Section 5) between 1982 and 2004 (626) than there were between 1965 and the 1982 reauthorization (490)."[71] In the very next paragraph of her dissenting opinion, Justice Ginsberg pointed out that "All told, between 1982 and 2006 DOJ objections blocked over 700 voting changes based on a determination that the changes were discriminatory."[72] She ended her review of the DOJ data by stating that "Congress recovered evidence that more than 800 proposed changes were altered or withdrawn since the last reauthorization in 1982."[73] A perusal of the DOJ database indeed reveals there have been a great number of Section 5 objections between 1982 and 2005. During that time frame, there have been more than 100,000 submissions and 753 objections.[74] In other words less than one percent of all Section 5 submissions have led to objections, resulting in jurisdictions making changes to their election systems. The submissions have become part of the norm for covered jurisdictions making changes to their systems, but for the vast majority, the changes conform to the VRA. The small fraction of changes certainly does not reflect an overintrusion by the federal government in the affairs of local government.

From the perspective of critical race theory,[75] SCOTUS, the Roberts majority specifically, uses the dual sovereignty and current data arguments to avoid speaking to the true issue at hand. Simply stated, the Supreme Court uses dual sovereignty and concerns about outdated data as a "racial shield," a protective device behind which they can hide avoiding any discussion of the racism that permeates the election processes across the nation. A "racial shield," as opposed to "racial code words,"[76] is a device that speaks to an actual political phenomenon that hides both the manner in which the phenomenon is executed and the substantive effect of that phenomenon on people. "Racial code words," on the other hand, is language one substitutes for a racial group rather than speak derogatorily of them; the word is designed primarily to create a negative image of that group to the general public or one's constituent group without explicit references to race. For instance, "illegal aliens or immigrants" are terms used at times as code words for Latinos. This term creates an image of unwashed individuals, desperate to arrive in the United States by avoiding all laws, to take the work of white working-class persons, and to avail themselves of the vast array of social services in this country. A "racial shield," such as political redistricting, speaks to a process that is legal, condoned by the Supreme Court; all state legislatures do it to gain a partisan advantage in their respective delegations and technology is used to model the large databases required to accomplish this task. The problem though is that in certain circumstances, such as the Texas redistricting process in 2011, the Latino population had to be manipulated in order to achieve a partisan advantage. This racial manipulation was performed consciously and diluted the worth of the Latino vote in various congressional districts. Another example of a "racial shield" recently used in Texas was the creation of a voter identification law to protect the integrity and security of the electoral process in the state, a commendable objective. The descriptor of the law appears simple and "high-minded," however, the problem is that the state used, as part of the strategy to create and pass this law, an argument stating that it was intended to prevent "illegal immigrants" from casting votes in Texas elections. Protecting the integrity and security of an election system is important in any democratic society, but to explicitly state that the law was designed to prevent, at best, a questionable phenomenon is another issue altogether. In this case, the intent to protect the election system was used as a shield to hide an attack on immigrants and the subsequent dilution of Latino voter strength in the state of Texas.

A "racial shield" then can best be described as a device used in the policy process allowing decision makers to divert the attention of others from issues having to do with discriminatory practices. In the case at hand, *Shelby County*, the court speaks of a theoretical governing concept, "dual sovereignty," and a purported methodological oversight as a way of shielding its review, the decisional process, and the entire jurisprudential discourse from the real issue at hand, racial purpose and discriminatory behavior in the election process. The use of a racial shield is one technique decision makers utilize to "systematically exclude events not perceived to be endemic to society."[77] In other words, rather than directly recognize that racial discrimination exists and is, therefore, a principal problem to be dealt with in the policy process, decision makers, in this case the Roberts majority, simply declare that "times have changed," and there is no longer a racism problem. The Court simply made a declaration, making racism disappear and found a technical problem as their rationalization for declaring Section 4(b) obsolete and inappropriately reauthorized by congress.

The rationale presented in *Shelby* by the Roberts majority provides fodder for those jurisdictions complaining about the strictures of Section 5. As clearly stated in the *amicus* briefs of the states in the Texas redistricting appeal, various jurisdictions feel that the federal government is being overly intrusive in state affairs or in an area specifically reserved to the state. This argument, however, in many of these states is an excuse they use to hide the racial intent important to the manner in which they redistrict at all levels and also create and institute various electoral devices.

SECTIONS 4 (B) AND 5 AND TEXAS

Although *Shelby* was decided after the Texas redistricting and Voter ID cases were heard, it did open the door for the state to resubmit redistricting plans and to implement the Voter ID law even if they were both found to be created with racial purpose. The principal reason that Texas was included under the coverage formula of Section 4(b), therefore making the state subject to preclearance under the VRA, was because of a 1975 amendment to the act adding the protection of language minorities if they constituted 5 percent of a jurisdiction's total population. This brought Latinos, Asians, and Native Americans under the protection of the VRA, requiring those jurisdictions to submit any changes to their election systems to DOJ or the DC District Court for preclearance. Although the 1975 amendment formalized coverage of Texas under the VRA, the state itself had a rich history of civil rights violations and would have been included under the original provisions of the VRA if appropriate deliberation had been given to the original process. Once covered under the VRA, Texas' record of racially discriminatory processes was vividly revealed. Since 1975, there have been 210 Section 5 objections alone in Texas, with 198 of these submitted between 1975 and 2006.

Although Texas did not come under VRA jurisdiction until 1975, it had been sued numerous times by African Americans for inhibiting access to the political process. African Americans had attempted to gain access to the state's electoral system and processes since before the Civil War to no avail. Before the Civil War they were generally denied access due to their inability to gain their freedom or to present acceptable evidence of freedom to the proper authorities. After the Civil War, intimidation by the Ku Klux Klan and the state government's refusal to approve the Fourteenth Amendment, the state commenced creating other barriers to the political participation of black persons. With the arrival of Reconstruction, African Americans ascended to many political offices in Texas as they did in other states through their alliances with Radical Republicans, but with the passage of the new state constitution in 1875 their advances began subsiding. Finally, through intimidation, gerrymandering, and the passage of new anti-participatory laws, African

Americans were completely eliminated from all state-level political offices with the final African American politician leaving office in 1897. Although African Americans were organized at the local level throughout Texas, they were not allowed to participate in the Democratic Party primary because of a 1923 state law that stated "negroes" were not eligible to participate in the primaries.[78] This was an example of the Jim Crow laws that proliferated throughout the southeastern part of the United States at that time. The law was challenged by an African American physician from El Paso, Texas, in 1923. Although Dr. Nixon lost at the district court level, he did win his appeal to the Supreme Court, *Nixon v. Herndon*,[79] where SCOTUS ruled the law in violation of the Fourteenth Amendment. Texas rewrote the law in an attempt at sidestepping the Court's ruling, declaring that political parties were private organizations and, therefore, could close their primaries to whomever they wished, particularly African Americans. The law was again challenged by another African American, Mr. Lonnie Smith, who also lost at the district court level but won at the Supreme Court in *Smith v. Allwright*.[80] Texas was found to be in violation of the Fourteenth, Fifteenth, and Seventeenth Amendments to the Constitution. Texas, still not wanting to give up the fight on this issue, allowed local Democratic parties to change their names and then hold private primaries with provisos that blacks would not be allowed to participate. Again, an African American brought suit and won at the Supreme Court, which ruled that the state's actions violated the precepts of the Fifteenth Amendment, *Terry v. Adams*.[81] Besides these early twentieth-century violations of the Fourteenth and Fifteenth Amendments, Texas imposed a poll tax on voters that also served as a barrier to not just African Americans but all low-income individuals including Latinos.

The history of the legal relationship between Latinos and the state of Texas is much different than that of African Americans. Part of the difficulty in including Latinos under the VRA was the manner in which they have been identified racially by American society and political jurisdictions generally. Latinos were not covered under any of the Civil War Amendments or the 1965 VRA for various reasons, including confusion as to their racial classification by the government and the manner in which Latinos were incorporated into the United States. This will be elaborated on in more detail in chapter 4 but deserves a mention here. Until the late 1960s, there was little understanding as to the specific ethnicity of Latinos outside the Latino communities themselves. The government of the United States classified Latinos for the first time in the 1930 census as "Mexicans"; in the 1940s, the U.S. government after a great deal of consultation with the Mexican government classified "Mexicans" as white.[82] The next instance where there was any attempt to lend sophistication to the Latino identifier by the Bureau of the Census was in 1970, and it has been refined every decennial census since. The 1970 Census classified Latinos as "persons of Spanish surname"; in 1980, the classification changed to include a question on race, followed by a question requesting individuals to identify themselves as "Hispanic" and then an option was added to further refine the category by adding a "Chicano" option for identification. In the 1990 census, a "write-in box" was added, and individuals were encouraged to elaborate on what Hispanic subgroup they felt they fit in. In 2000, the race and Hispanic questions were reversed with a reminder to answer both the race and ethnicity questions. Individuals could also choose more than one race if they wished. The identifier "Latino" was added as an option in 2000. Generally, the 2010 census questions remained the same as in 2000. This evolution of possible identification is interesting in itself as the continued "refining" of the Latino identifier partially has attributed to inaccurate counts of Latinos residing throughout the country. As an aside from a methodological perspective, this constant changing of identifiers makes gathering longitudinal data from the census bureau difficult, directly affecting the redistricting process and the manner in which the Texas legislature conceives of a voter identification law. Nevertheless, as mentioned earlier, Latinos were included under coverage of the VRA in 1975 when they were recognized as a "language minority" under the new Section 203 of the act. Again, findings to Congress that the electoral process for Latinos had been fraught with racial discrimination were required. As a result, a great deal of evidence showing the inequities in education, housing, health care, and election participation was placed into the public record, substantiating the need for coverage of the Latino community.

Another reason Latinos were not covered under the VRA originally was that during the era in which the VRA was being deliberated social science was dominated, and it still is to a great extent, by a "dual racial" analytical model. The American academy, as well as most national institutions, saw and see race relations as the tensions that existed and still exist between white and African American persons only. Little attention was being paid or is paid to the plight of Latinos. By the time the VRA was being considered for deliberation, the most prominent Latino civil rights activist was Cesar Chavez, founder of the United Farm Workers Union. Generally, unlike the African American Civil Rights Movement, Latinos have lacked for a central "leader" figure of the stature of Dr. Martin Luther King. The Mexican American Legal Defense and Educational Fund (MALDEF), the most prominent Latino civil rights public interest litigation firm, was not founded until 1969, well after the passage of the VRA. As a result, the only Latino civil rights litigation was brought by private attorneys on their own initiative or at the behest of organizations such as the League of United Latin American Citizens (LULAC) or the GI Forum, a Latino organization founded by World War II Mexican American veterans.

The history of Latino voting rights litigation in Texas is not as clear as that of the African American community. This is partially explained by the manner in which Latinos have been classified and have classified themselves racially. Nevertheless, Latinos have brought other civil rights lawsuits that laid the groundwork for their eventual protective inclusion of all civil rights laws including the VRA. The most important of these lawsuits was *Hernandez v. Texas*, 347 U.S. 475 (1954) which was issued two weeks before *Brown v. Board of Education*. The *Hernandez* decision was an appeal arguing that trials heard by juries in Texas were biased because they systematically excluded Mexican Americans. The Supreme Court voted unanimously in favor of Mr. Hernandez's appeal and ordered a retrial with an unbiased jury. The importance of this decision was that it extended Fourteenth Amendment protections to Mexican Americans, thus laying the foundation for their inclusion as a covered group in later civil rights laws.

The history of Latinos suing over election injustices is not as old as that of African Americans. The earliest case on record is *White v. Regester*,[83] was a combined African American and Latino challenge to the at-large election system Texas used to elect their state house of representatives. The suit only focused on the counties of Dallas and Bexar (San Antonio); African Americans challenged the system in Dallas County and Mexican Americans challenged in Bexar County. The court ruled that since *Hernandez* included Mexican Americans as a protected group under the Fourteenth Amendment, they had standing to bring the suit in *White*. The court ruled that, although at-large schemes were not in themselves unconstitutional, the two cases before the bench were based upon evidence brought under the *totality of circumstances* test.[84] The case against Bexar County was decided after the Supreme Court weighed evidence that the Mexican American community had been discriminated against in all areas of public life, particularly in the areas of education, health, housing, and politics.[85] Since *White,* the Latino communities throughout the state of Texas have brought more than 200 voting rights lawsuits on all jurisdictional levels including state, local, special, and school district.[86] If one considers that at least 150 Section 2 lawsuits and more than 200 Section 5 objections have been entered against Texas since 1975, one can easily conclude that this state is, without a doubt, one of the most formidable violators of the VRA of those states covered under the provisions of Section 4(b) that were struck down by the Roberts majority in *Shelby*. Between 1982 and 2006, the latest year identified in *Shelby*, "Texas has had the second highest number of Section 5 objections. . . . Only Mississippi had more."[87] During this time frame, DOJ objected 107 times to various redistricting schemes in the state, including ten at the statewide level.[88] In fact, Texas has been sued in statewide redistricting efforts after every census since 1990 inclusively.[89] During the twenty-four years of the Perales, et al., study, DOJ filed objections against Texas for annexations, various types of discriminatory election schemes, and changes in election polls, forms of ballots used on Election Day, and early and absentee voting, election dates, and voter qualifications.[90] It goes without saying that Texas possesses a rich history of attempting to sidestep provisions of the Voting Rights Act and dilute the votes of Latinos and other covered groups. A partial explanation for this can be found in the historical relations between Anglos and Latinos, which we will proceed to in the next chapter. Most important, however, was that the data on Texas were not even mentioned or considered in the *Shelby County* decision; yet this decision will directly affect the state and how it manages its election systems in the future. With its record of wholesale election discrimination, one can only speculate that *Shelby* will open the floodgates for more and more elaborate election discrimination schemes not only in Texas but across the nation.

WHY IS THIS IMPORTANT?

The discussion to this point is important for a number of reasons. There is no order of priority to these reasons, because they are all equally important to developing a method for understanding how racial purpose or intent can be hidden during a policy process. In the area of election policy in the state of Texas, racial intent was purposefully stated as a reason to structure the party primary process as a way in which to prevent African Americans from voting. The poll tax system that was found unconstitutional in *Harper v. Virginia Board of Elections*[91] was also used to create a barrier to the participation of poor people and people of color. This legacy is a reflection of the deep racial tensions that run throughout the history of Texas since before it became a state through the present day. Racial sentiments and prejudices, deeply embedded in the historical consciousness of Texas decision makers, find their way into the policy process and eventually written in to the very laws that govern how elections are conducted in the state.[92]

This process can be intentional as we will discover when we discuss the case of the 2011 redistricting process in Texas, but the most discouraging aspect of this is that racial purpose becomes part of the normal way of making a decision about the election process in this state. An essential part of the normalization process is that the racial rhetoric changes throughout the history of the process. In the early stages of the state's history, the rhetoric was clear and clearly stated; the process was designed to prevent people of color from voting. Now, the intent is hidden behind "racial shields" that speak to one topic making the decision appear race neutral when the opposite is the reality. Most important and devastating to advocates of voting rights and particularly to those individuals most affected by the policy is that "racial shielding" is modeled and legitimized by the highest court in the land. This is most evident in the *Shelby County* decision that will be used as the cited precedent for all jurisdictions wishing to pass legislation that will in the future inhibit and dilute the voting power of Latinos and other groups covered under the VRA.

This discussion is also important in view of the only guidance the Supreme Court has provided to date on the steps one must follow if they wish to provide evidence of racial intent. These steps were set forth in the *Village of Arlington Heights v. Metropolitan Housing Development Corporation*[93] and are the subject of the next chapter and lie at the heart of the proposed methodological techniques and research design used to identify racial purpose when it is directly left out of the decisional process.

NOTES

1. 42 U.S.C. §§ 1973 or Public Law 89-110, 91-285, 94-73, 97-205.
2. 446 U.S. 55 (1980).
3. 570 U.S.___(2013).
4. Nos. 11-713, 11-714, 11-715.
5. No. 11-713, 714, 715, p. 2.
6. Ibid., p. 17.
7. Ibid.
8. Ibid.
9. Ibid., p. 18.
10. 521 U.S. 898 (1997).
11. 505 U.S. 144 (1992).
12. *United States v. Sprague,* 282 U.S. 716 (1931).
13. Ibid., p. 19.
14. 507 U.S. 25 (1993).
15. 420 U.S. 1 (1975).
16. 429 U.S. 252 (1977).
17. This was recently the case in San Antonio, Texas when a sitting city councilwoman made biased comments against members of the gay community. The local and national gay communities have called for her resignation. She has found a great deal of support from members of the local Tea Party. *San Antonio Express-News,* Aug. 16–25, 2013.
18. 42 U.S.C. §§ 1973.
19. *Shelby County v. Holder* will be referred to interchangeably as *Shelby County* or *Shelby* throughout the remainder of this volume.

20. 565 U.S.__(2012).

21. 570 U.S.__(2013).

22. See particularly Kousser, J. Morgan. 1999. *Colorblind Justice: Minority Voting Rights and the Undoing of the Second Reconstruction* (Chapel Hill, NC, and London: The University of North Carolina Press).

23. Grofman, Bernard, Michael Migalski and Nicholas Noviello. "The 'Totality of Circumstances Test' in Section 2 of the 1982 Extension of the Voting Rights Act: A Social Science Perspective." *Law and Policy.* Vol. 7, No. 2, April 1985.

24. Senate Rep. No. 97–417, 97th Cong., 2d Sess. (1982), pp. 28–29.

25. Grofman et al., "The Totality of Circumstances Test," pp. 202–208.

26. 512 U.S. 974 (1994).

27. 431 U.S. 407 (1977).

28. For a thorough discussion of the *Shelby* decision see Richard L. Hasen's "Shelby County and the Illusion of Minimalism," *Legal Studies Research Paper Series No. 2013–116.* School of Law, University of California, Irvine.

29. The origin of the term Jim Crow is not clear but appears to have entered the popular lexicon in the early nineteenth century in reference to a specific minstrel show actor and used as a derogatory term for African Americans in that historical era. Jim Crow Museum of Racist Memorabilia, Ferris State University.

30. *Shelby County, AL. v. Eric Holder, et al.* 570 U.S. 15 (2013).

31. Sec. 4(b), VRA.

32. 383 U.S. 307 (1966).

33. *South Carolina v. Katzenbach*, 383 U.S. 301, 358–60 (1966).

34. 17 U.S. 316 (1819).

35. 521 U.S. 507 (1997).

36. 557 U.S.193 (2009).

37. 446 U.S. 156 (1980).

38. Hasen only points out the arrogance of the Roberts Court and possible future attacks on the VRA. My contention is that there appears enough language in the *Shelby County* decision indicating the possibility that attempts will be made to chisel away at the protections of the Fourteenth and Fifteenth Amendments.

39. Hasen, ibid.

40. Hasen, ibid, p. 18.

41. Thomas E. Mann and Norman J. Ornstein, *It's Even Worse Than It Looks: How the American Constitutional System Collided With the New Politics of Extremism* (New York: Basic Books, 2012).

42. "President Jackson's Proclamation Regarding Nullification," December 10, 1832.

43. Stanley Campbell, *The Slave Catchers: Enforcement of the Fugitive Slave Laws, 1850–1860* (Chapel Hill: University of North Carolina Press, 1970); Don E. Fehrenbacher, *The Slaveholding Republic: An Account of the United States Government's Relations to Slavery* (London: Oxford University Press, 2002).

44. 92 U.S. 542 (1876).

45. 412 U.S. 783 (1973); 384 U.S. 73 (1966).

46. 400 U.S. 112 (1970).

47. 446 U.S. 55 (1980).

48. *Cruikshank,* 542.
49. 446 U.S. 55 (1980).
50. 505 U.S. 144 (1992).
51. 521 U.S. 898 (1997).
52. *Dred Scott v. Sanford,* 60 U.S. 393 (1857).
53. 163 U.S. 537 (1896).
54. Peter Irons. *A People's History of the Supreme Court* (New York: Viking Press, 1999), pp. 157–165.
55. 347 U.S. 483 (1954).
56. These included many of the lawsuits that followed dealing with public accommodations such as *Heart of Atlanta Motel Inc. v. United States,* 379 U.S. 241 (1964).
57. *Regents of the University of California v. Bakke*, 438 U.S. 265 (1978).
58. Peter Irons, ibid.
59. www.donorstrust.org/AboutUS/MissionPrinciples.aspx.
60. www.projectonfairrepresentation.org.
61. Ibid.
62. 11–345 (2013).
63. *Grutter v. Bollinger* 539 U.S. 306 (2003).
64. March 7, 1965, Selma, Alabama a voting rights protest march from Selma to Montgomery of 600 marchers was met with violence from sheriff's deputies and white citizens, police dogs, and tear gas that was televised nationally and proved to be one of the most iconic moments of the voting rights movement. The march was led by a young John Lewis, now a member of congress, and the Rev. Hosea Williams of the Southern Christian Leadership Conference.
65. June, 1964. Three voter registrars, James Chaney, Andrew Goodman, and Michael Schwerner, were abducted and murdered by Ku Klux Klan members, one of whom was a deputy sheriff.
66. www.shelbyal.com.
67. Alexander Hamilton, James Madison, and John Jay. "Federalist 84." *The Federalist, The Gideon Edition.* Edited by George W. Carey and James McClellan. Indianapolis, IN: Liberty Fund, 2001. Irons, ibid. Pp 17–23. Also see Jay Wexler. *The Odd Clauses: Understanding the Constitution through Ten of Its Most Curious Provisions.* Boston: Beacon Press, 2011. Pp. 99–101.
68. Irons, ibid., pp. 464–84. Hasen, ibid., p. 31.
69. Her dissent was much longer than the majority opinion.
70. III, A at p. 13.
71. Ibid.
72. Ibid.
73. Ibid.
74. www.justice.gov/crt/about/vot/sec_5/obh_actv.php.
75. A clear and basic introduction of Critical Race Theory or CRT can be found in Richard Delgado and Jean Stefancic's *Critical Race Theory: An Introduction* (New York: NYU Press, 2012).

76. Eduardo Bonilla-Silva. *Racism Without Racists: Color-Blind Racism and the Persistence of Racial Inequality in America* (New York: Rowman & Littlefield Publishers, Inc., 2014). See particularly Chapter 2.

77. Henry Flores, *The Evolution of the Liberal Democratic State.*

78. Texas 1923, Article 309a.

79. 273 U.S. 536 (1927).

80. 321 U.S. 649 (1944).

81. 345 U.S. 461 (1953).

82. Patrick D. Lukens, *A Quiet Victory for Latino Rights: FDR and the Controversy over Whiteness* (Tucson: The University of Arizona Press, 2012).

83. 412 U.S. 755 (1973).

84. VRA, Section 2(b), amended, 1982.

85. 412 U.S. 768.

86. Nina Perales, Luis Figueroa, and Criselda G. Rivas "Voting Rights in Texas, 1982–2006." *Southern California Review of Law and Social Justice.* Los Angeles, CA: University of Southern California, Gould School of Law, Spring, 2008. pp. 713–59.

87. Ibid., p. 714.

88. Ibid., p. 714.

89. The author has served as an expert witness for plaintiffs in each of the last three statewide redistricting lawsuits that included state senatorial, house assembly, and congressional jurisdictions.

90. Ibid., pp. 731–46.

91. 383 U.S. 663 (1966).

92. Chandler Davidson. 1992. *Race and Class in Texas Politics.* Princeton, NJ: Princeton University Press.

93. 429 U.S. 252 (1977).

Chapter Two

In Search of Racism

This chapter speaks to a process that has evolved over a long period of time designed to hide a well-kept secret, that racism is alive and well in the United States generally but specifically in Texas and it predominates the public policy process. The search for racism cannot be limited by time frames that are only a few years in duration. The search for racism must encompass a long historical period covering many eras and generations. Contemporary racism may only be understood as the evolutionary end product of a long series of changing processes shielded by changing rhetoric. This strange phenomenon reared its ugly head during the preparation of testimony for the Texas Redistricting lawsuit of 2011, *Perez, et al. v. State of Texas*[1] and then repeated itself during the pre-trial preparation stage of the Texas Voter Identification lawsuit in July 2012, *Texas v. Holder, et al.*[2] The principal preparatory task was to generate research and prepare testimony based on the suspicion that "racial purpose" was an essential element in both the redistricting process and the manner in which the voter identification law was passed in the state legislature.

The fundamental problem was that at the initial stage of the research process in both cases there was no direct evidence that racism had played a role in either decision. Direct evidence is best defined as any documentation wherein racism is clearly identified in evidentiary material as the motive behind how congressional districts were drawn or the voter identification law was written. This type of evidence usually takes the form of memoranda, e-mail communications, or other types of documents where clearly stated language leaves no doubt that racism was at the core of the decision. In most voting rights cases this material is difficult to obtain because it has been hidden intentionally, protected as lawyer-client privileged material, or simply does not exist. In the two cases discussed here direct evidence of racial purpose was found in the redistricting case in a roundabout way but was nonexistent in the voter identification case. In the redistricting case circumstantial evidence of racial intent was uncovered during the discovery phase when Texas submitted the redistricting plans to the DCDC as part of the preclearance hearing process. Initially, Texas refused to release the e-mail evidence but was forced to by the DCDC.

CHOOSING A RESEARCH STRATEGY

One of the guiding principles of research is that every discipline appears to have unique techniques and preferences for some statistical tests over others. Each discipline, regardless of whether one is in the "hard or soft" sciences, prefers some strategies, techniques, and statistical tests over others. Generally, tradition dictates the choices in these areas and what is used today has been based on techniques that have endured a great deal of testing, evaluation, and commentary. Essentially, the techniques that predominate in a discipline have stood the test of time and evaluation by the academy, except in one area and this is the area of litigation research where the acceptance by the judiciary has made it difficult to pursue the traditional avenues of academic evaluation. Under the usual avenues of academic evaluation research techniques and statistical tests are measured on how well they perform over an extended period of time and in many different disciplines. The techniques themselves go through rigorous refereeing processes and are subject to debates in appropriate journals. Various scholars test and retest the techniques and perform replication studies for extended periods of time before the techniques are accepted by various disciplines. Each discipline also decides the standards for acceptance for each technique. Interestingly enough, some statistical tests, for instance, will have different standards of "proof" among disciplines depending upon the type and quality of the data under consideration. For instance, the use of a basic generalized linear regression technique uses different standards for acceptance of effects or levels of confidence depending upon whether one is a social or natural scientist. Social scientists generally measure the behavior of humans which is much more difficult to quantify than those variables or subjects studied by natural scientists where the measurements are more finite. The statistical technique is acceptable in both disciplines and the algorithms function the same way; the outcomes, however, are interpreted differently.

Litigation research is very different in many ways but principally the evaluators of research tend to be juries (composed of laypersons for the most part), judges and lawyers. Acceptance of the techniques or tests are based upon whether they can make the evidence clearly understood to the legal community and basically whether the techniques "will help the trier of fact (judges and juries) understand the evidence or to determine a fact in issue."[3] The aim of litigation research, in other words, is to substantiate the claims of one side in a given legal petition either for the defense or plaintiff. As a result the evidence and the expert who produces it must stand for rigorous cross-examination during depositions and trial. Given the advocacy nature of trials and the zealous representation for clients lawyers are sworn to perform, it goes without saying that this process can be extremely difficult and stressful for the experts. Generally, the areas of law run the gamut of everything from criminal to civil cases. Litigation research can cover everything from accounting practices, to mortuary sciences, to statistical techniques, to automobile accident investigation. In every case, evidence must speak to the facts of a given petition. The data, methodologies, and statistical techniques must meet standards of any given profession as well as those set forth in legal precedence. These standards have been set forth in what has come to be called the *Daubert Rule* that emanated from *Daubert v. Dow Merrell Pharmaceuticals*.[4] This decision led to a set of standards whereby expert testimony must use techniques that are based in "scientific knowledge" must "assist the trier of fact," and must present a judge with a clear standard upon which to base her decision. "Scientific knowledge" is defined as methodologies or techniques that are grounded in the "scientific method" and have been tested and accepted by the scientific community. The rules defined and accepted by the court are designed to prevent "junk" or "pseudo" science from being entered into evidence.[5]

The redistricting case did not pose a methodological challenge because direct evidence of racial purpose was available although it was difficult to obtain. The voter identification case was another matter altogether because, as the *House Journal* showed, the legislators denied the existence of racial purpose or intent. The lack of direct evidence in the latter case presented a research quandary because the methodological problem then became "how does one identify what the principal purpose of a policy is if it is intentionally hidden throughout the public policy process?" On a conceptual level this problem is tantamount to asking a researcher to create a research design or model to identify a principal variable missing from or hidden in the model. There are several ways in which to approach this problematic. One way is to create a model assuming that the variable exists and then simply letting the data point to the direction and existence of the missing variable. Another way is discovering missing data that directly point to the existence of the missing variable. Borrowing a technique from the world of statistics, one simply sifts through all the available data. If upon completion of the sifting process one has yet to uncover the missing variable, then one may identify the missing information as the missing variable or at least as information that can partially account for the missing variable. This is generally the situation when one concludes that the explanation in a statistical model may be due to the effects of unidentified intervening variables or may be the effects of spurious or unknown variables. In this instance, further research is required to test whether the effects of the variables originally excluded from the initial model do affect the behavior of the dependent variable or variables. In some special circumstances it may prove impossible to identify the missing information or variable for any number of reasons. For instance, it may be the case that there aren't sufficient resources, i.e., money, time, appropriate technology, and so forth, allowing the researcher to identify or gather the data. In the voter identification lawsuit this may have been the case when lawyers protected privileged information making the data unavailable. Most importantly, however, one must consider whether any of these methods violate the *Daubert Rule*?

If one peruses each of the methodological options one can easily determine that a good cross-examining attorney can charge an expert witness with not pursuing the scientific method and simply going through an exercise in speculation. However, litigation research in civil rights cases cannot be taken so frivolously because of the quality of life effects the outcome of a trial has on the well-being of a community of individuals who have been discriminated against for decades if not centuries. This is particularly true in situations where the rhetoric of racism has changed from one where direct references to race were used in one historical era to one where racial shields are utilized to hide the racial intentions of the decision makers.

GUIDANCE FROM THE
UNITED STATES SUPREME COURT

Since the first principle under Rule 702 is to provide information that will assist the court in understanding the facts of the case then it behooves one to look to the court for guidance as to what the court perceives as to the types of evidence that will assist in uncovering whether racial purpose lies behind a specific decision. The Supreme Court provided such guidance in *Village of Arlington Heights v Metropolitan Development Corporation.*[6] In this decision the Court found that racial purpose was not a motivating factor in the manner in which a local governmental unit applied its zoning laws. In its opinion the court did state, however, that racial purpose "demands a sensitive inquiry into such circumstantial and direct evidence of intent as available."[7] The court then went on and identified investigative areas where racial purpose evidence might be found. There are ten specific areas of inquiry and one very general one[8] that were modified for use in both of the Texas lawsuits discussed here and have come to be known as the *Arlington Heights* Factors.

Below are the factors as identified by the Court together with a brief explanation as to the type of data that speak to each of the factors. The most important issue is that voting rights litigation falls under the evidentiary rules of civil law which means that generally the "preponderance of the evidence" must substantiate the facts and the judge will be the determiner of when this standard is met. As a result voting rights litigation researchers seeking to provide information on racial purpose or intent must provide data on more than one of the areas listed below each of the *Arlington Heights* Factors *(AHFs)*. A shorter name has been inserted at the beginning of each *AHF* for brevity's sake.

Arlington Heights Factors

1. Disproportionate Impact (Disproportionate impact not sole determinant of invidious racial discrimination)
This is the factor under which much of the empirical information will be found but includes categories of information that speak to the nature of racially polarized voting, studies on differential turnout rates, changes in demographics in a specific jurisdiction, and so forth. With the exception of the racial polarization data most of these data are descriptive in nature. The racial polarization data are normally generated by a separate expert who gathers the appropriate information and then subjects the data to statistical testing using any number of techniques from double-regression, King's EI or R. Basically, racial polarization in the electorate can be defined as statistical evidence showing that racial or ethnic groups vote dramatically differently and prefer different candidates than each other. So, Anglos vote differently and prefer different candidates than do Latinos or African Americans. A clear pattern of these divergent voting patterns must be uncovered consistently over a lengthy period of time and covering a broad array of elections within the jurisdiction subject to the lawsuit. In Texas, for instance, evidence demonstrates that racial polarization exists at all jurisdictional levels in elections from presidential to special district elections regardless of whether the elections are partisan or not. Generally, these same patterns may be found throughout the United States but may be more intense in some regions because of a history of racial tensions in those areas. These data are generally produced using various types of regression analyses and, unless they are stark, subject to interpretation by attorneys and judges.

2. Racial Purpose Communications (Proof of discriminatory purpose negating judicial deference to other decisional factors)

This includes evidence from the record revealing racial purpose such as e-mail communications, all communications documents, agency reports, legislative records, memoranda and minutes of meetings, public utterances of decision makers, and so forth. This is the most important information because it will provide the most direct evidence speaking to racial purpose. Sometimes this information will not be uncovered through the normal *duces tecum.*[9]

3. Circumstantial and Direct Evidence (Sensitive inquiry into circumstantial and direct evidence of intent)

This may include both the historical record depicting past treatment of covered groups in all social areas; it may also include evidence of racial animosity surrounding the legislative environment. Evidence of this last sort may include video reports of the relationship between legislators and hate groups, racist demonstrations during or before a legislative session, racist outbursts by legislators during committee hearings, and so forth.

4. Effect on Population (Impact of official action bearing more heavily on one race than another)

This area includes the empirical data mentioned under number 1 above but also may include additional data on all areas of social life that fall under the *totality of circumstances* test. For instance in the voter identification case evidence concerning whether or not in-person voter fraud was being committed was used to discuss this category. The data should also include information concerning which racial group will be affected by the implementation of a law written in a certain manner. This variable will include economic impacts such as effects on wages or other sources of income; time spent away from work or school; age-related data; transportation costs; and, so forth. This is generally referred to as disparate impact analysis and purports to show how implementation of a policy will have an extremely different or "disparate" effect on specific racial groups. Data are arrayed showing how, for example, the transportation costs of obtaining a voter identification card are relatively more burdensome on Latinos and poor persons than Anglo and middle-class individuals. As of this writing, however, this technique is being challenged in the Supreme Court.[10]

5. Racial Patterns (A clear pattern, unexplainable on grounds other than race may emerge from the effect of state action, even when state action appears neutral)

This factor may contain some empirical data or it may not, depending on the substance, subject, and facts of the case. As an example during the Texas redistricting case a table was presented to the court indicating the number of individuals that had to be removed from one congressional district to achieve the apportionment ratio. The table also included how many individuals were moved, what racial group they belonged to, what their turnout rates were, and how different candidates would fare within the voting precincts included and excluded from the newly designed district. The table itself let a pattern emerge that could not be explained on grounds other than race.

6. Historical Background (Historical background of the decision revealing a series of official actions taken for invidious purposes)
The data used for any variables identified in this area are historical in nature and generally cover all public policy areas. Both old and recent historical records must be set forth. Essentially, by arraying the historical record in chronological order one may be able to develop a clear evolutionary pattern of any discriminatory purpose. Still, this factor is best substantiated through the presentation of direct evidence and is supplementary in nature.

7. Decisional Chronology (The specific series of events leading up to the challenged decision)
These data include information from various media types including internet sources (for example YouTube videos) to the legislative record. This may also include all attempts at communicating with authorities to correct a perceived discriminatory action from public petitions to attorney interactions. These data are information that represent the intensity and quality of race relations in the jurisdiction including examples of anti-immigrant rallies, castigating persons in places of employment or public places against the use of Spanish, maintenance of separate racial social groupings, and so forth.

8. Procedural Departures (Departures from the normal procedural sequences)
This may be produced through a construction of the legislative record outlining all procedures that went into the design, construction, and passage of a law. Compare the actual process with stated and published procedures and then simply present a comparison of the deviation to the courts. Here a presentation of a chronology and comparative analysis of how a certain policy was developed juxtaposed against what the "normal process" would look like. Evidence of the avoidance of conventional parliamentary procedures, unusual scheduling to either rush or delay matters, and avoidance of public hearings to minimize input from professionals, activists, or community members constitutes the heart of the evidence in this factor. Direct evidence may be derived from minutes of meetings, daily journals of legislative meetings, and public memoranda.

9. Goal Departures (Substantive departures too may be relevant particularly if the factors are usually considered important strongly favor a decision contrary to the one reached.)

These may be empirical data but not necessarily indicating how a particular public official or entity wishes to achieve a certain aim, i.e., fairly redistrict or protect the integrity of the ballot, yet their actions lead to other than the stated goals. The record may show that the original objectives or goals of a policy may not remain the same as the impact or "effect" data show. This difference may be the result of changing rhetoric as was the situation in the voter identification lawsuit when the law was initially intended to prevent fraudulent voting by illegal immigrants to one that was designed to protect the integrity and security of the ballot.

10. Legislative and Administrative History (The legislative and administrative history especially where there are contemporary statements by members in minutes, records, or reports. Where necessary some public officials may be called to the stand to testify as to racial purpose.)

This area is fairly clear if the public record is replete with both explicit racial commentaries by public officials. This may include hearsay evidence, innuendos, or the use of code words. One can then request the public officials to testify, either in court or in deposition, to determine their purpose. If they refuse or fall on "legislative privilege" then they can be challenged and, in extreme or special cases determined by the court, may be subpoenaed and compelled to testify under oath.

11. Alia.

The court was not clear about this factor other than stating that "the forthgoing summary identifies, without purporting to be exhaustive, subjects of proper inquiry in determining whether racial discriminatory intent existed."[11] One topic that is missing and may be included in this category is the history of voting and civil rights litigation in which the jurisdiction in question has been subject to before and since the passage of the VRA. For instance, Texas' record of 189 Section 5 objections displayed by type of offense and jurisdiction juxtaposed to the demographics of the specific jurisdiction is the type of evidence appropriate under this category. Additionally, if possible, uncovering any direct evidence of racial purpose in any Section 5 objection or Section 2 trial to lend depth to evidentiary production would be appropriate here. Finally, racial purpose or intent evidence found in the legislative record, city council meetings, county journals, or any coincidental committee meetings could be presented under this factor.

QUALITATIVE METHODOLOGICAL CONSIDERATIONS

Following the Court's guidance is very important for it gives the researcher a general road map to follow in preparing litigation research and it mirrors the evidence a court may find useful in understanding the case facts allowing it to make an appropriate judicial decision. The next step, however, in the development of a methodological strategy for uncovering the existence of racial purpose when it is hidden in the policy process, is to peel away the various layers of analysis that conceptually enclose the problematic and to place these layers within a greater theoretical construct. Good scientific research must be able to identify the cause/effect nexus in order to allow for generalizability and development of sound and reasonable conclusions concerning the relationship between the data and those same conclusions or observations. The courts also wish to draw a direct conclusion between the data and the facts of the case and a reason as to why the facts violate a specific rule of law or precedent. This last linkage is particularly important in disparate impact analysis where one must make a clear connection between purpose or intent and effect. The court's good intentions notwithstanding, the eleven *Arlington Heights* Factors can make data gathering burdensome and, in some cases, redundant. This will become evident as a discussion of each of the factors unfolds throughout this volume. In the final analysis the eleven factors will be reconstituted into four that prove to be more efficient and easily operationalized, while allowing each character to maintain mutual exclusivity. This reconstruction and definition is discussed in chapter 6.

There are at least three layers of analysis that must be considered before general qualitative data gathering can commence. Quantitative data gathering also depends on understanding how each of these layers are defined although some quantitative methods, already essential elements of voting rights litigation, will be gathered regardless because they have been defined as required evidence by some of the factors. As a result, the most robust research technique one may employ in presenting evidence in litigation research is what is known in the social science research community as a "Mixed Methods Research" or MMR, some scholars also refer to this approach as a "Multi-methods Research" approach. Social Science has begun to understand that combining quantitative with qualitative research methods provide more explanatory power to a comprehensive investigation. This technique not only provides research creating a broader picture of the data environment but also is well suited to fulfilling the data gathering guidance set forth by SCOTUS in *Village of Arlington Heights*. Some argue that MMR may tend to create conceptual problems making identification of variables, operationalization, and data gathering difficult. For instance Ahram recently argued that the integrity of the research might also be called into question because of "conceptual slippage"[12] however it appears that the multi-dimensionality of the racial purpose concept begs for the versatility of an MMR approach. Fundamentally the most important element of the approach is the initial stage when defining "racial purpose" together with its dimensions. The matrix below is a graphic

Table 2.1.   **Mixed Methods Research Matrix**

Research Area	Quantitative	Qualitative
Disproportionate Impact	X	
Racial Purpose Communications	X	X
Circumstantial and Direct Evidence	X	
Racial Impact on Population (Effect)	X	
Racial Patterns (voting, residential, etc.) Resulting From State Action in This Area	X	
Historical Background of Decision	X	X
Series of Events Resulting in Decision	X	X
Departure From Norm		X
Goal Other Than Stated Intent		X
Legislative and Administrative History of Decision		X
Alia		x

portrayal of how well suited MMR is to gathering and presenting data following the *Arlington Heights* Factors. As the matrix clearly indicates some factors require both quantitative as well as qualitative approaches while others may only require one or the other. Of the eleven factors seven require quantitative, seven qualitative approaches while at least three require a combined approach. Regardless, the matrix clearly indicates that MMR is a robust and thorough approach to developing litigation research leading to the identification of racial purpose.

THE POLITICAL CONTEXT AND THE *ARLINGTON HEIGHTS* FACTORS

The three principal layers demarcating the redistricters and legislators during the development of both policies requiring elaboration are the individual, political and social. These layers circumscribe the process used by decision makers when making a decision. In the cases discussed here each layer, acting simultaneously, affects the substance and process of the decision. For instance, a person's value system (moral, ethical, assumptions about race, gender, and so forth) directly affect the decision makers and the subsequent policy substance three ways.

It's best to give these approaches a nomenclature to ensure an easier understanding of how they function. These ways can best be described as "decisional mechanisms" and they allow the decision maker to create a heuristic or set of heuristics that assist in identifying the problem. For instance, drawing a congressional district to ensure that a political party controls the state's entire congressional delegation will be the guiding objective of a decision maker's task definition. Winning and winning regardless of consequences drives the decision maker's policy choices and methodological decisions when determining how to gerrymander. No consideration is given, or at least it is given little importance, to the disenfranchising effects on Latino voters. The legislators involved in determining the substance of the voter identification law were working under the operating assumption, this mechanism might be called an "a heuristic mechanism," that the costs of obtaining a voter identification card to Latinos was minimal and the process simple. For a wealthy or upper-middle-class, U.S. born Anglo Texan this may be true but for a poor, working-class individual with limited transportation options who may have difficulty obtaining the requisite documents proving citizenship, the process is costly, time consuming, and very difficult. The legislators do not understand the experiences of the poor, working-class Latino and assume that their social and economic situation is similar to their own. This failure of understanding causes the legislator to fall back on the only heuristic he or she possesses, his own understanding of economic and social reality, leading him to orient the policy in a way convenient to his or her social situation and not one suited to the social conditions of Latinos generally. This heuristic creates a false perception of the reality faced by individuals or groups of persons directly affected by the law. As a result the policy will be written creating a barrier to poor, working, Latino Texans from obtaining an appropriate voting registration document.

The second mechanism affecting the decisional process is that they limit the available policy options from which to choose. This mechanism—it can be called an "exclusion mechanism"—results in the exclusion from policy considerations such possible policy alternatives as universal suffrage or allowing noncitizens to vote. These two options lie outside the bounds of acceptable policy options within American political culture generally and Texas specifically and therefore would be excluded from the array of possible policy alternatives discussed during deliberations. This heuristic works in tandem with the first in that the decision maker assumes that voting is a privilege rather than defining it as a right. Working under this assumption will result in limiting the number of policy options available to those considering the substance of a voter identification law because it will exclude from the possible options those that could be based upon the notion of universal suffrage. In the redistricting case, assuming that one would absolutely ensure protecting the right of Latinos to elect a candidate of choice would lead to the consideration of different redistricting options. Considering, for instance, that the Texas congressional delegation should be structured proportionately according to the racial and ethnic demographics of the state would result in an entirely different redistricting process as well, although this latter alternative is excluded from the range of policy options.

Finally, the first two mechanisms will result in what the final policy, whether the redistricting or voter identification laws, will look like. Here the decision makers define the parameters of the policy with language that results in an implementation plan and process, this one is labeled an "implementation mechanism," that biases the outcomes in favor of those who look and think like the decision makers and against the interests of those groups and individuals who do not. Language is value-laden describing implementation criteria and processes that weigh more heavily on some groups as opposed to others.[13]

The three decisional mechanisms work on the individual decision makers and are directly affected by the three layers already mentioned. The individual layer considers the reasons and techniques various political players or decision makers make that have a racial purpose. The political layer includes an understanding of all systemic forces that affect the decisions individual politicians make. Finally, the social variables are those created by constituents, the media, generally societal that affect the decisional process. From a theoretical perspective, however, these layers represent essential elements of the structures and processes that make up the normal operations of a liberal democratic state.[14] As a result the decision maker and her actions must be placed within the institutional construct as well as within the construct of all the institutional arrangements that will affect her behavior and within which she must function and make decisions. This "decisional matrix" affects all decision makers because they cannot make a decision in a vacuum nor can any decision be objectively decided. A decision maker may have access to unlimited resources and be free of time constraints but this situation only exists within the theoretical world. The real world of politics, the world that dictates decisional tensions, mechanisms, institutional constructs, and inter-institutional arrangements, is fraught with subjectivity and personal biases driven by political, individual, and societal constraints and tensions. Before exploring this latter assertion a brief elaboration of the three layers is in order.

THE INDIVIDUAL LAYER

The use of racial shields allowing a decision maker to hide racial purpose or intent behind other policy variables or motives may be a simplistic manner in which to describe this phenomenon. Recently published work by Lee Smolin,[15] however, may lead one to consider that decision makers, when indicating they are making specific decisions using explicitly stated objectives and variables may really be basing their decision on a variable having multi-dimensions or characteristics or may have other unidentified or unintended objectives. This action may or may not be intentional on the part of the decision maker. If it is not intentional it may be the result of the political socialization process, the evolution of the political culture in one's community, or various issues or variables coming into play simultaneously on the decision maker or the process from outside the stated decisional model. Each dimension or characteristic cannot be separated away from the variable and cannot accurately be measured quantitatively because each characteristic exists as part of each other's essentiality. In other words, all of the variables that may affect any individual decision maker when making a decision may affect the decision maker or process simultaneously, placing a great amount of tension on the decision. The fundamental problem in litigation research is that all variables must be categorized and treated as categorically different with primary emphasis placed on trying to establish which is the principal variable affecting the decision. Or, even more simplistically, insisting that only one variable is the *raison d'être* for the decision.

This phenomenon plays an important role when attempting to understand racial purpose in the Texas redistricting and voter identification cases because it appears that decision makers have a stated goal yet appear to be hiding another goal, using the stated goal as a ruse, a "racial shield," as the actual intent or purpose of a policy. The concept of the "racial shield" will unfold throughout this work and be thoroughly explicated in the final chapter. In the two cases studied here the decision makers claimed that other outcomes, such as dilutive effects on the Latino population, were incidental or coincidental to those explicitly stated at the beginning and during the policy process. In some other cases this may be true and these effects are designated "externalities" or "spill-over effects." In the Texas redistricting and voter identification cases, however, the effects were so pronounced they could not be considered as externalities or coincidental occurrences but the result of a direct intention as uncovered during the trial.

Beyond the above conceptualization issue there are several other factors that may be the cause for overlooking variables in a decisional process including: 1) decision makers constructing heuristics when having access only to a certain or a limited amount of information; 2) decision makers controlled by an initial bias; 3) decision makers lacking resources and/or ability to gather the appropriate or any information to sort through; 4) decision makers having an overwhelming amount of information to sort through; or 5) the decision is affected by political pressures exerted in varying ways and to different degrees.[16] Fundamentally, uncertainty in the public policy process is created by the quality of available information, the political situation, time constraints placed on the policy makers and more. Regardless, uncertainty places a great amount of decisional stress on the policy makers, thus forcing them to rely on certain heuristics such as those described by Kahneman and Tversky in their groundbreaking research.

In states where historically there have existed social tensions among various races such as between Anglos and African Americans or Latinos, in Texas, white public policy decision makers, when confronting certain election policy decisions involving race, borrowing Kahneman's terminology, will be "anchored" in images, thoughts, and conceptions of what individuals of each race will qualitatively bring to the election process. In other words, they construct a racial heuristic based on the sociological environments within which they were raised, educated, trained, and function. This perception is colored by the depth and intensity of race relations in the specific region or state at the moment they are attempting to make their policy choices and decisions.[17] Strained racial relations leads to the creation of public policy structured in the biases generated through a history of racial discrimination.

Racism and acting with a "racial purpose" describes the relationship between Anglos and Latinos throughout the history of Texas. The domination of Latinos by Anglos has evolved stylistically from one overtly racist in the nineteenth century, where laws existed specifically restricting Latinos from voting, attending public schools, or holding certain professions or occupations,[18] to the subtle in the twenty-first century. Currently domination by Anglos is mystified by the use of code words, associating Latinos with terms such as "immigrants," "illegal immigrants," "undocumented," "noncitizens," and so forth.[19] These code words were utilized when state policy makers redistricted the United States congressional districts in 2011 and wrote and passed Senate Bill 14, the Voter Identification and Verification Law, also in 2011 in Texas. In the first situation Texas claimed that any appearance of racial intent was coincidental to the data. Although the state admitted that redistricting decisions were designed to ensure that the Republican Party retained control of the congressional delegation, the state insisted that there was no intention to discriminate against Latino voters during the process. In the latter case the state insisted it was passing a law to deter illegal immigrants from casting votes with the sole intention of protecting the security and integrity of the ballot.[20] Again, the state insisted that there was no racial intent underlying the process giving birth to the legislation.

E-mail correspondence acquired during the discovery process in a Section 5 challenge by Texas that was heard shortly after the redistricting trial held in San Antonio, Texas, however, revealed that Texas redistricters had acted with racial purpose during the redistricting process. The most probative e-mail is reproduced in its entirety below because it shows the intent of the redistricters, how they intended to pursue the racial gerrymander, and why they intended to do so. Mr. Eric Opiela served as a staff attorney to Speaker Joe Straus (R-San Antonio) through the fall and winter of 2010 and then transferred to the staff of a Republican congressman in Spring of 2011 while Mr. Interiano was the General Counsel to the Speaker of the State House of Representatives Joe Straus (R-San Antonio) at the time of this e-mail exchange.

From: Eric Opiela [mailto:eopiela@ericopiela.com] Friday, November 17, 2010 10:19 PM

To: Gerardo Interiano

Cc: Lisa Kaufman

Subject: useful metric

Just had a thought I needed to get out before I forget it. The raw data to calculate this is going to be in the PL 94-171 dataset we'll get in March (hopefully), but it would be really useful for someone to go in and calculate a ratio for every census block in the state of CVAP/Total Population, a ratio of Hispanic CVAP/Total Hispanic Population, a ratio of Spanish Surname RV/Hispanic CVAP, and a ratio of Spanish Surname RV/Total Hispanic Population (these last two have to be calculated with the voter file overlaid with census data). It also would be good to calculate a Spanish Surname Turnout/Total Turnout ratio for the 2006–2010 General Elections for all VTDs (I already have the data for this for 2006–2008 in a spreadsheet, just need to gather it for every VTD for 2010). These metrics would be useful in identifying a "nudge factor" by which one can analyze which census blocks, when added to a particular district (especially 50+1 minority majority districts) help pull the district's Total Hispanic Pop and Hispanic CVAPs up to majority status, but leave the Spanish Surname RV and TO the lowest. This is especially valuable in shoring up Canseco and Farenthold.

Mr. Interiano responded on November 19th at 6:17 AM by saying

I will gladly help with this Eric, but you're going to have to explain to me in layman's terms. Maybe you and I can sit down and go through this and you can show me exactly what you want next week or after Thanksgiving.

Mr. Opiela responded to Mr. Interiano 12 minutes later saying,

Happy to. Thanks Gerardo. Think of as "OHRVS" Optimal Hispanic Republican Voting Strength . . . a measure of how Hispanic, and Republican at the same time we can make a particular census block.[21]

As the e-mail reveals, Mr. Opiela had been thinking about creating a "nudge factor" to adjust census tracts across the entire state that would be used as the building blocks for the creation of congressional and state house districts, even to the extent of creating a technical-sounding name for the factor labeling it an "OHRVS" or Optimal Hispanic Republican Voting Strength measure. The reference to PL 94-171 was to the official census report that has the redistricting data. Both gentlemen agreed to work together on this indicating a degree of collusion. As Mr. Opiela's e-mail indicates he had consciously thought about how to manipulate the Hispanic population numbers in order to create districts that were 50+1% Hispanic majority but underperformed electorally. The level of detail developing seven ratios for every census tract in the state speaks to the sophistication and intent to manipulate Latino data to achieve their end. Most importantly, to claim that any dilutive effect that Latino voters suffered because of their actions was coincidental is ludicrous. In other words, the intention was to make the districts appear to pass VRA retrogression standards by making them majority Hispanic while actually creating districts where Latinos would turn out at low rates, resulting in the election of Republican candidates. This manipulation had the effect of diluting the voting strength of Hispanic voters in those congressional districts that, in effect, violated the VRA retrogression standards.

In the 2014 Section 3 (c) trial additional documents were uncovered showing how this procedure was applied to CDs 20 and 35 as well. CD20 is currently held by Joaquin Castro, the twin brother of Housing and Urban Development Secretary Julian Castro, a potential Democratic vice-presidential and presidential candidate. Mr. Lloyd Doggett holds CD35 and is a liberal Democrat who has proven to be a severe critic of both state and national Republican Party policies. The population manipulation was vividly depicted in the subsequent redistricting trial that will be discussed in chapter 5; however, the metric discussed by Mr. Opiela, after implementation, resulted in the movement of more than 600,000 persons to make a less than 150,000 person adjustment to one congressional district in order to protect a Republican incumbent. Essentially, this moved electorally high-turnout Latino precincts out of the district and replaced them with low-performing Latino precincts. This was accomplished on a precinct-by-precinct basis along the northern, eastern, and western boundaries of Congressional District (CD) 23. These graphics are available in chapter 3, where they are discussed as an appropriate exposition of an *Arlington Heights* factor. The end result was that the congressional district, CD23 in South and West Texas, was a Hispanic majority citizen voting-age-population district but would not perform as such. In other words, the majority Latino population within the district would not be allowed to elect a candidate of their choice. In effect, the racialization of the data resulted in a dilution of Latino voting power within the district. Frankly, if the court had not ruled against the redistricters and the State of Texas, the new district would most likely have returned Mr. Canseco to office, making it appear that Latinos had voted for a Republican candidate. As the turnout analysis produced during the trial demonstrated, Republicans had been losing ground to Latino voters for several decades, and they were not supporting Republican candidates regardless of whether or not the candidate was a Hispanic.

Mr. Opiela's decision to manipulate Hispanic voters for political purposes was driven by many reasons, one of which reflected his decision-making under both the individual and political beliefs and layers. His operating assumption was that Latino voters would not support Republican Party candidates. His suspicion was substantiated by the expert reports on racially polarized voting submitted during the trial. As mentioned earlier, these data showed overwhelming Latino preferences for Democratic Party candidates over many elections across many jurisdictions of the state.

Essentially, Mr. Opiela's action reflects two individual strands of thought, both carrying equal weight. One thought was based on how Latinos voted, the other on achieving a political gain. The decision reflects the construction of a heuristic on the part of Mr. Opiela because he assumed that Latinos would not, under any circumstances, vote for a Republican candidate. Simultaneously, Mr. Opiela was operating under the assumption that only Anglos would vote for a Republican candidate, an assertion he made in an e-mail dated May 30, 2011, when he said in reference to manipulating Latinos in CD23 that to "add Rs (which will be Anglos) and you put a neon sign on it telling the court to redraw it." The heuristic here was that Latinos and Anglos both vote only for candidates of specific parties when, in fact, the data on racially polarized voting revealed that these absolute beliefs are false. Not all Anglos vote for Republican candidates nor do all Latinos vote for Democrats. These observations were also reflected in the racial polarization data presented at trial by Dr. Engstrom. Furthermore, Mr. Opiela understood that if he went too far in his discriminatory behavior the courts would become suspicious. In fact, it was clear that he was aware that he might be violating federal law or the VRA. Nevertheless, Mr. Opiela bases the construction of his "nudge factor" metric and subsequent implementation on his racial heuristic, reflecting a racial purpose to his decision. This decision maker's thoughts, besides being driven by the needs of a political party, were on an individual level and exemplify the assertion that public policy decisions have various layers. This decision was made within the context of a political situation and within the confines of a political institution.

The individual layer in the decisional process surrounding the passage of the voter identification bill followed a different trajectory because there was no direct evidence in the form of e-mail correspondence speaking to explicit racial purpose statements. There was, however, the *Texas House Journal* of March 23, 2011, in which the members of the Texas House of Representatives debated and discussed the voter identification legislation where it appears that racism played a large part in the construction and design of the bill. For instance, all parties involved in the passage of the voter identification law denied that racial purpose was at the heart of the policy, as did the redistricters. The *House Journal* for the day of debate revealed that policy makers went through extraordinary measures in an attempt to avoid any discussion of race or whether their deliberations, and the final law, was in violation of the VRA or any federal law.

As an example of the refusal to discuss the possible violations of the VRA during the March 23rd session, Representative Patricia Harless, Republican Co-Sponsor of the bill, refused to agree that SB 14, the voter identification laws legislative nomenclature, had to abide by the VRA. In response to a question by Representative Richard Raymond, a Mexican American Democrat from South Texas, regarding the intent of the Voter ID Bill and whether she believed the VRA was still necessary, Rep. Harless refused to discuss the purpose behind the bill or discuss the VRA. She stated in response, "As I've said before, this is a federal issue to be decided by the federal courts. This isn't for us in the Texas Legislature to discuss right now."[22] A similar attempt to engage the Senate Committee of the Whole in a discussion whether Senate Bill 14 would violate the VRA was ignored.[23] The senators refused not only to discuss whether SB 14 was in violation of the VRA but also to even consider whether the bill may be in violation of the retrogression standards in Section 5 of the VRA. This, of course, all occurred before the *Shelby County* ruling.

On the day of debate the Republican leadership was directly confronted five times by various members of the Democratic minority as to whether the Voter ID law violated federal statutes. Each objection was rebuffed through parliamentary procedures. The Democrats attempted submitting fifty-nine amendments to the law yet only ten were accepted which dealt with only minor changes in wording. Of the remaining forty-nine, five were rejected outright, the other thirty-five were tabled, and ten withdrawn. The only three amendments sponsored by Democrats that received a vote on their substance failed along party-line votes. All five VRA-related amendments were tabled, all sponsored by racial minority members. All amendments were either passed or turned back along strict partisan lines, reflecting the sharp ideological division existing in this legislative body. The table below depicts the number of proposed amendments to the voter identification bill, the name of the sponsor, the sponsor's party identification, the status of the amendment, and the voting results where appropriate. As the data indicate, only four amendments were submitted by Republicans, all were approved, three of those without a vote. Of the fifty-nine Democratic-supported amendments, only six were sponsored or co-sponsored by an Anglo and three of these were by the same member, Representative Craig Eiland. Only two of the six amendments sponsored by Anglo Democrats were approved. Of the fifty-three amendments submitted by Latino or African American members, only eight were approved, four sponsored by a Latino member and four by African American members. Of the four amendments sponsored by Republicans, only two had a Latino cosponsor and these were amendments 7 and 28, both of which had more than forty sponsors.

Table 2.2. March 23, 2011, *Texas House Journal*, Roll Call Voting on Amendments to SB 14

Amend #	Sponsor	Race	Party ID	Status of Amend	Partisan Vote
1	Anchia	L	D	W	n/a
2	Anchia	L	D	W	n/a
3	Giddings & Bonnen	W	R	A	n/a
4	Turner	B	D	W	n/a
5	Hochberg	W	D	A	n/a
6	Y. Davis	B	D	W	n/a
7	49 cosponsors		R	A	n/a
8	Eiland	W	D	T	99Y 50N 1P
9 VRA	Alonzo	L	D	T	98Y 51N 2P
10	Y. Davis	B	D	A	n/a
11	Veasey	B	D	T	99Y 48N 2P
12	Dutton	B	D	T	100Y48N2P
13	Eiland	W	D	A	n/a
14	Raymond	L	D	W	n/a
15	Martinez	L	D	T	100Y49N1P
16 VRA	Raymond	L	D	T	101Y48N1P
17	Dukes	B	D	T	99Y49N2P
18	Dutton	B	D	T	98Y49N2P
19	Allen	B	D	F	54Y90N2P
20	Alonzo	L	D	A	n/a
21	Veasey	B	D	T	100Y48N2P
22	Gonzalez	L	D	W	n/a
23	Dutton	B	D	T	99Y49N2P
24	Martinez-Fischer	L	D	T	97Y50N2P
25	Hernandez Luna	L	D	T	99Y49Y2P
26	V.Gonzales	L	D	A	n/a
27	Miles	B	D	A	n/a
28	43 cosponsors		R	A	103Y44N2P
29	Dutton	B	D	W	n/a
30	Gonzalez	L	D	A	n/a
31	Dutton	B	D	T	99Y49N2P
32	Dukes	B	D	A	n/a
33	Dukes	B	D	W	n/a
34 VRA	Raymond	L	D	T	99Y48N2P
35 VRA	Raymond	L	D	T	100Y48N1P
36	Dutton	B	D	T	99Y48N1P
37	Hernandez Luna	L	D	F	48Y99N1P
38	Burman	W	D	F	48Y100N1P
39	Anchia & Strama	L & W	D & D	T	94Y47N1P
40	Menendez	L	D	T	98Y48N2P
41	Anchia	L	D	W	n/a
42	Walle	L	D	T	95Y52N2P
43	Rodriguez	L	D	T	96Y51N2P

(continued)

Table 2.2. *(Continued)*

Amend #	Sponsor	Race	Party ID	Status of Amend	Partisan Vote
44	Gallego	L	D	T	100Y49N1P
45	Anchia	L	D	A	n/a
46	Martinez	L	D	T	101Y46N
47	Alonzo	L	D	W	n/a
48	Bonnen, Bohen, Smith	A, A,A	R,R,R	A	n/a
49	Alonzo	L	D	T	100Y49N1P
50	Raymond	L	D	T	100Y46N1P
51	Gutierrez	L	D	T	100Y48N2P
52	Castro	L	D	T	99Y49N2P
53	Lucio	L	D	A	n/a
54	Alvarado	L	D	T	98Y49N2P
55 VRA	Veasey	B	D	T	99Y48N2P
56	Anchia	L	D	T	101Y48N1P
57	Anchia	L	D	T	99Y48N1P
58	Anchia	L	D	T	101Y48N1P
59	Dutton	B	D	A	n/a
60	Reynolds	B	D	T	99Y48N1P
61	Martinez	L	D	T	100Y44N2P
62	Strama	W	D	T	100Y49N1P
63	Eiland	W	D	T	100Y49N1P

As the data in the table indicate, only Latino or African American members sponsored amendments that would have modified the voter identification bill to ensure that the bill met the standards of the VRA. On the other hand, not one Anglo legislator sponsored any VRA-related amendment to the pending legislation. These individual decisions to support or not support VRA amendments were made within the context of a political dynamic that can only be uncovered by developing an understanding of the political layers enveloping the decisional process.

THE POLITICAL LAYER

One of the historical reasons for maintaining control over any electoral process is to control the public policy process. In the United States, controlling elections, either through their outcome or access to the ballot, has been seen as vital to political control.[24] The easiest and most efficient manner in which to maintain control is to ensure that only certain social groups have access to the voting booth. From the late seventeenth through the middle of the twentieth centuries, electoral controls were placed on African Americans, Latinos,

Asians, and Native Americans across the entire country. Some examples of barriers to participation, regardless of the group, included the outright denial of the franchise, use of literacy tests, imposition of poll taxes, tests proving good moral character and standing, and so forth. The principal reason for denial of the franchise to racial minority group voters may have been partially due to a fear that once elected to office African Americans would retaliate for the many centuries of slavery they endured; Latinos would retaliate for the manner in which they were treated after incorporation; Native Americans would retaliate because of the genocide inflicted on them; and, Asian Americans would retaliate for the manner in which they were brought to the United States and their subsequent treatment. Essentially, extending the vote to these groups of individuals was considered a risky undertaking because one could not guarantee how or why these groups would vote.

Underlying these fears was the belief that Anglos are dominant culturally, intellectually, and morally over the people of color who have been historically discriminated against in the United States. The engrained belief, structured deeply in American social ideology, that groups of people who are not white are less than equal on many levels, intellectually or morally for instance, has dominated the public policy process at all governmental levels throughout the history of the country. The birth, growth, and maintenance of racism in the public and political history of the United States have been amply documented.[25] Structuring race into the policy structure was intentional from the beginning of the nation through well into the latter half of the twentieth century and a principal reason the Civil Rights Acts, including the VRA, were passed in 1965.[26] Racism persists throughout a great deal of the American electoral system even though the VRA was passed with the intention of controlling these effects. For example, from 1982 through the end of 2013, there were 1,076 Section 5 objections recorded by DOJ. There were 198 objections entered against Texas, representing the most of all states originally covered by the VRA. Two tables document objections by state. As the data in Table 2.3 indicate, Texas had the most objections of any other state. Although Texas had the most objections, much smaller states such as Georgia and Mississippi were not too far behind. The second table details the 198 objections against Texas. Sixty-seven were for redistricting violations while eighty violations involved changes in the election systems, including objections to the numbered or place systems, reapportionment restructurings, and majority vote systems. The fifty-one violations listed under the "other" category included violations such as annexations, elimination of offices, moving of polling places, elimination of elected offices, and so forth.[27] The most important issue arising from these data is that local and state jurisdictions understand that their behavior in developing election policy for covered jurisdictions is subject to scrutiny by the national government. The data

Table 2.3. VRA Section 5 Objections by State, 1975–2013

State	Number of Objections	%
Texas	198	18.4
Georgia	178	16.5
Mississippi	173	16.1
Louisiana	148	13.8
South Carolina	121	11.2
Alabama	107	10
North Carolina	65	6
Virginia	33	3.1
Arizona	22	2
New York	13	1.2
California	6	.6
Florida	5	.5
North Dakota	4	.4
Alaska	1	<.1
Michigan	1	<.1
New Mexico	1	<.1

in Table 2.3 of Section 5 Objections indicate that Texas has had the most objections since Section 5's implementation, accounting for 18.4 percent of all objections between 1975 when it first came under coverage to the present. Finally, as if to speak to the state's reputation for persistence in violating the VRA, Texas's congressional, state senate, and house plans have been objected to in every redistricting year according to the database on DOJ's website.[28]

National government oversight, specifically either DOJ or a three-judge panel of the DCDC, does serve as a somewhat effective deterrent to electoral racial discrimination in those jurisdictions. Anecdotal evidence from interviews with election officials in San Antonio, Texas, and Bexar County indicate many Texas election officials have routinized DOJ submissions and are aware of the retrogression requirements of Section 5. Consequently, when considering changes to election processes or requirements, they normally have attorneys, generally specialists in this area of law, on retainer to the respective jurisdiction, to ensure that the proposed modifications do not violate either Fourteenth Amendment or VRA precepts.

As yet there is no centrally located database that track the number of Section 2 lawsuits brought in Texas, but interviews with two practicing civil

Table 2.4. Texas, VRA Section 5 Objections by Type, 1975–2013

Redistricting	Method of Election	Other
67	80	51

rights attorneys revealed that between the two of them they have sued various jurisdictions in Texas more than two hundred times. One civil rights attorney, who represented the plaintiffs in the first voting rights lawsuit brought against the state by Latinos, *White v. Regester*, joked once that at any given time there are more than two hundred Section 2 lawsuits waiting to be filed in Texas.[29] How accurate his observation was is not clear and his statement must be taken with a "grain of salt." Still this anecdote speaks to the broad extent to which voting rights are violated by jurisdictions throughout the state.

Within the United States political system, there are many ways to assert political control over the public policy process, one of the most important being gaining control of national congressional membership through the selection and election of candidates. Election, however, requires that the chosen candidates perform well electorally within their districts. Each district's design is based on data generated in the decennial census of total population. Controlling the ethnic and racial composition of the voting population within each district is the most technical method for ensuring political control of the state legislative process and each state's legislature.[30] The redistricting process also controls the design of each district, guaranteeing that the composition of the district is favorable to that party's incumbent or chosen candidate. Constitutionally this is legal;[31] what is not legal is intentionally manipulating the populations of groups covered under the VRA to achieve a political end.[32] During both the 2001 and 2011 redistricting efforts, the Republican Party in Texas controlled the policy process, and they ensured that the congressional districts were drawn in such a manner as to mathematically favor their candidates winning the vast majority of the state's congressional seats.

In both 2001 and 2011, lawsuits were brought against the state challenging the constitutionality of the congressional redistricting process with the federal courts ruling against the state both times. One of the telling pieces of evidence during each of these trials revealed that the Republican Party was losing voting support among the growing Latino population. The Republican Party's loss of support among Latinos is founded partially in the historical racial animosity that greeted Latinos during their incorporation into the United States in 1848.[33] Although Article IX of the Treaty of Guadalupe Hidalgo that ended the Mexican War between the two countries granted all Mexicans residing in the United States and their descendants American citizenship, there had been no enforcement mechanisms until the passage of Section 5 of the VRA[34] in 1965, particularly with the added amendment of Section 203 in 1974.

Besides congressional gerrymandering, another effective way in which to manipulate elections is to develop systems that control which potential voters can actually register and electorally participate. The state of Texas, along with other states, has instituted or attempted to institute strict voter identification laws since 2003. Texas's attempts began in 2005 with the express intent of deterring "illegal immigrants" from casting fraudulent votes, thereby ensuring the security and integrity of the ballot. By the time of the actual court hearing in July 2012, the words "illegal immigrant" had been dropped from the objectives of the law, and the intent was then declared to be to ensure the security and integrity of the ballot from the casting of fraudulent votes. Thus the state changed the rhetoric from the moment of the original passage of the bill until the voter identification law was challenged in the courtroom. In effect, the state had changed the racial rhetoric from an overt use of racial code words, *illegal immigrants*, to the use of a racial shield, *fraudulent votes*. Rhetorically, illegal immigrants became fraudulent votes. The language in the bill had been changed to hide the racial purpose of the law. States attempting to or having instituted voter identification laws are listed in Table 2.5.

The voter identification situation in Texas reflects a general trend across the nation. Since 2003, thirty-five states have created some form of a voter identification law. Of the ten states listed in the first column five are covered by Section 5 of the VRA[35] and nine of the ten are governed by Republican Party legislatures. The only one not controlled by Republicans, Wisconsin, has a "divided" representational system where each major party controls one of the chambers.[36] Of the eight states listed in the second column, the Republican Party controls seven. The only state listed in column two controlled by Democrats is Hawaii. The states listed in the "strict photo ID" category require that documentary photographic proof of citizenship be submitted to an appropriate state agency as a requirement for the issuance of a state voter photo identification card.[37] As the data in the table suggest, Texas's action appears to be part of a larger national movement toward narrowing access to voting in the United States. Of those states requiring the strictest controls, the Republican Party controls 74 percent. Of the thirteen states or parts of states covered by Section 5, twelve have instituted voter identification programs.

The interesting aspect of this trend appears that it is fueled by partisan interests and not for the generally stated interests of protecting the security and integrity of the ballot box. The Texas voter identification law was challenged in federal court as constituting a violation of Section 5. The DCDC concluded that the Texas Voter ID law was in violation of the VRA. The DCDC opinion, relying upon evidence presented during the trial, concluded that the burden of the law would fall more heavily on members of racial minority groups, the poor, younger voters, and the elderly. The state appealed to the United States Supreme Court, where the decision waited the outcome of the *Shelby County* decision. Once the Supreme Court declared Section 4(b) of the VRA unconstitutional, Texas declared that they would proceed with implementation of

Table 2.5. State Requirements for Voter Identification[1]

States that Request or Require Photo ID		States that Require ID (Photo Not Required)	
Strict Photo ID	**Photo ID**	**Strict Non-Photo ID**	**Non-Strict Non-Photo ID**
In effect:	*In effect:*	*In effect:*	
Georgia	Florida	Arizona	*In effect:*
Indiana	Hawaii	Ohio	**Alabama (1), (5)
Kansas	Idaho	Virginia	Alaska
Tennessee	Louisiana		Arkansas (9)
	Michigan		Colorado
Not yet in effect:	New Hampshire		Connecticut
Arkansas (9)	South Dakota		Delaware
*Mississippi (6)			Kentucky
*Pennsylvania (7)	*Not yet in effect:*		Missouri
**Texas (1)	**Alabama (1), (5)		Montana
Virginia (8)			North Dakota
*Wisconsin (2)			Oklahoma (3)
			Rhode Island (4)
			South Carolina
			**Texas (1)
			Utah
			Washington

* New voter ID law has not yet been implemented; state presently has no voter ID law in effect.
** New voter ID law has not yet been implemented; an older voter ID law remains in effect.

(1) In Alabama and Texas, current non-photo voter ID laws stay in effect for the time being. The new *photo* voter ID requirements will take effect after receiving preclearance under Section 5 of the Voting Rights Act. Texas was denied pre-clearance in December 2011. Alabama's new photo ID law has a 2014 effective date, and the state has not yet applied for pre-clearance. The Texas law was recently denied pre-clearance for a second time by a federal court in D.C.
(2) Wisconsin's voter ID law was declared unconstitutional on March 12, 2012. Dane County Circuit Judge Richard Niess issued a permanent injunction barring enforcement of the law, which the state has said it will appeal. Read the March 6 injunction and the March 12 injunction.
(3) There are some who prefer to call Oklahoma a *photo* voter ID state, because most voters will show a photo ID before voting. However, Oklahoma law also permits a voter registration card issued by the appropriate county elections board to serve as proof of identity in lieu of photo ID.
(4) Rhode Island's voter ID law takes effect in two stages. The first stage, requiring a non-photo ID, took effect on January 1, 2012. On January 1, 2014, a photo ID requirement will replace the non-photo ID law.
(5) Alabama's new photo ID requirement takes effect with the 2014 statewide primary election. The new law also requires preclearance. The delayed implementation date was intended to ensure that the timing of pre-clearance did not occur between the primary and general elections of 2012, thus creating voter confusion.
(6) Mississippi's new voter ID law was passed via the citizen initiative process. However, the language in constitutional amendment passed by MS voters on Nov. 8 is very general, and implementing legislation will be required before the amendment can take effect. The MS provision will also require pre-clearance under Section 5 of the Voting Rights Act before it can take effect.
(7) A state judge temporarily blocked enforcement of Pennsylvania's new voter ID law. It will not be in effect for the November 2012 election, and a trial on its permanent status will begin after the election.
(8) Virginia's strict photo ID requirement takes effect on July 1, 2014. Until then, a strict non-photo ID law remains in effect
(9) The new strict photo ID law in Arkansas will take effect on January 1, 2014, or when the funding to the Secretary of State for the issuance of free IDs for voting purposes has been appropriated and is available.

[1]*National Council of State Legislatures,* http://www.ncsl.org/research/elections-and-campaigns/voter-id.aspx.

the Voter ID law. A citizen immediately challenged this from Corpus Christi, Texas. The challenge is based upon the DCDC ruling and the "racial intent" provision in Section 3 of the VRA. This case was in the beginning stages of preparation during this writing.

The facts in each case will be presented in another chapter when both cases are extensively discussed; the important issue to be brought forth here, however, is that in both cases, the three-judge panel of the Federal District of West Texas sitting in San Antonio and a different three-judge panel in the United States District of Columbia, six different judges found that both the redistricting plan and the voter identification law violated the retrogression standards of Section 5 and the one-person, one-vote standard in the Fourteenth Amendment to the Constitution. After *Shelby,* Texas decided to leave the court-imposed plan in place, but the Latino Voting Rights Taskforce, who had brought the original redistricting challenge, requested that the federal court sitting in San Antonio review the state's action as a prerequisite to the state being placed back under Section 5 preclearance requirements based on the racial intent provision of Section 3. This trial was heard in August of 2014 and a decision was pending as of this writing.

The political layer then is one that can be collective in nature where the designs of a political party are intended to pursue a strategy ensuring control of the state apparatus by following tactics that include racial gerrymandering and creating a voter registration program that controls access to political participation by certain groups of individuals. This layer may also include the individual political ambitions of various political actors. For some, it was the preservation and strengthening of one's or a colleague's congressional district to ensure reelection. Some participants reinforced their political bona fides allowing them to pursue higher political office. This was the case for Mr. Opiela, who was a Republican candidate for Agricultural Commissioner of the state.[38] On a collective level, racial gerrymandering and restrictive ballot access is and was important to the viability of the Republican Party in Texas in light of the state's changing demographics.

THE DEMOGRAPHIC LAYER

The demographic variable that drove the public policy processes surrounding both pieces of legislation is one that is perceived to affect not only the political landscape of Texas but also that of the entire United States. This layer includes more than simply the growth rate and residential patterns of Latinos but also their historical voting patterns in presidential elections, and the relationship of both to the unique structure used in the United States to elect the Chief Executive. The first facet of this layer to discuss is the rapid growth of the Latino community in the United States. Essentially, the growth of the Latino population over the last forty years resulted in it overtaking African Americans as the largest minority group in the country. Between 1970 and 2010, the Latino community grew 28.8 percent, from 4.7 percent of the country's total population to 16.3 percent. Although Latinos can be found throughout the United States, they predominate in the western part of the country with most residing in five states: Arizona, California, Colorado, New Mexico, and Texas. The Latino growth in the West between 1970 and 2010 was 39.5 percent going from 11.3 percent to 28.6 percent in that region. One of the most significant pieces of datum uncovered by the Cervantes Institute in New York that speaks to the "Hispanization" or "Latinoization" of the United States is that there are almost 50 million Spanish Language speakers in the United States, making this country the second largest Spanish-speaking nation in the world, second only to Mexico. Although the Latino[39] community is very heterogeneous due to national origin, generational, linguistic, and cultural and class differences, the vast majority, 63.2 percent approximately, have national origin roots in Mexico. Another 9.2 percent are of Puerto Rican descent with Cubans, Salvadorians, and Dominicans each representing 3 percent of all Latinos respectively. Nevertheless, Latino national origin immigrants and descendants of immigrants come from twenty different Spanish-speaking countries, ranging from Argentina to Venezuela and Spain. There is some debate as to whether to count descendants from the Portuguese-, English-, or French-speaking countries of the Caribbean, so they are excluded from this discussion.

As opposed to the Latino population growth over the last forty years, the proportion of the national population identifying as African American in 1970 was 11.1 percent growing to 12.6 percent in 2010. This population dropped in the west from 4.9 percent in 1970 to 4.8 percent in 2010. The United States Bureau of the Census predicts that the nation will become a majority minority country by 2043 and by 2060, 57.3 percent of the total population will identify as one of the traditional minority groups.[40]

These descriptive data are important when one considers that although one can find Latinos residing throughout the United States, they reside principally in only a few states, generally those with large population concentrations and many of them in the West, considered the fastest growing geographical region of the country. Latinos also are slowly becoming a consistent voting group in those states having large numbers of Electoral College votes and, therefore, have developed the potential of becoming an important presidential constituency group. This latter contention is important because polling data available for Latinos since 1980 reveal that on average they support the presidential candidates of the Democratic Party at a 65 percent rate.

Table 2.6. Estimated Latino Support for Presidential Candidates, 1980–2012

Year	Source	Dem	Rep
1980	CBS News/NYTimes	56	37
1984	CBS	66	34
	NBC	68	32
	ABC	56	44
1988	CBS & ABC	70	30
	NBC	69	31
	LA Times	62	38
1992	VNS	62	24
	LA Times	53	31
1996	Unk	72	21
2000	Unk	62	35
2004	NEP	54	34
	WCVI	67	31.4
	Zogby Intl.	65	33
	Miami Herald	65	33
2008	WCVI	68.6	28.7
	CNN	67	31
2012	Latino Decisions	75	23

Table 2.6 shows the support given by Latino voters upon exiting the polls in each of the respective general elections identified. Obviously, the data are only as accurate as how well the sampling frame was constructed for each poll, and their accuracy is subject also to the usual methodological problems caused by the manner in which exit polls are executed. For instance, although not indicated in the table, some are telephone polls, some were conducted of voters as they exited voting locations, and at least one poll was conducted electronically using e-mail and cell phones. As a result, one cannot use the data in the table to understand Latino voting behavior from a scholarly point of view or to attempt to conduct any longitudinal conclusions. One can use the data, however, to develop a very general understanding for which party's candidates Latinos said they cast their ballots in a given election. Also, some of the polls were not designed to specifically sample Latinos but were aggregations of Latino respondents who haphazardly appeared in the national sample. This was the case for the polls conducted prior to 2004. The 2004 National Election Poll (NEP) was also an aggregation poll. The William C. Velasquez Institute (WCVI), Zogby International, and *Miami Herald* polls of 2004, however, were the first polls that sampled only Latino voters, giving a clearer picture of Latino presidential voting preferences. The data generated by NEP in 2004 back through the 1980 data reflect a varied pattern of Latino support for both Democratic and Republican Party candidates although the mean level of support is 62.5 percent for the Democratic and 32.58 percent for the Republican

candidates. The polls beginning with the WCVI 2004 poll through the Latino Decisions poll of 2012 show a more consistent pattern with Latinos supporting Democratic candidates at a 67.9 percent rate and the candidates of the Republican Party at a 30 percent rate. Overall, Democratic presidential candidates received the support of 64.3 percent of Latino voters and Republican Party candidates 31.7 percent. The polling history substantiates the conventional wisdom; Latinos generally support Democratic Party presidential candidates consistently at a rate that appears to be increasing more at every election.

The final piece of the demographic layer puzzle is to understand the relationship between the residential and voting patterns of Latinos during presidential elections. A perusal of the performance of Latino voters in the last two general elections and juxtaposing those results on the distribution of Electoral College votes reveals the importance of the Latino vote to presidential candidates of either party. Below are Tables 2.7 and 2.8 revealing how the states having approximately 90 percent of all Latino voters performed in the last two general elections. The first table reflects results from the 2008 general election as the data indicate 88.8 percent of all Latino registered voters resided in only fifteen states. These fifteen states accounted for 295 Electoral College votes and President Obama won thirteen of these states, losing only Texas and Arizona. As a result, President Obama was awarded 251 Electoral College votes from these thirteen states while needing only 270 to win the election. The data do not reveal whether the Latino vote determined the election outcome in each

Table 2.7. Table for Latino Performance in 2008 General Election and Distribution of Electoral College Votes

State	EC Votes	Cum CE Votes	LRVs	%LRVs	Cum % LRVs	Presidential Winner
CA	55	55	3263	28.1	28.1	Obama
TX	34	89	2441	21	49.1	McCain
FL	27	116	1380	11.9	61	Obama
NY	31	147	836	7.2	68.2	Obama
AZ	10	157	410	3.5	71.7	McCain
NJ	15	172	388	3.3	75	Obama
IL	21	193	385	3.3	78.3	Obama
NM	5	198	346	3	81.3	Obama
CO	9	207	225	1.9	83.2	Obama
PA	21	228	189	1.6	84.8	Obama
NV	5	233	131	1.1	85.9	Obama
MA	12	245	103	.9	86.9	Obama
OH	20	265	85	.7	87.5	Obama
MI	17	282	85	.7	88.2	Obama
VA	13	295	74	.6	88.8	Obama
15	295	295	10,341	88.8	88.8	

state, only that Latinos have a prominent electoral place in each state. In a close election, given their preference for Democratic Party candidates, however, it is conceivable that Latinos would be an essential part of that party's constituency.

The data in Table 2.8 is equally compelling and reflects the results of the 2012 general election. Unlike Table 2.7, the Electoral College Performance of 2012 reflects where Latino citizens reside as opposed to registered voters, so the comparison of the final outcome of the election and the Latino residential patterns is even more nebulous. The data indicate, like the performance shown in 2008, 88.8 percent of Latino citizens resided in seventeen states, fourteen of which were won by President Obama in the 2012 election, accounting for 243 Electoral College votes. Again, it is not possible to establish from the results to what degree Latinos played a significant role in the president's winning margin in each of these states. The only conclusion one can draw from the latter set of data is that Latinos generally are more concentrated in those states won by President Obama in 2012. Linking these residential patterns with the election results and the preference polling allows one to, at least, develop a strong suspicion that Latinos have become and will continue to be an integral part of the Democratic presidential electorate and prove a barrier that the Republican Party will have to overcome or control in future general elections.

Table 2.8. Table for Latino Performance in 2012 General Election and Distribution of Electoral College Votes

State	EC Votes	Cum EC Votes	Latino Citizens	%Latino Citizens	Cum % Latino Citizens	Presidential Winner
CA	55	55	6510	.279		Obama
TX	38	93	4867	.209	.479	Romney
FL	29	122	2250	.097	.576	Obama
NY	29	151	1548	.066	.642	Obama
AZ	11	162	989	.042	.684	Romney
NJ	14	176	773	.033	.717	Obama
IL	20	196	770	.033	.75	Obama
NM	5	201	544	.023	.773	Obama
CO	9	210	497	.021	.794	Obama
PA	20	230	407	.017	.811	Obama
MA	11	241	322	.014	.824	Obama
NV	6	247	302	.013	.837	Obama
WA	12	259	298	.013	.85	Obama
GA	16	275	238	.01	.86	Romney
MI	16	291	225	.009	.869	Obama
CT	7	298	220	.009	.88	Obama
MD	10	308	176	.008	.888	Obama
17	308	308	21,441	.888	.888	

Latino Decisions, the Latino polling organization, however conducted an analysis to determine whether and to what extent Latinos directly contributed to President Obama's victories and concluded that, at least in California, Florida, New Mexico, Colorado, and Nevada, Latinos provided the winning margins for the president.[41] The data concerning the 2012 election indicate that four new states have shown increases in their Latino populations, including Washington, Georgia, Connecticut, and Maryland. Latino Decisions declared that:

> The Latino vote share numbers across key states were even more pronounced, with Latinos exceeding the national average of 75% in most of the battleground states, including a remarkable 87% in Colorado and 80% in Nevada. The 66% of Latinos who voted for Obama in Virginia, 58% in Florida, and 82% in Ohio were also critical to the overall outcome of the race. At the end of the day, we estimate that the Latino vote led to a net margin gain for President Obama of +5.4%, and a +2.3% bump in the national popular vote. Consequently, if Latinos had split their vote evenly (50/50) in this election, President Obama would have lost the national popular vote. **For the first time in American history, the Latino electorate has a legitimate claim of being nationally decisive!** (emphasis in original)[42]

Latino Decisions' analysis attributed the historical support for President Obama to a lack of adequate Republican Party outreach and a perception that the Republican Party was not sympathetic to the interests of the Latino community, particularly the Republican Party's position on the immigration issue. Although most polls place the immigration issue relatively down the list of important concerns to Latinos, it was the anti-immigrant rhetoric and its tone that appeared to alienate Latinos from Republican candidates and their agendas rather than the substance of immigration policy.

THE THREE LAYERS AND POLITICAL STRUCTURE

All three layers functioned simultaneously on the Texas decision makers considering the redistricting process and the design of the voter identification law. On one level, the decision makers were motivated by political considerations insofar as ensuring that the policy alternatives they chose were the best to guarantee electoral control of the state apparatus in future years. At the same time, however, they could not ensure the long-term success of their party without acting with a racial purpose, because the one group that threatened and will threaten control of Texas' elected offices in future elections is Latinos. Finally, given the Republican Party's intransigence in their position on issues of concern to the Latino community and their inability to develop an appropriate outreach strategy, the only remaining path is to manipulate the election system to dilute the power of the Latino vote.

Although many layers possessing many variables affect every political decision, they are also made within the context of a structure of politics.[43] The structure, in turn, delimits the options available to decision makers. The complexity of how the structures are defined and function within which the Texas decision makers must make their policy choices partially explains how they reached their redistricting decisions and designed the voter identification law that eventually became Senate Bill 14.

Essentially, the political system may be understood as a complex matrix of institutions and institutional arrangements designed to create structural barriers to the full participation of some citizens and groups of people as opposed to others. These structural barriers are created at all levels of the political structure and are designed to exclude policy alternatives on three levels. The first level of exclusion in the redistricting process is to eliminate the high-performance Latino majority precincts from certain congressional districts in order to give Republican candidates a higher probability of succeeding. This level of exclusion would prevent the Latino community from electing a candidate of their choice in direct violation of the VRA. This effort was amply evidenced by the creation of the "nudge factor" and its implementation spoken of in the e-mail communications among the various Republican Party redistricters described earlier.[44] The structural barrier in the voter identification law limited the number and types of photo identification allowed for registration and also limited which agencies are allowed to issue identity cards if a citizen lacks the appropriate one. This will be thoroughly explicated when the case study of the voter identification lawsuit is discussed in chapter 5. Still, as an example, the law accepted concealed handgun identification cards and excluded student identification cards, thereby eliminating a group of voters that had a propensity for voting for Democratic candidates while including a large number of individuals who have a higher probability of voting for Republican Party candidates. This provision also carries an added burden on young Latinos as more and more of them enter university ranks. As an interesting aside, the defendant interveners in the Texas voter identification lawsuit were two young Latinas who were left with no appropriate identification under the new law. All they possessed were outdated high school identification cards. Their family could not afford automobile insurance, so they were prohibited from obtaining driver's licenses. Their situation will be discussed thoroughly in chapter 5 when their testimony during the SB 14 Section 5 hearing is presented.

Compounding the issuance of the new voter identification cards, limiting the issuing agency to the Department of Motor Vehicles at their regional of-

fices, which are few and far between in a state as large as Texas, created difficult transportation situations for poor and working-class individuals. First,
the issuance times were limited to normal operating hours, requiring working
individuals to take time off from work in order to stand in long lines or travel
long distances to obtain the cards. The long distances and limited number of
locations caused the poor and many of the working class to incur unnecessary
transportation costs. The vast majority of these individuals were Latinos. As a
result, both the manner in which the redistricting process was structured and
the voter identification card issuance process was designed weighed heavily
against Latinos, the poor, students, and young voters.

The second level of exclusion operates concurrently with the first. By
excluding policy alternatives compatible with the interests of the Latino community, the decision gives policy preference, a policy head start if you will, to
the Anglo or Republican candidates in the targeted districts. In the redistricting case, removing the high-performance Latino precincts and replacing them
with low-performance precincts gave Anglos a policy and thus an electoral
head start. The restriction of the types of acceptable identity cards and the
limitation of their places of issuance also gave Anglos a policy head start in
the voter identification and registration process. Both policy situations placed
the Latino community, as well as the young, poor, other minority groups, and
the elderly, at an electoral disadvantage, because these policies would have a
diminishing effect on the number of potential voters and, consequently, actual participants. Substantively, placing Latinos at a policy disadvantage has
the same effect as diluting their electoral power and the value of their vote.
On a qualitative level, this makes the Latino vote less valuable in the United
States election process than that of Anglos and may be a clear example of not
meeting the "one person, one vote" standard of the Fourteenth Amendment.

The third type of exclusionary structure is a filtering process created by
the political structure itself and is a combination of social attitudes and value
systems unique to the political culture of a given society or institution. This
translates into the exclusion of policy alternatives because they are not socially or politically acceptable. So, for instance, in Texas one will never see
universal voter registration discussed as a viable policy alternative or propor-
tional congressional representation based on ethnic or racial lines. In effect,
universal suffrage would require the inclusion of all individuals residing in a
given jurisdiction regardless of their citizenship status or whether they are in
the country legally. This type of policy alternative is anathema to the values
of a society that jealously guards its borders, deports millions of individuals
for being in the country illegally, and defines voting as a privilege of citizenship rather than a human right. These types of policy alternatives are filtered
out of the policy process simply because they are not even within the realm

of socially acceptable policy alternatives; they do not exist as essential parts of the United States', let alone Texas's, political values. These policy alternatives, as opposed to those in the first two categories, are eliminated during the socialization process and throughout the decisional processes where various other alternatives are weighed. Fundamentally, these policies are not even considered during the policy deliberations. For instance, Republican redistricters would not consider increasing the number of eligible Latino voters in some congressional districts because to do so would threaten the electoral viability of their candidates. This was stated in the e-mail between the redistricters when they stated that the "nudge factor" would assist the candidacies of "Canseco and Farenthold." In the case of Mr. Francisco Canseco, the 23rd Congressional District, this was accomplished by exchanging the high- with the low-performance Latino precincts; in Mr. Blake Farenthold's situation, the 27th Congressional District, the entire district was blatantly redesigned, changing its configuration from one principally located in South Texas ranging from Corpus Christi, Texas, to the Mexican border and having a large percentage of Latinos to one ranging northward and into Central Texas, where a majority of Anglos reside. These options were chosen because they were the best available to elect their candidates. Increasing Latino voter participation was not even considered viable because the decision makers understood, as reflected in all of the polling data, that it was futile to expect Latinos to support Republican candidates. The same can be said for the manner in which the voter identification card process was designed. Allowing for universal suffrage is not a policy alternative that is traditionally contemplated in the context of voter registration policies considered in the United States.

Principally, voting is perceived as a privilege rather than a right open only to those who can prove, using authorized identification, their citizenship. The franchise in the United States has historically been restricted, even to some citizens, and opened gradually. At the beginning of the nation, the franchise was originally approved only for property-owning, white males. There was even an attempt to restrict this to those owners having property of a certain value, but this proposal was defeated during the deliberations of the Constitutional Convention of 1789.[45] The franchise has been reluctantly opened to new groups of potential voters over more than two hundred years, requiring no less than six constitutional amendments and two federal voting laws. Although ballot access has opened dramatically throughout U.S. history, there are continuing attempts to ensure the narrowness of the opening through the passage of voter registration, voter identification, voter registration waiting periods, and the imposition of fees for acquiring voter registration documentation. The Brennen Center for Justice at the New York University School of Law reported that twenty-two states have passed or are considering passing new voter identification laws, eight states have passed laws requiring proof of citizenship, and two states have passed laws requiring criminal investigations in the event a potential voter falsely registers to vote.[46] Defining voting as a privilege of citizenship, rather than a right allowed to all residents within the United States, has a restrictive effect on voters, particularly for those groups subject or perceived to be subject to the restriction. For instance, if the law restricts access to citizens, then a state can require proof of citizenship in order to register. Those citizens, who have a difficult time obtaining that proof, whether from a lack of fundamental documentation, cost, or convenience, will not be able to obtain that proof easily. This process may weigh more heavily on Latinos who can be easily accused of being illegal immigrants as has often happened particularly along the border states with Mexico. The third type of exclusionary filtering, then, is normally attributable to the way in which a political culture defines certain rights of citizenship, physical and linguistic characteristics of citizens, and so forth. These characteristics are sometimes defined through scholarship, normal day-to-day communications, the professional world, the media, and judicial precedents, in short, in any arena of social discourse that defines cultural values. These values are culturally compatible with those learned in the home, one's educational environment, where one works, and so forth, finding their way into what is considered the normal world of policy discourse.

These policy selective mechanisms are institutionalized throughout the policy process in almost every political or bureaucratic institution. In the case of Texas, these filtering systems found their way into both the redistricting process and the legislative process that gave birth to the voter identification law. Although the policy alternatives selected as the final process are socially acceptable based on the general standards of acceptance, that is, they were passed through the normal legislative process and signed into law by the governor of the state, they are still biased against the interests of the Latino community. Redistricters and legislators can insist that they are only making political decisions based on partisanship, but the same policy is designed to dilute the voting power of Latinos. Essentially, the policy decisions designed to achieve a political goal were designed with racial purpose and intent.

NOTES

1. CA No. 11-CA-360-OLG-JES-XR.
2. CA No. 12-128.
3. Rule 702 of the Federal Rules of Evidence. Testimony by Expert Witnesses. (Pub. L. 93–595, §1, Jan. 2, 1975, 88 Stat. 1937; Apr. 17, 2000, eff. Dec. 1, 2000; Apr. 26, 2011, eff. Dec. 1, 2011.)

4. 509 U.S. 579 (1993).

5. These are now codified in Rule 702 of the Federal Rules of Evidence as Testimony By Expert Witnesses and state that

"A witness who is qualified as an expert by knowledge, skill, experience, training, or education may testify in the form of an opinion or otherwise if:

(a) The expert's scientific, technical, or other specialized knowledge will help the trier of fact to understand the evidence or to determine a fact in issue;

(b) The testimony is based on sufficient facts or data;

(c) The testimony is the product of reliable principles and methods; and

(d) The expert has reliably applied the principles and methods to the facts of the case."

(As amended Apr. 17, 2000, eff. Dec. 1, 2000; Apr. 26, 2011, eff. Dec. 1, 2011).

6. 429 U.S. 252 (1977).

7. Ibid., 564.

8. Ibid., 564–65.

9. This is the traditional subpoena issued before depositions requiring one side of the litigation to produce all the material and data they have concerning the facts. Each side "trades" information in this manner to expedite the process. Sometimes data or information revealed during *duces tecum* forces one side to attempt settlement.

10. *Mt. Holly Gardens Citizens in Action, Inc. v. Township of Mount Holly*, 658 F. 3rd 375 (3rd Cir. 2011) [2011 BL 233928].

11. Ibid., 564.

12. Ariel I. Ahram, "Concepts and Measurement in Multimethod Research," *Political Science Quarterly*, June, 2013. 66: 280–91.

13. These mechanisms have been elaborated on more in an earlier work by this author. Flores, Henry, 2003, *The Evolution of the Liberal Democratic State.*

14. Ibid., see particularly the discussions in chapters 3 and 5.

15. *Time Reborn: From the Crisis in Physics to the Future of the Universe* (New York: Houghton Mifflin Harcourt. 2013).

16. Kahneman, Daniel. *Thinking Fast and Slow.* New York: Farrar, Straus and Giroux, 2011. See also, Kahneman, Daniel, Paul Slovic, and Amos Tversky. 4th Printing. *Judgment under Uncertainty: Heuristics and Biases*. New York: Cambridge University Press, 2008.

17. Ibid.

18. This history has been chronicled by David Montejano in *Anglos and Mexicans in the Making of Texas, 1836–1986.* Austin, TX: University of Texas Press, 1987; Manuel G. Gonzales. *Mexicanos: A History of Mexicans in the United States.* Bloomington, IN: Indiana University Press, 2000; and Reynaldo Valencia, Sonia R. Garcia, Henry Flores and José Roberto Juárez. *Mexican Americans and the Law: ¡El pueblo unido jamás sera vencido!* Tucson, AZ: The University of Arizona Press, 2004.

19. Bonilla-Silva, *Racism without Racists.*

20. This argument arose, time and time again, on March 23, 2011, in the Texas State House of Representatives and recorded in the journal for that day.

21. *"The State of Texas v. United States, et al.,"* Case No. 11-CV-1303, Defendant's Exhibit DX304.

22. *Texas House Journal*, 82nd Regular Session, p. 988.

23. *Texas Senate Journal*, 82nd Regular Session, pp. 1017–19.

24. Gossett, 1997, *Race: The History of an Idea in America.* Olson, 2006, *The Abolition of White Democracy.*

25. Gossett, 1997, Olson, 2006, Segrest, 1994.

26. Oliver C. Cox. *Caste, Class and Race: A Study in Social Dynamics.* NY: Monthly Review Press, 1949; V. O. Key. *Southern Politics in State and Nation: A New Edition.* Knoxville, TN: The University of Tennessee Press, 1948, 1984; Chandler Davidson. *Race and Class in Texas Politics.* 1990; and J. Morgan Kousser. *Colorblind Justice: Minority Voting Rights and the Undoing of the Second Reconstruction.* Chapel Hill, NC: University of North Carolina Press, 1999.

27. www.justice.gov/crt/about/vot/sec_5/obj_activ.php.

28. www.justice.gov/crt/about/vot/sec_5/obj_activ.php.

29. Interviews with Messrs. Rolando Rios, Jose Garza, and George Korbel.

30. In the United States all congressional districts are designed by committees in each state legislature or a quasi-independent state commission. The only aspect of this provided by the national government is the apportionment ratio and the fundamental data upon which a district is designed. These latter data are derived from the decennial census.

31. *Davis v. Bandemer,* 478 U.S. 109 (1986).

32. *Balderas v. Perry.* Manipulating racial populations to achieve a political end is legal but only up to a certain point. Once it crosses a threshold considered injurious to the racial group, then the redistricting effort becomes unconstitutional.

33. Linda C. Noel, "'I am an American': Anglos, Mexicans, Nativos, and the National Debate over Arizona and New Mexico Statehood," *Pacific Historical Review,* (Aug, 2011), Vol. 80, No. 3, pp. 436.

34. This historical relationship has been chronicled extensively by David Montejano in *Anglos and Mexicans*, 1987.

35. Georgia, Arkansas, Mississippi, Texas and Virginia.

36. www.ncsl.org/documents/statevote.

37. Arizona's attempt at imposing proof of citizenship on the federal voter registration form was rejected by SCOTUS recently, *Arizona v. Inter Tribal Council of Ariz. Inc.* 677 F 3d 383, affirmed. No. 12-71 (June 17, 2013).

38. Mr. Opiela was defeated in the Republican Primary in March, 2014.

39. Although the choice of whether to refer to oneself as Hispanic or Latino is an individual choice, a great number of Latinos refer to themselves in national origin terms. I will use the terms Hispanic and Latino interchangeably for stylistic reasons throughout this book but will discuss the use of the terms in the next chapter.

40. Department of Commerce, United States Bureau of the Census. "The Hispanic Population 2010 Census Brief. Table 1. "Hispanic or Latino Origin Population by Type: 2000 and 2010," May 2011.

41. www.latinovotemap.org.

42. www.latinodecisions.org.

43. Flores, 2003, *Evolution of the Liberal Democratic States.*

44. E-mail between Mr. Opiela and Mr. Interiano.

45. Howard Zinn, 2003, *A People's History of the United States,* New York: Harper Collins; Charles A. Beard, 1914, *An Economic Interpretation of the Constitution of the United States,* NY: The Macmillan Company, Dover Edition, 2003, New York: Dover Publications, Inc.

46. Brennen Center for Justice, New York University School of Law, "Voting Laws Roundup, 2013," New York: New York, 2013. www.brennencenter.org.

Chapter Three

Racism, the *Arlington Heights* Factors, and Latinos

Using the *Arlington Heights* Factors *(AHFs)* as the road map for discovering racial purpose in voting rights litigation research requires a discussion of the forces that define racial purpose in the first place. Racial purpose or intent—the two are interchangeable legal terms—may be a single action of one decision maker or the result of the collective actions of a group of decision makers driving the creation of a certain law, statute, or public policy. Additionally, these decision makers are acting within institutional structures that affect the manner in which they make decisions. Finally, their actions are directly affected by the socialization processes they have been subjected to throughout their personal and professional lives. As a result, when a decision maker acts with racial purpose, that actor is displaying behavior that reflects the values and perceptions of the greater society and culture within which he or she works. A single act of racial intent is not a spontaneous occurrence, but is based in a relatively long history of social interactions that define the racial relations between Anglos and certain groups, in this case Latinos. In the final analysis, a decision maker acting with a racial purpose when developing, creating, writing, or implementing a public policy initiative of some sort, whether a law, statute, redistricting plan, and so forth, is reflecting the social values of his or her community or society.

A thorough understanding of how racial purpose in public policy decisions can be detected using the *AHFs* requires understanding the relationship between racism and racial purpose. This is particularly true when speaking of the political effects racial purpose have on Latinos. As a result, this chapter looks first at what racism is generally, where it originated, why it originated, what political roles it plays, and why it's important to understand in the development of public policy decisions in communities where it does appear.

One issue that muddles the picture of what role racial intent plays in the public policy arena is that the use of race has been seen by those who oppose policies such as affirmative action, the VRA, or civil rights generally as reverse discrimination, or preferential treatment for African Americans, Latinos, or other groups protected under national civil rights laws. Their fundamental argument is that creating programs or policies giving preference to members of minority groups discriminates against "white" people, because it takes away positions or resources that could have been used by either better-qualified or well-qualified white persons. Nevertheless, creation of preferences is not the same as creating laws that prevent against negative discrimination. Negative discrimination is the act of creating barriers that prevent individuals of some groups from having the opportunity of fully participating in some program. In voting rights, negative discrimination is the creation of barriers inhibiting or prohibiting voters, citizens, who belong to racial or ethnic groups who have been discriminated against historically, from either casting their rightful votes in elections or diminishing or diluting the value of their vote. Creating barriers to casting votes may include such activities as limiting the number of polling places, not having enough computers available to check voter registration, limiting the number of early voting days, limiting the number of voting hours on election day, restricting the vote to holders of certain types of identification, and so forth.[1] Diminishing the value of or diluting the worth of a vote occurs when representational districts are gerrymandered or, under certain circumstances, certain voting schemes such as at-large structures as opposed to single-member districts are implemented in some jurisdictions.[2] Either category represents negative discrimination because they exclude citizens from casting a vote, a fundamentally protected right,[3] and not allowing for full participation in the election process. This has the effect of giving more weight to some votes as opposed to others. In the voting rights context discussed here, this translates into placing more value on the votes of white persons over those of Latinos or African Americans. In effect a two-tiered system of citizenship is created where the franchise exercised by white persons represents the "gold standard" of citizenship because they can fully participate in the election process with ease and free of stressors. Examples of stressors are common to members of racial minority groups daily when encountering the "white world." For Latinos, these include being questioned about one's citizenship in various walks of life where a white person will not be; being subjected to undue surveillance in department stores or banks as opposed to the scrutiny a white person would undergo; or, even being eyed suspiciously or as a threat by white people encountered on the streets.[4] Latinos and others discriminated against in the voting process, then, are relegated to a lower, less equal tier of citizenship, because their votes are valued less than those of white persons under election schemes that deny, diminish, or dilute their vote.

In the discussion here negative discrimination is the act of drawing congressional districts or creating a voter identification law that constructs barriers to the participation of Latinos in the election process or inhibiting their ability to elect a candidate of their choice. These barriers have the effect of diminishing the value of Latino votes, thus substantively violating the "one person, one vote" constitutional principle.[5] The VRA was passed to prevent governmental officials from establishing barriers to participation, particularly in light of a history of discrimination that has plagued Latino voters since their incorporation. Texas history is rich with examples of systematic and systemic discrimination against Latinos in almost every walk of life. This discrimination has been chronicled by a large number of historians and sociologists and reported in books, court, and congressional testimony over the last fifty-plus years.[6]

Preferential treatment is not the issue in voting rights litigation; protection against negative discrimination is the issue at hand. Justice Roberts in his *Shelby County* decision declared that times have changed and blatant discrimination has all but disappeared.[7] To a certain extent, Justice Roberts is correct with the exception of incidents such as the murder of Mr. Byrd in Jasper, Texas, by two white supremacists in 1998; the days of racial lynchings, chained slavery, literacy, character, and one-drop blood tests have passed. On the other hand, the days of racial discrimination from the subtle to the not so subtle have not passed. One still encounters examples of direct voter intimidation and vote diminution and dilution along racial grounds throughout the country generally and Texas specifically. Where violent voter intimidation and overt tests were created specifically aimed at discouraging African Americans and Latinos from voting have pretty much disappeared, they have been replaced by other methods such as restructuring of congressional districts using ever more sophisticated statistical techniques and technological tools or the composition of a set of voter identification standards that are, in some cases, impossible to fulfill. The VRA cannot be construed as a law that creates preferential treatment for one group of citizens over another; it must be understood as a law designed to protect the rights of groups who have traditionally been prevented from fully exercising their franchise and having their vote valued equally with those of white persons. White voters enjoy "gold-standard citizenship;" the purpose of voting rights litigation is to extend and protect this gold standard to citizens who have historically been denied the standard.[8]

RACISM AS ROOT CAUSE OF RACIAL PURPOSE

The most complex aspects of determining racial purpose and its infusion into the public policy process are identifying or defining what racial purpose is and then identifying the linkages between racial purpose and the specific public policy. Essentially, acting with a racial purpose or intent in the policy process means that decision makers set as an important objective designing, constructing, and implementing a policy or program with the expressed intention of positively or negatively affecting individuals of a racial group. The discussion here focuses on the negative discrimination that occurred during the Texas redistricting process and during the design of the voter identification law that took place during the 2011 legislative session.

As stated in the introduction of this section, racism is the root cause of racial purpose. The starting point of this discussion, though, is defining what racism is and how it becomes part of the policy process: in short, identifying how racism becomes a central part of defining racial purpose or intent in the writing, design, and implementation of public policy. Racism in relationship to Latinos is a complex issue because of the unusual identity situation defining the social existence in which Latinos find themselves. In regards to Latinos, racism takes on a different color because society has never been clear as to whether Latinos are a separate racial category or ethnic group or some combination of the two. Regardless of conventional wisdom, racial categorizations are social constructs that have come down through history and that have been defined and refined by academics, governments, and the media over an extended period of time.[9] The identity that Latinos have has been concocted by American society over the last two hundred years and has gone through many iterations during that time; this history will be discussed in the next chapter. What is important here is that governments and society generally consider Latinos a separate, identifiable racial group.[10] And, as the Court pointed out in *Hernandez v. Texas,* Latinos are considered a racially identifiable group because society has designated them as such by treating them differently in various public accommodations.

Still, racism did not just arise out of the imagination of a few individuals who decided one day to just infuse a few policy decisions with a racial purpose although this may be the case in some instances. On the contrary, racism is an essential aspect of American culture and part of the way in which the social world defines every individual. Individuals define their social world by the way in which they define themselves racially and how others define individuals racially. A white person goes through life as a white person and interacts with the world around him, as such realizing a world of racial privilege. Black persons must interact with the world as black persons regardless of whether they feel otherwise, because they have been defined socially as a black person and treated in that manner by the world around them. Latinos are in the same situation as white and black persons. They interact with the world around themselves as Latinos and the world treats them as such.[11] This phenomenon is generally known as being "racialized" or "raced" and defines the social and political place of individuals in American society. This phenomenon is "hard-wired" into American culture and has become an essential thread of America's ideological tapestry.

Defining social issues in racial terms is not new and has been part of the American ideological and cultural fabric since the first European settlers arrived in the New World. In the beginning, racial differences were perceived as just racial differences where one group of individuals from a different part of the world and from different cultures were perceived and defined simply as different. Eventually, as lands were taken from Native Americans and more African slaves were introduced into the New World, a rationale for the subjugation of these people was needed. The first reasons were biblically based in that the subjugated people were considered heathens, not capable of making moral or ethical decisions. Those who were enslaved were deemed mentally inferior and incapable of ruling or governing themselves or any country. These early arguments were designed to allow for the removal of Indians from their lands and to keep Africans in a position to exploit for their labor. As America modernized and became a nation unto itself, its leaders were subjected to the ideas of the Enlightenment and the development of scientific racism, which flourished and was very popular among the well-educated, first in Germany and then England and France.

As Gossett[12] has pointed out, the origins of the concepts of race and racism are not clear and have been lost in the mists of history. Gossett discussed evidence that race theories existed as long as five thousand years ago in India and at approximately the same time in China. Racial theories evolved from nation to nation and from one historical era to another depending upon the relationship of a given country with another country or group of people who had been subjugated or with whom they had difficult relations. For instance, in the sixteenth century, both the English and Spaniards used racial theories defining indigenous people as inferior humans in order to justify conquering and enslaving the people of the Americas. It is not clear whether the first Africans imported into Jamestown in 1619, along with a cargo of indentured servants, were technically referred to as slaves. The first reference to slaves in the United States was in 1660 when a Virginia law set forth the difference between the terms served by "all Negroes and other slaves." This law and others passed by various colonies finally made it clear that Negroes would serve as slaves for the duration of their lives as opposed to "other slaves," presumably indentured servants and workers. Increasing importation of African slaves began around 1680 because the laws of indebtedness had changed in England; as a result fewer indentured servants and workers were arriving in the New World to perform menial labor. Consequently, increased importation of African slaves occurred and steadily flowed into the North American colonies until outlawed in the late eighteenth century.

An important element to legitimize maintaining a large population of slaves was to create racial theories that painted African people as less than whites. In late seventeenth-century New England, there is evidence that Africans were seen as less than whites and the justification usually revolved around issues of Christianity. Africans and Native Americans were seen as heathens or, as Cotton Mather concluded, the result of obscure workings of Providence.[13] According to Gossett, it appears that the only reason a rationale for slavery was discussed in the northern colonies was because the institution was being challenged by some individuals. In the southern parts of the New World, little discussion as to the social status of slaves occurred, so there appears to be no record of the development of a rationale for this institution or the horrid treatment of Africans and Indians.

While slavery flourished in the New World, a movement in the latter part of the seventeenth century unfolded when various thinkers in France began attempting to lend scientific credibility to racial theories. These efforts began as a way of attempting to understand the differences between Europeans, Africans, and Far Easterners. A science which would later become known as anthropology began attempting to classify the differences among people physically. The first classification of humans by race in France is generally attributed to François Bernier, a French physician, who described these differences in *Nouvelle division de la terre par les différentes espèces ou races qui l'habitent* published in 1684 four years before his death. Not until the next century was it established by Georges-Louis Leclerc, Comte de Buffon, a French naturalist, that "white" was the norm among races and the rest were deviations who, in his analyses of the "Negro race" in Africa, concluded that they had "little genius" and were unable to "count beyond the number three."[14] These treatises based on travel observations by educated Frenchmen were being written during the Age of Enlightenment when the scientific method was being born. So, every appearance of scientific rigor, as defined in eighteenth-century terms, was applied to all conclusions concerning race. The mental and social inequality of Africans was believed and professed by many of the original founders of the United States. Thomas Jefferson stated in one of his most important writings that "'in memory they are equal to the whites; in reason much inferior,' and 'in imagination they are dull, tasteless, and anomalous.'"[15] While the classification of humans was occurring, Charles Darwin was making his own observations on nature. Eventually, Darwin's methodology and his suspicions of the notion of natural selection were being published. It may or not have been inevitable, but eventually the two sets of observations melded and the first "scientifically structured" racial theories appeared in the West. Although theories of race began appearing in France, England and Germany in the eighteenth and early nineteenth centuries, what some generally attribute as the first scientific race theory, at least in the standards of that era they were considered scientific, was set forth by Joseph Arthur Comte de Gobineau in 1853.[16] He propagated the first theory of the "superior Aryan or Nordic race—blond, strong, intelligent, moral and brave" during an era when the European colonial powers were attempting to justify their centuries-old behavior toward the indigenous people of the Americas, Africa, and South Pacific. Generally, the propagators of racial theories attributed the dirt, grime, poverty, and an inability to communicate as clear evidence that Africans, Native Americans, and Far Easterners were not equal to the White European norm.

By the latter half of the nineteenth century, anthropologists, economists, and mathematicians had taken Darwin's theory of natural selection and discovered eugenics or the concept of manipulating genetics through selective social interaction. Essentially, the eugenicists wished to make natural selection positive by setting forth the notion of conscious selection as opposed to natural selection. Natural selection, in their perception, was too haphazard and chaotic a process and they wanted to ensure that only positive outcomes resulted from the evolutionary process. Consciously selecting individuals who were more intelligent, wealthy, and cultured to intermarry among themselves and discouraging those of lesser traits would necessarily lead to a better, more cultured human race. This perception eventually resulted in movements to segregate the less desirable elements of society from those of higher social standing and to discourage intermingling of any sort between the higher and lower social status groups.[17]

Although the initial eugenics movement activities occurred in Germany, the idea eventually found its way to England where it was championed by the nephew of Darwin, Francis Galton, and one of his acolytes, Karl Pearson.[18] The eugenics movement was part of what has come to be known as "scientific racism" which is a way of thinking about race based upon either pseudoscientific or misapplied scientific methods. From the middle of the nineteenth century through the end of World War II, scientific racism dominated much of sociological, anthropological, and social thought in the United States. Its origination is attributed to Charles Davenport, a prominent Harvard zoologist who published in Galton's and then Pearson's journals on this topic. Eventually, Davenport left academia to found what became the foremost eugenics and miscegenation research institute in the world, the Cold Springs Harbor Laboratory. Here he founded the Eugenics Record Office to study heredity and published one of the most influential college textbooks of the day on heredity and eugenics. Professor Davenport's conclusions on the intermarriage and intermixing of the white and black races were published in *Race Crossing in Jamaica*,[19] in which he concluded that interracial mixing would eventually lead to biological and cultural deterioration. His research and writing became popular in Germany in the early 1930s where "racial hygiene" had become the heart of racial thinking in that country. Davenport later partnered with Madison Grant, who was one of the founders of the American Anthropological Association. Grant, a lawyer with little training in anthropology, had published his most famous work *Passing of the Great Race* in 1916.[20] In this volume, Grant set forth his notion of miscegenation which went through many editions and like Davenport's became popular in Germany, particularly among Nazi ideologues. Fundamentally, Madison Grant contended that there was a hierarchy of races and that intermarriage and interbreeding would lead to cultural "suicide" in those countries where it was allowed to occur. Grant championed selective breeding and, as the Vice President of the Immigration Restriction League, provided statistical data for the Immigration Act of 1924 to set quotas on immigrants from Eastern Europe because he felt they were biologically inferior.[21] An example of Grant's views toward immigrants is evident in the excerpt quoted here because it clearly indicates that his perception went beyond biases against African and Eastern Europeans:

> What the Melting Pot actually does in practice can be seen in Mexico, where the absorption of the blood of the original Spanish conquerors by the native Indian population has produced the racial mixture we call Mexican and which is now engaged in demonstrating its incapacity for self-government.[22]

Grant was referring to the turmoil in Mexico occurring immediately after the Revolution of 1910 when government control passed from the hands of one autocrat to another and land-grabbing schemes prevailed. The social turmoil caused by the Mexican Revolution between 1910 and 1923 caused the first great outmigration of large numbers of Mexicans into the United States. It is not clear whether Grant had bothered to study the instability any country endures immediately after a revolution as extensive as the one Mexico underwent at the turn of the twentieth century before making his pronouncement. The history behind Grant, though, is interesting in that he remained the vice-president of the Immigration Restrictive League until his death. Throughout his tenure, the League successfully lobbied the federal government to create immigration quotas that biased immigration toward northern European immigrants and against immigrants from the Americas, Asia, and Eastern Europe. This is a clear example of racial purpose becoming an integral part of the public policy process in the United States beyond the Indian Removal Act of 1830, the Chinese Exclusion Act of 1882, and the Asian Exclusion Act of 1924. Other examples of public policy designed with a racial purpose or intent could be brought forth as well as a more substantial discussion of the development of racial thinking or scientific racism. This discussion, however, is intended as a brief overview of the historical development of this thinking and how it eventually found its way into the public policy arena in a negative way. Essentially, these examples of public policy were intended to discriminate against members of various racial groups to prevent them from participating in the American social world. Negative discrimination based on scientific racial theories was the philosophical and theoretical foundation upon which the logic for the separate but equal doctrine was upheld by *Plessy v. Ferguson*.[23] In other words, racial purpose, substantiated by scientific racism, has throughout the social history of the United Sates been used to create public policies that have a negative discriminatory effect on African and Native Americans, Asians of all nationalities, and Latinos.

RACIAL PURPOSE AND VOTING RIGHTS LITIGATION

The legal concept of racial purpose or intent has had a checkered jurisprudential history because, according to the Supreme Court, it is difficult to measure and also to determine its empirical relationship to the effect on a specific population. Generally, these concepts form a part of any civil rights litigation where a party claims that a specific policy has a discriminatory effect on them in some way. The petition then must show, depending on the area of law, that there has been a discriminatory purpose and an effect. These claims generally are brought under the equal protection clause of the Fourteenth Amendment. Nevertheless, the courts' rulings to date have resulted in plaintiffs having to provide evidence for both racial purpose or intent and the effect. The evidence required for effect is generally straightforward and is referred to as "disproportionate impact" or "disparate impact" analysis and includes evidence of how the challenged policy will affect a given community or racial group. The standard for proof of racial purpose, however, is not clear and has never been clear until recently when the courts have ruled that a proof of disparate impact is also proof of intent.[24] This, however, may be changing under the Roberts Regime as they set the evidentiary bar higher and higher for plaintiffs in civil rights litigation.

The jurisprudential history of racial purpose begins with the, ruling in *Yick Wo v. Hopkins*[25] where the Supreme Court ruled that a law that appears neutral superficially may "operate invidiously to discriminate against racial minorities."[26] This case had to do with the San Francisco Board of Supervisors granting construction waivers to Anglo-owned laundries but denying them to Chinese-owned laundries. The Court found that the law was implemented unevenly and defendants could not explain the difference, leaving the Court to conclude that the differences in treatment were due to "hostility to the race and nationality to which the petitioners belong."[27] The Court concluded that "a facially neutral classification was in fact racial."[28] Perry pointed out that "this evidentiary consideration 'has often been cited for the proposition that a racially disproportionate impact, if dramatic, will be sufficient to invalidate a law on equal protection grounds'."[29]

Thus, in *Yick Wo,* the Supreme Court concluded that "disproportionate impact occurs whenever official procedures relating to selection or entitlement to benefits produce a less favorable result for a protected group."[30] Beginning with the Court's ruling in *Yick Wo*, then, disproportionate impact equaled discriminatory intent. This formula remained until the late twentieth century in *Washington v. Davis*[31] when the court ruled that "plaintiffs must demonstrate that a law was conceived or maintained for a discriminatory purpose. Discriminatory purpose requires the plaintiff to show that the defendant acted out of a racial *animus* [italics in original], a desire to harm."[32] The Supreme Court, as it has done throughout its history, may have appeared to reverse course, but in reality it appears to have taken a step toward refining its position on this issue. As various legal theorists have posited, the search for discriminatory intent is a difficult one because the structure of the decision itself and the motivation of the decision makers must be considered beyond simply the impact of a policy.[33]

Taking this discussion to another level, there are several general stages in making a policy decision, including the general assumptions upon which the decision is being made; the motivation for the decision and/or that of the decision makers; the general quality and quantity of information that goes into the decision; how the policy is ultimately structured; how the policy is implemented; and, finally, how a policy is evaluated. Each and every stage of the decision is subject to the various decisional layers mentioned earlier in this volume affecting the individuals involved in the decision, the politics surrounding the decision, and the demographics within which the decision is being made. Finally, the institutional setting must also be considered as affecting the decision. Uncovering discriminatory intent or racial purpose in this decisional framework becomes a complex challenge that is both information- and cost-prohibitive.

Mitchell Rice argues that a race-dependent policy, one that is targeted to solve a specific issue where most of the subject population will be members of a specific race, will, by definition, have a racial purpose and will, also by definition, result in disparate impact on a specific racial group. In this instance, the proof of racial purpose is clear.[34] The policy has a clearly stated racial purpose, it is designed to specifically affect a racial group, and after implementation, it is shown to affect that racial group. The Court would view this as clearly a policy having a racial purpose or intent and then would inquire as to whether the policy served a "compelling governmental interest" before ruling. A more difficult proof arises when a policy is "facially race neutral" and whether the decision is race-dependent or intended to affect a racial group in some manner. Then the court must "look beyond the face of the decision and inquire into the actual considerations of the decision makers."[35] The compelling question then becomes "how does one enter into the minds of the decision makers to determine what their motivations are in making their decision or in designing a policy a certain way?"

The Court, aware of the institutional context within which a policy decision is made, has declared that it is easier to find discriminatory purpose in an administrative body as opposed to a legislative body. Generally, within a bureaucracy, it is easy to identify which individuals were involved in making a decision, while in a legislative body, it is not. Within an administrative body, motivation is easier to identify than within a legislative body because of all the bartering and individual political agendas that come into play. Finally, a court does not like to tread within the boundaries of an elected institution. In the United States system of government, the power vacuums that exist between the legislative, judicial, and executive branches are respected by each branch. To cross over into another institution's workspace and begin telling that branch of government how to perform its business is anathema to the political culture that governs inter-institutional arrangements in the United States. This latter consideration was evident when the Court ruled in *Washington v. Davis*[36] that, although an employment test was given to all applicants to join the Washington, DC, police department, two African American applicants were denied employment and the department did not act in a discriminatory manner. First, the court pointed out that they had never ruled that disparate impact was the only aspect of the petition that required evidence. Justice Byron White, writing for the majority, pointed out that the policy itself was racially neutral facially and that the plaintiffs needed to provide evidence of discriminatory intent on the part of the test makers and the department in order to prevail.[37]

Up until *Washington v. Davis,* the Court had vacillated between rulings whether discriminatory intent and effect or simply disparate impact was necessary for a plaintiff to prevail in any number of policy areas. For instance, in *Wright v. Rockefeller*[38] the court declared that a *prima facie*[39] case had to be made that discriminatory purpose existed when congressional districts were drawn by the New York legislature. The plaintiffs did not provide the court with evidence that the state legislature had acted with racial animus in drawing the Manhattan Congressional districts. The Court ruled the same way in *Fortson v. Dorsey*[40] saying that proof of discriminatory intent was necessary before they could find for the plaintiffs in a challenge to Georgia's state senatorial reapportionment plans. In 1968, the Court reversed course and ruled in *United States v. O'Brien*[41] that legislative motive on the part of the United States Congress could not be criminalized but the actual effect of the law may render the law unconstitutional.[42] In a subsequent decision, *Palmer v. Thompson,*[43] the court reiterated its position on the effect of the law being the most important element in proving a legislative action unconstitutional. However, in *Whitcomb v. Chavis,*[44] the court returned to its previous position that discriminatory intent in the legislative process was required in order to strike down a legislative apportionment plan. Finally, in a case that speaks specifically to Texas and the relationship of voting rights to Latinos in *White v. Regester,*[45] the court ruled that any alleged discrimination in reapportionment cases appeared to be the result of political partisanship rather than discrimination but that under certain circumstances the structure of multimember districts could have a disparate impact on minority populations. The structure itself, in this case at-large state legislative districts, coupled with a history of racial discrimination served to deny Latinos political access. This was the first time the court had sustained a claim of "vote dilution."[46] It appears that the differences in the Court's position over the years up until it ruled in *Village of Arlington Heights* were that it refused to look at discriminatory intent in the legislative process, and in redistricting and reapportionment cases it required that plaintiffs provide evidence that discriminatory intent was the motivating factor in the decisional process.

The Court's reluctance to seek racial intent from a legislative body's deliberations has merit beyond simply protecting the institutional privilege of an elected body. Part of the Court's reluctance may be based in the difficulty in discovering racial intent caused by the very nature of a legislative body's structure. Gathering evidence becomes prohibitive because of the convoluted decisional structures, both formal and informal, that govern the decisional process. For instance, the number of unofficial meetings where legislators and/or staff persons meet to discuss both legislative content and process are unknown. More often than not there were no official records of the meetings occurring or of what was discussed in those meetings. Also, the number, frequency, and intensity of meetings between representatives of interest groups who can influence policy decisions and legislators or their staff members may also be difficult to discern given the lack of official records of some of these meetings. Finally, the number of parliamentary procedures and institutional courtesies and customs affecting the decisional process are innumerable, particularly in a legislative body as large and old as that of Texas. As a result, aggregating a singular intention for a public policy may be, in itself, a methodological impossibility. This impossibility becomes even more impossible when legislators or their staff intentionally hide what their real motives are in composing or designing a policy.[47]

Although the Court was ruling that discriminatory intent must be proven in order to prevail in redistricting or reapportionment cases it was not providing any guidance as to how plaintiffs might proceed in providing the requisite evidence. The first hint provided by the Court in this vein was in *Washington v. Davis*, where the court indicated that "an invidious discriminatory purpose may often be inferred from the totality of the relevant facts, including the fact, if it is true, that the law bears more heavily on one race than another."[48] In Justice John Paul Stevens's concurring opinion he pointed out the relative impossibility of requiring "the victim of alleged effect discrimination to un-cover the actual subjective intent of the decision-maker, or conversely, to in-validate otherwise legitimate action because an improper motive affected the deliberation of a participant in the decisional process."[49] Essentially the Court admitted that it is difficult, if not impossible, to determine intent on the part of persons involved in writing or designing policy. The Court refined their guidance in *Arlington Heights v. Metropolitan Development Corp*[50] which was a rezoning dispute where African Americans alleged that the refusal to rezone a development to include mixed-income housing was a violation of the equal protection clause. The Court, ruling for the defendants, pointed out that although plaintiffs provided evidence of disparate impact or discrimina-tory effect they had not provided evidence of intent or racial purpose. Rather than just making the declaration, however, the Court pointed out that if the plaintiffs had provided racial purpose evidence they might have found it in the various areas that have been identified here as the *Arlington Heights* Fac-tors. This appeared to be an elaboration of what the Court was pondering in its *Washington v. Davis* opinion. The court was careful though to warn about investigating motive in legislative proceedings for fear of making "a substan-tial intrusion into the workings of other branches of government and placing a decision-maker on the stand therefore 'usually to be avoided.'"[51]

Following the *Arlington Heights* decision the Court became more strident in vote dilution cases that intent was the most important element to prove in an equal protection claim. A vote dilution case is one where petitioners al-lege that the election structure itself "dilutes" the value or worth of a covered group's vote. Generally, these petitions are submitted against jurisdictions that choose to structure their election system around an at-large representa-tive schema where all candidates run within an entire jurisdiction for specific places on a ballot. In a jurisdiction where covered groups represent a substan-tial percentage of voters, this percentage varies depending on the community and the extent of the density of their residential patterns, citizen members of covered groups claim that the at-large electoral scheme mitigates against their ability to elect a candidate of their choice. The mitigation is based on evidence that the larger group of voters, white citizens normally, traditionally vote as a block against candidates from covered groups such as African Americans, Latinos, Native and Asian Americans. In *City of Mobile v. Bolden,*[52] the Court ruled that even though the plaintiffs, in this case African Americans, provided evidence that white voters voted in blocks against black candidates and that the at-large election structure worked against the African American community's ability to elect candidates of their choice, it was just the "starting place" for the inquiry. Plaintiffs were still required to provide evidence of "purposeful discrimination."[53] Still, the only substantive guidance that the Supreme Court has provided plaintiffs with identifying evidence that substantiates proof of purposeful discrimination, the use of racial purpose or intent in voting rights litigation appears in the *Arlington Heights* Factors to which we now turn.

ARLINGTON HEIGHTS FACTORS AND LATINOS

One of the principal reasons for the production of this volume is that there has never been an explicit work on Latinos and voting rights litigation. The vast majority of the literature is based upon the experiences of African American voters. For example, the recent *Shelby County* decision was based on a community having a small percentage of African American voters, yet it is law that must be followed throughout the land. This decision directly affects the large Latino population in Texas where the relationship between Anglos, the political structures, and Latinos are markedly different than those of African Americans in Shelby County, Alabama. In future decisions, it behooves the Supreme Court to consider these differences when crafting decisions in this area of law, perhaps prompting the Court to make more narrow rulings.

   The differences between the social and political relationships between Anglos, the political structures, and Latinos in Texas are substantively different from those of African Americans in Alabama; yet the only guidance that exists in identifying racial purpose is the same for both. This guidance, which comes in the form of the *Arlington Heights* Factors, then must be met by evidence from the Latino community's experiences that are quite different from those of the African American community. Essentially, American voting rights laws have been interpreted by the courts from and through the experiential eyes of African Americans, and those of Latinos have been ignored or misunderstood or assumed to be the same as those of black persons in the United States. This disjuncture is said to be primarily caused by the notion that much of the social analyses performed in the United States is based upon a "dual-race model" of white-black relations rather than a "multi-racial analytical model" where other groups beyond African Americans and whites are included. The United States culturally is changing dramatically and quickly into a society that is multiracial, and the law must change accordingly. Consequently, the Supreme Court's opinions in future voting rights cases must reflect this understanding and concern for the different socio-historical experiences of the various groups petitioning the courts for redress in this area of law.

Further elaboration on the differences between Latinos and African Americans when it comes to their relationships with white persons and the political and legal structures of the United States is presented in the next chapter. Here, however, we turn to an elaboration of the *Arlington Heights* Factors and what evidence would need to be provided in support of a voting rights claim of racial purpose or intent from the Latino community. The factors originally identified in the *Arlington Heights* decision are modified here for brevity's sake and will be used throughout the remainder of this volume. The original factors as stated in the Court's opinion appear in parentheses.

Arlington Heights Factors

1. Disproportionate Impact (Disproportionate impact not sole determinant of invidious racial discrimination).
Under this factor, reports featuring racially polarized voting between Anglos and Latinos would form an essential aspect of the historical background of race relations within a jurisdiction. Racially polarized voting reflects the wide differences in political preferences existing between Anglos and Latinos in Texas. Although most racially polarized voting studies reflect differences in general elections, the report can and should present data from primary elections and any nonpartisan elections available. The most probative are primary and nonpartisan elections that allow further control of any political party effects. An example of a report of polarized voting reflecting the voting patterns in the 23rd United States Congressional District of Texas appears in Table 3.1. As the data in the table indicate, Latino support for Latino candidates is very high with the exception of the 2010 Eva Guzman election. Excluding the Guzman election, one can see that the ranges of Latino support are from 73.6 percent for Victor G. Carrillo in 2004 to a high of 99.6 percent for Cuellar in 2002. The polarization of the voters is shown by the contrasting amount of support from the non-Latino voters who are almost 100 percent Anglo in this district. If one controls for the Guzman and Carrillo elections, the support levels range from 12.1 percent for Cuellar in 2002 to 23.6 percent for Yanez in 2008. The Guzman elec-

Table 3.1.   US Congressional District 23 Endogenous Elections General Election Results Support by Race for Latino Preferred Candidates[1]

Year	Candidates	Election	% Latino Support	% Non-Latino Support
1992	Bustamante	US 23rd	84.7	18.3
1994	Rios	US 23rd	84.3	18.5
1996	Jones	US 23rd	78.03	19.15
1998	Jones	US 23rd	79.12	14.8
2000	Garza	US 23rd	84.6	16.8
2002	Cuellar	US 23rd	99.6	12.1
2002	Sanchez	Governor	85	16.7
2004	Carrillo	RR, Com, Pl 3	73.6	74.4
2004	Molina	CCA, Pl 6	80.5	20.6
2006	Alvarado	Lt. Gov.	77.6	21.7
2006	Molina	CCA, Presiding	81.9	24.5
2008	Noriega	US Senate	87.7	21.5
2008	Yanez	SC, Pl 8	91.5	23.6
2010	Chavez-Thompson	Lt. Gov.	89.9	17.1
2010	Uribe	Land Comm.	91.5	17.6
2010	Guzman	SC, Pl 9	16.8	81.3

[1] Estimates from 1992-2002 taken from Expert Report Table 1, *GI Forum v Texas* and are based on Double Regression Estimates. Those data on elections from 2004 through 2010 are linear regression estimates produced by State Attorney General's Office.

tion is an example of the animosity that Latinos have toward candidates representing the Republican Party. Guzman ran as a Republican for the Supreme Court after having been appointed by Governor Perry in 2008. She defeated another Latina in the Republican primary and then a Libertarian and an under-funded, poorly organized Anglo Democratic trial lawyer from East Texas in the general election of 2010. Still the Guzman election is clearly racially polarized. The Carrillo general election of 2004 for Railroad Commissioner was also unique as he was appointed to the commission by Governor Rick Perry in 2003, won the 2004 Republican Party primary in a runoff, and then defeated a Democratic Party candidate in the general election. Mr. Carrillo was a geophysicist for Amoco and also a gas and oil attorney having close ties to the energy sector. The title of the Texas Railroad Commission is a bit of a misnomer because its function is to regulate the price of oil and gas generated in the state. As a result, Mr. Carrillo was regarded generally as close to the energy sector but was defeated in the subsequent Republican Party primary by an unknown and under-financed Anglo candidate, 61 percent to 39 percent. Mr. Carrillo attributed his defeat to his Hispanic surname and castigated the voters of his party for being racially biased.[54]

The findings in Table 3.2 below, together with a qualitative analysis of each election, were part of the expert report for the plaintiffs in the 2011 Texas Redistricting lawsuit.[55] The report also pointed out how Latino preferences had been trending more and more in the direction of Democratic Party candidates over the eighteen years covered by the data. As the data indicate, support for the Latino candidate rose from 15.3 percent in 1992, his first election, to a high of 21.97 percent in 1996. Mr. Bonilla's support among Latinos began a steady decline in 1998 until 2002 when he received less than 1 percent of their vote. It is clear that Mr. Bonilla never was the choice of Latino voters throughout his tenure and was in danger of losing his seat given the changing demographics. It should be noted that the ethnicity of the candidate is not important to a finding of racial polarization, only that the votes of the racial groups differ greatly. Mr. Bonilla's only chance of survival was to change the boundaries of his district, ensuring inclusion of lower Latino turnout precincts and exclusion of the higher turnout Latino precincts in his district. The percentages in Table 3.2 were derived using double regression estimates[56] produced by a political scientist recognized by the court as an expert in this field and by the State Attorney General's Office. There were also research reports on differential turnout rates or the turnout rate differences between Anglos and Latinos in this district and changes in demographics.

2. Racial Purpose Communications (Proof of discriminatory purpose negating judicial deference to other decisional factors).
This factor includes evidence from the record revealing racial purpose such as e-mail communications, all communications documents, agency reports, legislative records, memoranda and minutes of meetings, public utterances of decision makers, and so forth. This is the most important information because it will provide the most direct evidence speaking to racial purpose. As noted earlier, sometimes this information will not be uncovered through the normal *duces tecum.*[57] An example of evidence that would fit under this factor are copies of e-mails transmitted between the Texas redistricters as they

Table 3.2.   U.S. Congressional District 23 Support by Race for Congressman Bonilla 1992–2002

Year	% Latino Support	% Non-Latino Support	S.E.
1992	15.3	81.7	.029
1994	15.8	81.5	.016
1996	21.97	80.9	.018
1998	20.85	85.2	.014
2000	15.4	83.2	.018
2002	.37	87.9	.01

were creating the "nudge factor" that would lead to the creation of Hispanic majority but low-turnout Hispanic congressional districts during the 2011 legislative session. The specific e-mail discussing the "nudge factor" was cited in an earlier chapter; nevertheless, the e-mail discusses how the metric is to be constructed and applied with the end goal of ensuring the election of two Republicans to Congress, Messrs. Canseco and Farenthold. The e-mails, together with the subsequent responses, reveal collusion to manipulate the Hispanic vote because the operatives felt that they would not support Republican candidates. In a later e-mail, one of the operatives states that the only reliable Republican voters are Anglos. These e-mails provide direct evidence that the redistricters had a racial purpose to their redistricting efforts, albeit a racial purpose to achieve a political end, still a racial purpose.

3. Circumstantial and Direct Evidence (Sensitive inquiry into circumstantial and direct evidence of intent).

This may include both the historical record depicting past treatment of covered groups in all social areas; it may also include evidence of racial animosity surrounding the legislative environment. During the redistricting trial, the plaintiffs began their racial purpose presentation with a montage of YouTube snippets taken during state house and senate hearings and a Tea Party rally, sponsored by a state house member that was designed to present to the court the intense racial animosity that pervaded the legislative session during which the redistricting and voter identification laws were being considered. One clip showed a Texas State Senator excoriating a Latino male who was presenting his testimony before a senate transportation subcommittee in Spanish. The senator said that he was insulted that the man was speaking Spanish, and the man responded that, although he spoke English, he preferred speaking in Spanish, his native language, saying he felt more comfortable using his native language in such a formal setting. The witness also pointed out that he was accompanied by a professional interpreter to translate his comments into English for committee members. Another snippet showed a Tea Party rally on the steps of the state capitol; an event of this nature must be sponsored by a member of the legislature in this instance it was house member Leo Berman (R-Tyler, Texas). The main speaker at the rally pointed out that the reason that meaningful immigration legislation was not possible in the legislature was because there were "36 Hispanic elected legislators," so they all had to be eliminated from office. Testimony was also entered that there were five pieces of legislation requiring English as the official language of Texas and approximately one hundred other pieces of legislation having something to do with immigration entertained during this session. The evidence was submitted to give the court a feeling of the intense level of racial tension and animosity that surrounded the session where both redistricting and voter identification laws were being considered. These types of data, although anecdotal, speak more to the sociological effects that a legacy of racism has on a community. The racial outbursts are examples of the deeply engrained sociological attitudes that some Anglo elected officials have toward Latinos.[58]

4. Effect on Population (Impact of official action bearing more heavily on one race than another).
This area includes the empirical data mentioned under Factor One but also may include additional data on all areas of social life that fall under the *totality of circumstances* test. For instance in the voter identification case, evidence concerning whether or not in-person voter fraud was being committed was used to discuss this category. The data should also include information concerning which racial group will be affected by the implementation of a law written in a certain manner. This variable may include economic effects on voters seeking identification cards such as effects on wages or other sources of income; time spent away from work or school; age-related data; transportation costs; and, so forth. This is generally referred to as disparate impact analysis and purports to show how implementation of a policy will have an extremely different or "disparate" effect on specific racial groups. Data are arrayed showing how, for example, the transportation costs of obtaining a voter identification card are relatively more burdensome on Latinos and poor persons than Anglo and middle-class individuals. As of this writing, however, this technique is being challenged in the Supreme Court.[59]

5. Racial Patterns (A clear pattern, unexplainable on grounds other than race may emerge from the effect of state action, even when state action appears neutral).
This factor may contain some empirical data or it may not, depending on the substance, subject, and facts of the case. As an example during the Texas redistricting case, Table 3.3 was presented to the court indicating the number of individuals that had to be eliminated from one congressional district to achieve the apportionment ratio. The table also includes how many individuals were moved, what racial group they belonged to, what their turnout rates were, and how different candidates would fare within the voting precincts included and excluded from the newly designed district. The table itself let a pattern emerge that could not be explained on grounds other than race, that race was the principal variable in the redesign of CD23.

The table depicts the total number of individuals who were moved in and out of Congressional District 23 in order to achieve the reapportionment number after the 2010 census. In the second column, third row is the new reapportionment number of 698,488; this number was derived by dividing the total national population by the number of congressional seats. As a result, each

Table 3.3. Population Additions and Subtractions US CD23 Differences Between C100 and C185

Area	Tot Pop	2010 Tot Regs Vtrs	2010 Latino Regs Vtrs	2010 % Latino Regs Vtrs	2010 Non-Latino Regs Vtrs	2010 % Non-Latino Regs Vtrs	2010 Latino Turnout	2010 Non-Latino Turnout
C100	847,651	449,172	233,372	52.0	215,800	48.0	24.9	39.4
C185	698,488	367,371	198,709	54.1	168,662	45.9	22.9	41.6
Diff	−149,163	−81,801	−34,663	2.1	−57,138	−2.1	−2.0	2.2
Areas Moved into CD23	231,514	110,307	67,863	61.5	42,444	38.5	16.2	35.7
Areas Moved out of CD23	380,677	192,108	102,526	53.2	89,582	46.7	23.0	33.7
Diff	149,163	81,801	34,663	8.3	47,138	−8.2	−6.8	+2.0

congressional district in Texas under the new redistricting plan was required to have 698,488 individuals exactly. The row immediately above that cell in the table indicates 847,651 was the number of individuals who actually resided in the old CD23 as reflected in the 2010 census counts. The state was required to reduce the population by 149,163 individuals in order to reach the number required under the new plan. The old plan, referred to as the "benchmark" plan, is numbered C100 while the new plan, approved by the state legislature and signed into law by the governor, is referred to as C185. This latter plan is the one challenged in the federal district court in the *Perez v. Perry* suit of 2011.

The benchmark CD23 had been a matter of contention in previous redistricting lawsuits in 2003 and 2006 and had changed hands between candidates of both parties due to the redistricting changes. This seat was held by a Republican, Francisco "Quico" Canseco, as a result of the 2008 election when he ran against a badly organized incumbent Ciro Rodriguez who, in turn, had won the seat from a Republican incumbent after the 2006 redistricting lawsuit. As the data in column five of the table indicate, 52 percent of all registered voters in the district were Latino under the benchmark C100 plan, while under the C185 plan this number increased to 54.2 percent. These numbers, however, are mitigated by the turnout figures which appear in the last two columns. Although Latino registration increased by 2.1 percent the actual Latino turnout rate, calculated from the 2010 general election, decreased from 24.9 percent to 22.9 percent, a full 2 percent. Compounding this situation the data in the last column shows that non-Latino turnout increased from 39.4 percent in C100 to 41.6 percent in C185, a 2.2 percent increase. The decrease in Latino turnout and increase in non-Latino turnout in the new CD23 represented a full 4.2 percent turnout reversal for Latinos. Essentially, CD23 was redesigned to increase the number and percentage of Latinos but to include only low-participating Latino voters. High-participating Latino voters were replaced in CD23 with low-participating Latino voters. As a result, CD23 in C185 gave the appearance of being "more Latino" but its actual potential performance would not be; performance here being determined by either an increase or decrease in the Latino turnout rate.

This shift from a congressional district that appeared as a Latino majority district would not perform as such was accomplished using the "nudge factor" discussed in the e-mail, cited earlier, between the two Republican redistricters. As the data in the second column indicate, in order to construct the new district, the redistricters moved more than 612,000 individuals to achieve the 149,163 reduction required to reach the new apportionment numbers while still keeping the district appearing as a Latino majority district yet friendly to Republican candidates. As the e-mail indicated, the redistricters wanted to construct a district that would be helpful electorally to Mr. Canseco. Nevertheless, aiding Mr. Canseco meant decreasing the performance potential of the Latinos in the new CD23 because Mr. Canseco was not the preferred candidate of Latinos in the district. As an interesting aside Mr. Canseco lost his reelection bid in 2012 to a Latino Democrat, Mr. Pete Gallegos, by only a 4.7 percent margin.

The process that the redistricters went through to achieve this transformation required measuring election precincts along the boundaries of the old CD23 seeking precincts that were majority Latino but that had a history of underperformance. It is clear that the redistricters systematically searched for precincts that had a majority of Latino registered voters but that also had a history of low voter turnout. The movement of all precincts resulted in dramatic geographical differences between the old and new CD23s. Most important, however, was that it created the illusion that CD23 had been transformed into a stronger Latino performing district when, in fact, the potential voting power of Latinos had been intentionally diminished.

This process resulted in changes made along the boundaries of the fourteen counties along the borders of CD23. The changes resulted in the geographical reconfiguration in El Paso County in the west; the addition of Loving, Winkler, Ward, Crane, Upton, Reagan, Schleicher and approximately half of Sutton Counties on the northern boundary of the district; the removal of almost half of Maverick County and the additions of portions of Atascosa and LaSalle Counties and all of Frio County in the South; and, the inclusion and exclusion of various parts of Bexar County. The changes to the congressional district were distinct and the changes appear in Figure 3.1 below.

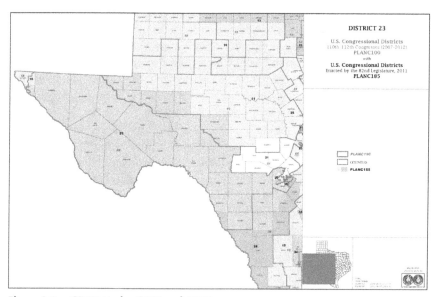

Figure 3.1. CD23 Under C100 and C185
Texas Legislative Council

In order to demonstrate the changes made to CD23 by the redistricters from Plan C100 to C185 it is important to discuss the modifications in great detail. This discussion is essential to show the precise nature with which the redistricters pursued the strategy set forth in the "nudge factor" e-mail. Although there is no evidence as to the order that the redistricters accomplished their mission the data that gave the initial hint that something was amiss was that many of the adjoining congressional districts, specifically 16, 20 and 28, were also overpopulated in the benchmark plan and were required to shed population to meet the new apportionment standard. When restructuring CD23 the redistricters not only removed populations from the adjoining districts and placed the overpopulations in CD23, they also removed other areas of CD23 and replaced the missing populations in the original districts. In effect the machinations were clear evidence that the redistricters were simply trading populations between the various districts. The question then surfaced as to which populations were being moved and what was or were the unique characteristics of those populations that made them ripe for selection. Below is a table of the southern and western regions of Texas indicating the overpopulation figures for the identified congressional districts under the benchmark plan. As the map indicates, CD16, wholly contained in El Paso County in the far west, was overpopulated by 58,939 individuals; CD23 by 149,163 persons; CD20 in Bexar County by 13,144 individuals; and, CD28 immediately adjacent to the east and south of CD23 by 153,336 persons. It appears that some of the overpopulation from some of the districts was used to create a new congressional district to the east of CD23, CD35, under Plan C185. This latter district is not depicted in the map because it did not exist under the benchmark plan and was one of the four new congressional seats allocated to Texas after the 2011 reapportionment.

There was no evidence uncovered as to whether a specific geographical area was given priority during the restructuring of CD23 or if the redistricters began their restructuring from one end of the district or another. Consequently, this discussion will begin by looking at the far western boundary of the district in El Paso County and work eastward concluding the analysis in Bexar County.

Table 3.4.   C100 South Texas Congressional Districts: Population Deviations

District	Population	Ideal Population	Deviation
15	787,124	698,488	88,636
16	757,427	698,488	58,939
20	711,632	698,488	13,144
23	847,651	698,488	149,163
27	741,993	698,488	43,505

Source: Texas Legislative Council. C100 Block Equivalency File.

EL PASO COUNTY

The 16th Congressional District lies wholly within El Paso County and as of the 2010 Census was found to be overpopulated by 58,939 individuals in the benchmark plan. How much population was moved out of CD16 into CD23 and vice versa is depicted in Table 3.5 below.

As the table indicates 32,880 registered voters were moved into CD23 while another 6,381 were moved from CD23 back into CD16. Of those numbers 29,043 or 88.3 percent of the removed registered voters were Latinos; of those returned to CD16 from CD23 4,863 or 76.2 percent were Latino. The unique characteristic of the registered voters resulting in their selection is found in their participation levels. The data in the table points out that the participation rate of those Latino registered voters added to CD23 was 11 percent, while that of the Latinos removed from CD23 was 3.9 percent higher or 14.9 percent. So, even though more Latino registered voters were added to CD23 those who were had lower participation rates than those who were removed. In itself, this "trade-off" in this geographical area means little; however, in the aggregate the effect would prove something else. Finally, as the map in Figure 3.2 indicate the population shifts changed the far western boundary from one that had run north and south to one that ran roughly east to west.

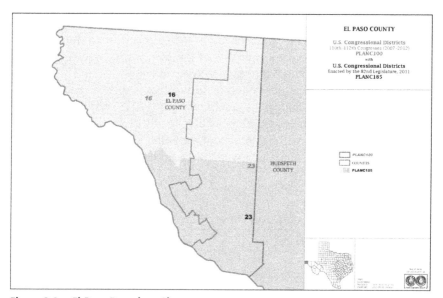

Figure 3.2. El Paso Boundary Changes
Texas Legislative Council

Table 3.5. Population Exchange Between CD16 and CD23, El Paso County

	Tot Reg Vtrs	Latino Reg Vtrs	% Latino Reg Vtrs	Non-Latino Reg Vtrs	% Non-Latino Reg Vtrs	Latino Turnout	Non-Latino Turnout
Moved into CD23	32,880	29,043	88.3	3,837	11.7	11.0	10.9
Moved out of CD23	6,381	4,863	76.2	1,518	23.8	14.9	20.8
Difference	26,499	24,180	12.1	2,319	-12.1	-3.9	-9.9

THE WEST

Describing this area of CD23 as the west is a slight misnomer because the area really lies along the northern boundary of the district and adjacent to CD11, still it is in what is commonly known as "West Texas." Seven counties and approximately half of another were added to CD23 under Plan C185. This addition is highlighted in Figure 3.3. Congressional District 11 became overpopulated after the 2010 Census by 12,194 individuals. The population that was moved from CD11 into CD23 accounted for 19,158 registered voters, 6,925 or 36.1 percent were Latino while 12,233 or 63.9 percent were non-Spanish surnamed. The data in Table 3.6 below indicate that there were almost twice as many non-Latino registered voters added to CD23 from CD11 and their turnout rate was 16.7 percent higher than that of the Latino voters. Data of what percentage of the non-Latino voters were African American was difficult to obtain because voters in Texas do not register by race, but a perusal of the population figures provided by the Texas Legislative Council based in census reports revealed that only 3.5 percent of the non-Latino population in these counties was African American. The registration rate for

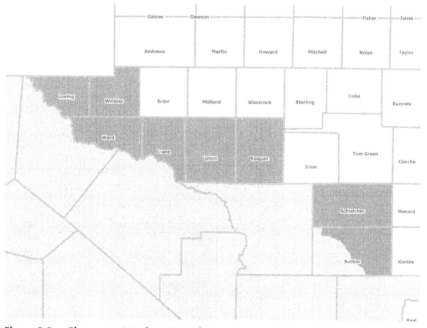

Figure 3.3.   Changes to Northern Boundary
C100 and C185 Boundaries from Texas Legislative Council; County Boundaries from 2010 Census via Caliper Cooperation

Table 3.6. Population Added to CD23 from CD11

	Tot Reg Vtrs	Latino Reg Vtrs	% Latino Reg Vtrs	Non-Latino Reg Vtrs	% Non-Latino Reg Vtrs	% Latino Turnout	% Non-Latino Turnout
Moved into CD23	19,158	6,925	36.1	12,233	63.9	22.9	39.6

the non-Latino population was 74.4 percent as opposed to 40.6 percent for the Latino voters who were added to CD23. Essentially, the redistricters added more Anglo registered voters who voted at much higher rates than the Latinos who were also added to CD23 from the same counties.

THE SOUTH

The southern region of CD23 that was affected by the redistricting included the southern portion of Maverick County along the border with Mexico and portions of Atascosa and LaSalle Counties as well as the entirety of Frio County. Maverick County was nearly halved with the southern portion of the county assigned to CD28. Frio and portions of Atascosa and LaSalle were switched from CD28 into CD23. These changes are depicted in Figure 3.4. The data in Table 3.7 below show the number of registered voters, Latino and non-Latino, and their respective turnout rates. The data indicate that 33,487 total registered voters were added to CD23 from CD28 while 12,322 were removed. Fully 64 percent of the registered voters added or 21,426 were

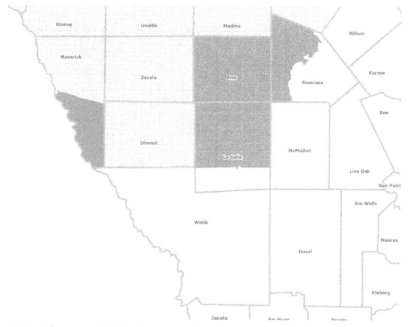

Figure 3.4.   Changes to the Southern Boundary of CD23
C100 and C185 Boundaries from Texas Legislative Council; County Boundaries from 2010 Census via Caliper Cooperation

Table 3.7. Population Changes to Southern Region of CD23

	Tot Reg Vtrs	Latino Reg Vtrs	% Latino Reg Vtrs	Non-Latino Reg Vtrs	% Non-Latino Reg Vtrs	% Latino Turnout	% Non-Latino Turnout
Moved into CD23	33,487	21,426	64	12,061	36.0	17.5	41.8
Moved out of CD23	12,322	11,230	91.1	1,092	8.9	20	22.8
Difference	21,165	10,196	−27.1	10,969	27.1	−2.5	19.0

Latinos while the remaining 12,061 or 36 percent were non-Latinos. Of the 12,322 removed from CD23 into CD28, 11,230 or 91.1 percent were Latinos with only 1,092 or 8.9 percent non-Latinos. Finally, the data indicate that the voting participation rate for those Latinos moved into CD23 was 17.5 percent as opposed to 19.8 percent for those moved out of the district. The turnout rate for the non-Latinos added to the district was 41.8 percent while the rate for those removed from the district was 22.8 percent.

Several observations can be made of the population switching made in this area of CD23. First, although more Latinos than non-Latinos were moved into CD23 from CD28 the number of non-Latinos moved into the district was almost 1,000 more than the number of Latinos removed from the district. This slightly lowered the percentage of Latino registered voters in CD23. The participation rate of those Latinos added into CD23 was lower than that of the Latinos moved into CD23. Complicating the turnout rate scenario is the fact that the participation rate for the non-Latino registered voters moved into CD23 from CD28 was almost doubled from 22.8 percent to 41.8 percent. The turnout rate differences reveal a "participation gap" between Latinos and non-Latinos that was exacerbated by the movement of voters in this region. Under C100 the "participation gap" between non-Latino and Latino voters was 2 percent, 27.3 percent for Latinos and 29.3 percent for non-Latinos. After redistricting, the "participation gap" expanded from 2 percent to 17 percent, 23.6 percent for Latinos to 40.6 percent for non-Latino voters. Clearly, a pattern begins emerging where CD23 under Plan C185 is having increased numbers of Latinos but they are Latinos who participate less than those removed from the district. Simultaneously, those non-Latinos added to CD23 have higher participation rates than those removed.

BEXAR COUNTY

The largest numbers of registered voters moved into and out of CD23 during redistricting came from Bexar County (San Antonio). On one level this may appear an obvious observation given that Bexar County is the largest urban area in the region and initially the changes may appear cosmetic in nature because all changes were made within the county boundaries. The data in Table 3.8 below, however, tells another tale. As the data in the table demonstrate 173,405 registered voters were removed from various parts of CD23 into four different congressional districts, 20, 21, 28 and the new 35. It should be noted that the existing congressional districts were also overpopulated even though receiving additional registered voters from CD23. Of the 173,405 registered voters moved out of CD23, 86,433 or 49.8 percent were Latinos and 86,972 or 50.2 percent were non-Latinos. The data in Table 3.8 also show that 24,782 voters in Bexar County were added to CD23. Of these, 10,469 or 42.2 percent

Table 3.8. Population Changes to CD 23 in Bexar County

	Tot Reg Vtrs	Latino Reg Vtrs	% Latino Reg Vtrs	Non-Latino Reg Vtrs	% Non-Latino Reg Vtrs	% Latino Turnout	% Non-Latino Turnout
Moved into CD23	24,782	10,469	42.2	14,313	57.8	23.5	33.8
Moved out of CD23 into CD20	112,212	53,714	47.9	58,498	52.1	24	34.4
Moved out of CD23 into CD21	10,677	2,052	19.2	8,625	80.8	37.2	44.6
Moved out of CD23 into CD28	8,815	3,589	40.7	5,226	59.3	23.7	31.8
	41,701	27,078	64.9	14,623	35.1	22.7	26.8
Total moved out	173,405	86,433	49.8	86,972	50.2	23.9	34
Difference	−148,623	−75,964	−7.6	−72,659	7.6	−.4	−.2

were Latinos and 14,313 or 57.8 percent were non-Latinos. The turnout rates for the Latino voters removed from CD23 was 23.9 percent, that of the Latino voters who were placed back into CD23 was 23.5 percent. On the other hand, the participation rates for the non-Latino voters were 34 percent for those removed and 33.8 percent for those added into the district.

APPLICATION OF THE METRICS

It was not discovered how the redistricters determined the threshold standards for how many Latino or non-Latino voters to move until the Section 3 (c) trial was heard in August 2014. The method utilized by the redistricters to transform CD23 required that they meticulously pick and choose election precincts around the periphery of the district carefully selecting those precincts that served the strategy set forth in the "nudge factor" e-mail. The two variables utilized as the "metrics" were the percentage of Spanish surnamed registered voters in a precinct and the support levels of those voters for Latino candidates in ten elections. The elections, exogenous to the district, covered general elections from 2002 through 2010 and appear in Table 3.9 below. The table compares how the "Hispanic Choice" candidate in Plan C100 performed in CD23 under both plans C100 and C185.

The ten elections, labelled here "OAG10 Races," were selected by the Office of the State Attorney General (OAG) and were chosen because all of the candidates were the Latino preferred candidate in their respective statewide elections. As the data in the fifth column demonstrates only three of the statewide Latino candidates would have prevailed in CD23 in Plan C100 where 52 percent of all voters were Latinos. Under CD23 in Plan C185 having a 54.1 percent Latino registered voter population the Hispanic preferred candidates performed even worse, prevailing only once. Essentially, the redistricters chose ten statewide elections featuring Latino candidates who ran against an Anglo between 2002 and 2010. In the fourth column are the names of the candidates winning the majority of Latino votes statewide in their respective elections thus being deemed "Hispanic Choice." These elections were reaggregated so that the results appearing in the table are based on votes cast within the jurisdictional boundaries of CD23 under the benchmark C100 Plan. The data in the fifth column clearly show that the Latino preferred candidates prevailed in only three of the ten elections. The last column shows that the Latino preferred candidate prevailed only once in ten elections in the CD23 configured under C185.

In two of the e-mail communications among the redistricters it was discovered that they were choosing which precincts to include or exclude from not

Table 3.9. OAG10 Races Comparison of CD23 in C100 and C185 by OAG10

Year	Election	Contest	Plan 100 Hispanic Choice	Plan 100 Prevailing	C185 Prevailing
2002	General	Governor	Sanchez	Sanchez 50.2	Perry 50.7
2004	General	RailRd Comm	Scarborough	Carillo 52.8	Carillo 54.03
2004	General	Crt of Criml Appls	Molina	Keasler 50.7	Keasler 53.2
2006	General	Lt. Gov.	Alvarado	Dewhurst 53.2	Dewhurst 56.7
2006	General	Crt of Criml Appls	Molina	Keller 50.4	Keller 53.4
2008	General	US Senator	Noriega	Noriega 52.0	Cornyn 50.1
2008	General	Supreme Crt	Yanez	Yanez 55.3	Yanez 50.8
2010	General	Lt. Gov.	Chavez-Thompson	Dewhurst 56.6	Dewhurst 58.3
2010	General	Land Comm	Uribe	Patterson 55.1	Patterson 57.5
2010	General	Supreme Crt	Bailey	Guzman 58.1	Guzman 58.2

only CD23 but also from CDs 20 and 35 using the OAG10 Races.[60] Given the evidence it is abundantly clear that the redistricters were using a strategy born out of the communications revealed in the "nudge factor" e-mail to guide their work with the purpose of creating congressional districts that were majority Latino registered voter but where the Latino voters would be outvoted by the Anglo or non-Latino minority. Although, the stated intention was to create districts where a Republican would win the redistricters pursued no other alternative to success but through the dilution of Latino voting power.

6. Historical Background (Historical background of the decision revealing a series of official actions taken for invidious purposes).

The data used for any variables identified in this area are historical in nature and generally cover all public policy areas and are data produced through normal historiography. For instance, the public record in jurisdictions throughout the state of Texas and reports from the United States Bureau of the Census reveal policies that created segregated schools where Latino children were forced to attend public schools through the secondary level that had been specifically set aside for their education.[61] These schools were known in each school district as "The Mexican School." In smaller school districts a separate "Mexican Classroom" was set aside for the education of Latino children. Various Tax Appraisal Districts throughout the state also have copies of land titles indicating that land in certain parts of cities or counties throughout the state could not be sold or resold to any Latinos.[62] Although both policies were stopped through court order in the 1960s, the legacy was to set back the educational progress of Latinos in Texas for generations and to establish segregated neighborhoods that remain segregated to this day. These neighborhoods, originally segregated through racial covenants, are now racially segregated structurally through custom, property values, and the inability of low-income Latinos to purchase property of higher values.[63] Most important, however, is that the generations of individuals who enacted the policies are still alive and have transmitted their perceptions of Latinos to their progeny. Anti-Latino chauvinism still exists in Texas, and various individuals continue their efforts at writing it into policy in laws that wish to make English the official language of the state or instituting any number of anti-immigrant laws, one of which is the voter identification law. The reason the voter identification law or anti-immigrant laws are seen as anti-Latino is based simply in the fact that the largest number of immigrants in the United States having arrived either legally or otherwise come from Latin America with the vast majority, estimated at upward of 60 percent by the Immigration and Customs Enforcement Service, coming from Mexico. The largest expenditures for border security have been spent on the Mexican border to build the fence and to populate the border with guards and enforcement agents. The voter identification and verification law or Senate Bill 14 was originally intended to discourage illegal immigrants from Mexico from casting fraudulent ballots in elections in the United States. More of the overall history of discrimination against Latinos in Texas is presented in the next chapter. Nevertheless, there is sufficient historical evidence to show that there has been a continuing history of discriminatory behavior on the part of governments at all levels within the state and individuals since the incorporation of Latinos into the United States beginning in 1836.

7. Decisional Chronology (The specific series of events leading up to the challenged decision).
These data include information from various media types including Internet sources (for example, YouTube videos) to the legislative record. This may also include all attempts at communicating with authorities to correct a perceived discriminatory action from public petitions to attorney interactions. These data are information that represent the intensity and quality of race relations in the jurisdiction, including examples of anti-immigrant rallies, castigating persons in places of employment or public places against the use of Spanish, maintenance of separate racial social groupings, and so forth.

Examples of these types of data appear in the discussion under Factor Three that included a discussion on the YouTube videos used as evidence during the redistricting trial. A more substantive example of the type of evidence that may be applicable under this factor, however, is the debate and discussion record surrounding the passage of SB 14 when it was presented in the State House for consideration on March 23, 2011. This day saw sixty-three separate attempts to amend SB 14, four submitted by Republican house members and fifty-nine by Democrats (see Table 2.2). All four of the Republican amendments passed. Of the fifty-nine amendments sponsored by Democrats, ten were adopted without a vote, three failed on a floor vote, and thirty-eight were tabled. Of the thirty-eight tabled, five were specific references to the VRA. The five VRA amendments were sponsored by either Latinos (four) or African Americans (one). Minority members of the house sponsoring forty-three of the fifty-nine amendments were identified as Democrats; no Republican minority members sponsored any amendments to SB 14. Of the forty-three amendments sponsored by minority members, thirty-four were tabled, one failed on a vote, and eight were adopted.

All five amendments that referred to the VRA were tabled though there were passionate, sometimes sarcastically comical, discussions in each instance. All of the adopted amendments were not controversial, several were grammatical or syntactical changes, while the remainder were re-stipulations of various requirements that exist under current law such as no fees for requesting duplicate voter identification cards, ensuring that provisional ballots were available in polling places, or stating that if any part of SB 14 were to be legally struck down the other parts would remain legal.

In the final analysis, it was clear that the House leadership did not want to discuss any possibility that some aspect of SB 14 violated or could be in violation of the VRA. In each of the five instances when a VRA-related amendment was sponsored, there was no substantive conversation, simply a motion to table followed by a voice vote on the motion. Other times, either a Latino or African American representative, when making the motion to amend SB 14, would attempt to engage in a debate or discussion with Representative Harless, the Republican sponsor, she would declare "she was not so advised," declaring no knowledge of the topic such as when one member asked her if she thought discrimination still existed in Texas. It should be added that Rep. Harless also refused to cooperate during her deposition prior to the trial, claiming "legislative privilege."

The five amendments that were intended to change SB 14 so it would not violate Section 5 of the VRA included the following in the order they were presented and can be found in Table 3.10 in that same order. The first attempt was Amendment 9 which was an effort at grandfathering in all voters over the age of 65. Representative Roberto Alonzo, the amendment's sponsor, pointed out that many older minority voters might not be able to provide the supporting identification in order to obtain a new voter identification card under the provisions of SB 14 as initially submitted. Mister Alonzo attempted to have the age lowered from 70 to 65 to allow a higher number of older minority vot-

Table 3.10.   March 23, 2011 Texas House Journal Roll Call Voting on VRA Amendments to SB 14

Amend #	Sponsor	Race	Party ID	Status of Amend	Partisan Vote*
9	Alonzo	Latino	Democrat	Tabled	101Y 48N 1P (99R, 2D)-Y, 48D- N, 1R-P
16	Raymond	Latino	Democrat	Tabled	100Y 49N 1P (99R, 1D)-Y, 49D-N, 1R-P
34	Raymond	Latino	Democrat	Tabled	101Y 48N 1P (98R, 3D)-Y, 48D-N, 1R-P
35	Raymond	Latino	Democrat	Tabled	100Y 49N 1P (99R, 1D)-Y, 49D-N, 1R-P
55	Veasey	African American	Democrat	Tabled	99Y 48N 2P (98R, 1D)-Y, 48D-N, 2R-P, 1D-A

*Vote to table amendment. A "Yes" vote represented a vote against the submitted amendment. A "P" designated a member as present but not voting "Y" or "N."

ers to apply and receive voter ID cards under the new rules. He engaged in a farcical conversation with Rep. Mark Veasey, an African American member from Fort Worth now in the U.S. House of Representatives, on the history of racial discrimination throughout Texas' electoral history in order to make a case for his amendment but was cut off when a vote on tabling the motion was called.

Representative Richard Raymond, a Latino Democrat from South Texas, sponsored the 16th Amendment that was designed to strike down an aspect of SB 14 that potentially violated the VRA in that it was designed to require voters without SB 14–approved identification to provide documentary evidence that their employer would not allow them time off from work to obtain the requisite identification. The prospective voter also was required to show, the employer's refusal to allow the voter to seek identification notwithstanding, documentary evidence that a Department of Motor Vehicle Office where he could obtain the proper identification was not open for at least two consecutive hours beyond the worker's times of employment. Representative Raymond sought to engage Representative Van Taylor, who was one of the bill's sponsors, in a discussion concerning whether or not this provision would be in violation of the VRA to no avail. Eventually, a motion from the floor to table the proposed amendment was entertained by the chair.

Representative Raymond also sponsored Amendments 34 and 35 that were attempts to change SB 14 to ensure it was not in violation of the VRA. Amendment 34 was a statement declaring SB 14 "legally unenforceable if it does not comply with Section 5, Section 203, and Section (4) (f) (4) of the Voting Rights Act."[64] The bill's sponsor, Representative Harless, immediately responded that "the Voting Rights Act either does or does not apply to various sections of this bill. This is for the Supreme Court to determine not the Texas Legislature. I move to table."[65] Representative Raymond then attempted to engage Representative Harless in debate as to whether the VRA was good law and whether it was still necessary in 2011. She refused to engage in the debate by charging Representative Raymond with "putting words into my mouth," "I don't think this is the place to debate that," or stating that they had already discussed the topic. Representative Veasey then interjected facetiously asking Representative Raymond why he thought Representative Harless refused to address the issue. Mr. Raymond responded by saying that he thought she did not wish to admit that her bill had voting rights implications for millions of Texas voters, particularly members of minority groups. The conversation ended with the restated motion to table by Representative Harless.

Amendment 35 was similar to 34 in that it was an attempt by Mister Raymond to insert an amendment that declared "Sections 203 and 14 (f) (4) of the Voting Rights Act apply to this section."[66] The amendment was to ensure compliance in the voter identification education portion of SB 14 by ensuring that the bill complied with the language protection requirement set forth in Section 203 of the VRA. Representative Larry Phillips moved to table complaining that he felt the amendment would lead to too much federal oversight. He added that he wasn't sure if "those sections (203 and 14 (f) (4)) apply to this, that will be up to the—that will be up to, ultimately, the Supreme Court to determine, and that's who we need to let determine."[67] Mr. Raymond tried to engage Mr. Phillips in the same manner as he had Ms. Harless concerning whether the VRA applied or not to the state of Texas. Mister Phillips pointed out that "I want this (SB 14) to comply with federal laws, and if the voting rights laws that are in effect apply to this and they're constitutional, the supreme court will uphold it, and if they don't they won't." He then went on before Mister Raymond could respond by stating that:

> the federal government passes the laws that they do, and we're either going to follow those laws or not. We either have to or we don't, and that's part of the debate that is going on across this nation of what we do and we do not want to—we don't want to incorporate—we're trying to stop federal laws that we don't agree with."[68]

This discussion was ended by another tabling motion. Representative Veasey submitted Amendment 55, which was intended to allow the old registration card to stand if the new voter identification card in SB 14 was found to violate the VRA. Ms. Harless again pointed out that the issue was a matter for the Supreme Court and not the Texas legislature, and the discussion was cut short by another tabling motion.

Each of the discussions surrounding the amendments that specifically referenced the VRA provided several interesting themes that kept repeating themselves. The first was a complete refusal to enter into a debate as to whether SB 14 or any provisions under discussion violated all or part of the VRA. Secondly, each of the sponsors who spoke in defense of SB 14 pointed out that they felt that it was not the Texas legislature's role to determine whether SB 14 complied with the VRA. In actuality, the sponsors felt that the Supreme Court needed to act to determine whether the VRA was constitutional. Finally, it appeared, particularly in Mister Phillips's comments, that they were determined not only to force the Supreme Court to act on the constitutionality of the VRA but to do so by invoking the Tenth Amendment to the Constitution insinuating that the VRA represented federal government intervention in a state issue. Representative Harless was vehement in her refusal to discuss whether she felt racial discrimination still existed in the state and whether or not the VRA was still an essential law. Both Harless and Phillips did admit that the VRA was important and effective and necessary at one time in history but then fell short of even saying whether it was still needed; instead they switched their comments, stating that this was a matter for the Supreme Court to adjudicate. Most importantly, the record indicates an unwillingness on the part of legislators to even discuss the topic of whether SB 14 or any of its provisions were in violation of the VRA. In fact, one suspects that most of their responses were rehearsed with the principal strategy being to create a situation that would result in a constitutional challenge to the VRA. The data in Table 3.9 also indicate that all five amendments were tabled along partisan lines. This session had fifty Democrats and one hundred Republicans. The data in the last two columns reflects the number of partisans voting for or against the tabling motions for each of the five amendments.

8. Procedural Departures (Departures from the normal procedural sequences).
This Factor may be produced through a construction of the legislative record outlining all procedures that went into the design, construction, and passage of a law. Comparing the actual process with stated and published procedures and then simply presenting a comparison of the deviation to the courts. Here a presentation of a chronology and comparative analysis of how a certain policy was developed juxtaposed against what the normal process would look like. Evidence of the avoidance of conventional parliamentary procedures, unusual scheduling to either rush or delay matters, and/or avoidance of public hearings to minimize input from professionals, activists, or community members constitutes the heart of the evidence in this factor. Direct evidence may be derived from minutes of meetings, daily journals of legislative meetings, and public memoranda.

9. Goal Departures (Substantive departures, too, may be relevant particularly if the factors usually considered important strongly favor a decision contrary to the one reached).
These may be empirical data but not necessarily indicating how a particular public official or entity wishes to achieve a certain aim, that is, fairly redistrict or protect the integrity of the ballot, yet their actions lead to other than the stated goals. Changing the goals of the voter identification bill is discussed during the review of the trial in chapter 5 and then again in chapters 6 and 7. The record may show that the original objectives or goals of a policy may not remain the same as the impact or "effect" data show. This difference may be the result of changing rhetoric as was the situation in the voter identification lawsuit when the law was initially intended to prevent fraudulent voting by illegal immigrants to one that was designed to protect the integrity and security of the ballot.

10. Legislative and Administrative History (The legislative and administrative history especially where there are contemporary statements by members in minutes, records, or reports. Where necessary, some public officials may be called to the stand to testify as to racial purpose).

This area is fairly clear if the public record is replete with both explicit racial commentaries by public officials. This may include hearsay evidence, innuendos, or the use of code words. One can then request public officials to testify, either in court or in deposition, to determine their purpose. If they refuse or fall on legislative privilege, then they can be challenged and, in extreme or special cases determined by the court, may be subpoenaed and compelled to testify under oath.

11. Alia.

The court was not clear about this factor other than stating that "the forthgoing summary identifies, without purporting to be exhaustive, subjects of proper inquiry in determining whether racial discriminatory intent existed."[69] One topic that is missing and may be included in this category is the history of voting and civil rights litigation in which the jurisdiction in question has been subject to before and since the passage of the VRA. For instance, Texas's record of 198 Section 5 objections displayed by type of offense and jurisdiction juxtaposed to the demographics of the specific jurisdiction may be the type of evidence appropriate under this category. Additionally, if possible, uncovering any direct evidence of racial purpose in any Section 5 objection or Section 2 trials to lend depth to evidentiary production might also be appropriate here. Finally, racial purpose or intent evidence found in the legislative record, city council meetings, county journals, or any coincidental committee meetings could be presented under this factor.

RACISM, RACIAL PURPOSE, LATINOS, AND THE VRA

Race is a social construct that defines relations between groups. The concept of race was concocted as a device to allow humans to designate one group of persons as different from another based on cultural, language, sometimes religious grounds. Beginning in ancient times and culminating in the contemporary era, a hierarchy of races has developed upon antiquated and old prejudices based on nothing more than religious or pseudo-scientific beliefs. These beliefs have found their way into contemporary cultural ideology and are manifested in a multitude of ways. Nevertheless, this social categorization of people defines how various groups interact with each other, but, more often than not, racial definitions determine whether one group interacts positively or negatively toward the other group or groups. For instance, in popular culture, one sees African Americans, Latinos, Native Americans, and so forth depicted by various caricatures based on stereotypes springing forth from the imaginations of individuals who have these racial stereotypes embedded in the manner in which they view racial groups generally. As a result, some ra-

cial groups' work ethos, their family cultures, their propensity toward criminal behavior, their intellectual sophistication, or their ability to participate
rationally in the political world are based on racial stereotypes popularized in
every sort of medium from pop-cultural to academic. In regards to Latinos,
examples of the former, the now infamous cartoon depictions of the "Frito
Bandito" used to advertise a popular brand of corn chips in the late 1960s
and early 1970s, were withdrawn after a Mexican American media watch
group mounted a national protest. In the latter category, an example of racial
stereotypes that were created in the academic world can be found in the works
of Oscar Lewis,[70] Patrick Moynahan,[71] Edward Banfield,[72] and Michael Harrington[73] when they developed their research that defined the families of the
poor as a dysfunctional culture predetermining the behavior of subsequent
generations. The most important contribution of academicians, however, was
that they developed a theory that became popular that worked to the detri-
ment of racial minority groups. Essentially, they came to a conclusion that the
poor, who included all minority groups, could not define their world in future
terms; as a result they lived for the present and pursued economic strategies
based on the gratification of present-time needs. Planning for the future,
defining the world in future terms was not possible because the demands
of daily survival prevented that way of thinking. This working assumption,
although discredited in the 1990s and early part of the twenty-first century,[74]
formed the basis for the policies that eventually formed the core of what came
to be known as President Lyndon Johnson's "War on Poverty" in 1964. The
centerpiece of President Johnson's "war" was the Economic Opportunity Act
and programs such as Head Start, Volunteers in Service to America, and the
Job Corps, all designed to "lift the poor" out of poverty. Nevertheless, the
cultural assumptions of those academics who created the "culture of poverty"
were the basis upon which the programs were designed and constructed. The
cycle itself was believed to be never ending as long as the poor remained
within their family structures. The most important assumption was that if
you could break the cycle of poverty, then these individuals could become
contributing members of society. Policy makers thus learned to define and
embrace these stereotypes of the poor from their families, in school, through
their media exposure, and through sharing them with peers throughout their
professional lives.

Racial stereotyping has found its way into the public policy formation
process and subconsciously or, sometimes, consciously defines the way in
which policy makers define a policy issue, assists the policy maker in arriving at a specific design of a policy addressing the issue, and directs the
manner in which a policy is implemented. When arriving at a public policy
decision, images of race determine the orientation of specific public policies,

particularly those that will have either positive or negative effects on a racial group. Racial purpose or intent subsequently creeps its way into the policy process as a working assumption, because the decision makers determine, either consciously or subconsciously, that the targeted racial group requires to be treated in either a positive or negative discriminatory manner.

To reiterate, negative discrimination involves writing policy that creates barriers excluding individuals from participating or having access to public goods or services that all citizens have a fundamental or required right to, such as essential public safety services, public education, and voting. Positive discrimination is the creation of laws or policies protecting access to the goods, services, or rights fundamentally protected or required by law. Access requires protection where access has been denied through discriminatory practices historically.

In the world of voting rights, the principal problematic lies in determining and identifying how racism finds its way into and becomes embedded in the public policy process. This has become difficult for at least three reasons. The first is that racism and its public expression has changed dramatically over the last fifty years. Racist terminology has evolved from the overt and explicit to the subtle and unspoken. Whereas once Latinos were referred to as "spics," "mescins," "beaners," and "greasers," now they are referred to by code labels such as fraudulent voters or illegal aliens. The second reason is more technical. Until recently, in jurisprudential history, there has been little guidance as to the sort of evidence the Court was willing to entertain to identify or define racial purpose or intent; this they finally did in *Arlington Heights.* The third reason is simply that judicial voting rights decisions together with the intellectual discourse surrounding litigation in this area are oriented around a dual-race analytical framework. In other words, judges and scholars view civil rights generally, but specifically view voting rights issues through lenses that divide the social world in two, black and white. This leaves Latinos, together with other excluded racial and ethnic groups, in an analytical netherworld. Although the Supreme Court does make decisions that generally stand as the law of the land that are applicable to the entire nation, they do make particularized decisions when they feel that the circumstances dictate, referred to as narrowly tailored decisions. The Court may wish to consider narrowly tailored decisions in some situations where Latinos are concerned.

The Court showed great wisdom in issuing its guidance in *Arlington Heights* as a methodological road map around the three barriers creating the problematic of identifying racial purpose in civil rights litigation. The most important aspect about this is, however, that the Court must consider is that the case for Latinos may be treated differently than that of African Americans or other racial or ethnic groups covered under the VRA. The rationale for this argument is multifaceted, but it includes the facts that Latinos have a different social and political history than African Americans; Latinos experience and have experienced a different type of discrimination throughout their time in the United States; and Latinos are perceived and treated differently than any other racial group in the United States by Anglos. The unique social and political place of Latinos in the United States and Texas comprise the discussion in the next chapter.

NOTES

1. Examples of these types of barriers occur periodically in almost every election across the United States. In some cases such as in Florida, minimizing the number of days available for early voting has been codified into state law. The lack of a sufficient number of computers occurred in Florida during the 2000 general election and arose during the post-election suit brought by the NAACP against the state. In some local jurisdictions, zealous election judges will declare that persons of some groups have lost their right to vote and then will turn the voters away. This occurred in Killeen, Texas, during the 2004 general election an African American woman was told this by an election judge. A local poll watcher challenged this action and the judge relented.

2. *Thornburg v. Gingles,* 478 U.S. 30 (1986).

3. *Bullock v. Carter,* 405 U.S. 134 (1972).

4. Examples of these have been at the heart of Cornel West's writings, especially *Race Matters,* Boston, MA: Beacon Press, 1993. See also Paul L. Wachtel's *Race in the Mind of America: Breaking the Vicious Circle Between Blacks and Whites,* New York: Routledge Press, 1999; Joe R. Feagin and Karyn D. McKinney, *The Many Costs of Racism,* New York: Rowman & Littlefield Publishers, Inc., 2003; and Sherene H. Razack, *Looking White People in the Eye,* Toronto: University of Toronto Press, 1998.

5. *Reynolds v. Sims,* 377 U.S. 533 (1964).

6. Some of the better known histories or sociological studies are included in the following works. Carey McWilliams, *North From Mexico: The Spanish-Speaking People of the U.S.* (New York: Greenwood Publishers, 1968); Rodolfo Acuña, *Occupied America: The Chicano's Struggle Toward Liberation* (New York: Harper & Row Publishers, 1972); David Montejano, *Anglos and Mexicans in the Making of Texas, 1836–1986* (Austin, TX: The University of Texas Press, 1987); Mario T. Garcia, *Mexican Americans: Leadership, Ideology and Identity, 1930–1960* (New Haven, CT: Yale University Press, 1989); Chandler Davidson, *Race and Class in Texas Politics;* Manuel G. Gonzales, *Mexicanos: A History of Mexicans in the United States* (Bloomington, IN: Indiana University Press, 1999); Reynaldo Valencia, Sonia R. Garcia, Henry Flores, and José Roberto Juárez, Jr., *Mexican Americans and the Law;* and, Ian F. Haney López, *Racism on Trial: The Chicano Fight for Justice* (Cambridge, MA: Harvard University Press, 2003).

7. *Shelby County,* ibid., 13–14.

8. Olson makes a similar argument in his *The Abolition of White Democracy* pointing out that white persons enjoy full-citizenship because of the social privilege they enjoy as opposed to the lower status of African Americans and Latinos.

9. Ashley Montagu, *Man's Most Dangerous Myth: The Fallacy of Race,* 6th ed. (Walnut Creek, CA: AltaMira Press, 1997); Kenan Malik, *The Meaning of Race: Race, History and Culture in Western Society* (New York: New York University Press, 1996).

10. *Hernandez v. Texas,* 347 U.S. 475 (1954).

11. Lani Guinier & Gerald Torres, *The Miner's Canary: Enlisting Race, Resisting Power, Transforming Democracy* (Cambridge, MA: Harvard University Press, 2002); Olson, ibid.; Segrest, ibid.; Sherrow O. Pinder, *Whiteness and Racialized Ethnic Groups in the United States* (New York: Lexington Books, 2012); Eduardo Bonilla-Silva, *Racism and Racists: Color-Blind Inequality in America,* 4th ed (New York: Rowman & Littlefield, 2014).

12. Gossett, 1997, see particularly the first chapter, pp 3–16, for a review of the early origins of racism.

13. Gossett, ibid, p. 31.

14. George L. Leclerc Buffon, *Natural History, General and Particular*, translated by William Smellie (3rd ed.; London, 1791), VIII, 34–35 cited by Gossett, Ibid., pp. 32–37.

15. Thomas Jefferson, *Notes on Virginia.* In *The Writings of Thomas Jefferson* (Washington, 1903) cited in Gossett, p. 42.

16. Arthur de Gobineau, 1853, *An Essay on the Inequality of the Human Races.* Translated by Adrian Collins (London: William Heinemann, 1915).

17. Pat Shipman, *The Evolution of Racism: Human Differences and the Use and Abuse of Science* (New York: Simon and Schuster, 1994). See particularly chapter 6.

18. Pearson is considered one of the modern fathers of statistics who developed the concept of the "Bell Curve" and also Pearson's Product Moment Correlation Coefficient.

19. Washington, DC: Carnegie Institute, 1929.

20. New York: Scribner's.

21. Tucker, William H. *The Funding of Scientific Racism: Wickliffe Draper and the Pioneer Fund* (Champagne Urbana: University of Illinois Press, 2007).

22. Grant, ibid., p. 17.

23. 163 U.S. 537 (1896).

24. *Shaw v. Reno,* 509 U.S. 630 (1993).

25. 118 U.S. 356 (1886).

26. Mitchell F. Rice, *The Discriminatory Purpose Standard: A Problem for Minorities in Racial Discrimination Litigation?,* Boston College Third World Law Journal 6 (1986) no. 1/2. http://lawdigitalcommons.bc.edu/twlj/vol6/iss1/2.

27. Ibid., 374.

28. Rice, ibid., 2.

29. Note, *Proving Intentional Discrimination in Equal Protection Cases: The Growing Burden of Proof in the Supreme Court,* 10 N.Y.U. Rev. L. & Soc. Change 435, 438 (1980/1981). Cited in Rice, ibid., 2.

30. Michael J. Perry, *The Disproportionate Impact Theory of Racial Discrimination,* 125 *University of Pennsylvania Law Review* 541 (1977).

31. 426 U.S. 229 (1976).

32. Rice, ibid., 7.

33. Rice, ibid., 4.

34. Rice, ibid., 4.

35. Rice, ibid.

36. 426 U.S. 229 (1976).

37. *Washington v. Davis*, 238–39, 246.

38. 376 U.S. 52 (1964).

39. A *prima facie* case is one where sufficient evidence is presented that the court can rule irrefutably in favor of the plaintiff.

40. 379 U.S. 433 (1965).

41. 391 U.S. 367.

42. Rice, ibid., 8.

43. 403 U.S. 217 (1971).

44. 403 U.S.124 (1971).

45. 412 U.S.755 (1973).

46. Rice, ibid., 9.

47. Flores, 2003, *Evolution of the Liberal Democratic State,* ibid.

48. Davis, 426 U.S. at 242.

49. Davis, 426 U.S. at 253.

50. 429 U.S. 252 (1977).

51. 429 U.S. 268 footnote 18. Cited in Rice, ibid. at 18.

52. 446 U.S. 55 (1980).

53. Ibid. at 66.

54. Victor Carrillo, *Letter to Supporters,* March 5, 2010.

55. Flores, Henry, undated, "Expert Report Submitted on Behalf of MALDEF in GI Forum v. Texas," Table 2.

56. Grofman et al.

57. This is the traditional subpoena issued before depositions requiring one side of the litigation to produce all the material and data they have concerning the facts. Each side "trades" information in this manner to expedite the process. Sometimes data or information revealed during *duces tecum* forces one side to attempt settlement.

58. http://www.youtube.com/watch?v=hNKWISYPdZ4.

59. *Mt. Holly Gardens Citizens in Action, Inc. v. Township of Mount Holly,* 658 F. 3rd 375 (3rd Cir. 2011) [2011 BL 233928].

60. E-mails exchanged between Messrs. Ryan Downton, Doug Davis, Gerardo Interiano on May 27, 2011 and May 28, 2011. Subject: election analysis.

61. Montejano, 1987, *Anglos and Mexicans,* Ibid. San Miguel, Guadalupe, Jr., *"Let Them all Take Heed": Mexican Americans and the Campaign for Educational Equality in Texas, 1910–1981,* Austin, TX: University of Texas Press, 1987. Ricardo R. Fernandez and Judith T. Guskin, "Hispanic Students and School Desegregation." In Willis D. Hawley, ed., *Effective School Desegregation* (Beverly Hills, CA: Sage, 1981). Henry W. Cooke, "Segregation of Mexican-American School Children." In

Wayne Moquin with Charles Van Doren, ed. *A Documentary History of Mexican Americans* (New York: Praeger, 1971).

62. Montejano, 1987, *Anglos and Mexicans,* ibid.

63. Flores, *Evolution of the Liberal Democratic State,* ibid.

64. *Texas House Journal*, March 23, 2011, p. 987.

65. Ibid.

66. Ibid., p. 991.

67. Ibid.

68. Ibid., p. 993.

69. Ibid., 564.

70. *Five Families: Mexican Case Studies in the Culture of Poverty*, New York: Basic Books, 1959.

71. *On Understanding Poverty: Perspective on the Social Sciences,* New York: Basic Books, 1969

72. *The Unheavenly City,* Boston, MA: Little, Brown, 1970; *The Unheavenly City Revisited: A Revision of the Unheavenly City,* Boston, MA: Little, Brown, 1974.

73. *The Other America: Poverty in the United States,* New York: Simon & Shuster, 1962.

74. Goode, Judith and Edwin Eames (1996). "An Anthropological Critique of the Culture of Poverty." In G. Gmelch and W. Zenner. *Urban Life*. Waveland Press; Small, M. L., Harding, D. J., Lamont, M. (2010). "Reconsidering Culture and Poverty." *Annals of the American Academy of Political and Social Science* 629 (1): 6–27.

Chapter Four

Latino Identity, Whiteness, and Dual-Race Theory

The political place of Latinos possesses a unique history due to the manner in which Latinos became incorporated into the political culture of the United States, the heterogeneous nature of Latino culture and people, the racial hierarchy of both Latinos and the United States, and the very different nature of Latino identity. Latinos were incorporated into the United States through treaties where either Mexico or Spain lost large geographical areas and the negotiated treaties included provisions guaranteeing citizenship and concomitant rights to all Latinos who came under control of the United States as a result of those treaties. For instance, Puerto Ricans were incorporated as a result of the treaty between Spain and the United States that ended hostilities between the two countries in 1898. The United States also acquired Cuba, Guam, and the Philippines under the same agreement. In some cases, such as a result of the negotiations that led to the signing of the Treaty of Guadalupe Hidalgo, no special or unique laws such as constitutional amendments were required ensuring Latinos a right to the franchise; this was automatically granted as a result of the treaties. The diverse nature of Latino culture and people, however, presented both Americans and Latinos with difficulty in determining the place of Latinos within the social and racial hierarchy that defined American culture. This resulted in Latinos having what some have characterized as an "ambiguous racial identity"[1] that places them somewhere between African Americans and Anglos (whites) in the racial social hierarchy of the United States. This ambiguity results in both Anglos and Latinos, and also African Americans, being confused as to what the legal, political, and cultural place of Latinos is. This is manifested in the manner in which Latinos are treated in various areas of law, including voting rights. Finally, this ambiguity and subsequent unequal treatment of Latinos has relegated them to a second-tier level of citizenship where the top tier, "the gold standard of citizenship," is open only to white people within the United States.

UNIQUE HISTORY OF LATINOS

The proposition that racism is an essential element of acting with racial purpose or intent in both the Texas redistricting process of 2011 and the construction of the voter identification bill of the same year requires delving into the history of racism itself and how it came to play a role in the election public policy process. Acting with racial purpose is not, although it can be, normally the action of an individual performing a racist action, rather the action is a reflection of a long history of racism and racial ideology that is part of the fabric of a community's or society's culture. To completely understand a racist action, one must understand the history behind that action and the totality of the environmental forces causing the action. Texas's record of lawsuits based on racial discrimination or prejudicial behavior toward Latinos in many public policy areas reflects this history and also how deep racial ideology is embedded in the manner in which Texans make public policy decisions. For instance, in *Hernandez v. Texas,*[2] the Court ruled that Latinos had been systematically excluded from petit and grand juries in Jackson County Texas over a forty-year period of time; in *Cisneros v. Corpus Christi Independent School District,*[3] the federal district court ruled that Latinos had been systematically discriminated against in public schools in the state; and, in *White v. Regester,*[4] the Court ruled that the at-large election structure governing state assembly elections mitigated against Latinos electing a candidate of choice. In other areas where lawsuits were not brought, however, there was explicit discrimination against Latinos. For instance, cemeteries were traditionally segregated with Latinos buried in one area and away from the area where Anglos were laid to rest. Many restaurants would only serve Latinos through windows at the back of the establishment, denying them seating anywhere on the premises. Public swimming pools were generally closed to Latinos except for one day a week after which the pool would be cleaned before Anglos returned. Residential areas of cities and towns included racial covenants in real estate titles ensuring that Latinos could only purchase homes in one part of a city. Even in the realm of the social and recreational life of a community, one finds segregated nightclubs, dance halls, and grocery stores as well as churches. Although most of the segregated institutions were slowly eliminated throughout the 1960s and 1970s, one still finds vestiges of these institutions in the manner Latinos are treated in certain venues such as in high-end shopping or entertainment venues, where one is either survcilled by a store's security or is told that the prices may be too high for the Latino to afford so they should shop elsewhere. On a more sophisticated level and one weighing heavily on the ability of Latinos to participate in the public life of the state are the challenges to the University of Texas's affirmative action admissions plan by Ms. Abigail Fischer that reached the Supreme Court in 2013, the Voter Identification Card case, and the 2011 congressional redistricting lawsuit. Each of these three lawsuits have embedded within them racial ideology based on the same crude racism once found in the examples of racism in jury selection, housing, school, swimming pool, and social discrimination generally that exemplify the relations between Anglos and Latinos in the state.

THE BEGINNING OF ANGLO/
LATINO RACE RELATIONS

The history of the relations between Anglos and Latinos in Texas begins in 1821 when Stephen F. Austin crossed the Sabine River into Mexican Territory to begin the process of bringing American immigrants under an agreement with the Mexican Government, to settle in this new land. As part of his agreement, Austin pledged to abide by all Mexican laws and learned Spanish, became a Mexican citizen, and pledged loyalty to his adopted country.[5] Austin was a slaveholder, and he populated his Texas colony with mostly Southern slaveholders who brought their slaves with them.[6] Although Austin owned slaves, he was ambivalent to the institution. At one point in his life, he cursed the institution; in the end, he championed Texas entering the Union as a slave state.[7] These early pioneers eventually created propaganda leading to more and more settlers coming into Texas, establishing the foundation for a "relationship that, although frequently violent and tense, has led to a situation that today may be characterized as a form of integration."[8] Other historians have likened the relationship between Anglos and Latinos in Texas to those of the Israelis and Palestinians on the West Bank, French Algeria, or the Pre-Mandela South African regime.[9]

The cultural clash between Anglos and Latinos throughout the Southwest and particularly in Texas was caused by a number of issues. For one, Anglos arriving in Texas had come for a variety of reasons including running from unrepayable debts in other cities and states; some immigrated to Texas seeking renewed economic fortunes; and, others were simply pioneers who sought new beginnings or opportunities in order to create a better life for themselves as opposed to what they had experienced before. What the new immigrants were expecting upon their arrival in Texas is not clear, what they encountered was completely unexpected. They did not find themselves in a land where they were totally free to pursue their ambitions; rather they arrived in a new country and nation altogether. They arrived in Texas discovering a country that expected them to agree to be loyal and obey the laws of Mexico. Mexico was in the process of outlawing slavery, which did not go over very well with the slaveholding immigrants, who had imported large numbers of slaves to perform the heavy manual labor required in farming enterprises. Also, asking loyalty to another country irritated some Americans. Finally, the new immigrants encountered new systems of landownership, taxation, and public governance. What had been thought of as a new land that could be exploited freely with only Native Americans to contend with was, in reality, a land that was already occupied by Mexican ranchers and small landowners, merchants, and a highly organized governing system. The Anglo settlers, who were almost all religious Protestants, came into a region that was religiously dominated by a powerful Roman Catholic Church. Instead of arriving in a region where the new immigrants could pursue whatever economic activity they wished, they found themselves subject to new rules, laws, and policies based upon Spanish/Mexican culture, not Southern and American. A clash was inevitable.

In less than ten years after the arrival of the first Anglo settlers in Texas, revolts against Mexican authorities began; the first was known as the Fredonian Rebellion of 1827.[10] This rebellion occurred in Nacogdoches, Texas, by Anglo immigrants who had quarrels with the local authorities over land titles. Eventually, the rebellion was suppressed by the Mexican military supported by immigrants from other Texas colonies who wanted better relations with the Mexican government. Still, this incident was a harbinger of the Texas War of Rebellion[11] that led to Texas independence. Once independence was established, land dispossession began officially sanctioned by the new government and escalated after Texas was annexed by the United States in 1845. The original immigrants who came to Texas had agreed to abide by Mexican laws and to swear loyalty to the Mexican government, yet within ten years, the state had become an independent nation and within another ten, a state in the Union. As soon as Texas had gained its independence from Mexico in 1836, a series of actions began that has been characterized as a process where Mexicans were dispossessed of their lands, expelled from numerous cities, towns, and counties, and murdered by vigilantes and Texas Rangers.[12]

Land displacement proceeded along both legal and extra-legal means and saw millions of acres of ranch and sheep grazing ranges transferred from the hands of Mexican landowners, both large and small, into the hands of Anglo ranchers. Some lands were obtained through cash transfers, some by raids during which all Mexican males would be shot dead, and the women and children run off the property.[13] Nevertheless, land displacement was accompanied by massive expulsions and violence. Between 1836 and 1845, Mexican families were forcibly displaced from Victoria, San Antonio, Goliad, and Refugio. After Texas joined the Union, more expulsions occurred in Austin, 1853 and 1855; Seguin, 1854; Matagorda and Colorado Counties, 1856; and Uvalde in 1857.[14] In San Antonio, Juan Seguin, who was the last Latino mayor prior to Henry Cisneros, was forced to leave in 1842 because he and his family had received murder threats. It should be noted that Mr. Seguin had fought on the side of the Texans during the 1836 War.[15] By the end of the 1840s, more than two hundred Mexican families had been forced to leave San Antonio, Texas.[16] Most of the displaced Mexican families fled to Mexico or to communities along the border south of the Nueces River, which had been the northern border recognized by Mexico but not the United States. Race relations were so acrimonious that between the middle of the nineteenth century until 1920 the Texas Rangers stationed a battalion-sized force in the region between the Nueces and Rio Grande Rivers. During this time frame, the indiscriminate shooting and murder of Latinos was not uncommon and even received mention in a 1922 editorial in the *New York Times* that noted that "the killing of Mexicans without provocation is so common as to pass almost unnoticed."[17] The maltreatment of Mexicans by Texans during this historical period was known as far away as Argentina in the 1940s.[18]

The hatred that passed between Anglos and Latinos in Texas, from the founding of the Republic through the Depression Years, was characterized by lynchings,[19] shootings, and murders fomented on both sides, with the majority instigated by Anglos. Even the Texas Rangers, a law institution that is revered today, were known to indiscriminately kill Mexicans to the extent that their behavior drew a diplomatic complaint from the president of Mexico himself.[20] It should be noted that prior to World War II the Mexican government was the only champion that Mexican immigrants or Mexican Americans had in lodging complaints of ill-treatment or discrimination. Although the Mexican government was concerned principally with the treatment of their countrymen in the United States they did speak out against racist actions against Mexican Americans as well. The intense animosity between Anglos and Latinos of that era is aptly described in a quote by the historian Frederick L. Olmstead when he commented after his journey through Texas and the southern border:

The mingled Puritanism and brigandism, which distinguishes the vulgar mind of the South, peculiarly unfits it to harmoniously associate with the bigoted, childish, and passionate Mexicans. They [Mexicans] are considered to be heathen; not acknowledged as "white folks." Inevitably they are dealt with insolently and unjustly.[21]

Although the depth of the animosity that began and described the relationship between Anglos and Latinos in Texas is difficult to communicate in a
few short paragraphs, it is clear that racism and racial intolerance were at the
foundation of the beginning of the relationship between these two groups.
This tension which found its way into the policies governing land tenure resulted in a restructuring of the social and class hierarchy in Texas. Control of
the economy and public institutions passed from the hands of Mexicans into
those of Anglos; land and small businesses also transferred hands between the
two groups. Latinos, those who were not forced to leave their homes or who
fled in fear for their lives, eventually had to live in narrowly defined neighborhoods of cities and towns. The population of the modern day borderlands
along the Texas-Mexican border is predominantly Mexican not only because
the region lies next to Mexico but because the core group of the founding
populations arrived from other parts of Texas during the relocation actions of
the middle nineteenth century. The most important aspect of this narrative,
though, is to show that the relations between Anglos and Latinos in Texas,
since their inception, have been defined along intensely antagonistic racial
lines. Once Anglos took over the reins of government, public policy decisions
in a broad array of policy areas were designed, written, and implemented
with racial purpose just as the land dispossession and Mexican relocation
processes were.

The dispossessions and forcible relocations violated the substance and meaning of the Treaty of Guadalupe Hidalgo that ended the war between the United
States and Mexico. This war that still burns in the memories of contemporary
Mexicans resulted in the loss of fully half of Mexico's landmass to the United
States. Texas was lost after the War of Secession in 1836. This was a large
enough land loss, but after the 1845–1848 war, Mexico ceded what are now
the states of Arizona, California, Colorado, Nevada, New Mexico, and parts
of Wyoming, Oregon, and Utah. Not only did this represent a loss of a large
geographical area, but it represented a loss of a great deal of natural resource
wealth that has made that part of the United States the richest and fastest growing to this day. Most importantly, however, a large number of Mexican citizens
were left behind.[22] The actual number of *olvidados* varies; depending upon the
study and author, it is generally agreed that more than 75,000 Mexican nationals remained in the United States after the signing of the treaty.[23]

Little attention is paid to the provisions of this treaty because it normally
is not covered in traditional history textbooks and left out almost entirely of
high school and university-level American history courses. More attention
should be given to this because, at a minimum, it resulted in the largest geographical acquisition that the United States ever made in the construction of
this country. The treaty gave the Mexican nationals who remained behind,

los olvidados, a year to decide to repatriate. If they chose to remain in the United States, then they were granted automatic citizenship together with all rights and privileges guaranteed by the Constitution. These rights were also to be extended to all descendants of these first Mexican American citizens. Unlike African Americans who were given citizenship upon the abolition of slavery, or Native Americans who were treated as a sovereign people, Mexican Americans became full U.S. citizens subject to the equal protection of the Constitution before the passage of the Civil War Amendments.[24]

Although war between Mexico and Texas ended in 1836 with the signing in May of that same year of the Treaties of Velasco between President Burnet of Texas and General Santa Anna of Mexico, the treaties were never ratified by the Mexican government. There were two treaties: one public, the other private. The differences between the two were personal. In the public one, a specific timetable for withdrawal of Mexican troops from Texas together with a statement and timetable as to the method of their withdrawal was set forth. Additionally, there was an article describing an exchange of prisoners of war. The private treaty, which was not to be disclosed unless the public one became an issue, set forth trade agreements that Mexico and Texas would undertake. The principal problem with the treaties was that the Mexican government declared that Santa Anna did not have the government's authority to sign the treaty because he had been removed from power after being captured by the Texans at the Battle of San Jacinto that ended hostilities in 1836. The Mexican government, which was fighting other secession wars at the same time with other Mexican provinces, was too weak to counterattack the Texans. In fact, until the Treaty of Guadalupe Hidalgo, the Mexican government did not recognize Texas as a republic. During the war with Mexico, Texas declared itself a republic and eventually was annexed by the United States in 1845.[25]

RACIALIZED THINKING AND THE MEXICAN PROBLEM

The land dispossessions and Latino relocations that occurred throughout the southwestern United States after the Mexican American War of 1845–1848 were the result of greed and rationalized through the use of racial stereotypes of Latinos. These stereotypes are reflected in public statements made by various politicians, academics, and race theorists that appeared in newspapers and journals between the middle of the nineteenth century through the late 1920s. Some of the racial hatred between Anglos and Mexicans in Texas was due to the atrocities committed by both sides during the war of 1835–1836.[26] However, once the war, land dispossession, and relocations were over, the question then became what was to be done about the "Mexican Problem."[27]

The "Mexican Problem" appears defined as lack of educational attainment, crime rates, welfare dependency, and inadequate housing that resulted from the Mexican American landless and unemployed by the land disposessions, relocations, and restructurings of the agricultural economy. The basic economy of Texas began changing as more farmers emigrated from various parts of the United States and changed the economy from one based primarily on cattle production to agriculture. The dispossessed and relocated Mexicans were integrated into the new economy as low-wage farmhands. The transformation of the labor force is depicted in this excerpt from Montejano's work demonstrating the changes between 1850 and 1900.

> The Mexican rural population was equally divided in thirds among ranch-farm owners (34%), skilled laborers (29%), and manual laborers (34%). By the turn of the century, the top two tiers had shrunk—ranch-farmer owners comprised 16 percent of the Texas Mexican population, skilled laborers 12 percent—and the bottom tier of manual laborers had expanded, comprising 67%, or two of every three adult Mexicans.[28]

Essentially, the social structure of the Mexican American community was inverted, "turned upside down" between 1850 and 1900. Over a fifty-year period, they were transformed from a people characterized as landowners and skilled laborers into a community that was predominantly composed of manual or unskilled laborers. Along the border, between the Nueces and Rio Grande Rivers where many of the dispossessed and relocated settled, there began a period of lawlessness and violence that caused the state government to station an entire battalion of Texas Rangers until 1927. The stationing of the Rangers did more to enhance the violence than anything else, and they were removed eventually after a legislative inquiry revealed the extent of their incitement and participation in violence against Mexicans and Mexican American citizens.[29]

Although greed may have been the principal motivating factor behind the land dispossessions and relocations of the nineteenth century, it was race and racial or racialized thinking that provided the public and superficial rationale for the discriminatory actions of Anglos in the early stages of their relations with Latinos in Texas. According to Montejano, race thinking is characterized by several elements, including "Texas history and folklore, previous experience with other races, biological and medical theories, and Anglo-Saxon nationalism."[30] Race and racial or racialized thinking, all treated here as the same, is a deeper and more broadly defined way of seeing another group of people using superficial physical differences from which to draw opinions concerning their behavior and culture. Racialized thinking also uses one's own culture as the norm against which to judge others. Montejano's construct includes mythological beliefs, life experience, egoistic perception, combined with one's scientific understanding of race, culture, ethnicity, and/or religion. Placing this into an historical context led Anglos of the middle to late nineteenth and early twentieth centuries to believe that "Mexicans were lazy, shiftless, jealous, cowardly, bigoted, superstitious, backward and immoral."[31] Race thinking was and is always a two-way street though, because Mexicans of that era saw Anglos as "arrogant, overbearing, aggressive, conniving, rude, unreliable, and dishonest."[32]

Race relations between Anglos and Latinos were exacerbated by the clash of the two cultures that McWilliams depicted vividly and is best described by quoting him at length.

> The Mexicans knew nothing of self-government, while the Americans, it was said, traveled with their "political constitutions in their pockets" and were forever "demanding their rights." Although tolerant of peonage, the Mexicans were strongly opposed to slavery. The Anglo-Americans, most of whom were from the Southern states, were vigorously pro-slavery. The Anglo-Americans were Protestants; the Mexicans were Catholic.[33]

As Prof. Samuel Lowrie described it in 1932, "cultural differences gave rise to misconceptions and misunderstandings, and misunderstandings to distrust, distrust to antagonism, and antagonism on a very considerable number of points made conflict inevitable."[34] The inevitable conflict began almost immediately upon the introduction of the two cultures and continues through this day. It was the most violent at the beginning of the Republic with the level of violence remaining high through the end of the Great Depression of the 1920s and 1930s, tapering off with the beginning of World War II. Gaining control of the political, economic, and social structures of Texas allowed Anglos to gain the superior position in a power relationship with Latinos—a power position that came to be defined in racial terms.

What came to be known as the "Mexican Problem" was created and defined by Anglos in Texas. The "Mexican Problem" is important to understand because its perception and definition gave birth to contemporary thinking about Latinos and also gave birth to the manner in which public policy toward Latinos was conceptualized in the twentieth century. Montejano attributes the creation and substantive definition of the "Mexican Problem" to the social structure created after land dispossessions and relocations and the subsequent social restructuring of the Latino community. Essentially, as Latinos became landless and were forced to live in other areas of the state, they ended up at the bottom of Texas's social structure.

Increasing numbers of immigrants from Mexico, which also inflated and exacerbated the imaginary Mexican problem, bolstered the creation of the new Latino working poor. The Mexican immigrants had been forced off of their lands due to the push of the social turmoil created by the Mexican Revolution and the pull of the new and exploding agricultural economy of South Texas.[35] The years between 1900 and 1930 saw the first big waves of Mexican immigration. Most of these immigrants crossed the border before the establishment of the Immigration and Naturalization Service (INS) agency, and the border was considered open so there are no official numbers as to how many immigrants managed to cross in that time frame. However, McWilliams noted that in 1900 71,062 immigrants had crossed from Mexico and that number rose to 683,681 by 1930.[36] Grebler, Moore and Guzman reported that Mexican immigration between 1900 and 1910 numbered 23,991 and rose to 487,775 by 1930.[37] Both sets of numbers are estimates but give an indication of the degree of movement from Mexico into the border region of the United States generally. It was estimated by the INS that between 1900 and 1930, Mexico lost approximately 1.17 percent of its population annually to the United States. Although a great number of immigrants crossed to work in the fields as agricultural workers, they also came to "cut brush, to build railroads, and to work in the copper mines."[38]

What was characterized as the "Mexican Problem" was reinforced by a combination of anti-immigrant hysteria coinciding with a series of reports and master's degree theses written concerning the social problems of the latest group of immigrants to arrive in the United States.[39] What the studies reported was the:

> inadequacies and the weaknesses of the Mexican character. The data "proved" that Mexicans lacked leadership, discipline, and organization; that they segregated themselves; that they were lacking in thrift and enterprise. . . . That Spanish-speaking children were "retarded" because, on the basis of various so-called intelligence tests, they did not measure up to the intellectual caliber of Anglo-American students.[40]

Montejano, in his seminal work, vividly depicts the race hysteria that gripped the United States generally and Texas specifically in a chapter aptly entitled "The Mexican Problem."[41] He points out that the hysteria was promulgated in both the "popular and academic literature" of the period between the turn of the twentieth century and 1930. Mexican immigration was described as a "deluge" that would soon overwhelm Anglos in the Southwest. "Eugenicists pointed out with alarm that Mexicans were not only intellectually inferior— they were also quite 'fecund.'"[42] Prominent Texas historian William Leonard "predicted that the coming of Mexicans would have disastrous effects for rural Texas" because "society in the Southwest cannot easily adapt itself to the handling of a second racial problem."[43] For Leonard, the first racial problem was that of the African American poor, former slaves, and descendants of slaves, who also made up part of the working poor landscape. Interestingly enough, Leonard pointed out the strange "racial place" Mexicans found themselves in "for Mexican immigrants, . . . They are not Negroes. . . . They are not accepted as white men, and between the two, the white and the black, there seems to be no midway position."[44] Leonard's perception is interesting because it portends the unique racial place Mexicans in Texas found themselves in until the Supreme Court made its landmark ruling in *Hernandez v. Texas.* The other racial place Latinos found themselves in was emphasized by Texas sociologist Max Handman when he stated "American society has no social technique for handling partly colored races. We have a place for the Negro and a place for the white man: The Mexican is not a Negro, and the white man refuses him an equal status."[45] In his final analysis, Handman concluded that this situation may "mean trouble." Finally, a Texas labor historian of that era, Ruth Allen, placed the entire Mexican problem into a clear context for Texas policy makers when she stated,

> When the Negro had begun to rise out of the semi-peonage of the one-crop farm and a vicious credit system, we brought across the Rio Grande horde after horde of Mexican peons even more ignorant and helpless than the Negro. One can only marvel at the temerity of a people who, faced with the gravest race question of all time, have injected into their civilization a second group, alien in background and language, and not readily assimilable.[46]

Adding to the race hysteria, Allen concluded her argument by noting that Anglo-Saxons needed to directly face the race question or "let the Negro and the Mexican take upon us a terrible vengeance for years of exploitation, deprivation, and oppression."[47] Allen's observations and conclusions are prescient because she articulated the underlying fear of racists, racist behavior, and policy makers acting with a racial purpose. Essentially, one must discriminate or suffer the consequences of what will happen if oppressed races or racial groups gained or regained power.

The arrival of World War II found that racial purpose had become a way of life for Texas policy makers at both the local and state levels of government. Farmers were encouraged to increase Mexican immigrant workers to keep the costs of labor down. The continuing influx of immigrants, not a deluge but a steady stream, combined with the higher birthrates of both immigrants and Mexican Americans, created a young population in dire need of education. Whether to educate Mexicans and to what extent became a topic of debate among growers, politicians, and educators. The growers wanted no or minimal education; the politicians wanted some but were unsure as to the degree; and the educators wanted an educational level that was market driven.[48] As a result, in rural communities you found the emergence of a dual-school system within the traditional school districts, which led to the creation of Mexican schools where children of immigrant workers and Mexican Americans were educated. Most of the rural schools ended in grades four through six depending on the district. The creation of separate schools for Mexican children was important to the agricultural economy because it ensured the creation of an unequal educational system that, subsequently, ensured the creation and maintenance of an adequate manual labor supply. It was clear to growers that if Mexican children were to gain an education, they would eventually want to be supervisors, managers, or owners, resulting in the importation of more Mexicans to perform the fundamental menial fieldwork.[49]

The Great Depression gave birth to national cries for the deportation of Mexican workers, a policy that saw the outmigration of large numbers of Mexicans only to rise again with the coming of World War II when the need for more labor in the fields and industry increased. What followed was the formalization of the influx of Mexican workers with the creation of the Bracero program that allowed American corporations to contract with the Mexican government for workers to replace those who joined the military to fight in World War II.[50] The end of hostilities found the continuation of the Bracero program for a number of years. When it ended one finds an increasing number of undocumented workers that continued until 2007.[51]

After World War II, the "Mexican Problem" was addressed through a combination of formal and informal processes leading to the social isolation of Latinos in Texas. At the same time, post–World War II also saw Latinos begin to reverse the discriminatory trends through a series of community-based initiatives and federal court decisions. The isolation was the result of several discriminatory practices working in concert. Which practice was foundational is a matter of debate but one of the most significant came in the form of segregated communities through the use of racial covenants written into real estate and land titles restricting what land and where Latinos could purchase. As a result in small Texas towns, one discovers the heart of any Latino community can be found in one particular section such as in the cities of Amarillo, Odessa, Lubbock, Rock Springs, Uvalde, Kerrville, Seguin, Victoria, and Corpus Christi. Texas's large cities also reflect racially segregated residential patterns that were initially established through the use of racial covenants. These covenants were eliminated with the passage of the Federal Fair Housing Act of 1968[52] which was part of the Civil Rights Acts of 1964. Still, segregated residential patterns that were established at the beginning of the twentieth century are impossible to unravel because they have become and form the bases and centers of Latino neighborhoods and communities. Those segregated communities coupled with increasing real estate values and traditional lending processes help fortify continuing segregation. Besides the historical nature of racial segregation acting in concert, there are "red-lining" lending practices where banks and mortgage companies refused to offer loans to Latinos to purchase homes in certain areas of cities and towns. These practices, coupled with the exercise of some real estate agencies of only showing properties in certain parts of some neighborhoods for purchase by Latinos, have led to a continued pattern of racial segregation in most Texas communities to this day. Segregated residential patterns lead inevitably to segregated school systems in the state.

In Texas, all education is local. In other words, public education is based in a system of independent and consolidated school districts that are locally based and dependent upon the local property tax structure for funding. Some school districts cover an entire county geographically; others, particularly in sparsely populated areas, consolidate many small districts into one large one; while in the urban counties there will be combinations of large numbers of independent and consolidated school districts. For instance, San Antonio, Texas, has fifteen independent school districts in the city and seventeen total in the county. Funding for all operations and salaries is dependent on a tax levied against the property value within each school district together with funds distributed by state and federal governments. Nevertheless, local property taxes make up the most substantial portion of income for each school district. As a result, those districts that are property wealthy, as in energy-producing areas, will generate more revenues than those which are property poor. This difference has been the subject of a number of lawsuits beginning with *San Antonio Independent School District v. Rodriguez*[53] at the federal court level and continuing through *Edgewood Independent School District v. Kirby*[54] in the Texas State Supreme Court. In both decisions, the courts ruled that the Texas state school funding system was unfair and led to disparate funding for the state's public schools.

The two cases were markedly different. Families in the poorest school district in the state, at that time the Edgewood Independent School District, brought the Rodriguez lawsuit. The petition claimed that the school funding system violated the Fourteenth Amendment of the Constitution and denied the children of this property poor district equal protection of the Constitution by denying them equal access to a fundamental right—education. The Court agreed with the plaintiffs that the school funding system was unfair, producing unequal amounts of revenues based on varying property values in each district. The Court first pointed out that although the districts were property poor, there was not an identifiable class of poor people who lived within that district and incomes varied as did the opportunity to provide for the education of children. The Court then addressed the issue as to whether education was a constitutionally protected right. The court pointed out that education, at least through the twelfth grade, was a state requirement and not a right guaranteed by the Constitution. Public education is essential to the maintenance of a socialization process that introduces and inculcates individuals into the political culture of a society and the state is only responsible for providing a minimal level qualitatively. Essentially, in the *Rodriguez* case, the court ruled that there was no class of low-income persons who had petitioned the court for redress. Rather, the group was composed of individuals with varying incomes who happened to live within the jurisdictional boundaries of property poor school districts. Equally important, the Court ruled that education was not a constitutionally protected right but a state requirement for those between certain ages.

A generation passed before representatives of the same school district decided to bring suit against the State of Texas in state court on the public educational funding system. The plaintiffs argued that the existing property tax funding system violated an important precept of the state constitution. The constitution mandates that "it shall be the duty of the Legislature of the State to establish and make suitable provision for the support and maintenance of an efficient system of public free schools."[55] The plaintiffs argued that the tax system based upon unequal property values was inefficient and in violation of the spirit and meaning of the state constitution. The Texas State Supreme Court agreed with the plaintiffs and ordered the state legislature to restructure the public school funding system.

Although the state courts have continuously ordered the state legislature to correct the educational funding disparity, reform opponents have consistently created additional barriers that have extended the litigation. Not until 1993 did the state legislature pass a school financing scheme that attempted to address the disparate funding scheme. It was popularly known as a "Robin Hood" scheme after the mythical medieval English bandit, because it took excess revenues, generated under a funding scheme controlled by the state government, as opposed to the local school district, from property wealthy districts and distributed them to poor districts. An option allowed a property rich district to "adopt" a poor district with which it shared its excess revenues. Eventually, this scheme was deemed "unfair" to rich districts, and a new scheme was enacted in 2006. This scheme, again, was challenged as being unfair and another scheme was developed by the legislature. As of the end of 2013, another lawsuit was filed by property rich school districts to ensure that the new public school funding cuts remain in place in light of a district court's decision that the funding scheme is constitutionally suspect.[56] When the inequitable school funding structure will be settled to every party's or potential party's satisfaction is only a guess, but in light of the long history governing this issue, there apparently is not the will by the state leadership to change a system that continues to ensure the unequal distribution of educational services throughout the state.

The racially discriminatory laws that ensured the continuing segregation of municipal facilities throughout Texas continued to be maintained into the latter half of the twentieth century in Texas, and there were not any attempts by local government to remove them until the 1950s. For instance, in San Antonio where there were no official governmental ordinances that established or protected segregation, the first moves to integration were taken by the four large military installations which integrated their on-site recreational and social facilities. This example was then followed by the Archbishop of San Antonio, Robert E. Lucey, who ordered all parishes, parochial, and secondary Catholic schools to integrate. This diocesan order was extended to the Catholic universities in San Antonio. Finally, under the changing times and pressure from the local NAACP chapter, the City Council appointed a committee to study the issue. The committee returned a recommendation not to pass an ordinance outlawing segregation but to pass a policy of voluntary integration by all businesses in the city. The government passed an ordinance eliminating segregation of all municipal parks, golf courses, and tennis courts in 1954, but did not extend this to swimming pools, buses, railroad stations, and all municipal buildings until 1956. The voluntary integration of business continued slowly:

> July 4, 1963, nearly two-thirds of all hotels, restaurants, and other places of public accommodation had agreed to desegregate voluntarily. "These businesses accounted for nearly 95 percent of all hotel rooms, 90 percent of all motel rooms, and 90 percent of all restaurant meals served in San Antonio. . . . Three months later, only twenty-six restaurants and five motels had refused to participate in the voluntary program."[57]

To this day, San Antonio has been considered one of Texas' most liberal cities and a model for integration in the state.

Throughout the segregation era, Latinos were considered white for official counts but subject to various types of segregation rules very different from those imposed on African Americans. For instance, although Mexican Americans were allowed to attend white schools, they were relegated to either a separate Mexican school within the Anglo school districts or, if schools were too small, a special "Mexican classroom."[58] African Americans, on the other hand, were segregated into a separate school system that was not disbanded until after *Brown*. Although, segregation in schools was found unconstitutional in 1954 by the Supreme Court, it persisted in Texas long after for Latinos because of the unique racial place assigned to them between Anglos and African Americans. What caused the integration may provide lessons for those who raise the question as to when racism will ever end in the United States. Although integration took an inordinately long time, it did finally spread to all businesses and public facilities in San Antonio by the end of the twentieth century. There are still very exclusive private dinner and country clubs that are only minimally integrated in the city and surrounding county. Nevertheless, the city of San Antonio, in Latino historical and sociological circles, has always been seen as the "center of the Mexican middle class" in the United States. Educational and business opportunities did arise for Latinos in San Antonio but are still controlled to a certain extent by social and private relations among Anglos. For instance, in November 2013, a lawsuit was filed by a Latino businesswoman against Exxon-Mobil for manipulating the sale of filling stations away from Latino and minority buyers and into a situation more favorable to Anglo buyers.[59] The lawsuit argues that Exxon-Mobil recruited minority bidders to fulfill federal requirements under Small Business Administration (SBA) provisions only to structure the bidding process so only Anglo businessmen could take advantage of the bidding.

RACIAL PURPOSE AND LATINOS

The succinct and necessarily superficial presentation of the historical relations between Anglos and Latinos in Texas reveals a relationship defined along racial lines. It is a unique relationship because of the distinct racial place Latinos find themselves in, white but not white, people of color yet not of color. Needless to say, Latinos find themselves being used as a buffer race between Anglos and African Americans. Throughout the history of Texas, integration has been achieved by counting Latinos as white, which often caused widespread confusion among Latinos, policy makers, and individuals conducting research in these matters. Although Latinos had been counted among persons identified as "white," they were treated as "others" by Anglos generally. This was clearly demonstrated in the *Hernandez* suit of 1954. Even though Latinos were considered white, they were not treated as such by Anglos or the government.

The brief history presented here, however, serves as an important function when addressing the principal goal of this volume, the presentation of a model that demonstrates "racial purpose" where there appears to be direct evidence of such. The history above addresses the requirements of *Arlington Heights* Factors 3 and 4. As a reminder, Factor 3 is Circumstantial and Direct Evidence (Sensitive inquiry into circumstantial and direct evidence of intent) and Factor 4 is Effect on Population (Impact of official action bearing more heavily on one race than another). Fundamentally, the court had great foresight in developing these two factors for a very simple reason. Racial purpose or intent if identified as one action on the part of one individual could be considered an aberration and not part of a systematic pattern of racism. A history of racial purpose, thinking, and behavior between two groups of people can be seen as both a pattern of race relations but also an essential element in the basic cultural ideology of a society. In other words, long-standing patterns of discriminatory behavior reveal more than just the actions of one individual. Long-standing patterns of racially discriminatory behavior indicate that these patterns are essential elements of the manner in which a society views and interacts with certain groups of people. Where racially discriminatory behavior exists on a societal level, one can conclude that racial thinking and behaving is a normal part of that society's social and ideological *weltanschauung*.

A society's *weltanschauung* allows a society to determine its belief systems and makes countries, states, cities, and communities define themselves socially and politically in ideological terms. This is embedded within a society's ideological mechanisms that assist in propagating the *weltanschauung* from one generation to another. This propagation is generally accomplished through the family structures, schools, religion, and the media and work or peer groups. The *weltanschauung* gives individuals a definition to their lives and an orientation of why they perform the duties they do on a daily basis. In the public policy process, the *weltanschauung* assists decision makers in the identification of problems that must be addressed, how the policy is designed to address the identified problem, and how to implement the policy that has been designed. The entire process may appear objective on one level because of the methods used to achieve the identified goals, but the assumptions giving birth to the policy, how data are identified and variables operationalized, and how the policy is implemented are not.

Latinos in Texas have been subject to racism, racial thinking, and racist behavior since the beginning of the Republic in 1836. For the first 110 years of the relationship between Anglos and Latinos, there were concerted efforts to openly restructure the Latino social order through land dispossessions and forcible relocations. Schools were intentionally segregated as were residential patterns in every town and city in the state. Latinos were excluded from the use of many municipal facilities and services such as serving on juries and voting in some communities. Essentially, the conscious and overt discriminatory practices levied against Latinos before 1950 relegated them not only to the lowest social rung in the state but simultaneously ensured that they were denied full citizenship, the gold standard of citizenship, in Texas. The gold standard of citizenship includes all rights and privileges that go along with citizenship, but also it includes the ability to enjoy those rights and privileges free of any intimidation or struggles to exercise them. Denial of property rights, service on juries, and political representation defined the citizenship status of Latinos. After 1950, Latinos struggled to gain equal citizenship with Anglos through litigation for the removal of racial covenants, restoration of jury service, elimination of the poll tax, and imposition of single member representational districts. The 2011 redistricting process and voter identification law provided a regression in the quality of citizenship for Latinos. The redistricting process was a political relocation, moving Latinos from one congressional district where they enjoyed the ability to elect a candidate of their choice to another, where they would become politically mute. The voter identification law literally dispossessed Latinos, low-income persons, the old, and young voters of their citizenship by limiting the types of identification cards allowable to vote.

One indicator of how healthy a group's citizenship is can be found through a perusal of socioeconomic indicators such as those that Montejano used to describe the inversion of the Latino social order between 1850 and 1900. Between 1910 and 1940, the Mexican origin population of Texas grew from 7.1 percent to 11.5 percent of the state's population. In 1950, the Latino origin population of Texas stood at 13.3 percent, increasing to 37.6 percent in 2010. The Latino population of Texas has regenerated itself through many decades of immigration and high birthrates and is now in a position to warrant more political representation than they currently have, but the redistricting processes utilized since 1974 have only marginally worked in their favor. Economically, Latinos have remained at the bottom of the income rung, have poverty levels over 20 percent, dropout levels of more than 50 percent at the primary and secondary schools, and still reside in severely segregated communities. Any economic improvements have been marginal at best since 1950 for Latinos in Texas, revealing a legacy of when their social structure was upended.

In the two cases discussed here, ideological orientation played a great role in how the redistricting process was designed and executed and why and how the voter identification law was passed. The redistricting process was designed initially to ensure that one political party stayed in control of the Texas state congressional delegation and the various state assemblies. The voter identification process was designed to protect the integrity and security of the state election system from fraudulent voting by undocumented immigrants. Since the political party in numerical control of the state legislature is responsible for redistricting, the first step was to protect as many of the controlling party's incumbents as possible by ensuring that each Republican congressional district had a population that would support the incumbent or candidates of their party. In those districts that were marginal, the redistricters reverted to manipulating the population of voters both favorably and not disposed to support Republican Party candidates. This was accomplished through the elimination of Latino voters from several districts and the inclusion of Anglo voters; the rationale was that Latinos would not support Republican candidates and the only reliable Republican voters were Anglos. Without a dissenting thought, the redistricters assumed that all Latinos voted Democratic and all Anglos voted Republican. This is racial thinking at the most fundamental level. In the voter identification case, illegal immigrant hysteria that has been part of Texas cultural ideology since almost the beginning of relations between Anglos and Latinos drove the decisional process for the creation of the voter identification law. Racial thinking dominated the selection of the types of personal identification that would be acceptable to election judges and deemed impossible or, at least, problematic for illegal immigrants to acquire, including a military identification card, driver's license, and a concealed gun identification card. Latinos sued the State of Texas, in both cases two three-judge panels, one sitting in San Antonio, Texas the other in Washington, D.C., ruled that the redistricting process was performed with racial intent. A three-judge panel in Washington, D.C., also ruled against the voter identification card law because of its deleterious effects on members of minority groups, the young, the poor, and senior citizens. The discussion now turns to an analysis of the two trials in the continuing search for racial purpose.

NOTES

    1. Laura E. Gomez, "Off-White in an Age of White Supremacy: Mexican Elites and the Rights of Indians and Blacks in Nineteenth-Century New Mexico," In Michael A. Olivas, ed., *"Colored Men" and "Hombres Aquí": Hernandez v. Texas and the Emergence of Mexican-American Lawyering,* Houston, TX: Arte Público Press, 2006.

    2. 347 U.S. 475 (1954).

    3. 457 F2d 142 (1972).

    4. 412 U.S. 755 (1973).

    5. Gregg Cantrell, *Stephen F. Austin: Empresario of Texas* (New Haven, CT: Yale University Press, 1999), p. 7.

    6. Ibid., p. 9.

    7. Ibid.

    8. Montejano, *Anglos and Mexicans,* 1987, p. 3.

    9. Fehrenbach, Theodore Reed (T.R.), *Lone Star: A History of Texas and Texans* (New York: Macmillan, 1968).

    10. Cantrell, *Stephen F. Austin,* 1999, pp. 179–88.

    11. This is generally referred to by Mexicans as the War of Secession.

    12. Montejano, *Anglos and Mexicans*; McWilliams, *North from Mexico,* pp. 98–114; Acuña, *Occupied America,* pp. 35–71.

    13. Montejano, *Anglos and Mexicans,* pp. 50–74.

14. Ibid., pp. 26–30. Olmstead, Frederick L., *A Journey through Texas; or, a Saddle-Trip on the Southwestern Frontier* (New York: Dix, Edwards & Co., 1857; repr., Austin, TX: University of Texas Press, 1978).

15. Montejano, *Anglos and Mexicans,* p. 27.

16. Ibid.

17. November 8, 1922.

18. Ruth and Leonard Greenup, *Revolution Before Breakfast: Argentina, 1941–1946,* Chapel Hill, NC: The University of North Carolina Press, 1947, p. 249.

19. Richard Delgado, "The Law of the Noose: A History of Latino Lynching," *Harvard Civil Rights–Civil Liberties Law Review* 44, (2009): 297–312.

20. Emma Tenayuca and Homer Brooks, "The Mexican Question in the Southwest," *Political Affairs* (March, 1939): 259. Walter Prescott Webb, *The Texas Rangers: A Century of Frontier Defense* (Boston and New York: Houghton Mifflin, 1935; reprint, Austin, TX: University of Texas Press, 1965), p. 478. McWilliams, *North From Mexico,* pp. 110–14.

21. Olmstead, *A Journey through Texas,* 1978, p. 455.

22. In Mexican lore, these are referred to as *los olvidados* or the forgotten ones. See Alfredo Mirandé, *Gringo Justice* (Notre Dame, IN: University of Notre Dame Press, 1987), p. 9.

23. McWilliams, *North from Mexico,* 1968, p. 52.

24. Articles VIII and IX, Treaty of Guadalupe Hidalgo, 1848.

25. Gonzales, *Mexicanos,* 1999, pp. 58–75; Acuña, *Occupied America,* 1972, pp. 19–23.

26. McWilliams, *North from Mexico,* 1968, pp. 98–117; Montejano, *Anglos and Mexicans,* 1987, pp. 38–39, 50–98.

27. In some parts of Texas the "Mexican Problem," stated as such still lingers. In a job interview this author participated in at a prominent Texas university in 1983, he was asked what he thought should be done concerning the Mexican Problem. After he responded that he did not know there was a problem with Mexico, the questioner responded by indicating that the problem was that of all the crime caused by teenage Mexicans on this side of the border in El Paso, Laredo, and Del Rio, Texas. The author concluded that the questioner, who was an adviser to Governor William Clements on the Mexican Problem, assumed that where ever there were large numbers of young Mexican Americans, some would perceive a "Mexican Problem."

28. Arnoldo DeLeón, *The Tejano Community, 1836–1900* (Albuquerque: University of New Mexico Press, 1987), cited in Montejano, *Anglos and Mexicans,* 1987, p. 73.

29. Julian Samora, Joe Bernal, and Albert Peña, *Gunpowder Justice: A Reassessment of the Texas Rangers* (Notre Dame, IN: Notre Dame University Press, 1979), pp. 65–66.

30. Montejano, *Anglos and Mexicans,* 1987, p. 161.

31. McWilliams, *North from Mexico,* 1968, p. 99.

32. Ibid.

33. McWiliams, *North from Mexico,* 1968, p. 100.

34. Samuel H. Lowerie, *Cultural Conflict in Texas, 1821–1835* (New York: Columbia University Press, 1932). Cited by McWilliams, *North from Mexico*, p. 100.

35. McWilliams, p. 206. Montejano, *Anglos and Mexicans*, 1987, pp. 179–96. After its own independence from Spain in the 1820s through the Revolution of 1910 Mexico was a very unstable country at one time fighting four different independence movements among its own populace. Its integrity as a stable country did not occur until the decades after 1910. As a result, it was too weak to fight the incursions of the United States. A great deal of Mexico's peasant and working classes emigrated to the United States seeking social and economic stability.

36. McWilliams, *North from Mexico*, p. 163.

37. Leo Grebler, Joan W. Moore and Ralph Guzman, *The Mexican-American People: The Nations' Second Largest Minority* (New York: The Free Press, 1970), p. 64.

38. McWilliams, p. 162.

39. McWilliams, pp. 206–07.

40. McWilliams, ibid.

41. Montejano, pp. 179–96.

42. Ibid., p. 180.

43. William Leonard, "Where Both Bullets and Ballots Are Dangerous" *Survey,* October 28, 1916, pp. 86–87. Cited in Montejano, p. 181.

44. Ibid.

45. Max S. Handman, "Economic Reasons for the Coming of the Mexican Immigrant," *American Journal of Sociology,* 35, No. 4 (January 1930): 601–11. Cited in Montejano, p. 158.

46. Ruth Allen, *Chapters in the History of Organized Labor in Texas,* Austin, TX: University of Texas Publications, 1941, p. 14; Ruth Allen, *The Labor of Women in the Production of Cotton,* Austin, TX: University of Texas Publications, 1931, pp. 238–39. Cited in Montejano, pp. 181–82.

47. Ibid.

48. Montejano, *Anglos and Mexicans,* pp. 191–95.

49. Paul S. Taylor, *An American-Mexican Frontier: Nueces County, Texas* (Chapel Hill: University of North Carolina Press, 1934; reprint, New York: Russell & Russell, 1971). Paul S. Taylor, "Mexican Labor in the United States: Dimmit County, Winter Garden District, South Texas, *University of California Publications in Economics* 6, no. 5 (1930): 293–464. Cited in Montejano, pp. 192–93.

50. See McWilliams, Montejano, Gonzales, and Garcia for discussions concerning the *Bracero program.*

51. Jeffrey S. Passel, D'Vera Cohn, and Ana Gonzalez-Barrera, "Net Migration from Mexico Falls to Zero—and Perhaps Less," *Pew Research Center,* April 23, 2012.

52. Sec. 800, 42 U.S.C. 3604.

53. 411 U.S. 1 (1973).

54. 777 S.W.2d 391 (1989).

55. Article VII, Section 1, "Support and Maintenance of System of Public Free Schools," *Texas Constitution,* 1876.

56. *The Texas Taxpayer & Student Fairness Coalition, et al. v. Michael Williams, Commissioner of Education, et al.* Cause No. D-1-GN-11-003130 in 200th District Court of Travis County, Texas.

57. Robert A. Goldberg, *Racial Change on the Southern Periphery: The Case of San Antonio, Texas, 1960–1965,* 49 J. S. HIST. 349 *passim* (1983); Robert A. Goldberg, "The Challenge of Change: Social Movements as Non-state Actors," *Utah Law Review,* 1, (2010): pp. 65–79.

59. Montejano; Gonzales.

60. Patrick Danner, "Bidder: Sale of gas stations a 'charade.'" *San Antonio Express News, Business, Technology & Gadgets,* Saturday, November 30, 2013, p. B1.

Chapter Five

"Do Citizens Select Legislators or Do Legislators Select Their Constituents?"[1]

The two cases discussed in this chapter are the Texas Congressional Redistricting Case, *Perez v. Perry*, and the Texas Voter Identification Case, *Texas v. Holder*, heard in 2011 and 2012, respectively. The former was heard by a three-judge federal court panel in the Western District of Texas sitting in San Antonio, the latter by a three-judge federal court panel of the United States District Court of the District of Columbia. The redistricting trial had a companion trial, *Texas v. Holder* heard almost simultaneously by another three-judge panel of the DCDC. This latter trial, technically a hearing, was one where the state of Texas was submitting the redistricting plan to the judicial panel for preclearance. The state did not wish to submit the redistricting plan to Department of Justice (DOJ) because they felt they could not get a fair hearing from the Attorney General. This decision was based on deep partisan differences given that the Texas AG was a conservative Republican having to appeal to President Obama's Attorney General's Office. Texas felt they could get a better hearing before a judicial panel than the Obama Administration's Attorney General. This strategy did not work as the DCDC panel ruled that the redistricting plan was retrogressive and violated Section 5 of the VRA. This panel also ruled that no further action would be taken subsequent to the hearing in San Antonio.

Both the redistricting and voter identification cases were classical voting rights lawsuits, because in both cases it was claimed that the state's actions violated various provisions of the VRA. The redistricting claim was not new. The State of Texas had been sued in every round of redistricting since the imposition of single member congressional and state assembly districts in 1974.[2] In each round of redistricting, Latino and African American plaintiffs argued that the state did not draw representational lines that maximized electoral opportunities for candidates of their choice.

WHY WAS THE STATE OF TEXAS
SUED OVER THE REDISTRICTING PLANS?

Before delving into what occurred during the trial, it is important to understand why the lawsuit was brought initially. There were eleven plaintiffs originally with one dropping out prior to the trial. Although each plaintiff filed a separate suit, all were consolidated by the Western District of Texas in order to expedite a decision. The State of Texas was under pre-*Shelby* Section 5 preclearance supervision. Thus the state was required to submit any changes to election laws or procedures to either DOJ or the United States District Court of the District of Columbia to ensure that there would not be any retrogression. The state attorney general, Mr. Greg Abbott, declared that DOJ was too political and felt he could not obtain a fair evaluation. As a result, the state submitted all of their redistricting plans to the DCDC for review. This happened almost simultaneously with the trial that opened in September 2011. The hearing before DCDC did not commence until after the conclusion of the trial in San Antonio, and DCDC pointed out that the District Court had ruled the redistricting of both the state House and Congressional plans in violation of the VRA so deferred to that court's ruling. The Texas Attorney General then sought relief from the Supreme Court, who pointed out that the state needed to answer to the District Court's decision before they ruled.

The plaintiffs in *Perez v. Perry*, the redistricting lawsuit heard in San Antonio beginning September 6, 2011, argued that besides the state failing to seek preclearance under Section 5, the redistricting plans violated Section 2 of the VRA, the "one person-one vote rule" delineated in *Reynolds v. Sims*, the Fourteenth Amendment's "equal protection clause," and were drawn with "racial intent." Although there were ten plaintiffs, many of the plaintiffs argued different aspects of the claims, for instance, the Mexican American Legislative Caucus felt that the state chamber's redistricting processes as codified over the years were violated by excluding the recommendations and perceptions of minority legislators in violation of the Fourteenth Amendment. The Latino Redistricting Task Force, represented by MALDEF, felt that there were violations of the "one person, one vote" rule and the Fourteenth Amendment. The MALDEF attorney, Ms. Nina Perales, pointed out in her opening comments that the state failed to create additional minority-majority districts in the urban counties of Harris (Houston), Dallas–Fort Worth, and in the Rio Grande Valley. She also pointed out that the redistricters had acted with racial intent in creating a "sham" Latino majority district, CD23, in south and west Texas. One plaintiff represented by a private attorney, Mr. Dave Richards, argued that the state constitution's provision that county lines not be cut during the redistricting process, what is known as the County-Line Rule, violated the "one person, one vote" rule.[3]

A BRIEF ORGANIZATIONAL NOTE

Before delving into the trial itself, a brief word as to how the arguments are presented here because the order of the witnesses' testimony has been changed in this volume, as opposed to the order in which they appeared at trial, for organizational reasons and readability. The narrative begins with opening statements by both sides and then is followed by the presentation of the plaintiffs' arguments. In the actual trial, all plaintiffs argue their sides, presenting their lay witnesses first followed by their experts. Here all of the lay witness testimony is presented first followed by all of the experts. The actual order in which they appeared in the trial is maintained. The plaintiffs' side of the argument is then followed by the defendant's side, lumping together lay and expert witnesses similarly to the order of the plaintiffs' presentation. The case study concludes with the closing arguments for both sides followed by observations and conclusions on the points of law and supporting evidence by the author. It must be noted that some of the lay witness testimony has been excluded because of their lack of substance and failure to address a particular point of law that was being argued. This trial, like many civil trials, was placed on the clock by the presiding judge with each side allotted a certain number of hours while the entire trial was to be conducted over a two-week period of time. The judges decided that they would work beyond the normal workday hours if necessary on some days and on the middle Saturday as well.

PEREZ V. PERRY: THE REDISTRICTING CASE

The judge's question which appears as the title of this chapter directed at the attorney who oversaw the congressional redistricting process for the state of Texas was rhetorical, but it speaks to the essence of the state's redistricting process that caused it to be overturned by the Federal District Court of West Texas. The trial during which Judge Rodriguez posed his query began on September 6, 2011, in San Antonio, Texas to a packed gallery. In attendance were several United States Representatives, community leaders representing many of the most important Latino, African American, and Asian American organizations throughout the state, reporters from both local and national news agencies, junior law firm staffers, and the curious general public. There was standing room only on this September morning because of the unique nature of the trial; specifically what the issues would speak to and the trial itself represented another, very important, chapter in the history of race relations in the state.

The singular defendant, the State of Texas, was represented by eight different attorneys with only five present on opening day, while the nine plaintiffs were represented by nineteen attorneys, all of whom were present when the gavel marked the opening of deliberations. The plaintiffs included several individuals and organizations and were represented by some of the most important civil and voting rights attorneys in the nation. Several plaintiff attorneys had argued important cases, and won, before the United States Supreme Court and were well known to everyone in the courtroom including the three judges. Supporting the plaintiff attorneys were several expert witnesses each of whom had more than thirty years' experience in testifying before the court in voting rights matters. One plaintiff attorney even mentioned as an aside to one of the experts that for once the plaintiffs had more resources available for this type of trial than the state.[4]

The judicial panel, required under the VRA, was composed of Judges Orlando Garcia and Xavier Rodriguez, both district judges of the Western District of Texas, and Judge Jerry E. Smith, a Circuit Judge from the 5th Circuit Court of Appeals. All three are veteran judges and well thought of by attorneys and their colleagues. Judge Garcia had been appointed by President Clinton while the other two were appointed by Republican presidents. Judge Smith was appointed by President Reagan while Judge Rodriguez was appointed by President George W. Bush. The attorneys representing the plaintiffs were a who's who of voting rights law and included Jose Garza, Nina Perales, Rolando Rios, Gerald Hebert, Dave Richards, Renea Hicks, and Gary Bledsoe, to name a few. Just these seven attorneys had more than 220 years of voting rights litigation experience at the highest levels.

The trial began punctually with opening statements from plaintiff attorneys. Mr. Garza, representing the Mexican American Legislative Caucus (MALC), began by noting that each decade since single member districts were imposed on Texas by the court in *White v. Regester,* minority voters had sought relief from the redistricting of the state. Mr. Garza, participating in his third round of congressional redistricting, argued that the state had violated the "one person, one vote" principle set forth in *Reynolds v. Sims,*[5] redistricting criteria set forth in *Gingles v. Thornburg,*[6] the Fourteenth Amendment's "equal protection clause, and accused the state of *cracking, stacking, and packing*[7] the minority community to achieve a political end. Mr. Dave Richards followed; pointing out that the "county-line" rule for redistricting in Texas was protected by the "10 percent deviation rule" that inhibited the ability of redistricters to create additional minority state representative districts. Ms. Nina Perales succeeded, arguing that Latinos had been responsible for more than 60 percent of the total population growth in the state over the last decade, yet Texas had not seen fit to create additional house or congressional districts to accommodate that growth. She argued that "racially polarized voting" still existed in the state, which reflected the legacy of racial discrimination. Ms. Perales also noted the disappearance of traditionally majority Latino House District (HD) 78, the gerrymandered Congressional District (CD) 23, and the avoidance of the creation of majority Latino HDs and CDs in various other parts of the state. Messrs. Rios and Bledsoe argued that the redistricting process did not follow the traditional steps created during earlier redistricting efforts, pointing out the compressed time within which the legislature had rushed the process through from beginning to conclusion and the lack of transparency of the process generally. And, Mr. Hebert argued that the plan had not been precleared according to the requirements set forth in Section 5 of the VRA and the resulting product, the new congressional and house plans, were retrogressive and a step back from the levels of political representation Latinos had achieved in the 2006 court-imposed plans.

The state's lawyers, all working from within the Attorney General's office,[8] argued in their opening statements the opposite. Essentially, Mr. David J. Schenck,[9] who headed the state's defense team and a well-respected Texas litigation attorney, argued that times had changed in Texas and racial animosity had disappeared. He argued that racial polarization in the electorate no longer existed, regardless of whether 78 percent of minority voters supported the same candidate and voted cohesively over time. Mr. Schenck also argued that the state had not intentionally racially gerrymandered the districts in the two chambers at question in the trial.

THE PLAINTIFFS' ARGUMENT

The Lay Witnesses

The trial began with the plaintiff attorneys presenting their witnesses first as is the practice in most trials. The plaintiffs have the opportunity to present their claim while the defendant has the responsibility of discrediting plaintiff claims during cross-examination. The first plaintiff witness was State Representative Trey Martinez-Fisher, who was the chair of the Mexican American Legislative Caucus (MALC). Martinez-Fisher spoke principally to the apparent refusal of the redistricting committee to communicate with those parties, minority group legislators and their representatives mostly, to discuss proposed districts or changes to districts. Representative Martinez-Fisher also pointed out that the chairperson of the redistricting committee, Representative Burt Solomons, had directed all legislators to communicate with each other to ensure coordination in the redistricting process. Chairperson Solomons was also clear in his direction to those counties having more than one representative district. In these multi-districted counties, the representatives were to reach a collective decision as to how all of the districts within those counties were to be drawn, and the county-wide plan, supported by a consensus of the representatives, would be submitted to Chairperson Solomons. Mr. Solomons pointed out that the consensus of the county delegation would speed up the approval process when the overall state House plan would be presented for a vote before the entire House. Martinez-Fischer declared in his court testimony that, despite the chairperson's directions, only two of the county delegations, Bexar and El Paso, those having a majority of Democratic Party representatives, followed his direction. Martinez-Fischer argued that those delegations having a majority controlled by Republicans, such as Harris and the Dallas-Fort Worth metroplex, refused input from the Democratic representatives of their counties. There was also the refusal of Representative Aaron Peña, who had changed from the Democratic to the Republican Party just prior to the session during which redistricting occurred, to participate in the Rio Grande Valley caucus's meeting. Instead, Representative Peña, who was appointed to the House Redistricting Committee prior to his party switch, relied on the redistricters' efforts at drawing a district for him after giving them separate instructions as a member of the committee. Representative Martinez-Fischer also pointed out that the House Redistricting Committee refused input from MALC even though MALC had submitted a separate House plan and several Congressional demonstration plans showing how additional minority districts could be drawn. Martinez-Fischer further noted that the principal reason it was important to ensure legislative input from representatives of the minority community was because this was one manner by which public policy could be influenced by Latinos, African Americans, and other minorities. Basically, Mr. Martinez-Fischer's argument was that if racial minorities were not represented by candidates of their choice, then their voices would not be heard in the chambers of the statehouse or the national legislature.

Two other lay witnesses were offered by MALC, and they spoke to the multi-ethnic communities of Harris County and the Alief Independent School District, who traditionally worked together on policy issues and in political campaigns. Essentially, this argument was presented to show the court that various racial groups, specifically Latinos, African Americans, and Asians, were politically cohesive. Showing the court that segments of various minority communities who live in close proximity are politically cohesive, that they vote the same way, and there is evidence that they work together toward similar political ends, is important if one wishes to make a Section 2 argument. If there is not enough of one minority group who can make up the majority of the population in one district, then one cannot meet the first prong of the *Gingles* Test.[10] However, by pooling populations of different minority groups, either living together or in close proximity, and together comprising the majority population in an area, it is possible to make an argument that a new representative district can be drawn in that area.

The next several lay witnesses spoke to the legacy and history of racism in the state. The first to testify was Joe Bernal, a former state senator and member of the State Board of Education, author of a critical study of the Texas Rangers, university and high school teacher and long-time community activist in San Antonio, Texas. Mr. Bernal colorfully described his experiences in attempting to use public swimming pools during his youth only to be turned away because he was Mexican. He also provided testimony on the refusal of restaurants in New Braunfels and Lubbock, Texas, to serve him and some companions. Bernal also spoke to the burden placed on Latino voters by the $1.75 poll tax[11] and annual registration required prior to their abolition. Mr. Bernal as well provided evidence from his master's thesis on the unfairness of the school financing system's reliance on the states' property tax laws. The following witness, Mr. Alex Jimenez, also provided substantiating testimony to Mr. Bernal's as to the legacy of racism in the state.

The Hidalgo County Judge, Mr. Ramon Garcia, noted the need for the creation of an additional state representative seat in the Rio Grande Valley, pointing out that the lack of adequate representation weakened the ability of the population to influence policy in the state capitol. He particularly noted that the "County-Line Rule" mitigated against the creation of an additional state representative district. Judge Garcia pointed out that the Rio Grande Valley was one large community of interest, and the "County Line Rule" established a barrier against the creation of the required new representative district. He also spoke to the need for an additional congressional district in that region.

Mr. David Saucedo, Maverick County Judge, testified to the devastating effects to his county's ability to influence policy when it was split in half in the new congressional redistricting plan. Historically, Maverick County had always been kept whole in one congressional district or another. Mr. Saucedo pointed out that his county was 95 percent Latino and by placing half in two different congressional districts, the state had literally halved the Latino community and consequently diluted their voting power. When queried from the bench if it wasn't advantageous to be represented by two different congressmen in Washington, Judge Saucedo responded that splitting his county between two congressmen prevented the county from presenting a unified front on policy issues.

Former United States Representative Ciro Rodriguez, who had represented CD23 during his tenure, pointed out that the congressional plan developed by the state, specifically speaking to the new CD23, split many Latino communities of interest. Mr. Rodriguez focused his comments on the Latino community on the south side of San Antonio, noting how this community had always been entirely contained within a specific congressional district allowing it to become an important voting community able to influence congressional, state, and local elections because of its cohesiveness as well as the high participation rates of Latinos. The new CD23, on the other hand, split the south side community three ways, placing each portion into a separate congressional district.

The next several witnesses were presented by attorneys representing the NAACP and focused on several issues including the unresponsiveness of the House Redistricting Committee, racial gerrymandering, the ability to draw minority coalition districts, and the refusal of Anglo house members of the Harris County delegation to work with their minority counterparts in the building of a consensus redistricting plan for their county. The first witness was State Representative Sylvester Turner who pointed out that Chairperson Solomons had directed the urban county delegations to work together to construct a consensus plan for their counties. Mr. Turner testified that the Anglo Harris County representatives, led by Ms. Patricia Harless, had not consulted with any minority representatives of the county when producing the county plan. When Mr. Turner attempted to complain to Representative Solomons, he was shunted off to a staff member, Mr. Solomons refusing to meet with him. Representative Turner noted how the plan was presented in record time with little public input. He pointed out that the redistricting bill was filed on April 13th with public hearings on the 15th and 17th; the committee voted on the bill on the 19th and the full House was presented with the final vote coming on the April 24th. Only eleven days passed from initial filing to the final vote. Mr. Turner declared that besides the unresponsiveness of all those in control of the redistricting process, the decision makers rushed through the entire legislative process in violation of all traditional norms.

Representative Turner testified that after he had been told that Chairperson Solomons could not meet with him, he met with Mr. Gerardo Interiano, Counsel to the Speaker of the House and responsible for overseeing the house redistricting process, who told Mr. Turner that it was already too late to make substantive changes to the plan. Mr. Turner concluded that the entire process was closed to minority input, the outcome had been predetermined, and the process overly rushed to ensure minimal access by anyone outside of the process. Representative Turner indicated that the same unresponsiveness and shuttered process surrounded the development of the congressional plan. Finally, Mr. Turner felt that this particular legislative session was dominated by intense racial tensions due to the fact that several major pieces of legislation were argued during the session, including the Voter ID Bill, Sanctuary Cities, Public School Financing, the Early Voting Bill, and more. NAACP then presented lay witnesses who spoke to the coalition building by community leaders from the Latino, African American, and Asian communities in various counties, particularly Dallas and Harris. Travis County community activists were also presented noting the coalition building between the Latino,

African American, and Anglo communities in support of policy and candidates who were the choices of the minority community. The County Judge of Travis, Mr. Sam Briscoe, noted that, without this coalition, no minority candidate could be elected to office.

The final set of lay witnesses presented by the plaintiffs included several congresspersons and other community leaders who could not testify earlier. Congresswoman Eddie Bernice Johnson (D30–Dallas), testifying on behalf of the NAACP, declared how her new congressional district had been "packed" with minorities, particularly a prison. She noted that she thought every prison and jail in the county had been placed in her district, an issue that she communicated to the redistricters who ignored her input. Ms. Johnson pointed out that the redistricters did the same to two other African American congresspersons, Mr. Alexander Green (D9–Houston) and Ms. Sheila Jackson Lee (D18-Houston) representing Harris County, information she obtained after conversations with both of her colleagues. Congresswoman Johnson also described the coalition-building efforts of the minority communities of Dallas County with whom she has worked for more than forty years.

Congressman Henry Cuellar (D28–San Antonio/Laredo) pointed out that he met with Congressman Lamar Smith (R21–San Antonio) to submit his preferences for the redistricting of his district. He said that he thought he had a deal with Mr. Smith on the exclusion of Guadalupe County from his district. Guadalupe County, which lies to the north of San Antonio, is 79.8 percent Anglo, and Mr. Cuellar had never received more than 45 percent of the vote in that county. Mr. Cuellar pointed out that he had opened an office in the county, where one had never been opened before, opened a neighborhood office, brought a great deal of federal dollars to that part of his district, yet was generally shunned by its voters.

Congressman Green reiterated the lack of cooperation with members of Congress on the part of the state redistricting committee, the continuing existence of racially polarized voting in the state, and how minority-majority districts were "packed" with more minority voters. Mr. Green pointed out that if all the excess minority group populations from each congressional district in Harris County were pooled together, there could be an additional district drawn in the county. He also noted something particularly interesting: the way the new minority districts were configured split some of the old constituent neighborhoods, creating situations where communities of interest had to be reconstructed, a process that takes a great number of years. This created the situation, in Mr. Green's perception, that minority legislators might not be able to win future elections in the new districts because the new minority communities would be politically unorganized. Coalition building and subsequent cohesive voting patterns required a great deal of developmental work in order to create new communities of interest in place of those that had existed in earlier districts. Essentially, this round of redistricting had dismantled old coalitions and entirely new ones had to be established, a process that tended to dilute the voting strength of the combined minority community until new coalitions could be reestablished.

Mr. Green's suspicion was corroborated by several other lay witnesses who were presented by plaintiff attorneys. This was the general theme of the testimony presented by Ms. Sylvia Gonzalez, Past National Vice President of LULAC, and Bishop James Dixon, a community activist from Harris County. They both spoke to the coalition building of Latinos, African Americans, Asians, Muslims, and Jews around issues of employment, police brutality, jail discrimination, and economic development.

Generally, the lay witnesses presented by the plaintiffs created the background and painted the portrait for the three-judge panel of the history of racism and how it continued throughout the redistricting process. The major themes voiced by these witnesses included the lack of responsiveness on the part of the state redistricting committees and the national congressional liaison, the persistence of racially polarized voting, racial gerrymandering in the form of "packing" and "cracking" of minority communities, the conflict between the state's "County Line Rule" and the VRA's Section 2 requirements, the need for increased political representation in light of the exploding minority population, and the intense racial animosity surrounding the legislative session during which redistricting was conducted.

The Experts

There were nine expert witnesses presented by the plaintiffs including political scientists, historians, demographers, and an attorney. Each expert presented research on one or two specific areas including "racial purpose or intent," racially polarized voting patterns, the history of racism and its legacy in the state, the technical redistricting process using the state's software system, the relationship between the Republican Party and Latinos and African Americans, why the VRA was still required in Texas, and the relationship between redistricting and public policy. All of the experts had extensive experience in voting rights litigation with more than three hundred years and hundreds of cases of participation among them. Many of the experts were well known by the court and all attorneys present.

The first expert, Dr. Jorge Chapa,[12] a demographer, presented evidence on the population growth of Latinos over the last decade. Dr. Chapa also presented evidence on educational attainment levels, voter registration and participation, income and poverty levels of Latinos noting a clear lack of progress during the previous decade. The next expert was Dr. Morgan Kousser,[13] a historian who had written a groundbreaking work on the VRA in the southeastern United States. Dr. Kousser presented statistical analyses of elections throughout the state over the previous decade indicating the persistence of racially polarized voting. Dr. Kousser used Ordinary Least Squares, Weighted Least Squares, and Ecological Inference techniques to cross-substantiate his findings. He also presented analyses of the shapes of congressional districts that led him to believe there was racial intent behind the strange shapes of many districts. He pointed out that the drawing of an odd-shaped district required a great deal of effort. In other words, Dr. Kousser felt that creating a strangely shaped district was a conscious act that required a great deal of planning, mathematical calculations, design work with highly specialized software, and extensive resource allocation. He specifically noted that the splitting of Maverick County was what raised his initial suspicion. Dr. Kousser concluded his testimony by pointing out that he felt that racial gerrymandering was conducted, and, therefore, from a social scientific perspective, was a clear violation of the one person, one vote principle.

Dr. Kousser was followed by Mr. Ed Martin, a Democratic Party consultant who provided evidence of racial gerrymandering. He described for the court how minority communities were "cracked" and "packed" in both Dallas and Harris Counties. He also noted that by elimination of the "County Line Rule" additional minority majority house districts could be drawn in Dallas-Fort Worth, Harris, and El Paso Counties as well as in the valley in the Hidalgo/Cameron County region.

Dr. Henry Flores[14] was the first expert for the Latino Redistricting Task Force, and his testimony spoke exclusively to the allegation that the state had acted with "racial purpose or intent" in the redistricting process. Dr. Flores presented his testimony using the *Arlington Heights* Factors as a road map for his research. He, like Dr. Kousser, indicated that the strange configuration of some of the House and Congressional districts spiked his initial suspicion that the state had acted with "racial purpose." The proof of racial purpose is, by definition, mostly qualitative in nature. As a result, Flores's testimony began with a collage video made up of various YouTube snippets intending to demonstrate for the Court the intense level of racial animosity surrounding the legislative deliberations in this particular session.

The video began with a clip showing the president of the Texas Tea Party speaking at a rally on the steps of the Texas State Capitol. A demonstration of this sort requires sponsorship by a member of the legislature; if not sponsored, the demonstration must be held off the grounds. In this case it was discovered, after several queries, that the demonstration had been sponsored by Representative Leo Berman (R-Tyler), one of the most ideologically conservative

Republican members. The snippet captured the Tea Party president saying that the reason that no "good" immigration legislation could be passed in the state house was because there were too many Latino representatives.[15] As a result, the Latino members had to be eliminated from the legislature.

Another film fragment featured State Senator Chris Harris (R-Dallas) excoriating a Latino citizen for making a presentation to the Transportation and Homeland Security Committee during public hearings surrounding the proposed SB 9 which would have granted police the power to check one's immigration status upon a routine traffic stop.[16] The citizen was making his comments in Spanish but was accompanied by an interpreter who was translating his remarks into English for the committee members and the gallery. Senator Harris asked the citizen how long he had resided in the United States and whether or not he could speak English. The Latino citizen indicated that he could speak English and that he had been in the United States for twenty-three years. The citizen continued indicating that, although he spoke English, his primary language was Spanish; as a result, he felt more comfortable making his speech in Spanish because of the importance and formality of the proceedings. This response triggered a vehement condemnation on Senator Harris's part, who screamed at the Latino that he was in the United States and English was the language of government. The senator continued, saying that he felt insulted by the use of Spanish in the committee hearing. Although there were more than these two snippets of the collage, the judges and gallery saw the entire video; they were the most demonstrative exemplifying the intense racial animosity that blanketed this entire legislative session.

Dr. Flores then provided testimony concerning the rushed nature of the redistricting proceedings that also included examples of the unresponsiveness of both the chairman of the redistricting committee and the redistricters to the suggestions and recommendations of national and state minority legislators. One particularly blatant example of this unresponsiveness was when a senatorial privilege was denied Senator Rodney Ellis (D) of Houston, an African American, who asked for a several-hour delay in a committee hearing to accommodate his travel to the state capitol. His request was completely ignored when normally time would have been made to allow his appearance before the committee. This denial was not simply an example of the rushed process and unresponsiveness, but is particularly glaring given Senator Ellis's seniority and standing within the Senate.

This was then followed with an analysis of several congressional and state house districts demonstrating racial intent in the redistricting process itself. The most glaring examples of racial gerrymandering occurred in Congressional Districts 23 and 27. Dr. Flores began his presentation with a discussion of CD23, noting immediately the splitting of Maverick County where traditionally the county had been wholly included in a particular congressional district in every round of redistricting previously. The expert witness produced a table (Table 3.3) he had constructed that depicted the total population moved in and out of CD23 by the redistricters.

The first observation made of the data in the table is in the third column, in the second row of the table at the top shows CD23 had grown to a total population of 847,651 as reported in the 2010 census. Congressional District 23 had become overpopulated between 2000 and 2010, requiring a reduction of 149,163 in order to reach 698,488, which was the new apportionment ratio.[17] Following column two down to the fifth row reveals that the redistricters added 231,514 persons from the geographical areas outside the district. In column two, row six of the table the data show that the redistricters removed 380,677 individuals from the benchmark plan. The redistricters manipulated 612,191 individuals in order to reduce the old CD23 population to the required apportionment ratio. The remainder of the table presents the Total Registered Voters, Latino Registered Voters (SSVR), Latino Registered Voters and the turnout rates for both Latino and non-Latino voters from the 2010 general election. The other most telling data are the turnout rates by race set forth in the last two columns. As the turnout rate data indicate, reconfiguring CD23 resulted in a "participation gap" between Latino and non-Latino voters. Under the benchmark C100 Plan Latino turnout in 2010 stood at 24.9 percent, under the reconfigured C185 Plan Latino turn out fell by 2 percent to 22.9 percent. The non-Latino turnout rate moved in the opposite direction from the Latino turn out rate. Under C100 the non-Latino turnout rate was 39.4 percent increasing 2.2 percent to 41.6 percent under the C185 Plan. Essentially, there was a 4.2 percent additional widening of the participation rates between Latino and non-Latino voters resulting in the creation of a "participation gap" in the new district. The data in the table make the redistricters' intentions clear. Under Plan C185, CD23 was reconfigured to have a higher percentage of Latino registered voters going from 52 percent to 54.1 percent while at the same time having Latino voters turn out at lower rates than they did under the benchmark C100 Plan. Rather than making a few adjustments to reduce the district's population to the apportioned ratio, the redistricters systematically went around the entire perimeter of the district selecting specific election precincts for either exclusion or inclusion in the new district. The systematic manipulation of Latino voters speaks to Dr. J. Morgan Kousser's suspicions concerning the complex nature of redistricting and how deliberate and conscious the act of district boundary manipulation must be.

On the surface, this type of data manipulation lies at the heart of any redistricting process. In this specific case, however, in order for the redistricters to achieve their political end, they manipulated the Latino populations of many counties.

How they manipulated the populations and why they did so in the exact manner in which they did was revealed in several e-mails that had surfaced during the discovery phase of Texas' Section 5 appeal in the DCDC case discussed earlier.

Congressional District 27 was interesting visually because it was one congressional district that went from being a Latino majority district to one where Latinos were in the absolute minority. It is not clear, given the existing e-mail instructions, if the redistricters intended doing to CD27 what they did to CD23. The problem is that originally CD27 was a Latino majority district that had always elected a Latino Democrat to Congress. Mr. Blake Farenthold[18] had barely beaten a weakened thirteen-term Democratic incumbent by 799 votes in the 2010 general election marking an important partisan win for Republicans. It was not clear to the redistricters if Mr. Farenthold could hold his seat in subsequent elections; as a result, CD27 had to be reconfigured to ensure his reelection. Originally, CD27 was anchored by Nueces County, Corpus Christi, Texas, and spread southward to the Mexican border, a region heavily Latino and strongly Democratic. The redistricters completely dismantled CD27. They still anchored the district in Nueces County, Mr. Farenthold's home county; but, instead of working with the southern counties, they shaped the district northward all the way to the eastern part of Travis County. Dr. Flores indicated that this was further evidence of racial gerrymandering and an obvious attempt at diluting the Latino vote. When later queried, the redistricters would admit that they had structured the new CD27 to guarantee Mr. Farenthold's reelection, but they said that they had avoided retrogression under the VRA by creating CD35, a majority Latino district in another part of the state.

One of Dr. Flores's conclusions concerning the manner in which both CDs 23 and 27 were reconfigured by the redistricters was that whoever redrew the districts was extremely meticulous in identifying the exact precincts to use in the reconstitution process. The meticulousness speaks to a deliberate effort at identifying which Latino majority precincts were chosen for exclusion or inclusion in both congressional districts. The level of detail work, discussed in chapter 3, spoke to the conscious effort of the redistricters to act with a racial purpose by manipulating the Latino voter population to the advantage of current and future Republican candidates in both districts. Dr. Flores concluded his testimony by demonstrating that additional Latino majority Texas House districts could have been drawn by the redistricters if they wished in Nueces and El Paso Counties and the Hidalgo/Cameron County region.

The next expert presented by MALDEF on behalf of the Latino Redistricting Task Force was Dr. Richard Engstrom[19] from Duke University, who provided testimony on racially polarized voting in seven specific counties and a fifty-two-county-wide region covering the 2006, 2008, and 2010 general elections. The seven counties analyzed by Dr. Engstrom included El Paso,

Nueces, Bexar (San Antonio), Dallas, Harris, Tarrant (Fort Worth), and Travis (Austin). Engstrom also studied racially polarized voting in the three general elections noted in CDs 23 and 27 and HDs 33 and 78. The statistical techniques utilized by Dr. Engstrom included EI or Ecological Inference[20] and multivariate regression where appropriate. In the latter instance, appropriateness was governed by the presence of two or more large minority populations within the analyzed jurisdictions such as in Dallas, Travis, and Harris Counties but not in CDs 23 and 27 or HDs 33 and 78. Professor Engstrom defined racially polarized voting as a consistent pattern of high percentages of racial minority group voters voting differently than Anglo voters in the same elections. Essentially, minority voters tend to prefer different candidates than Anglo voters in the same election. This pattern must be consistent throughout a large number of elections and over elections covering different periods of time. Thus, an analyst investigating the existence of racial polarization in elections will base his conclusion over a large number of elections covering more than one election year. Dr. Engstrom also produced research on Latino participation rates in all of the elections he studied: the four representative districts for the benchmark, the legislatively approved districts, and the districts proposed by the Latino Redistricting Task Force. This latter analysis allowed him to determine how likely it would be for Latinos to elect their preferred candidates in the various types of plans at question in the trial. Engstrom concluded that there was a high degree of racially polarized voting in all of the jurisdictions he studied, and Latino voters remained strongly cohesive in all of the regions he discussed. He also discovered that African American and Latino voters voted together in all general elections. An example of Engstrom's research appears in Tables 5.1 and 5.2.

The data in Tables 5.1 and 5.2 are excerpted from Professor Engstrom's report submitted on behalf of the Latino Redistricting Task Force. Only one segment of his data is shown here for brevity's sake. His full report ran to sixty-one pages, and the racial polarization data was reported in two tables that were seventeen pages long. Here only his findings for Bexar County (San Antonio) are presented. He produced regression, bivariate and multivariate, analyses on 169 elections conducted between 2008 and 2010 that occurred in fifty-nine counties, fifty-two in South Texas and the remainder in the state's large urban counties of Bexar, Dallas, El Paso, Nueces (Corpus Christi, Tarrant (Fort Worth), Travis (Austin), and Harris (Houston). The bivariate regression estimates for Bexar County indicated that all but one election were racially polarized. Engstrom discovered that fully 91 percent and 90 percent of all elections subjected to bivariate and multivariate regression analyses, respectively, were racially polarized. His analyses of elections occurring before 2008 had appeared in his reports for the 2003 and 2006 redistricting lawsuits.

Table 5.1. Bivariate Analysis Percentages of Group Support Point Estimates and Confidence Intervals

Election and Jurisdiction Office and Candidate Party Affiliation	Latino Voters	Non-Latino Voters
Bexar County (San Antonio)		
2010 General Election	86.6	24.2
Lt. Governor *(Chavez-Thompson)* D	84.4–89.0	22.5–25.8
2010 General Election	91.6	24.0
Land Commissioner *(Uribe)* D	88.9–94.5	21.8–26.1
2010 General Election	16.3	70.3
Supreme Crt., Pl. 9 *(Guzman)* R-Incumbent	13.8–18.7	68.3–72.2
2010 Dem. Primary	87.4	60.7
Lt. Governor *(Chavez-Thompson)*	85.9–89.0	59.2–62.2
2010 Dem. Primary	90.4	46.3
Land Commissioner *(Uribe)*	88.9–92.0	44.6–48.0
2010 Rep. Primary	24.4	14.2
Governor *(Medina)*	20.5–28.1	12.9–15.4
2010 Rep. Primary	80.7	31.0
Railroad Commissioner *(Carrillo)*	76.9–84.6	29.7–32.1
2008 General Election	88.7	29.6
U.S. Senate *(Noriega)* D	87.3–90.2	28.12–31.2
2008 General Election	91.4	31.1
Supreme Crt., Pl. 8 *(Yanez)* D	89.7–93.1	29.4–32.7
2008 General Election	91.8	27.3
Crt. Criminal Appeal , Pl. 4 *(Molina)* D	90.3–93.3	25.8–28.8
2008 Dem. Primary	85.3	55.2
U.S. Senate *(Noriega)*	84.2–86.4	53.6–56.8
2008 Dem. Primary	89.5	31.7
Supreme Crt., Pl. 7 *Cruz)*	82.2–90.8	30.0–33.4
2008 Dem. Primary	93.2	44.9
Supreme Crt., Pl. 8 *(Yanez)*	91.9–94.6	43.1–46.6

Nevertheless, Dr. Engstrom's findings clearly indicate a consistent pattern of racial polarization between Anglos, Latinos, and African Americans in the state. Although the percentages change slightly from year to year or election to election, the pattern remains.

The Latino Task Force's final expert witness was Dr. Andres Tijerina,[21] who presented historical research on official and unofficial racial discrimination against Latinos in several policy areas including elections, education, and housing. Dr. Tijerina provided testimony tracing both official and unofficial efforts that various public officials and private individuals put forth in attempts at manipulating and diluting Latino voting power. He began his analysis with the Hidalgo Rebellion of 1913 and culminated his comments describing the deleterious effects of the poll tax on Latino voters. Dr. Tijerina

Table 5.2. Multivariate Analysis Percentages of Group Support Point Estimates with Confidence Intervals

Election and Jurisdiction Office and Candidate Party Affiliation	Latino Voters	African American Voters	Other Voters
Bexar County (San Antonio)			
2010 General Election	78.3	73.8	9.6
Lt. Governor *(Chavez-Thompson)* D	76.9–76.6	59.9–90.4	7.4–11.7
2010 General Election	82.8	72.3	8.18
Land Commissioner *(Uribe)* D	81.1–84.4	52.2–89.0	5.9–10.3
2010 General Election	23.7	14.1	84.9
Supreme Crt., Pl. 9 *(Guzman)* R. Incumbent	22.3–25.1	3.8–23.3	82.7–87.2
2010 Dem. Primary	86.0	65.2	60.2
Lt. Governor *(Chavez-Thompson)*	84.5–87.5	57.8–72.8	55.2–64.6
2010 Dem. Primary	86.4	9.76	54.01
Land Commissioner *(Uribe)*	84.8–88.1	.5–18.0	51.8–56.1
2010 Rep. Primary	21.3	24.1	11.1
Governor *(Medina)*	19.2–23.3	15.3–32.0	8.6–13.4
2010 Rep. Primary	63.2	37.0	25.7
Railroad Comm. *(Carrillo)*	60.8	25.1–48.0	22.8–28.5
2008 General Election	83.2	70.0	21.9
U.S. Senate *(Noriega)* D	81.5–84.9	52.8–90.9	19.4–24.3
2008 General Election	86.0	81.4	21.2
Supreme Crt., Pl. 8 *(Yanez)* D	84.4–87.6	68.2–97.5	18.9–23.4
2008 General Election	85.7	71.2	18.4
CC, Pl. 4 *(Molina)* D	84.1–87.5	53.9–92.6	15.9–20.8
2008 Dem. Primary	83.6	37.6	57.1
U.S. Senate *(Noriega)*	82.4–84.9	28.7–46.7	55.3–59.1
2008 Dem. Primary	85.6	28.3	32.5
Supreme Crt. Pl. 7 *(Cruz)*	84.3–87.0	8.9–44.1	30.5–34.5
2008 Dem. Primary	89.2	46.3	43.6
Supreme Crt. Pl. 8 *(Yanez)*	87.7–90.7	31.3–59.3	41.4–45.8

also spoke of the use of violence, including lynchings, as a weapon to intimidate the Latino community into silence and not participating politically. Finally, he presented research on efforts used to manipulate the Latino vote, including the King Ranch's infamous "corralling Mexican voters," through the use of slating groups by "progressive" political groups in urban areas to minimize ballot access and control the Latino vote. "Corralling" was the act of collecting all of the Mexican ranch hands and placing them into a corral, one normally used to control ranch animals, and then marching them all down to the voting locations and ensuring that they all voted for whom the King family wanted elected. This prevented Mexican voters in those counties, residing within the King Ranch's confines, from casting ballots independently and freely. Slating was the act of controlling, through secret ballot, who could be a candidate for city offices, thus limiting the choices available to voters during elections and leaving little choice for voters. The Hidalgo County Rebellion of 1913 was an attempt by white professionals and small ranchers and farmers to overthrow the "bossism" that was kept in power by local machines through the manipulation of the Mexican vote. The revolt of the white middle class ended up overturning the political elites. However, the new participation rules made it illegal for Mexicans to vote in elections from that time on. Most of these types of manipulation tactics were overturned in the 1960s and 1970s, but, as Dr. Tijerina pointed out in his testimony, their effects were felt in several policy areas. Specifically, the policy to educate or not to educate Latinos that grew out of that era created and established Latinos as a permanent underclass to this day. Additionally, this affected Latinos' ability to influence economic development polices in various cities and towns, resulting in the creation of poor living conditions in the neighborhoods heavily populated by Latinos throughout the state.

The next expert was sponsored by the attorney representing LULAC, the League of United Latin American Citizens, the oldest Latino civil rights organization in the nation. The expert, Mr. George Korbel,[22] presented evidence on the use of redistricting technology and the RedAppl system used by state redistricters. Korbel spoke to the substantive significance of splitting of Maverick County, the racial gerrymandering of the new Latino majority CD35, and the selective packing of minority populations in districts already having majority-minority populations. Korbel also used as an example of extreme gerrymandering how redistricters split the City of Austin into six different congressional districts.

Korbel, who has been actively involved in four rounds of state redistricting in Texas, spoke to the issue of the "rounding down" of the number of state House seats that were allocated to Harris County. The constitutional rule points out that if the reapportionment ratio determines that a fraction of a district is calculated, then the actual number of districts assigned to the county while avoiding the "County Line Rule" will be rounded to the nearest number possible. The reapportionment district allocation for Harris County determined that the county was to be allotted 24.4 house seats in the new redistricting process. Ensuring that no seats broke or cut the county's jurisdictional boundaries, the redistricters, under direction of the Chairperson of the Redistricting Committee, was to round down and allocate only twenty-four seats to the county. Korbel pointed out that in earlier redistricting efforts the state had rounded up, ensuring that the African American or Latino communities of Harris County were assigned an additional seat. Mr. Korbel interpreted the reduction as retrogression under the VRA when the redistricters reduced the number of seats in Harris County from twenty-five to twenty-four. In this instance, the redistricters would point out later in the trial, the County Line Rule and the state constitution required that they round down rather than up.

The NAACP's[23] political science expert witness Dr. Richard Murray,[24] presented testimony on the political situation of African Americans in Houston, Texas, and the surrounding area including Fort Bend County which is directly adjacent to Harris County on the southwest. Murray also provided evidence of the political cohesion of African Americans and Latinos in Dallas County and began his presentation by discussing the relationship between race and politics in Texas from a historical perspective through the present day. Murray identified the commencement of the contemporary relationship between race and politics in the state when the Republican Party stopped outreach to the African American community during the Goldwater Presidential campaign. According to Murray, Goldwater refused to support the VRA and Nixon pursued his "Southern Strategy" by supporting segregationists in the South.[25] The Texas Republican Party chose to consolidate its power by developing its base among Anglos rather than racial minority groups. Murray stated that Texas Anglos are "much more old stock Anglo Saxon, much more conservative. So it sets up a politics in our state that has become more polarized now along Anglo versus minority patterns."[26] According to Murray, Anglos continue to pursue political strategies to ensure domination of the political process in light of the changing demographics, and this strategy has exacerbated the already extreme polarization in the state. Blacks and Latinos have become politically cohesive because they both suffer similar histories of racial discrimination in areas of the economy, health care, and the criminal justice system. Murray also presented evidence that the African American and Latino communities of Harris County were "cracked" to ensure the creation of four Anglo state house districts. He saw this as a clear intent to diminish minority voting power. He produced exhibits demonstrating strong electoral cohesion between Latinos and African Americans in both Dallas and Harris Counties. Murray also presented evidence showing how every existing house and congressional minority district was overpopulated and unnecessarily manipulated, leading him to conclude that redistricters were "very skilled at minimizing statewide opportunities for minority voters by a variety of techniques."[27] In Dr. Murray's estimation he felt that the racial gerrymandering practiced by the state tended to minimize the effectiveness of minority legislators and was the principal reason for the existence of the VRA. In another part of his testimony, Murray pointed out that the United States Constitution required redistricting to be conducted using total population and encouraged the Court to consider this option because the data normally used for redistricting derived from the American Community Survey (ACS) undercounted minorities and could account for the outmigration of large numbers of people.

The next expert was presented by the attorney for the Rodriguez plaintiff, Mr. Renea Hicks. The expert, Dr. Steven Ansolabehere,[28] presented testimony citing that only 44 percent of all Hispanics state-wide resided in Latino majority districts of any sort.[29] He also pointed out that 88 percent of whites are assigned to white majority districts and only 500,000 African Americans end up being placed in minority majority districts.[30] Essentially, Dr. Ansolabehere concluded that Latinos, African Americans, and whites were treated differently when assigned to various representative districts throughout the state. This maldistribution combined with the intense nature of racially polarized voting in the state presents whites with better opportunities of electing candidates of their choice. For Professor Ansolabehere, this was clear evidence of racial gerrymandering in the form of packing and cracking of minority communities to give whites undue representative advantages. Dr. Ansolabehere then used evidence from Tarrant, Dallas, and Nueces Counties to demonstrate his observations. This expert concluded that Hispanic and black population growth areas were being split and placed in white majority districts,[31] noting that racial intent was clearly evident in the manner in which the district boundaries were drawn and how minority populations were manipulated within and between districts to allow Republicans to gain an upper hand.

The final expert presented by plaintiff attorneys was Dr. Alan Lichtman,[32] who testified on behalf of the Queseda plaintiffs. Lichtman studied the political cohesiveness of Latino and African American voters in the state and found them highly cohesive. He also noted that his research discovered that Latino voters cast their ballots for Anglo Democrats and against Latino Republican candidates normally. His research also supported Dr. Ansolabehere's conclusion that the state's redistricting plans were very carefully crafted to maximize Anglo voter preferences as opposed to those of minority voters.[33] Finally, Lichtman pointed out the importance of creating accurate representational districts for Latinos and African Americans, demonstrating a direct link between representation and public policy input particularly in areas affecting economic development, education and welfare.

THE DEFENDANT'S RESPONSE

The Lay Witnesses

The first lay witness presented by the State of Texas was Representative Burt Solomons (R-Carrollton),[34] who was Chair of the House Redistricting Committee during the 2011 legislative session. Mr. Solomons testified that he had carried the Sanctuary Cities bill that allowed police officers to stop and ask the citizenship status of individuals routinely stopped. He testified that he announced to House members that redistricting was intended to be a member-driven process. Mr. Solomons felt that all members should have input as to what their districts should look like and, if their district was in a county having multiple districts, the entire delegation should reach consensus as to how all their districts should be configured. Representative Solomons indicated that he invited all who wished to have input in redistricting to visit with him or his staff, specifying that only one group actually made an appointment to visit with him on this issue. He said that MALDEF, represented by Ms. Nina Perales, Vice President for Litigation, met with him for thirty or forty minutes over the Latino Redistricting Task Force's redistricting wishes.[35] He indicated that he was the person responsible for making the decision to round down the number of state house seats in Harris County, saying that he based this on state constitutional dictates.[36] Mr. Solomons also testified that there was one public hearing on the State Board of Education redistricting plan and one on the House plan.[37] Under cross-examination by Mr. Jose Garza, attorney for the Mexican American Legislative Caucus, Mr. Solomons stated that the reason another Latino majority district could not be drawn in the Cameron/Hidalgo County region was because he would have to break the state constitutional mandate that county lines must be respected, otherwise known as the County Line Rule. In an interesting exchange, Attorney Garza asked, "You need a federal judge to tell you that the federal Voting Rights Act trumps the Texas Constitution's county line rule; isn't that correct?" To which Mr. Solomons replied, "More specifically, U.S. Supreme Court, because the county line rule is not only here in Texas, but it is elsewhere." Mr. Garza countered with "So it wouldn't be enough if this Court gave you such an order; you would need the Supreme Court to tell you that?" And Representative Solomons replied, "I would like the law to tell me what I should do and shouldn't have done, yes."[38] Mr. Solomons's testimony on this topic corroborates earlier testimony given in depositions as well as the content of certain e-mails to the effect that, regardless of the outcome of the trial proceedings, the state intended to appeal the case all the way to the Supreme Court in order to have a better chance at obtaining a favorable ruling. Mr. Solomons's comments concerning the County Line Rule also made it clear that there was not a great deal of concern for VRA implications during the redistricting process on the part of the legislative leadership or redistricters under their supervision.

This lack of concern for VRA provisions was also reflected in his responses to both Mr. Garza's and Ms. Allison Riggs's[39] queries concerning whether or not Representative Solomons had been aware of the rapid growth of minority populations throughout the state and whether he or his redistricters had thought about the possibility of increasing the number of majority-minority districts. Mr. Solomons indicated that he had been aware of the growth rates generally, but he had not considered increasing majority-minority districts. In fact, Mr. Solomons stated that he did not get involved in the day-to-day technical aspects of redistricting leaving those to responsible staffers.

Judge Smith asked Representative Solomons if he had given instructions or if he had heard of anyone else giving instructions to the staff concerning drawing district lines in the House or Congress to ensure "the greatest chance as possible for incumbents to be reelected." The judge was attempting to clarify information from some of the redistricters[40] that it was their impression that incumbent protection was one of Chairperson Solomons's wishes. To which Mr. Solomons replied, "I never said that. I don't believe I said that to anybody."[41]

The next lay witness was Representative Larry Gonzales (R-Round Rock) who spoke to the openness of the consultation process, pointing out that Representative Solomons was open to all members and he had not had trouble gaining access to the Chairman or any of his staff concerning redistricting matters. He also testified that he felt that Latinos were trending generally conservatively ideologically and would soon support more Republican politicians. This last contention was provided with no data or research.

Defendant Experts

Two individuals responsible for redistricting, Mr. Ryan Downton, who oversaw the state house redistricting process and drew some districts himself, and Mr. Gerardo Interiano, who was responsible for the congressional plan, were the state's redistricting experts. Mr. Downton was General Counsel to the Texas House Redistricting Committee.

Mr. Downton testified that Texas went from thirty-two congressional districts to thirty-six due to increased population growth as determined by the 2010 census. He pointed out that the first priority was to draw districts in areas that had experienced growth such as in North and Central Texas and the Harris County/Houston areas.[42] Mr. Downton said he received demonstration maps from Congressmen Joseph Barton (R6–Ennis) and Lamar Smith (R21–San Antonio) and MALDEF prior to beginning his work. He also received other maps from MALC and other groups as he was proceeding through the drawing process. He attempted to construct a majority Latino congressional district in North Texas, specifically the Dallas–Fort Worth area, but said that he "could not make the numbers work"; and, with a Republican super majority in the state house, he did not think there was the will to construct a Latino majority district that would vote Democratic unless forced to do so by VRA requirements.[43] Mr. Downton was queried by Judge Xavier Rodriguez to explain why he could not draw a majority Latino district in North Texas given Congressman Smith's request to do so. Downton replied that he tried, but because of citizenship levels and high percentage of underage Latinos, he could not construct a majority district for Latinos. Judge Rodriguez asked if Mr. Downton thought Congressman Smith had erred in his belief that the majority Latino district could be drawn in North Texas. Downton replied that he didn't think the congressman was mistaken, saying that he thought the congressman had just drawn one that he thought was 50 percent +1 district for Latinos.[44] This point is important because there appears throughout the testimony of expert witnesses on both sides that such a district could be drawn in North Texas.

Mr. Downton testified that one can command, through a drop-down menu, RedAppl software to shade block level areas of maps by partisanship based upon Senator McCain's performance in the 2008 general election. If the senator won a majority of votes in a certain block or precinct, the redistricter or anyone working on the map would see that area shaded in the color red. The color blue indicated that a precinct had voted for President Obama. Downton was asked by his attorney if he had opened and activated the color scheme for race or ethnicity while he was drawing the map. Downton replied that he had not.[45] Downton was then asked by his attorney to look at the map submitted by Representative Solomons and discuss any differences between that map and the Congressional plan passed out of the Senate. The attorney requested that Downton discuss changes between the two maps; Downton replied that he noticed that there were two Hispanic communities in Fort Worth, one in the north the other in the south, that had been split up and placed in two different districts. At this point he indicated that he rectified the situation by placing both communities in the same district. Here Judge Rodriguez intervened in the testimony and the following exchange took place. It is cited in its entirety because it appears that Mr. Downton contradicts his earlier testimony that he had not used the racial or ethnicity shading while redistricting.

JUDGE RODRIGUEZ: Well, at what point did you turn on the race feature again or the ethnicity feature? Because you did 136,[46] and that gets passed by the Senate, so now we are looking at the House consideration. At any point, did you turn the ethnicity or race feature on to see whether or not you would be in compliance with the Voting Rights Act?

THE WITNESS: Yes.

JUDGE RODRIGUEZ: And at what point did you turn the feature back on?

THE WITNESS: Well, as far as the feature, we were always—we were conscious of the numbers, and so we would look at them throughout the process before moving forward with the map. When we initially put the first map out, our analysis wasn't complete. . . . In north Texas, we had looked at drawing that Hispanic district, so we used Hispanic shading to try to figure that out. Once we weren't able to do that, then it was back to the political function of how to balance the districts. And we didn't—honestly didn't think about ethnic shading at that point, because it was a political decision. After that map was released and we started—we got some comments saying, "Hey, you split the Hispanic population," then we pulled up the shading and saw, yes, they are right. We did split the Hispanic population. Can we put it back together?[47]

Immediately after this exchange, both Mr. Downton's attorney and Judge Smith asked several questions to direct the witness's testimony back to the notion that he had made strictly a political and not a racial decision.[48] Nevertheless, Mr. Downton, as a result of questioning by both Judge Smith and his attorney, revealed that he had drawn majority Latino districts in an area of Central Texas anchored in Bexar County and extending north to Travis County that became CD35 while also ensuring that CD20, wholly contained in Bexar County remained a majority Latino district.[49] During these exchanges, there is a continuing effort by Judge Smith to ensure that even though race or ethnicity was being considered in the drawing that there was a partisan reason behind the decisions. The attorney then concluded this portion of Mr. Downton's testimony by indicating how a majority Latino district in El Paso was bolstered by changing the western boundary of adjacent CD23 and how adding Dimmitt, Zavala, and half of Maverick Counties ensured maintenance of a majority Latino population in this latter district.[50]

Mr. Downton's testimony then moved to discuss the Texas House redistricting plan where he reviewed the construction and approval of those plans from the urban counties beginning with those in the Dallas–Fort Worth metroplex. After discussing the political dynamics and interaction between the Republican and Democratic House members over the plan, he noted that the Democratic Representatives, Messrs. Lon Berman (Fort Worth) and Mark Veasey (Dallas), did not vote to support the final product.

Moving to Harris County, Mr. Downton discussed the decision of reducing the total number of districts from twenty-five to twenty-four given the apportionment ratio being calculated at 24.41. He emphasized to the Court, even during questioning by Judge Rodriguez, that this was a legal decision provoked not by arithmetic calculation but state constitutional mandate.[51] Mr. Downton pointed out to the Court that the only disagreement to this decision came from the Democratic members of the Harris County delegation. This redistricter's testimony then moved to the question of how the various districts within Harris County were drawn. First, the Republican members ensured that they received the areas that they wanted and then they tried to pass a unified plan only to have the minority members complain on the floor of the House. The debate was recessed and the Harris county delegation met separately to discuss their differences. The Democratic members were told that they could not change any of the Republican districts only their own. After various changes were made among the minority districts, the plan was resubmitted for approval by the entire House. At this point, some minor changes were made to some of the Republican districts to accommodate the concerns of one of the African American members. Throughout his testimony on this topic, Mr. Downton reiterated concerns with violation of the VRA to the Harris County delegation with some of the proposed changes as part of the guidance he gave them.[52]

Mr. Downton was then cross-examined by Ms. Perales of MALDEF representing the Latino Redistricting Task Force. The questioning centered on the efforts Mr. Downton pursued to ensure compliance with the VRA when he was drawing various congressional districts. His testimony indicated that, although he was making partisan decisions, they were based in the fact of moving Hispanic or Latino populations in and out of various districts. Ms. Perales focused her questioning on Mr. Downton's efforts at creating a situation to ensure Mr. Canseco's reelection in CD23 by referencing the e-mail from Mr. Opiela where the Hispanic metric was discussed. It was clear from the e-mail and Mr. Downton's testimony that the effort to ensure reelection for both Messrs. Canseco and Farenthold could not be accomplished without manipulating the Latino population in or out of the benchmark districts. Mr. Downton admitted that CD27 could have been drawn to ensure that it was a Latino majority district but was drawn in the new configuration to guarantee Mr. Farenthold's reelection. Moreover, he continued, if CD27 had been configured as a Latino majority district, it is highly probable that Mr. Farenthold could not have prevailed in his subsequent reelection effort. Mr. Downton concluded this portion of his testimony by stating that he did not see a violation of the VRA in redesigning CD27 in the manner he had because of the "swap" with CD34 in another part of the state.[53]

Mr. Downton agreed with the attorney for the Queseda plaintiffs that Chairman Solomons had a goal to draw districts that would reelect as many Republican members as possible.[54] Under cross-examination, Mr. Downton disagreed that House District 149 in Harris County that had elected the first Asian American, Mr. Herbert Vo, several times was a majority-minority district and was therefore dismantled because it was not protected by the VRA.[55] Asked by Messrs. Rios and Hebert if he had attempted to combine Latinos and African Americans into a combined minority-majority district in Dallas County Mr. Downton responded that he had not thought of it nor did he try.[56] Under cross-examination by Ms. Perales, Mr. Downton agreed that an additional Latino majority Congressional district in Cameron County could be drawn and still place Congressman Farenthold in a district extending north that would allow him to get reelected.[57]

The state's next redistricting witness was Mr. Gerardo Interiano, who was Counsel to the Speaker of the Texas State House and responsible for overseeing the House Redistricting plan but also had a substantial effect on the congressional plan that was approved by the House. The first issue addressed by Mr. Interiano was to explain the constitutional provision behind the decision to award Harris County twenty-four rather than twenty-five house districts. He said that the apportionment ratio was determined by dividing the total 2010 population of the state by 150, the number of house districts; this calculation determined the "ideal district size." This last number was divided into the total population of Harris County to determine the number of districts for the county, which was 24.41. According to the Constitution, each county was to get as many as nearly as possible to the determined allocation. In Mr. Interiano's opinion, this meant that Harris County would be allocated twenty-four seats.[58]

He then discussed the County Line Rule, pointing out that the approved plan cut only one county jurisdictional boundary or line in order to comply with the "one person, one vote" rule. Mr. Interiano differentiated between the County Line Rule and the assignment of excess population to other counties from a county having excess population after all of the population had been assigned to districts wholly within the county's boundaries. The excess population was to be assigned to counties adjacent to the population from which the excess came.[59] Mr. Interiano was very specific in stating that the Constitution required that excess population only be assigned to an adjacent county and not split among various others.[60] This testimony is important because Mr. Interiano was really saying that the principal reason why additional minority-majority districts could not be drawn in various parts of the state was due to the County Line Rule and the narrowness of the rule governing the assignation of excess population. It is apparent that the County Line Rule may have been broken to accommodate excess population. In other words, the rule may not be broken to create a district where groups protected by the VRA might have an opportunity to elect a candidate of choice but can be broken to manage excess population. Mr. Interiano demonstrated both rules by discussing the redistricting of the house seats in the Cameron/Hidalgo Counties area. When it came to discussing Representative Aaron Peña's (R) HD 41, Gerardo Interiano agreed that he placed more Anglo Republicans in the district in order to ensure Mr. Peña a better opportunity of being reelected. Mr. Interiano took this moment to point out that he had been explicitly directed by Representative Solomons and Speaker of the House Joe Straus (R-San Antonio) that the districts were to be drawn to allow all incumbents, regardless of party, an opportunity for reelection.[61] Even the elimination of one district in Harris County was designed to ensure all incumbents had an opportunity to be reelected because two incumbent Democrats were paired in a new district.[62] He ended his direct testimony by explaining how the demonstration plans submitted by various plaintiffs in the lawsuit did not meet constitutional muster by either having excessive county line cuts or distribution of excess population in more than one county.

Mr. Interiano's cross-examination was begun by Ms. Perales of MALDEF, who started by getting Mr. Interiano to agree that at the beginning of the redistricting process both he and Chairperson Solomons had reviewed a racial block voting report.[63] Ms. Perales asked Mr. Interiano if he could not draw a Latino majority district within the constraints of the County Line Rule, he would not; Mr. Interiano replied that he would not draw such a district if it did not comply with the state constitution.[64] However, she was specific and made him admit that he would not draw a district that did not comply with the County Line Rule.

Mr. Interiano was then queried as to the e-mail he received from Mr. Eric Opiela concerning what had to be accomplished to ensure that CD23 was a majority Latino district that would give Mr. Canseco an opportunity for reelection. Ms. Perales had Mr. Interiano read the e-mail[65] where the metric was discussed to ensure that more Anglo Republicans were added into the district to assure Mr. Canseco's reelection but not enough to incur legal scrutiny.[66] Mr. Interiano then agreed that a public hearing on the congressional plan with a map offered by the chairperson of the committee was not held until after the regular session adjourned. He also indicated that the formal hearing, where the committee voted on the House plan held on April 19, was conducted without a video broadcast.[67] Under cross-examination by Jose Garza, legal counsel for the Mexican American Legislative Caucus, Mr. Interiano admitted that the House plan passed by the legislature had the same number of County Line cuts as at least three other plans reviewed by the committee.[68]

Mr. Rick Gray then cross-examined Mr. Interiano concerning the 10 percent deviation rule. The rule itself means simply that any district must be drawn within 10 percent, in any combination, of the mean apportionment for all districts. In the case of Texas, the apportioned population for its state house districts was 167,000, so a district must be drawn within plus or minus 10 percent total deviation, of the mean. Attorney Gray asked Mr. Interiano if he operated under the 10 percent deviation assumption as he constructed districts wholly contained within a county. Mr. Interiano responded that he had not. Mr. Gray then asked Gerardo Interiano if he had ever tried to minimize the deviation if it was close to 10 percent. Mr. Interiano responded that he had not. The most important characteristic was to ensure that the County Line Rule was not violated.[69] He, however, pointed out that it really was not his decision to manipulate the 10 percent deviation but that of the county delegations, he simply followed the directions of the county delegations.

Mr. Gray then asked Mr. Interiano about HD 41, which was, at that time, represented by Mr. Aaron Peña (R). Rick Gray noted that each of the other three wholly contained House districts, within Hidalgo County,[70] were overpopulated by between 7,700 to 4,000 individuals, while HD 41 was underpopulated by 7,399 persons. Mr. Gray inquired if this was because Mr. Interiano had been given the direction guaranteeing the reelection of all incumbents; in response, he replied that was true.[71] Attorney Gray informed Mr. Interiano that in earlier testimony it was noted that the manner in which HD 41 was created more favorably for Mr. Peña was to include as many Anglos as possible from all parts of Hidalgo County. Then Mr. Gray asked Mr. Interiano if it were not true that this could only be accomplished by drawing down at the precinct level and to actually split some of the precincts. Gerardo Interiano agreed with Attorney Gray on this latter point. Then Mr. Gray asked him that if he had been working at the precinct level did he not use the race or ethnicity shade because "you have to have the race shade on because you're doing it by race at that level because there is no political data at that level, correct?" Mr. Iteriano said, "I did not have that shading available. No sir." Upon this response, Judge Rodriguez chimed in asking that if he didn't have the race shade on, how he had drawn the districts. To which question, Mr. Interiano said that he was surrounded by members of the legislature who were instructing him as to which precincts to include or exclude from their districts. Then the following exchange ensued.

JUDGE RODRIGUEZ: So during those discussions was ethnicity or race brought up at all?

THE WITNESS: No, sir.

JUDGE RODRIGUEZ: No one mentioned that this is a white neighborhood?

THE WITNESS: No, sir.[72]

This exchange, as to whether the race shading was on as Mr. Interiano drew HD 41, is vague but raises the question whether Interiano, sitting looking at his computer screen working at the precinct level with the race shading on the screen, was ignoring it as he was being given directions on which precinct performed for Republicans or Democrats. It is not clear how one can avoid looking at color shading on a computer screen that indicates what the percentages of a particular race is in each precinct and instead make changes to district boundaries by taking verbal directions from nontechnical individuals.

The final expert for the state was Dr. John Alford,[73] who agreed that elections in Texas were very racially polarized but insisted that both African Americans and Latinos were partisan voting. He did admit that generally voting in Texas was a function of race. He pointed out that African Americans voted cohesively with Latinos when they were both voting for Democratic candidates. Dr. Alford pointed out that voting is partisan because neither blacks nor Latinos vote for Republican candidates regardless of their race.[74] He also noted that he did not understand how only one of the four new congressional districts in the state was a minority opportunity district given the great deal of Latino growth that had occurred over the last decade.[75] He admitted that there was no gain in total minority opportunity districts between the benchmark and Plan 185.[76] When his testimony moved on to the situation with a discussion of how CDs 23 and 27 had been reconstituted, he agreed that CD23 had not been drawn appropriately after an intercession by Judge Garcia.[77] Dr. Alford also agreed that CD23 was not an "effective minority district in the newly adopted plan, but it does remain a majority district."[78] Judge Garcia asked Dr. Alford how he would have advised the redistricters when they were restructuring CD23. Alford pointed out that he would have advised the redistricters to not "mess with the 23rd." Instead he said that they just "fiddled around with the 23rd enough to cause all of us to be here talking about the 23rd."[79]

Under cross-examination by Mr. Gary Bledsoe concerning the intersection of race and voting in Texas, Dr. Alford indicated that he had been approached by a group representing the Republican Party who asked him to construct minority districts in the state. It was clear from Professor Alford's discussions with the members of the group that there was a clear intent to pack as many minorities into Democratic districts to ensure more Republican victories. As a result, Dr. Alford concluded that from the beginning of redistricting in the state, there has always been a clear connection between race and partisan politics.[80]

THE CLOSING ARGUMENTS

As closing arguments go, the ones in this case were not extraordinary. The plaintiffs generally, with one exception, addressed the points of law they had based their arguments on, substantiating their arguments with various pieces of evidence or exhibits that spoke to their points. The lawyers for the State followed the same pattern, only they simply argued the positions they had staked out to defend, substantiating their positions with what they thought were the appropriate data. Nine plaintiff and two defendant attorneys made their closing arguments over a period that covered a day and a half with the plaintiffs using eight hours on the ninth day of the trial and the defense using half of the tenth day.

The plaintiff attorneys argued various points of law including violations of the one-person, one-vote principle expounded in *Reynolds v. Sims,* the Fourteenth

Amendment equal protection clause, Section 2 of the Voting Rights Act, and that the State had acted with racial purpose or intent. The State, on the other hand, argued that they did no such thing. In fact, the State argued that if there were any violations, they were coincidental.

The State did argue two very interesting points. The first was that times had changed and that racial discrimination in the electoral process no longer existed. At one point, one of the defense attorneys alluded to the notion; they did not formally argue that if minority groups were not electing candidates of their choice, it was because they were not voting in large numbers. Not being able to elect a candidate of choice, therefore, was not a function of State action but of voter inaction. The other foreboding issue argued by the State that may lead this case, once it is reargued, to the Supreme Court was the lead attorney for the State, Mr. David Schenck's, argument that maybe Section 2 had either outlived its usefulness or had become so overused that it needed reinterpretation.

Mr. Garza, lead attorney for the Mexican American Legislative Caucus (MALC), began the closing statements for the plaintiffs by restating his two claims. He argued that the State had violated the one person, one vote principle through the inconsistent use of the 10 percent deviation and County Line Rule. He argued, in a brief exchange with Judge Smith, that both of these state-level principles had been employed to ensure the reelection of incumbents while providing a disadvantage to Latinos.[81] Garza, citing the research by Dr. Kousser,[82] pointed out that a much higher percentage of Latino majority districts were overpopulated while Anglo majority districts were underpopulated because of the manner in which both the 10 percent deviation and County Line Rule were applied. Judge Rodriguez asked if the other districts in Hidalgo County had suffered the disadvantage because of the way District 41, Representative Peña's district, had been drawn, to which Garza replied that was the example he was describing.

Speaking to his second claim, that the County-Line Rule violated Section 2 of the Voting Rights Act, Mr. Garza stated that the previous night, as he was preparing his closing comments, he noted the inconsistency with which the State had determined whether to round up or down the number of districts in those counties requiring multiple districts such as Harris, Dallas, El Paso, and Hidalgo Counties. Here the argument reached an interesting level because both Judges Garcia and Smith engaged Attorney Garza in a discussion as to whether the VRA superseded the County Line Rule. From a constitutional law point of view, this can be argued simply by posing the question as to when does federal law "trump" state law. Citing *Strickland v. Bartlett,* Mr. Garza argued that if plaintiffs can demonstrate a Section 2 district but are prevented from doing so by a "whole county line rule" then state law must yield to the VRA.[83] Mr. Garza argued that this rule prevented the drawing of additional Latino majority districts where they could be drawn to meet the first proof of the "three-pronged" *Gingles* Test. In response to Judge Smith, Attorney Garza argued that state subdivision lines must be respected as long as "they don't conflict with the court's obligation to remedy the violation.[84] After this exchange, Mr. Garza represented research from Dr. Kousser on racially polarized, cohesive, and block voting that comprised the remaining two prongs of the *Gingles* Test that must be met to prove a Section 2 violation. When Attorney Garza moved to his discussion of the "totality of circumstances" proof required that normally follows the *Gingles* proof, he was asked by Judge Smith if there was any research or data "that shows that those disadvantages directly impact the opportunity to participate in the electoral process?"[85] The judge was asking this because Mr. Garza had presented information concerning the socioeconomic disadvantages characterizing the state's Latino community. It appeared that Attorney Garza could not give the judge the information he wished because Judge Smith ended by indicating that he still did not understand "how it is that an individual or group of less educated or are below poverty line less able to be encouraged to register and encouraged to go vote and otherwise participate or run for office or whatever it might be?"[86]

Mr. Rick Gray, attorney for the Perez plaintiff, made his closing arguments by stating that he supported Mr. Garza's claims but wanted to emphasize the claim that the State had violated the "one person, one vote" principle. Mr. Gray cited *Vieth v. Jubelirer*[87] that "the equal population principle remains the only clear limitation on improper districting practices and . . . we must be careful not to dilute its strength."[88] Rick Gray said that the State's inconsistent application of the 10 percent deviation rule and County Line Rule were the bases of the violation. Adherence to both of these rules allowed redistricters to pack minorities into some districts just to assure the reelection of incumbents and also violated traditional redistricting principles as set forth in *Karcher v. Daggett.*[89]

Ms. Nina Perales succeeded Mr. Gray and argued two claims. She argued that the State had diluted the voting power of Latinos in contradiction of Section 2 of the VRA through the manner in which the state redistricted. Perales's second argument was that the State violated the equal protection clause of the Fourteenth Amendment because Latinos received disparate treatment and were intentionally discriminated against during redistricting. She noted that all conditions existed that would allow for the drawing of more Latino majority districts in certain regions of the state, but the State failed to do this because of the manner in which they drew districts in Nueces, Hidalgo-Cameron, and El Paso counties. Perales's argument was focused on both the House and Congressional districts drawn in the mentioned counties.

Ms. Perales referenced expert reports from Drs. Richard Engstrom and Andres Tijerina as she presented her arguments for all three regions. Dr. John Alford, the State's expert, was also cited on several points including racially polarized voting. She provided the court with demonstration districts, racially polarized voting data, information on cohesive voting patterns, and Anglo block voting which met all three prongs of the *Gingles* Test. Finally, she used citations from *Bartlett v. Strickland, Campos v. City of Houston* and *LULAC v. Perry* to substantiate her claims from a constitutional law perspective. Ms. Perales did speak about the possibility of drawing additional minority districts in the Dallas-Fort Worth and Harris County areas, but they were not a part of her claim, only that these possibilities existed.

In speaking to the Congressional map, Ms. Perales focused on CDs 23 and 27, showing how they had been manipulated using the "Optimal Hispanic Republican Voting Strength (OHRVS)" performance metric cited in the Mr. Eric Opiela's e-mail. Noting that drawing a district to ensure incumbent protection diluted the voting power of Latinos in those districts, a clear violation of Justice Kennedy's pronouncement in *LULAC v. Perry.*

Ms. Allison Riggs representing the NAACP spoke to the constitutionality of coalition districts citing *LULAC v. Clements,*[90] *Overton v. City of Houston,*[91] *Brewer v. Ham,*[92] *Campos v. Baytown,*[93] and *LULAC v. Midland I.S.D.*[94] She also underlined the reasons Latinos, African Americans, and Asians are politically cohesive in Texas. Attorney Riggs noted that racially polarized voting was not racist; it only meant that groups of individuals from specific races tended to vote in similar patterns and different from other races. Nevertheless, she did bring up a crucial point in noting that the empirical data, statistics that identify racial polarization in elections, cannot be separated from the qualitative causes for those data. In other words, racial polarization in an electorate is the end product of a long history of racial discriminatory and disparate treatment levied against racial minority groups. Intentional discrimination in redistricting will simply exacerbate an already racially polarized community.[95]

Following Ms. Riggs, Mr. Gary Bledsoe, representing African American congresspersons, pointed out that racial polarization is also an artifact of the "Southern Strategy" begun during the Goldwater era and brought to fruition during the Nixon administration to woo the white southern vote. Part of that effort was to support anti-civil rights positions in every public policy area in an effort to win the votes of conservative southern white voters. This drove African Americans away from the Republican Party into the ranks of the Democratic Party, thus causing the entanglement of race and partisanship. In Texas, race and partisan affiliation are politically the same and cannot be separated and Mr. Bledsoe laid the blame in the lap of Republicans.[96]

Mr. Gerry Hebert representing the Quesada plaintiffs agreed with all of the colleagues who preceded him and focused his argument on the "intent question posed in *Shaw v. Reno, Johnson v. Miller,* and *Vera v. Bush.*"[97] Mr. Hebert pointed out that the state's redistricter, Mr. Ryan Downton, admitted that he used race throughout the redistricting process. He argued that the redistricters improperly redistricted in that they denied minority legislators' requests for including their offices in their districts while accepting and granting ludicrous requests from Republican legislators. In this latter case, he put forth the examples of Representative Marchant wanting his "grandbabies'" school included in his district and Representative Granger's political campaign headquarters placed in her district. He also pointed out that Congressman Lamar Smith, who was the congressional liaison for redistricting, requested several condominiums that had a great number of Republicans placed in his district together with the San Antonio County Club.[98] Congressman Smith's request was also granted. Hebert finished his argument describing the lack of proportionality in redistricting, noting that even though the state's population increases over the last decade were due primarily to the growth of minority populations, they were denied additional seats in both the state House and in the state's congressional delegation. Hebert was the last of the plaintiff attorneys to present closing statements.

The state's first attorney, Mr. David Schenck, who focused his arguments on the congressional plan only, argued that the state had increased the number of minority-majority congressional districts by one over the benchmark plan. He noted that all the state was required to do was to make the district majority-minority, not make it one that elects any particular candidate a certain way. The election of candidates is the responsibility of the electorate, not that of the redistricters. Mr. Schenck noted that the manner in which plaintiff attorneys were arguing Section 2 was inappropriate in that the creation of more minority-majority districts by stretching and combining minority groups would just lead to more segregation. He also pointed out that the state was not compelled to draw coalition districts. Schenck emphasized that, even if the state wanted to draw coalition districts, the only place they were required to do so would be where cohesive voting occurred. The problem is that cohesive voting must occur in all elections including primaries. He argued that using Section 2 itself to create a quota system is a violation of the Fourteenth Amendment. Mr. Schenck finished his argument by stating, "We need to make sure that the VRA is being read in a way that's consistent with the Constitution, by making sure that we limit the remedy of race-based districting so we don't end up with districts where people are thinking they represent people of one race."[99]

Mr. David Mattax then concluded the state's arguments by discussing the House redistricting, pointing out that the state had every intention of drawing additional minority majority districts, but they could never reach the required majority population threshold. This was caused because the state had to adhere to the County Line Rule. He argued that creating an additional minority district in Hidalgo County would disenfranchise Anglo voters. They were all placed in HD 41 so they could elect a candidate of their choice. Here Judge Rodriguez said that the HD 41 redistrict, however, involved moving 95 percent of all Latinos into other districts to accommodate that change. To which Mr. Mattax agreed.

Mr. Garza was allowed to rebut and noted that *Bartlett v. Strickland*[100] said that "It is a common ground that state election law requirements like the whole county provision may be superseded by federal law" when there is disparate treatment of protected groups. He also argued that the decision in Harris County to go from twenty-five to twenty-four house seats was within the discretion of redistricters, but it was a racially discriminatory decision.

Mr. Schenck's rebuttal was foreboding in that he argued that the plaintiff's attempt to use Section 2 to increase the number of minority districts "looks like they are trying to increase segregation. . . . Section 2 is causing segregation."[101] He argued that Section 2 is being liberally overextended beyond its original intent and is only designed to cure invidious discrimination which has already been corrected. Essentially, Mr. Schenck's Section 2 argument was designed to awaken the Supreme Court that a review of this section of the VRA may be due if not in this case, a future one.

TEXAS V. HOLDER—SENATE BILL 14: THE TEXAS VOTER IDENTIFICATION AND VERIFICATION ACT[102]

This matter, before a three-judge panel of the DCDC in Washington, was a Section 5 hearing. Texas, being under Section 5 coverage at that time, was required to submit any change to its election procedures or policies to either DOJ or the DCDC for preclearance to insure against retrogression. As in the redistricting case the Attorney General of Texas, Mr. Greg Abbott, had declared that he did not wish to submit to DOJ because, in his estimation, they were too political and he did not feel that Texas could receive a fair review. This was purely a political estimation because the Obama administration's DOJ had only objected to a little more than 1 percent of all Section 5 submissions. Nonetheless, Texas chose to request a review of SB 14 or the Texas Identification and Verification Act by the United States District Court for the District of Columbia.

The trial began on July 9, 2012, in the courthouse of the United States District Court for the District of Columbia before a three-judge panel presided over by District Judge Rosemary Collyer, who was already familiar with the parties because she had presided over the Section 5 hearing the previous year of the Texas Redistricting Plan. President George W. Bush appointed Judge Collyer to the court in 2003. The senior judge was David S. Tatel, appointed to the D.C. Court of Appeals by President Clinton in 1994, and President Obama appointed the third judge, Robert L. Wilkins, in 2010.

Judge Collyer welcomed all of the parties who, in turn, introduced themselves. There were eight plaintiff attorneys, three of whom were from a private law firm in Chicago who specialized in civil appeals; the remaining five were from the Texas Attorney General's office. There were eight attorneys representing the United States government from Mr. Holder's staff and thirteen attorneys representing various Defendant Interveners. An essential element in Judge Collyer's opening statement was placing both sides on notice that each was allowed only ten hours to present their case, and each defendant intervener was allotted five hours. This allocation of time included the direct testimony of all witnesses, lay and expert, cross-examination, together with any time used to put forth motions, and opening and closing arguments. At the beginning of each trial day, Judge Collyer would review the number of hours each side had remaining after their previous day's arguments.

THE OPENING ARGUMENTS

The Plaintiffs

Mr. Adam Mortara of the Chicago law firm of Bartlit, Beck, Herman, Palenchar and Scott, LLP presented the opening argument for the State of Texas. Mr. Mortara made it clear from his opening sentence that his strategy was going to be portraying Senate Bill 14[103] as a commonsensical piece of legislation noting that identification cards were used widely for a broad array of transactions that all persons take part in every day. He also stated that his team would show that Senate Bill 14 was not written with the intent or purpose of "denying or abridging the right to vote on account of race or color and in the case of Hispanics"[104] as a language minority. Mr. Mortara noted that, in his perception, there were two questions at stake in the hearing. The first was whether Senate Bill 14 "has a discriminatory effect" and it "was enacted with a discriminatory purpose."[105] As an aside, this was an interesting statement by Attorney Mortara because it appears that he wishes to lead the court back to the specifications of the *Bolden* decision where Section 2 plaintiffs were required to show both that a challenged law had a discriminatory effect and a purpose. After Congress rewrote this portion of the VRA in 1982, they made it clear that a showing of effect was an indication that a defendant had acted with racial purpose. Essentially, Congress made it clear in the 1982 revision that effect and purpose were one and the same. Mr. Mortara made it clear that he would attempt to show that effect and purpose were two different issues requiring two different findings of fact.

Adam Mortara continued his opening arguments by saying that there were four reasons why the state would prevail in the hearing. The first was that the law was written so all could take advantage of it, because the State of Texas had placed no fees on the acquisition of the identification cards; the cards were free. Secondly, he noted that the social science literature available at that time all showed that there was no effect on participation by anyone because of the existence of a voter identification law, citing studies of the implementation of voter identification in both the states of Indiana and Georgia. Then Mr. Mortara revealed his second strategy in that he intended to discredit the expert witness for the government, Dr. Steven Ansolabehere, by putting forth research performed indicating that the effects of voter identification laws were negligible. The third reason that Texas would prevail was that the database DOJ used to present its case was flawed in that it was composed of data that attempted to correlate the voter registration list obtained by the Texas Secretary of State Office with the state's Driver License lists obtained from the Texas Department of Motor Vehicles (DMV). Mr. Mortara pointed out that the database had not been properly cleaned by Dr. Ansolabehere, resulting in a large number of individuals in the database who had either moved from the state or been deceased. This was the same mistake that had proved fatal to the claimants in the Indiana voter identification law challenge.[106] The last reason Attorney Mortara identified as to why the Federal Government would not prevail is that when performing their analysis of the types of identification available to voters in Texas, DOJ had not included the state identification cards only federal.

Mr. Mortara then said that DOJ was basing their arguments on the *Arlington Heights* Factors (*AHFs*) arguing that the Federal Government were using them in a formulaic manner and "without reflection or wisdom or common sense and leading to a sort of ipso facto conclusion of race discrimination."[107] He noted that using the *AHFs* without thoughtful contemplation "is a real danger when you look at the list."[108] Finally, Adam Mortara pointed out that "DOJ likes to base its judgments on unusual deviation from procedures" and he continued by saying that this would be a problematic way of looking at the way in which Texas passed the legislation because the state senate had the reputation of "normally" not following procedures during their deliberations. He stated that they did not do so when considering Senate Bill 14 because of the obstinacy of the Democrats in both the 2009 and 2011 legislative sessions.

The Defendants and Interveners

Ms. Elizabeth Westfall delivered the opening argument for the United States that was clear and to the point that Texas would not be able to meet their burden of proving that Senate Bill 14 would not have a retrogressive effect. She noted that Dr. Ansolabehere's research uncovered that 1.4 million registered voters in the state lacked the types of identification required by the new voter identification law.[109] Moreover, a disproportionate number of the 1.4 million registered voters were Latinos or African Americans. Attorney Westfall noted that Ansolabehere's research had gone unrefuted by plaintiffs and was "fatal" to their case.[110]

Finally, Ms. Westfall stated that Dr. Morgan Kousser would provide testimony showing that the unprecedented growth of minorities in the state caused the state legislature to act with racial purpose. This would prove, according to Ms. Westfall, by showing that the state Senate passed the law through irregular manipulation of the legislative process over objections by minority legislators as a response to problems that would not be corrected by the law,[111] advancing legislation that became more strict as it evolved, and continuously rebuffed efforts that would have eliminated discriminatory effect from the bill.[112]

The Plaintiff Witnesses

The first witness the State of Texas put forth was Mr. Brian Keith Ingram, Director of the Elections Division of the Texas Secretary of State. Mr. Ingram provided evidence on the voter registration process and the management of the Texas Election Administrative Management System that houses the master database of all registered voters in the state. As of the trial date, there were 13,196,388 persons in the database. In the last audit prior to his testimony in 2007, the State Auditor found between 23,000 and 26,000 deceased persons and felons still on the list. Ingram declared that an actual statewide voting history for each voter did not exist prior to 2011.

Mr. Ingram pointed out that because of the ease with which ineligible voters can cast a ballot SB 14 was formulated. There were cases of deceased voters casting ballots. Ingram also noted that it is very easy for any individual to simply pick up anyone's voter registration card and cast a vote because the card has no photo, and there is not a requirement to show a photo identification card when voters present themselves to vote. Additionally, there is no requirement for a perfect match of names. Texas Admin Code 81.71 only requires similar or familiar difference between names to allow someone to cast a vote.

Mr. Ingram was asked by DOJ, in a supplementary request to their Section 5 submission, to match a voter registration list with one from the Texas Department of Public Safety in order to determine race and ethnicity of registered voters with driver's licenses or state identification cards. "We could not match, could not prove that 795,000 registered voters had an ID." He said he expressed this concern to DOJ in his report.[113] The State's attorney asked Mr. Ingram if he was aware of DOJ research matching the voter registration list to the driver's license roll and that Justice had discovered 1.9 million voters who had no driver's license or state issued identification card. Mr. Ingram responded that he was made aware of the research during the Section 5 application process and he looked into it. He discovered that both his and his wife's names were on the list even though they were both registered and had driver's licenses.[114] Under cross-examination, he admitted that some citizens who were deemed ineligible on the voter registration list only denied that they were citizens to avoid jury duty. Mr. Ingram also admitted that the current registration process was free. He further declared that the voter registration list is always out of date because it changes daily and must be subjected to periodic maintenance to remove deceased, felons, individuals who have left the jurisdiction, and mental incompetents.[115]

Mr. Ingram also noted another issue with the list that in any given year the list contained between 1.5 and 2 million suspended voters. These were individuals who moved yet the state had not been officially notified of their moving. Additionally, voters who did not respond to follow-up requests for updates to their registration were listed on the suspension list. This latter category included persons whose registration card had been returned to the Secretary of State by the mail. According to law these could not be forwarded and the voter was placed on the suspension list. The state then sent a follow up request for information to update the voter's file.

Under cross-examination, Mr. Ingram agreed that impersonating a voter on the suspension list is impossible because one was required to discover which voter was suspended. He also admitted that SB 14 could not prevent all noncitizens from voting.[116] After identifying the list of approved identification in SB 14 including driver's licenses, election identification cards, personal state identification cards, U.S. military identification cards, U.S. citizenship certificate with a photo all of which had not expired within the previous sixty days, he also noted that a U.S. passport and a Texas concealed handgun permit were allowed. Ingram admitted that noncitizens could obtain a driver's license and a U.S. military identification card. He also admitted that anyone sixty-five years of age or older could vote by absentee/mail-in ballot and was not required to use a photo identification for this process.[117]

Under cross-examination, Mr. Ingram stated that he thought SB 14 was good legislation and needed to be implemented to prevent in-person voter fraud. Mr. Chad Dunn, the cross-examining attorney, then said that Ms. Ann McGeehan had said during her deposition that she did not think it was her job to try and push legislation. Ingram said he had not read her deposition so could not comment on her opinion.[118] Mr. Dunn then asked Mr. Ingram about pending legal decisions against Texas because of alleged violations of the National Voter Registration Act (NVRA). These violations included that a voter registrar, registered in one county, could not accept voter registration applications from a voter in another county. Another violation was that it was a crime for a deputy registrar to turn in an incomplete registration application. He did acknowledge that Harris County had rejected 68,000 registration applications prior to the 2008 general election, and that a consent decree had been entered against Harris County in this matter. Then he rejected Attorney Dunn's contention that many counties in Texas had created, on an *ad hoc* basis, many barriers to voter registration over the years. Mr. Dunn then noted that any registered voter can challenge the registration of any voter and noted that some counties in the state were writing policy to enshrine this process. Mr. Dunn noted that he brought up this issue because Mr. Ingram's attorney had noted that registering to vote in Texas was easy.[119]

Mr. Ingram was then asked about the responsiveness of his office to complaints from Latino citizens who had complained that they had been denied the right to vote for lack of photo identification. Attorney Dunn asked Mr. Ingram of two specific cases that had been filed with his office and Mr. Ingram responded that he had not heard of them. Then Attorney Dunn asked Mr. Ingram if he had only heard of the cases that supported SB 14 and not current law? To which Mr. Ingram said that was not true.[120]

Attorney Dunn then raised the issue of the allegations of in-person fraudulent voting in the Donna Howard case. Ms. Howard is a state representative; some consider her a moderate Democrat, others a liberal, and she represents District 48 in Austin, Texas. Her 2010 reelection campaign against a retired professional football player who was running as a Republican ended with her winning by sixteen votes out of 51,000+ cast. After a recount, her victory was reduced to twelve votes. Her opponent requested an investigation by the Texas House of Representatives that conducted hearings that took the form of a trial in front of the entire chamber and culminated in March 2011 when Representative Howard was declared a winner by four votes.[121] Mr. Ingram stated "There was rampant in-person voting in that election, that's how *those* (emphasis added) people vote, yes." Mr. Dunn pointed out that the "investigation found no violations." To which Mr. Ingram stated "There was not enough found to overturn race."[122] Presumably he meant illegal ballots, but this was not clear from his testimony.

Mr. Dunn asked Mr. Ingram if he did not think it was unusual that during the legislative session during which SB 14 was being considered, redistricting and changing voter registration requirements were also being considered. To which Mr. Ingram responded "it is what it is."[123] Attorney Dunn concluded his questioning by asking Mr. Ingram if he was aware that more than two million Latino citizens and three-quarter of a million African Americans had not been registered to vote. Ingram said he was not aware of those numbers.[124]

The next three witnesses for the State of Texas included Mr. José Luis Aliseda, Jr. who at the time SB 14 was being considered by the legislature was the Republican State Representative of District 31 which includes eight counties extending from Atascosa County, southeast of San Antonio, Texas, to Starr County on the Mexican border. The second witness was Major Forrest Mitchell, a Criminal Investigator in the Special Investigations Unit of the Texas Attorney General's Office. Senator Thomas Williams, who was a joint author of Senate Bill 14, followed Major Mitchell.

Representative Aliseda was asked to testify by the state because he had strongly supported the House version of SB 14 with examples of in-person voting fraud during his floor speech. He had also been the County Attorney of Bee County where he had prosecuted voter fraud. He complained that one reason he was in favor of SB 14 was because he had found it almost impossible to prosecute in-person voter fraud given the current law not requiring photo identification. Mr. Aliseda indicated that as county attorney he had been informed that noncitizens had cast ballots in some elections. His final complaint was that he discovered that in some Texas counties there were more individuals listed on the voter registration rolls than actual population reported in the census.

During his cross-examination, Mr. Aliseda indicated that one cannot tell if a person is registered by simply looking at them, that voting by noncitizens was "not a big problem in Texas," and voting by undocumented workers isn't a problem in Texas because people who were "here illegally would be worried about 'getting caught.'"[125] Mr. Aliseda finally admitted that all he had stated on the floor in support of SB 14 concerning voter fraud was misleading or inaccurate. Everything he testified to in deposition and on the stand was hearsay, and he had no substantive evidence to support his concerns. Mr. Freeman, the cross-examining attorney, then said that Mr. Aliseda had testified that he had been told that noncitizens had voted in his county, but he never used this information in committee or on the floor supporting SB 14. Then Attorney Freeman concluded his cross-examination by pointing out that noncitizens have driver's licenses so they could vote, and SB 14 could not stop this type of in-person fraud. Mr. Aliseda agreed to this as well.[126]

Major Mitchell was asked about a number of voter fraud prosecutions his office had referred or pursued since 2004, and he said there had been fifty convictions but only five in-person fraud cases had been sent for prosecution. Under cross-examination Major Mitchell said that he knew of no cases involved where noncitizens attempted to cast ballots in any elections. Mr. Rosenberg for the defendant interveners had Major Mitchell review the five cases of voter fraud that had been prosecuted since 2004 and found that only two were of in-person fraud.[127]

The next lay witness for the State was State Senator Thomas Williams, who represented District 4 that covers portions or all of six counties to the north and east of Houston, Texas. Senator Williams was a joint author of SB 14. He presented a history of voter identification card legislation going back to 1997. He pointed out that SB 14 was designed "to prevent in-person voter fraud, and to shore up people's confidence in our electoral system, protect the integrity of the ballot box."[128] He stated that he had ordered Ms. Ann McGreehan to create a database that correlated state's voter registration rolls and the driver's license databases during the Senate Hearings of SB 14 but never received a report.[129] He also admitted that during the hearings, held as the Senate meeting convened as a Committee of the Whole, testimony had been provided "concerning the disproportional impact of SB 14 on minority voters."[130]

Under cross-examination by Ms. Abudu, Senator Williams said that he had chaired the Senate committee on Transportation and Homeland Security during the 2011 session.[131] Attorney Abudu asked Mr. Williams, "Would you agree that any law that decreases the voter participation of minority voters could lead to Anglos remaining a majority in the legislature?" To which the senator replied, "I haven't considered that before." Ms. Abudu followed up by asking, "Well, considering it now, would you agree that is a possibility?" Senator Williams responded, "I guess it is a possibility."[132] Attorney Abudu then, attempting to refine the senator's response, entered into the following exchange with Mr. Williams:

Q. Uh-huh. And if it is indeed established that Senate Bill 14 has a negative and disparate impact on minority voters, would you still support Senate Bill 14?

A. I don't believe that's what the record is going to show.

Q. Well, if the record does establish that, would you still support Senate Bill 14?

A. I think that all voters were affected equally by this requirement, and that we're giving a free election identification certificate away, and that no one will be disfranchised.

Q. I would like you to answer my question, please.

A. That's the best that I can answer it.[133]

Essentially, the senator refused to answer the question as to whether he would support SB 14 if he were confronted with data indicating that the implementation of the bill would hurt minority voters.

The State then called the first of its two expert witnesses, Professor Thomas Sager, who was a Professor of Statistics at the University of Texas at Austin in the Department of Information, Risk, and Operations Management in the McCombs School of Business. Professor Sager's responsibility was to critique the defendants' expert's, Dr. Steven Ansolabehere, methodology in the construction of a very large database. The database in question was one that Professor Ansolabehere had constructed to identify which Latinos and African Americans had a photo identification card as specified in SB 14. The purpose for constructing this database was to determine whether SB 14 was retrogressive according to Section 5 standards.

The database in question was constructed by comparing the state list of registered voters to the driver's license and state identification card database. The former database was normally compiled by the Secretary of State's Office while the latter was constructed and maintained by the Texas State Department of Public Safety. Professor Sager critiqued Dr. Ansolaberhere's technique as faulty for two fundamental reasons. The first was that Professor Ansolabehere had cleaned the databases, removing deceased individuals, felons, those having duplicate Social Security numbers, and individuals who had moved out of the state before conducting his sweeps. A *sweep* was a computerized search based upon identifiers common to each dataset. Each sweep would be run and a separate dataset with common information fields from each dataset would be created. After all three sweeps were conducted, the final dataset was supposed to identify all registered voters who possessed either a driver's license or a state-approved identification card.[134] Dr. Ansolabehere's three sweeps were, in the order they were conducted, matching Social Security numbers; matching first and last names and date of birth; and, matching middle names to the first and last names and date of birth.

The second criticism was the manner in which Professor Ansolabehere had defined his sweeps and the number of sweeps that were conducted. Sager said that he used three databases as had Dr. Ansolabehere, plus the 1.5-million-person dataset that Dr. Ansolabehere had developed from his analysis. The voter registration roll included more than 13 million names while the driver's license database possessed more than 26 million together with the 800,000 from the "license to carry list."[135] Sager felt his technique was more thorough because he added an additional, better-defined, sweep, thus increasing the probability of greater coverage. Professor Sager's four sweeps included the first two of Dr. Ansolabehere plus a third sweep using the last four integers of the Social Security number together with the first and last name. The fourth sweep used by Professor Sager was using the last four of the Social Security number plus date of birth. Professor Sager indicated that Dr. Ansolabehere's methodology was biased toward Hispanics while his was not. Additionally, Professor Sager pointed out that Dr. Ansolabehere had cleaned the voter registration and driver's license databases before he used them. Dr. Ansolabehere removed from the driver's license file all duplicate records having the same Social Security numbers, deceased drivers, and all drivers where the license had expired more than sixty days before. In other words, he removed many records that could have been used during additional sweeps. While Dr. Ansolabehere's methodology yielded 1.5 million individuals who did not have identification or driver's licenses, including Ingram and his wife who testified earlier concerning this inconsistency. Most important, Professor Sager pointed out that Dr. Ansolabehere's methodology was biased structurally, yielding more women and Hispanics in the dataset of 1.5 million showing not having any acceptable types of identification cards under SB 14. Both biases were due to the name matching function. Women were using their married names on some applications while using their maiden name on another. Latino names varied depending upon the language use of first names and spacing issues for last names appearing on different applications for the same individual. Under cross-examination, Professor Sager admitted that the reason he arrived at a different result in his analysis from Professor Ansolabehere was not because Dr. Ansolabehere's methodology was incorrect but because the two methods were different.[136] Additionally, Professor Sager could not take issue with Dr. Ansolabehere's conclusion that "the voter identification requirement will affect whites and minorities differently, and the differences are substantial."[137]

The plaintiff's last expert, who testified out of turn due to some travel complications, was Dr. Daron Robert Shaw, Distinguished Teaching Professor at the University of Texas, Austin. Professor Shaw was asked to critique Dr. Steven Ansolabehere's article in *PS* that appeared in 2009 focusing on a survey Professor Ansolabehere had conducted as to whether voters who were asked to present photo identification were subsequently allowed to vote.[138] The survey also asked nonvoters if lack of proper photo identification was one of the possible reasons for their not voting. Dr. Ansolabehere's findings pointed out that "while quite a few people were asked to present identification at the polls, almost nobody was excluded from voting once they were asked for photo identification."[139] Of 36,500 individuals who were asked for photo identification, only twenty-five were not allowed to vote nationwide; when the survey was administered, only Indiana had a photo identification card requirement.[140] Of the nonvoters, "virtually nobody said they didn't vote because they didn't have the proper identification."[141]

Professor Shaw indicated that he performed a follow-up study because of the onset of SB 14. He pulled 2,750 Texas cases as well as data from Indiana and Georgia. The "idea was to see if we could get some measure of compatibility" among all three states.[142] He noted that 87 percent of voters polled said they participated in primaries in 2008 in all three states. Fully 99 percent of all respondents in Indiana and Georgia indicated that they had been asked for photo identification compared to 60 percent of Texas respondents. Only 1 percent in Georgia and Texas were not allowed to vote after showing identification, none in Indiana. By race, 15 percent of blacks in Georgia were not allowed to vote. Professor Shaw found disparate rates of identification card possession in all states but did not specify what they were. After his analysis and review of the scholarly literature, he concluded that there would be no measureable effect on voter turnout if SB 14 were to be implemented.[143]

The research that Dr. Shaw was asked to perform for this trial was to survey a sample of the 795,000 individuals from the DOJ file who indicated that they did not have photo identification in three areas: possession, their attitude toward possession of voter identification, and basic demographics. He completed 1,238 interviews in a general group and 600 each in Hispanic and African American unique samples. In the general group, he found that 95 percent possessed SB 14 acceptable photo identification, and he obtained the same percentage in the Hispanic sample. Dr. Shaw also surveyed Ansolabehere's 1.9 million list of individuals who might not have driver's licenses or licenses to carry firearms. He created four subsamples, one each for Anglos, African Americans, Hispanics, and a general sample. There were 1,000 cases in his general sample, 530 in the Anglo sample, and 600 each in the Hispanic and African American samples. Professor Shaw found that 91 percent of his Anglo sample, 93 percent of African American, and 92 percent of Hispanic samples all possessed one of the two forms of identification. He also discovered that the search firm, Catalist, was only 70 percent accurate in identifying African Americans for that sample, indicating a 30 percent error rate making that sample problematic. In other words the Catalist methodology correctly identified whether someone on the list was an African American 70 percent of the time. In short, Catalist misidentified individuals as African American when they were not 30 percent of the time. Finally, Dr. Shaw noted that although possession of driver's licenses was lower for Hispanics than Anglos, their possession rates were higher when it came to passport and citizenship certificates.[144] A great deal of Dr. Shaw's criticism was directed at the quality of Ansolabehere's 1.9 million list of individuals who indicated that they did not possess SB 14-specific identification. Professor Shaw noted that there were many individuals on the list who were deceased or did not have phone numbers making the creation of the samples he used for his surveys very difficult.[145]

Mr. Freeman from the United States Attorney General's office performed the cross-examination of Dr. Shaw, reviewing his sampling techniques as opposed to Professor Ansolabehere's in relationship to the initial survey Dr. Shaw had conducted as a replication of Dr. Ansolabehere's. Dr. Shaw admitted that he had not included any individuals using cell phone numbers, so his survey was skewed toward older voters and non-minorities.[146] Although Professor Shaw's study indicated that 90+ percent of minority voters he contacted indicated that they had photo identification, they were difficult to contact. His general survey subsample demographics did not match up to those of the population he was sampling, indicating a high error rate. Professor Shaw admitted that this was the main reason he did not attempt to weight his sample.[147] Dr. Shaw also admitted that after reviewing the social science literature available on this topic, he concluded that it was unlikely that stringent photo identification requirements would lead to higher turnout.[148] He also admitted that his conclusions concerning the study of the effects of photo identification in Texas when compared to the studies in Indiana and Georgia were faulty because all three states had different policies and much different demographics.[149] Finally, Attorney Freeman had Dr. Shaw review four scholarly articles on the relationship between voter identification and turnout of minority voters where all studies indicated that any stringent photo identification laws would lead to either lower registration or turnout rates or both.[150]

Mr. Rosenburg, the lead intervener attorney, then asked Professor Shaw about his political polling background. Dr. Shaw admitted that he had been recruited and worked for Karl Rove on the Bush campaign in 2000 and worked for Bush/Cheney Reelect and the Republican National Committee as Director of Election Studies.[151] This was clearly an attempt by Mr. Rosenburg to align Shaw ideologically with the Republican Party.

Defendants and Defendant Interveners

In this trial, the defendant was the United States of America as well as Eric Holder in his capacity as Attorney General of the nation. The interveners were various, including the Mexican American Legislative Caucus, the NAACP, and two teenage Latino twin sisters from San Antonio, Texas. The two lay witnesses for the United States Government were two state representatives who had played significant roles during the hearings surrounding the passage of SB 14 during the 2011 legislative session. The first witness was State Representative Trey Martinez-Fischer, (D-San Antonio), who was the sitting chairman of the Mexican American Legislative Caucus (MALC). He was followed by State Representative Rafael Anchia (D-Dallas), who had asked substantive questions during the House deliberations and who had submitted several amendments to SB 14 that were summarily rejected during the hearings.

Mr. Martinez-Fischer pointed out that MALC was concerned about the difficulties minority communities would have in ballot access if SB 14 were implemented, indicating that certain populations did not have proper identification including driver's licenses. Additionally, Representative Martinez-Fischer indicated that some counties were so large geographically that some citizens would be required to make a two-hundred-mile round-trip just to visit a Department of Public Safety (DPS) office in order to apply for a voter identification card. Mr. Martinez-Fischer added that some of the large urban areas, such as San Antonio, Texas, which he used to illustrate his point, did not have a sufficient number of DPS branches to service the large populations in those areas. He noted, for instance, that there were only three offices in all of San Antonio and the largest area where Latinos and African Americans lived didn't even have an office. Mr. Martinez-Fischer noted that the DPS office in his district often had waiting times of two hours or more with no facilities to make waiting comfortable in the hot summer months. He pointed out that MALC had tried to add new locations to SB 14, such as county courthouses, to no avail because the bill's sponsors rejected them.

The examining attorney, Mr. Jose Garza, representing MALC, asked Representative Martinez-Fischer about the justifications offered for SB 14. He responded by stating that in the 2005 and 2007 legislative sessions, the talk was about how SB 14 was needed to prevent immigrants from committing voter fraud. The conversation began shifting in 2009, although there was still talk about preventing immigrants from voting, to simply preventing voter fraud. The language changed again in 2011 to one of protecting the integrity and security of the ballot box. Mr. Martinez-Fischer noted that the shift in justification together with the way legislative procedural changes surrounding the rules of how SB 14 was going to be considered concerned him that there was more than ballot security to SB 14. Attorney Garza asked Mr. Martinez-Fischer if minority legislators voiced these concerns during the legislative process, to which the representative answered affirmatively. He pointed out how under normal situations the legislature always passed a bill of "unintended consequences" to cover unforeseen externalities caused by the initial legislation. Minority legislators attempted to amend SB 14 to protect minority populations by supporting this type of legislation to no avail. This was very disheartening in light of the fact that between 750,000 and 1.5 million Texans could possibly be disenfranchised by SB 14.

Mr. Garza then asked Mr. Martinez-Fischer to outline the change in legislative procedures surrounding the passage of SB 14. The representative noted that the governor had declared SB 14 emergency legislation, which lifted the constitutional requirement that no legislation could be passed during the first sixty days of the session. A Select Committee was formed to hear only this one bill, eliminated the two-thirds vote rule to suspend or change rules, expedited committee hearings (the bill passed through all committee processes in six days), and the chair and vice-chair were chosen ahead of time. The creation of the select committee also suspended all rules governing the appointment of members based on seniority that eliminated the possibility of many minority legislators from participating on the committee. Finally, when the legislation reached the House floor, all attempts to amend by minority members were rebuffed.[152]

"Tagging" was not allowed in Select Committee, but once legislation reached the House floor, it was initially stopped by a parliamentary point of order motion, which required it to go all the way back to the Select Committee, then printing, then the Calendar Committee before reaching the floor again. Generally a process of this sort takes a great deal of time; this time it took two days from the parliamentary objection to its reintroduction on the floor of the House.[153] When Representative Martinez-Fischer was asked about his impressions after the House floor debate and final passage of SB 14, he responded by saying:

> You know, but again, at the end of the day when you look through all the rationale, you think it has something to do about voting, but you know, there's been lots of discussion about the author of the bill that says that voter ID is *immigration policy* (emphasis added). And so anybody who thinks voter identification legislation is good immigration policy then maybe voter identification and voting in elections was *not the primary place* (emphasis added). And, frankly, if you're looking at illegal immigration, in the State of Texas you're looking at immigration concerning people that look like me.[154]

Representative Rafael Anchia (D-Dallas) representing State House District 103 was the next lay witness for the MALC defendant interveners. He pointed out that there had been no public testimony presented during any hearing for SB 14. He was then asked if there had been any change in the justification for voter identification legislation since he had been in the legislature. Mr. Rafael Anchia noted that he had been on the House Elections Committee in 2005, 2007, and 2009 but was excluded this time around. He testified that initially voter fraud was the focus of the legislation, and then it changed to in-person impersonation, but then as research developed "there was a subtle confluence of the discussion of voter impersonation at the polls with other issues."[155] He discovered through research that the vast majority of voter fraud occurred with mail-in ballots, "official oppression, there were concerns about collusion with election officials. . . . There was bribery."[156] Then,

> after the 2007 session and going into 2009 and beyond, the justification for the bill moved from impersonation, then to non-citizen voting—illegal immigrant

voting, essentially—and then became about the integrity of elections and preventing the disenfranchisement of validly cast votes by avoiding invalidly cast
votes.[157] . . . Around 2009 and 2011, you start to hear a lot less of the illegal
aliens voting and more of integrity of elections.[158]

Mr. Garza, the examining attorney, then asked, "Did the House examine
whether voter ID would preserve the integrity of elections?" Mr. Anchia
responded, "Not as far as I can tell."[159] He continued, pointing out that SB
14 and the new voter identification card was supposed to be "some failsafe
mechanism for preventing voter impersonation at the polls." He then cited the
example of how during this aspect of the discussion in the committee hearing
DPS brought a bunch of fake IDs into the hearing, and "we asked members
to distinguish between real and false and it was interesting." Many members
could not distinguish between the authentic and false identification cards.

> There were many IDs that had been picked up by DPS that were actually quite
> real looking. And we wondered aloud if, in fact, a photo ID requirement, even
> when you did have a valid driver's license in front of you, would prevent im-
> personation to the extent it did exist.[160]

The defendants then presented Dr. Morgan Kousser,[161] who had been charged
with determining whether the "intentions of the legislature in passing SB 14
were racially discriminatory."[162] The examining attorney, Mr. Richard Dell-
heim, asked him if he had reached a conclusion after his research, to which
Professor Kousser replied that he had.[163] He briefly discussed his methodology
that he had outlined in the volume he authored entitled *Colorblind Justice,*[164]
and answered that his methods had never been criticized in any scholarly journals. He spoke to the extent and intensity of racial polarization in elections of
the decade between 2000 and 2010 that he and other experts in the redistricting
trial had testified to. Dr. Kousser then spoke to the changes in legislative procedures that occurred during both the 2009 and 2011 sessions, making it more
difficult for opponents of SB 14 to inhibit its passage. For instance, he noted
that the "chubbing" process and two-thirds rule had been eliminated. Kousser
also pointed out that Governor Rick Perry had deemed SB 14 emergency
legislation that allows the legislature to hear and pass the bill within the first
60 days of a session. Generally, this declaration is only made for emergency
legislation requiring a quick response by the state government to some crisis or
extreme need. Following this, the Lieutenant Governor, Mr. David Dewhurst,
placed SB 14 at the top of the list of all legislation, ensuring that it would be
heard and acted on first before all previously filed bills. Dr. Kousser indicated
that this was a departure from normal procedure and an indicator of racial
intent as outlined by the Supreme Court in *Arlington Heights.*

Returning to his previous discussion concerning the intensity and depth of racial polarization in the state, Dr. Kousser noted that it was difficult if not impossible to separate partisanship from racial voting. "There's a high correlation between partisanship and race that a bill that has partisan effects would have racial effects" he noted.[165] Continuing, he noted that "a bill that disfranchises Democrats and particularly affects poorer people has a very disproportionate effect on minorities. It's impossible to separate these two."[166] These observations elicited the following exchange with the circuit court jurist, Judge David Tatel.

Judge Tatel asked Professor Kousser,

> when you have, say, a Republican legislature that wants to protect its power by disenfranchising Democrats, the effect of that is also where you have polarized voting to disenfranchise minorities. . . . As a scholar researching this, how do you sort out the motive? How do you determine in a situation like that whether the motive was partisan or racial? What are the scholarly approaches to answering that question?"[167]

Dr. Kousser responded by creating a hypothetical indicating that if a study had been conducted ahead of time by either the DPS or Secretary of State's offices and it was found that a bill had a deleterious effect on minorities and then the state implemented such a bill, then the case is clear. Judge Tatel responded "Really. Tell me why." To which Professor Kousser, in turn, responded, "Because the anticipation of the [negative] effect would have been apparent to everybody." Judge Tatel then observed:

> "Yeah, but if their purpose—suppose their purpose is totally partisan. They're Republicans wanting to maintain control, and they find out that—yeah, they do a study, and they find out that as a result of this they're going to disenfranchise a large number of Democratic minorities. Does this mean their motive is racial?"

Professor Kousser responded, "If they're disproportionately disenfranchising minorities, yes, I think it does." Judge Tatel then concluded this discussion by noting that he was still uncertain as to this issue and asked the examining attorney to elicit responses to address his concern.[168]

Professor Kousser's testimony then moved to a discussion of how the reasons for SB 14 had changed over the years. He noted that in 2011 alone the bill was advertised as one that would prevent illegal aliens from voting to one where the bill was to restore confidence and integrity of the political process. Dr. Kousser noted that he was skeptical of the last two reasons in light of the fact that Republicans had been winning overwhelmingly in the state in recent years and could not understand why there was a lack of confidence in the electoral process. He also noted that there had been no discussion concerning protecting the integrity of the political process.[169]

The defendant interveners then introduced Ms. Victoria Rose Rodriguez, a young Latina who had just graduated from high school, as their next lay witness. She noted that SB 14 would negate her ability to register to vote because the bill did not allow for the use of student identification cards. Neither she nor her twin sister possessed a driver's license because the automobile insurance costs would be prohibitive for their parents. Finally, they lived a great distance from the local DPS office and would have a difficult time getting there to obtain a voter identification card under the current system. The only identification card that had a photo of her was that issued to her in high school, but that was now obsolete because she had graduated. As a result, all she had to identify her was a birth certificate that did not have her current address so she could not prove her residency with that document. Asked how she had boarded the plane in San Antonio, Texas, ridden the railroad from Baltimore, checked in to the hotel, and entered the secured federal courthouse in Washington, she responded with her expired high school identification card.[170]

The next lay witness for the interveners was the Reverend Baziel Peter Johnson of Dallas, Texas. Reverend Johnson had a career as a civil rights activist beginning in the era of voter registration drives in Louisiana in the 1960s and currently headed a nonprofit organization to promote nonviolence in Texas. He principally testified to the state of violent race relations in Texas and spoke to several instances of forced segregation and beatings that were racially motivated in East Texas. He also spoke to an incident in Sulphur Springs, Texas, which is a small community almost due east of Dallas halfway to Texarkana, where a young black man was thrown from a pickup truck during an altercation with a white man who had made disparaging remarks because the black man was seen in a public place with his white girlfriend. He was horribly disfigured losing much of his face in the process. This incident, which occurred in 2007, was still being adjudicated in 2013 and had been ruled a nonracial incident by the Texas Rangers.[171] He spoke of the burning down of three black churches in East Texas and of black persons afraid to go out after dark in the small communities of East Texas for fear of violence.[172]

The next lay witness was State Senator Rodney Ellis of Houston, who testified to the unusual procedures that were instituted to ensure the passage of SB 14. Senator Ellis was the senior senator in the chamber, having served for twenty-two years. He spoke to the differences between his ten-year struggle in passing the James Byrd Crime Control Act and how quickly SB 14 had been passed. Senator Ellis pointed out that this was primarily true because the senate leadership were more disposed to getting their bill passed than his;

as a result they changed many of the traditional procedures to ensure quick passage of SB 14, including having the governor declaring it emergency legislation and lifting of the two-thirds rule for bringing a bill to the floor for action.[173] Asked if he had tried to modify SB 14 through the submission of amendments, and he responded that he had, including one allowing the use of public university student identification cards, same-day registration, and a measure seeking information as to whether SB 14 would have disparate effects on racial or ethnic minorities in the state.[174] Senator Ellis indicated his disappointment that none of his amendments were even given consideration. He did speak of his disappointment in his fellow senators in their failure to support his amendment on allowing the use of public university student identification cards because he had supported the license to carry identification card in hopes that other senators would support his bill. They did not.[175]

All of Senator Ellis's amendments were tabled by the Senate, including one where he had sought information on the disparate effects on racial and ethnic minorities. He pointed out that his request would not have delayed SB 14 or changed its implementation but was made in light of the Secretary of State's failure to respond to his request for similar information prior to consideration of SB 14. Mr. Ellis pointed out that he did not feel that this was an extraordinary request but one that any senator would make to ensure that there were no unintended consequences or effects on certain populations. When he asked Senator Fraser for the disparate effects information the senator, who was reluctantly carrying SB 14, responded to Mr. Ellis by stating "I'm not advised. Ask the Secretary of State." This led Senator Ellis to conclude that the state knew full well that SB 14 would have a disparate impact on racial minorities and that the voter identification bill had been designed and passed with racial intent or purpose.[176]

Senator Ellis was followed by Mr. Randall "Buck" Wood, who was an elections attorney with over forty years of experience, having interviewed more than two thousand individuals in elections that had been contested before election courts during his years of experience. He stated that he had "never seen anybody impersonate someone else. I've heard of maybe one instance of it in forty-some odd years, but it really can't be done. You can't impersonate someone who has already voted because you will get caught." Mr. Wood also noted that one is required to know who an individual voter is and know that the individual would not vote before attempting to impersonate that voter, an almost impossible situation. Finally, he made it clear that almost all illegal voting that he was familiar with was done by mail-in ballot.[177]

Mr. Wood was followed by Dr. Henry Flores, an expert witness for the interveners, who was charged with providing research into whether the state had acted with racial purpose in the construction and passage of SB

14.[178] Dr. Flores[179] presented information concerning the rapidly changing demographics of the state and how it was quickly becoming more Latino. Texas had already become a majority-minority state but would be a majority Latino state within decades. He noted that the changing demographics was the principal reason behind the passage of SB 14, citing comments from the *House Journal* by Representative Patricia Harless where she stated that "the population demographics were changing and they had to pass that bill to stop it."[180] Professor Flores also noted that this coincided with comments from the public record during the 2005, 2007, and 2009 legislative sessions where it was publicized that voter identification was important to stopping massive voting fraud by illegal immigrants.[181] After conducting his own research into voting fraud, Dr. Flores discovered one or two cases of voting fraud by mail-in ballot between 2000 and 2011, and concluded that there was not sufficient evidence of voting fraud for this to be the real reason behind passage of SB 14. Finding no other empirical reason for SB 14, Professor Flores concluded that the voter identification legislation had morphed into an anti-immigrant bill particularly in light of all the racial and anti-immigrant rhetoric that had pervaded discourse in the 2011 legislative session.[182] Professor Flores noted, "And as we've heard from testimony earlier today, it's pretty hard to do in-person voting fraud as it is, let (alone) done by an individual, let (alone) done by masses of undocumented persons coming across the border at any given time."[183] He continued by looking at how the anti-immigrant rhetoric washed over the local Latino citizen communities because "Where do illegal immigrants or undocumented workers come from in the State of Texas principally? They come from Mexico, they come from Latin America, so SB 14 in my own mind turned into an anti-immigrant bill . . . as a result, I concluded that race was at the heart of SB 14."[184]

Part of Dr. Flores's research design in investigating the racial purpose of SB 14[185] was to look at and attempt to understand the effects of the social, cultural and political environment on the political players as they considered SB 14. Dr. Flores noted that the 2011 legislative session was one of the most racially acrimonious he had witnessed in over thirty years of observing the state legislature. There were approximately one hundred anti-immigrant bills submitted during the session[186] including three attempting to make English the official language of the state. Dr. Flores, in order to show the anti-Latino-immigrant nature of much of the legislation, pointed out that there had even been a bill prohibiting remittances to Latin American countries and Mexico but not to other countries of the world including Asia, Africa, or Canada.[187] He also gave examples of how the immediate environment outside the legislature was racially charged when he gave an example of the Tea Party demonstration, sponsored by a conservative member of the legislature, declaring that the reason that no good anti-immigrant legislation could be passed in Texas was the presence of elected Hispanic officials and they had to be removed.[188]

The examining attorney, Mr. Jorge Sanchez of MALDEF, asked Dr. Flores more about his methodology and to explain to the court what the concept of *anchoring* was. Anchoring, which is a concept borrowed from the world of decision-making theory, is a heuristic device that decision makers create to base a judgment or decision on. Lacking any empirical evidence but facing the situation where a decision is required, decision makers will construct a heuristic that creates a rationalization for their decision. Lacking evidence of voter fraud in this case, Texas legislators fell back on a heuristic based upon a long history of racial tensions and stereotypes that had governed their perceptions of Latinos throughout history. Driven by the fear of the rapidly changing demographics, knowing that they could not attract Latinos to their legislative agenda, state legislators constructed the voter identification bill that would build another barrier against the political participation of Latinos and other minorities. The heuristic of racial intolerance, xenophobia, poor race relations, and a history of bad treatment of Latinos drove the state legislature to design SB 14 in such a way as to make it difficult for Latinos to register and vote. The inability to attract Latinos to the agenda of the Republican Party was evidenced by the continuing intense levels of racially polarized voting. The silence and other avoidance tactics used during the passage of SB 14 as appearing in the various daily legislative journals was simply a way of indicating that the state policy managers did not want any input from minority legislators. Silence and avoidance had become racist acts, shielding the racial intent of decision makers, as opposed to the overt acts of discrimination seen in earlier historical eras.[189]

The interveners offered another expert who criticized Dr. Shaw's response rate as being too low and, therefore, not yielding useable information for the various surveys he performed off of Dr. Ansolabehere's database of 1.9 million individuals. Two state senators, Carlos Uresti and Wendy Davis, then followed this expert. Mr. Uresti, who represents one of the geographically largest state senatorial districts in the United States that is 70 percent Latino and 5 percent African American, addressed the same issues as did Senator Ellis as to the changes in procedures and the unavailability of information that was forthcoming from either Senator Fraser or the Secretary of State's Office. Senator Davis, representing a district in Tarrant County centered in Fort Worth, Texas, that is approximately 40 percent minority and had been a center of dispute in the redistricting trial concluded in 2011, spoke to the procedural irregularities her two colleagues had addressed but also added testimony on the fiscal aspects of SB 14. She noted that this was the first time that a legislative item had been brought to senators without an accompanying fiscal report. Generally, when a bill is brought to the senate for consideration, it is accompanied by a report from the Legislative Budget Board that outlines the costs of implementation. In the case of SB 14, the Lieutenant Governor suspended the rule, so no fiscal report accompanied the bill. Senator Davis indicated that she had asked for a report and was told that the amounts were minimal because most of the cost would be covered by Help America Vote Act (HAVA)[190] funds.[191] She pointed out that the amount of money from HAVA, which was $2 million, was earmarked in a fiscal note during the 2011 session and designated for voter education efforts through the purchase of media time. Senator Davis felt this was inadequate because in her campaign, centered in the Dallas–Fort Worth media market, she had spent $1.1 million, which was considered a small media buy. As a result, she pointed out to her colleagues that $2 million would not go far enough to educate voters throughout the state. Additionally, she noted that no funds had been set aside for the education of election judges on the requirements of SB 14.[192] She was then questioned as to funding for the Department of Public Safety where she pointed out that DPS had been cut by 5 percent during the 2011 budget, requiring it to close eighty-one offices. Davis did note, however, that there was a provision in the budget to create six "super DPS centers" for the total amount of $65 million. The problem here was that all six were to be centered in the urban areas of Dallas–Fort Worth, Houston, San Antonio, and Austin; none would be located in rural areas.[193]

Senator Davis's testimony then continued to the thirteen amendments she had put forth during the debates, all of which were rejected or tabled during the debate. The ones she was most concerned about were those that protected the ability of indigent individuals to obtain either the voter identification card or the underlying documents. Davis noted that although the voter identification card was supposed to be free, many individuals did not possess the underlying documents required to apply for the identification card. These auxiliary documents were expensive to those who were poor or had very low incomes. Her amendment would have allowed an indigent person to obtain the underlying documents free of charge.

Another amendment was simply to have the DPS personnel inform each applicant that the voter identification card was free upon their arrival at the application office. Senator Davis also offered amendments allowing for the use of expired driver's licenses or other underlying documents during the voter identification application process. The only amendment that was revived was her amendment to allow indigent individuals to obtain free underlying documents. Senator Duncan, a Republican from the panhandle of Texas, felt that this was a worthy amendment, so he sponsored it after it had been tabled and it passed. Eventually, however, when SB 14 went to Conference Committee, this particular amendment was stripped by the House conferees.[194]

One of the most interesting amendments sponsored by Senator Davis was one that would clarify the name situation that some married women found themselves in by having either their married or original name (maiden) on their driver's license while having their other name on their voter registration card. This amendment would have allowed an election worker or judge discretion in determining whether the specific voter involved was the same person on both cards. This amendment was tabled in the Senate. What made this amendment interesting was that in the first election where photo identification was required, Ms. Davis found herself caught in this conundrum and was required to cast a provisional ballot.[195] In the end, Senator Davis felt that Senate Bill 14 would have a disparate effect on minorities and women voters.[196]

The U.S. government concluded its portion of the trial with two experts. The first, who were the closing witnesses on the fourth day, was Dr. Alan Lichtman of American University.[197] Professor Lichtman's charge was to review all of the expert reports to determine whether there was evidence of racial intent. Dr. Lichtman was a "rebuttal witness" so did not perform any primary research for this trial. He reviewed Professor Sager's critique of Dr. Ansolabehere's work and concluded that a great deal of what Sager said was accurate but it did not affect Dr. Ansolabehere's conclusions, noting that both found that SB 14 would have disparate effects on Hispanics. Dr. Lichtman did point out, however, several flaws in Professor Sager's methodology noting that Sager was not able to account for certain qualitative characteristics underlying the data used in his analyses, including the discretion of poll workers which can sometimes be driven by stereotypes they may have of minority voters and the unique construction of Latino names that allows for easy mismatching.[198]

Moving to Dr. Shaw's research, he noted that Shaw found disparate treatment of Hispanics in that the surveys that were conducted discovered higher percentages of Latinos and African Americans, as opposed to Anglos, were asked for photo identification in the elections studied.[199] Dr. Lichtman also noted that Dr. Shaw's surveys lacked internal validity checks, were conducted within too compressed a time frame, and suffered from poor response rates at 2 percent. Each of these flaws, noted Professor Lichtman, were fatal to the surveys, but combined negated the usefulness of Dr. Shaw's findings. Dr. Lichtman characterized the survey methodology as "so far out of line with reality checks that no reliable conclusions of any kind can be drawn from the survey."[200]

Dr. Lichtman's testimony concluded when Mr. Hebert, one of the examining attorneys, took him back in an attempt to address Judge Tatel's principal concern of whether partisanship or race were the driving forces behind SB 14.

Hebert asked Professor Lichtman the question that "Judge Tatel brought up with Dr. Kousser, which was how do you as an expert unravel issues of intent when it comes to issues of partisanship and race?" Dr. Lichtman responded by stating, "That can only be achieved if SB 14 had a disparate impact on the ability of minorities who are heavily Democratic to vote. So you could choose the partisan end only by knowingly and intentionally discriminating against minorities." Professor Lichtman noted that this is "much easier in Texas to use minorities as a proxy for Democrats because … voting is so highly polarized along racial lines in Texas."[201]

The last witness was Dr. Stephen Ansolabehere, whose database had been the focus of the plaintiff's criticism. As Mr. Mortara pointed out in his opening arguments and Mr. Hughes would point out in his closing, the plaintiffs felt that the entire Section 5 review of the Department of Justice would stand or fall on the quality and substance of Professor Ansolabehere's research. Dr. Ansolabehere was charged with developing a database that would allow DOJ to determine the retrogressive effects of SB 14 on Latinos and African Americans in Texas. This was accomplished through the construction of a database that identified those registered voters who possessed three of the identification cards required in SB 14: a driver's license, a state identification card, or a license to carry a concealed handgun. Dr. Ansolabehere indicated that his methodology was to merge the databases, which were obtained from the Texas Department of Motor Vehicles, with the database of registered voters obtained from the Secretary of State's Office. The merge was intended to identify and create a list of those individuals who appeared on the registered voter list but did not appear on any of the other three. The next step was to determine the racial identity of the individuals on this last list. Professor Ansolabehere indicated that he had attempted to obtain a list of all individuals in the state who had a military identification card but was unable to get this information from the Department of Defense.

The final list of names amounted to 1.5 million individuals who were registered voters but did not possess any of the three forms of photo identification specified in SB 14. Dr. Ansolabehere then contracted with Catalist, a private data-management consulting firm, to use their proprietary algorithm to determine the percentage of African Americans and Latinos in the database. This step was necessitated because Texas does not register voters by race, so it is impossible to determine the race or ethnicity of voters in this manner. He did avail himself of the list of Spanish Surnamed Registered Voters maintained by the Secretary of State's Office to assist in the identification of Latino registered voters. This latter database, however, is determined through the use of a master Spanish surnamed list maintained by DOJ and shared with the states. In the final analysis, Professor Anoslabehere discovered that of all registered voters in the state, 61.5 percent were Anglo or White, 11.6 percent were Black, and 23.6 percent were Hispanic. Of those on the Voter Registered No Identification (VRNID) list, the list of those registered voters not having the requisite photo identification derived after the merging of all databases, 51 percent were Anglo or white, 16 percent black, and 29 percent Hispanic. Another set of registered voters that Dr. Ansolabehere developed, one he labeled the "Ambiguous List," was composed of registered voters over sixty-five and those whose identification cards had expired; of these, he discovered that 49 percent were Anglo, 17.6 percent black, and 30.3 percent were Latino. This led Ansolabehere to conclude that the photo identification card requirement as set forth in SB 14 had a disparate effect on minority voters. Although when he isolated those voters over sixty-five who did not have photo identification, he found the statistical effect reversed and Anglos were the most affected by this requirement.[202]

Although Professor Ansolabehere admitted during cross-examination that his methodology was flawed to a certain extent in light of the manner in which he either excluded or included certain groups for analysis, that is, deceased voters or voters who moved out of the state, he still felt that his data supported his final conclusion concerning SB 14. In the end, Judge Tatel noted that his research still did not assist the court in answering the legal question.[203]

THE CLOSING ARGUMENTS

The closing arguments in a Section 5 hearing are designed to allow both sides to summarize their arguments showing why they should prevail. The judges, on the other hand, are looking for information and argument that will allow them to answer a legal question. The closing for Texas was presented by Mr. John M. Hughes of the Chicago firm of Bartlitt, Beck, Herman, Palencher and Scott, LLP, who argued that SB 14 would not "deny or abridge the right to vote on account of race or color or because of membership in a language minority group."[204] Mr. Hughes then began presenting the four reasons he felt this way, beginning with pointing out that existing social science literature indicated that there was no disparity proven in either Indiana or Georgia's implementation of their voter identification law. Attorney Hughes attempted to present two other reasons but both Judges Tatel and Collyer interrupted him, pointing out that what the court was seeking was evidence on whether or not SB 14 was retrogressive according to Section 5 of the VRA. The final point made by Judge Tatel was one that he kept returning to throughout the hearing when he asked, "What about a mixed motive that's partially racial?" And, whether, if it was, did it violate the retrogression standard of Section 5. Mr. Hughes agreed that it did.

Michael Coangelo, from the Department of Justice, presented the closing argument for the United States, pointing out SB 14 was "exactly the type of bill Congress had in mind when it passed the Voting Rights Act."[205] He argued that the *Arlington Heights* Factors laid the groundwork for the determination of racial purpose. Mr. Coangelo first argued that the large population growth of Latinos motivated the passage of SB 14 as declared by Representative Patricia Harless in her comments in the legislature. Additionally, SB 14's passage was characterized by unusual changes in procedures that accelerated the legislative process.[206] Mr. Coangelo pointed out that even with the criticism leveled at Dr. Ansolabehere's research it still stood given the weaknesses of the research the plaintiff experts had used to develop their critiques. Judge Tatel also interrupted him with his continuing concern over whether the entire passage of SB 14 was based on partisanship or race. Mr. Coangelo responded that "it's important to remember that on the record here and the reason that the *Arlington Heights* Factors for example, look at whether the stated goals were in fact the goals is that if you conclude they are not, you can conclude that something else is going on and perhaps most likely racial discrimination."[207] Judge Tatel responded, "Right." Attorney Coangelo continued:

> I think an important element of that question is that the record here not only shows that the Texas legislature or the legislators who supported the law were giving other reasons aside from partisanship. The record actually shows that they expressly disclaimed any reliance on partisanship. Our deposition designations include deposition testimony from the Senate bill sponsors saying that partisanship was no part of our purpose.[208]

Mr. Coangelo directed the court to look at the expert reports of Drs. Kousser and Flores as evidence for racial purpose pointing out that their research went unrefuted by the plaintiffs.

Judge Tatel then moved on to the question of retrogression, noting that Dr. Ansolabehere had not been able to gather data on federal identification cards, so he was resting his expert report solely on state identifications. He asked Mr. Coangelo how the court was able to pass judgment or reach a legal conclusion with only half the required information. Attorney Coangelo pointed out that Ansolabehere had attempted to gather data from Department of Defense, Secretary of State, and Homeland Security to no avail, so his analysis had to be based solely on state-level data.[209]

After discussions on Section 2 and retrogression standards under Section 5 that had been adjudicated throughout the years in relationship to poll taxes and the changing of polling places in covered states, the discussion turned to the SB 14 case specifically. Judge Tatel was curious if the distance and cost burdens incurred by indigent persons in Texas were enough to meet the retrogression standard, and Mr. Coangelo indicated that they were. Then the judge asked if Texas had ameliorated the process by making identification cards and their underlying documents free and expending money to substantially change the distance or transportation issues faced by indigents. If Texas had provided amelioration for the cost and distance burden, then what should the court conclude? Mr. Coangelo said that Texas would still not have met the retrogression standard because what SB 14 was proposing was tantamount to a "re-registration" process that, as a double process, would retrogress the voting strength of those bearing the most burden anyway. Judge Tatel then asked if it was possible for any covered state to have a voter identification card system. Attorney Coangelo pointed out that that was not the case, but each case was different and had to be treated as such. In this case, Texas simply failed the test of Section 5 particularly in light of the complete rejection of corrective amendments submitted by Senator Davis in the Texas State Senate and minority legislators in the Texas House.[210]

Defendant intervener attorneys Rosenburg and Hebert followed with the former presenting a statistical solution to the database issue that haunted the proceedings and Mr. Hebert presenting a classical argument highlighting the political and electoral damage SB 14 would do to the Latino and African American communities who had fought so hard and long for this right. Although Mr. Hebert's presentation was emotion-filled, he did provide the court with a summation of the testimony brought by all of the lay witnesses to remind the court of the human element in a case of this nature.

Mr. Hughes returned for his rebuttal but could only point to the social science literature as substantiation for Texas's petition. Both Judges Collyer and Tatel attempted to enter into a discussion of the differences between the Texas situation and the two states covered in the literature, Georgia and Indiana, but Attorney Hughes kept trying to make his point that DOJ had not made its case on retrogression. At one point, Mr. Hughes argued that Section 5 was burdensome and capricious but would not get involved in an extended discussion with the judges on this topic.

SUMMARY AND CONCLUSION OF BOTH CASES

Both cases had different beginnings, substances, and endings. The redistricting lawsuit was one brought by a group of voters against the State of Texas and was a constitutional claim based on the Fourteenth and Fifteenth Amendments to the Constitution and Section 5 of the Voting Rights Act. The voter identification lawsuit was a hearing petition by the State of Texas seeking preclearance under Section 5 of the Voting Rights Act. Many of the same actors were present and participated in both lawsuits because of their expertise and experience. Both matters required similar findings insofar as elements of proof are concerned. Under Section 5, as noted earlier in this volume, racial purpose and discriminatory effect must be shown by one of the petitioners. Discriminatory effect is clear; all one must show is that the policy under review has a disparate impact on a covered population. Racial purpose, on the other hand, is still a proof in evolution. The courts to date have let proof of purpose or intent remain a logical conclusion of effect. Essentially, if discriminatory effect is present, then, the courts have concluded, one may assume that there was a racial purpose. This conceptualization, however, particularly in light of the retreat on voting rights the current Roberts Court is making, is tenuous at best. As a result, a concerted effort to provide a stringent, disciplined social science conceptual design upon which a proof of racial purpose can be based is essential. This is the subject of the next chapter.

Although both of the cases were decided in favor of Latino and African American communities, they obviously had different conclusions. The Federal District three-judge panel in San Antonio, Texas, that oversaw the redistricting lawsuit ruled against the State of Texas, indicating that the state had acted with racial purpose and had designed a congressional and state house plan that diminished the voting power of Latinos and African Americans. The Court ordered the State to redraw the jurisdictional boundaries for both delegations to better reflect more equitable outcomes. The State appealed to the U.S. Supreme Court, who ruled that the three-judge panel had made an error in its directions to the State but that they were substantively correct and Texas had to abide by their ruling. This resulted in the court overseeing negotiations between the State Attorney General's Office and plaintiffs' attorneys over the redrawing of both maps. Neither side was completely satisfied with the outcome, but both settled on one recommended by the Court so that elections could proceed in 2012. The State of Texas was also ordered to decide whether to accept the Court-ordered plans as permanent or to develop other redistricting plans in the 2013 legislative session. The State decided to use the Court-ordered plan as the permanent one, with some modifications, until the 2020 round of redistricting. However, several plaintiffs were not satisfied with the modifications that resulted in the filing of additional suits by various plaintiffs with a trial heard in the summer of 2014.

The SB 14 Section 5 hearing was decided in favor of the Justice Department and the defendant interveners. The three-judge District of Columbia panel ruled that there was sufficient empirical evidence brought forth by Dr. Ansolabehere and his critics to indicate retrogression under Section 5 and refused preclearance to Texas. SB 14 or its subsequent edition was not brought forth in the 2013 state legislative session. However, as soon as the *Shelby* decision was handed down, Texas Attorney General Greg Abbott ordered the immediate implementation of SB 14. The first election that required photo identification was a midterm election in the Fall of 2013 that only dealt with some state constitutional amendments, and there were only a sprinkling of complaints of deleterious effects. In one case that received some publicity, State Senator Wendy Davis was not allowed to vote because her driver's license included her maiden name, Wendy Russell Davis, while her voting registration card had her listed as Wendy Davis. She was forced to sign an affidavit attesting to her identity before she was allowed to vote.[211]

NOTES

1. Judge Rodriguez asked this during the cross-examination of the redistricter who was responsible for drawing the Congressional Plan on the fourth day of the trial, Sep. 9, 2011. It appears that the question may have mirrored the judge's frustration as to the politics that underlie the Texas redistricting process and was meant rhetorically. This statement appears in the Bench Trial Transcript at page 1002.

2. *White v. Regester.*

3. Each of the plaintiffs' opening statements which outline their basic arguments in the trial can be found in the Bench Trial Transcript of *Shannon Perez, et al. v. Rick Perry, et al.,* No. SA: 11–CV–360, Sep. 6, 2011, pp. 7–52.

4. Much of the narrative of this and the subsequent trial are taken from the trial transcripts, trial exhibits, and depositions from the various witnesses, interviews and the author's notes. The author was one of the expert witnesses appearing in both the redistricting and the voter identification trials. This particular comment was made to the author by one of the civil rights attorneys as the trial was about to begin.

5. 377 U.S. 533 (1964).

6. 478 U.S. 30 (1986).

7. All of these terms are professional redistricting jargon that provides colorful descriptors of what redistricters have done in order to deny minority communities of equal representation during the drawing process. *Cracking* is the intentional splitting of minority communities by drawing district lines through the community, thereby splitting their potential votes among various districts. *Stacking* is the act of taking a minority community and adding it on to another district. *Packing* is designed to increase the percentage of minority voters within a district.

8. It should be noted that the Attorney General (AG) had participated in the 2003 redistricting trial but did not show up for any sessions of the 2011 trial.

9. Mr. Schenck was Deputy Attorney General for Legal Counsel in the AG's office. He was considered chief legal counsel to the AG now in private practice.

10. Ibid., *Thornburg v. Gingles*, chap. 3, p. 95.

11. Michael Phillips asserts that the poll tax was passed for racial reasons in his "Texan by Color: The Racialization of the Lone Star State," in David O'Donald Cullen

and Kyle G. Wilkerson, eds. *The Texas Right: The Radical Roots of Lone Star Conservatism.* College Station, TX: Texas A & M University Press, 2014, pp. 10–14.

12. Dr. Chapa is a Professor of Demographics, Immigration and Immigration Policy at the Institute for Government and Public Affairs at the University of Illinois at Urbana-Champaign. His testimony appears at pp. 170–205.

13. Dr. Kousser is a Professor of History and Social Sciences at the California Institute of Technology (Cal Tech) and specializes in the intersection of race and politics in the South. He is the author of the award-winning *Colorblind Justice: Minority Voting Rights and the Undoing of the Second Reconstruction* (1999). His testimony appears in the Bench Trial Transcript at pp. 205–313.

14. Dr. Flores is the Distinguished University Research Professor in the Institute for Public Administration and Public Service at St. Mary's University in San Antonio, Texas. This was his third round of redistricting trials testifying as an expert and is a specialist in racially polarized voting, discerning racial purpose, Latino voting behavior, and Latino politics. His testimony appears at pp. 431–87.

15. Ibid., http://www.youtube.com/watch?v=hNKWISYPdZ4

16. Ibid.

17. The apportionment ratio is determined by dividing the entire population generated by the 2010 census by the total number of districts in the U.S. House of Representatives, 435. This figure, for 2010, was 698,488 and is the number used to draw each congressional district throughout the nation. This figure is, in turn, divided into the total population of each state to determine how many seats in the national House it will be allocated with the assumption that each state is required to have a minimum of one representative district regardless of the size of the state. As a result some small states that have less of a total population than the reapportionment ratio have only one U.S. Representative and two senators such as Wyoming or Alaska. Texas experienced the highest growth of any state and was awarded four additional districts, thus the debate, during the trial, of where to place additional seats and which new districts would have a majority-minority population.

18. Mr. Farenthold, although a conservative Republican, is the nephew of a well-known liberal Democratic former Texas politician, Francis "Sissy" Farenthold, who ran for Texas Governor in 1972 and 1974 and was considered as the vice presidential candidate for her party in 1972, losing the nomination to Senator Thomas Eagleton of Missouri.

19. Dr. Engstrom is one of the foremost statistical testifying experts in voting rights cases and was testifying in his third round of Texas redistricting. His testimony appears in pp. 487–548.

20. EI is a technique developed by Gary King at Harvard University. He explicates his technique in *A Solution to the Ecological Inference Problem: Reconstructing Individual Behavior from Aggregate Data* (Princeton, NJ: Princeton University Press, 1997).

21. Dr. Tijerina teaches at Austin Community College and is considered a very well-respected historian of Mexican Americans in Texas.

22. Korbel is an experienced civil rights attorney in Texas but appeared as an expert in this case. He argued the now famous *White v. Regester* case in 1974.

23. National Association for the Advancement of Colored People.

24. Dr. Murray is a Full Professor of Political Science at the University of Houston and has written one of the most influential texts on Texas politics that is in its sixth edition. He has also authored one of the few studies on the politics of Houston, Texas.

25. This also is covered by Ian Hardy-López in his *Dog Whistle Politics.*

26. Bench Trial Transcript, p. 865.

27. Ibid., p. 1057.

28. Dr. Ansolabehere is an expert on public opinion, the media, elections and representations and teaches in the Department of Government at Harvard. His testimony appears on pp. 1095–1144.

29. Bench Trial Transcript, p. 1124.

30. Ibid., p. 1125.

31. Ibid., p. 1136.

32. Dr. Lichtman is a history professor at American University in Washington, D.C., and is an expert in vote dilution, racially polarized voting, political history, and the application of research methods to voting rights cases. This was Dr. Lichtman's third appearance in a Texas redistricting trial. His testimony appears in pp. 1209–1262.

33. Bench Trial Transcript, pp. 1237–38.

34. Rep. Solomons did not seek reelection in 2012 and returned to the private sector as a lobbyist.

35. Bench Trial Transcript, p. 1665.

36. Ibid., p. 1667.

37. Ibid., p. 1571–75.

38. Ibid., p. 1593.

39. Ms. Riggs is a staff attorney for the Southern Coalition for Social Justice and was one of the attorneys representing the NAACP during the trial.

40. They had testified earlier and their testimony will be covered shortly.

41. Bench Trial Transcript, pp. 1634–35.

42. Bench Trial Transcript, pp. 903–904.

43. Ibid., p. 906.

44. Ibid., pp. 907–908.

45. Ibid., p. 910.

46. "136" was a reference to Congressional Plan 136 (C-136) that had come up earlier in Mr. Downton's testimony. Ibid., p. 912.

47. Ibid., pp. 912–13.

48. Ibid., pp. 913–15.

49. Ibid., pp. 916–20.

50. Ibid., p. 921.

51. Ibid., pp. 930–31.

52. Ibid., pp. 931–39.

53. Ibid., p. 973.

54. Ibid., pp. 995–96.

55. Ibid., pp. 1008–1009.

56. Ibid., pp. 1010–12.

57. Ibid., p. 1023.

58. Ibid., pp. 1419–20.

59. Ibid., pp. 1424–26.

60. Ibid., p. 1426.

61. Ibid., pp. 1426–27.

62. Ibid., p. 1427.

63. Ibid., p. 1443.

64. Ibid., p. 1447.

65. Cited in chapter 2, p. 71.

66. Bench Trial Transcript, pp. 1460–61.

67. Ibid., pp. 1463–64.

68. Ibid., pp. 1472–73.

69. Ibid., pp. 1473–74.

70. There are four House districts wholly within Hidalgo County and another that absorbs the excess population of Cameron County. All districts with the exception of House District 41 were represented by Democrats. Mr. Peña, who represented 41 during the 2011 session, was a Democrat but switched parties at the beginning of his term. He did not win reelection to his seat in 2012.

71. Bench Trial Transcript, 1478.

72. Ibid., pp. 1478–80.

73. Dr. Alford is an Associate Professor of Political Science at Rice University who is an expert in elections and voting behavior and has testified for defendants in many voting rights cases. This was Dr. Alford's second round of redistricting.

74. Bench Trial Transcript, pp. 1789–91.

75. Ibid., p. 1832.

76. Ibid., pp. 1835–37.

77. Ibid., p. 1838.

78. Ibid., p. 1839.

79. Ibid., p. 1841.

80. Ibid., p. 1935.

81. Bench Trial Transcript, pp. 1966–1968.

82. Ibid., p. 1968.

83. Ibid., p. 1983.

84. Ibid., pp. 1983–84.

85. Ibid., p. 1996.

86. Ibid., p. 1997.

87. 541 U.S. 267 (2004).

88. Bench Trial Transcript, p. 2001.

89. 462 U.S. 725 (1983).

90. 7:1988cv00154 (W.D. Tex.).

91. 564 S.W.2d 400 (1978).

92. 944 F2d 902 (1991).

93. 840 F2d 943 (1988).

94. 812 F2d 943 (1987).

95. Bench Trial Transcript, p. 2088. This is an argument treated in political science theory literature by Haney-López in his *Dog Whistle Politics* and Cullen and Wilkerson in *The Texas Right*.

96. Ibid., pp. 2098–2125.

97. Ibid., p. 2147.

98. San Antonio Country Club was immediately across the street from the congressman's district line and is reputably the club of "old San Antonio money."

99. Ibid., p. 2226.

100. 129 S.Ct. 1231

101. Bench Trial Transcript, p. 2318.

102. *Texas v. Holder, et al.,* No. 12–128 (July 9, 2012)

103. Senate Bill 14 will also be referred to as the Texas Voter ID Bill throughout this discussion.

104. Bench Trial Transcript, p. 6.

105. Ibid.

106. *Crawford v. Marion County Election Board,* 553 U.S. 181 (2008).

107. Ibid., p. 38.

108. Ibid.

109. Ibid., p. 42.

110. Ibid., p. 43.

111. She did not indicate what these problems were but they may have been a reference to the senate's concern that undocumented aliens were crossing the border to cast fraudulent ballots, which is an argument that had no basis in fact but was used as a public relations ploy on the part of those favoring Senate Bill 14.

112. Bench Trial Transcript, p. 43.

113. Bench Trial Transcript, p. 71.

114. Ibid., p. 75.

115. Ibid., p. 80.

116. Ibid., p. 88.

117. Ibid., pp. 94–95.

118. Ibid., p. 112.

119. Ibid., pp. 114–18.

120. Ibid., p. 118.

121. Tim Eaton, "UPDATED: Rep. Donna Howard Addresses House," *Austin American Statesman, Statesman.com,* March 22, 2011. This was an updated article from the original and was updated to add her speech at the conclusion of the hearing.

122. Bench Trial Transcript, pp. 120–21.

123. Ibid., p. 122.

124. Ibid., p. 123.

125. Ibid., pp. 202–14.

126. Ibid., pp. 214–17.

127. Ibid., pp. 255–57.

128. Ibid., p. 289.

129. The timing of this request was debated in the courtroom and it came to light that Senator Williams had requested this report after SB 14 had been approved. The basis for his request, according to the trial transcript, was that he wanted to see if rural voters in West Texas had appropriate identification. Yet it appears originally in the transcript that his request was made during the SB 14 hearings.

130. Ibid., pp. 307.

131. This is an interesting fact because it was during one of the committee hearings of this committee where the YouTube video was filmed of Senator Harris deriding a witness for using Spanish to present his testimony. Senator Williams was the presiding officer during the particular session when the incident occurred. The video was used in the redistricting lawsuit and is referred to early in this chapter.

132. Bench Trial Transcript, p. 323.

133. Ibid.

134. A Texas State identification card looks very similar to a Texas driver's license. The principal difference is that each is labeled either as a driver's license or identification card.

135. The license to carry list is a list of all individuals who possess a photo identification permit allowing them to carry a firearm openly in Texas.

136. Bench Trial Transcript, p. 446.

137. Ibid., p. 452

138. Ibid., p. 707.

139. Ibid., p. 708.

140. Ibid.

141. Ibid., p. 709.

142. Ibid.

143. Ibid., pp. 712–15.

144. Ibid., pp. 721–32.

145. Ibid., pp. 733–45.

146. Ibid., p. 746.

147. Ibid., p. 774.

148. Ibid., p. 786.

149. Ibid., p. 787.

150. Ibid., pp. 788–93.

151. Ibid., p. 813.

152. See discussion in chapter 3, pp. 125–29.

153. Ibid., pp. 480–83.

154. Ibid., p. 495.

155. Ibid., p. 557.

156. Ibid., p. 558.

157. Ibid., p. 559.

158. Ibid.

159. Ibid.

160. Ibid., pp. 559–60.

161. Dr. Kousser had testified in the earlier redistricting lawsuit.

162. Bench Trial Transcript, p. 581.

163. Ibid., p. 582.

164. Ibid., p. 11, n.14.

165. Ibid., p. 594.

166. Ibid., p. 595.

167. Ibid., p. 599.

168. Ibid., p. 601.

169. Ibid., p. 602.

170. Ibid., pp. 656–58.

171. Ibid., p. 838. The disposition of this case can be found at *Wright v. Weaver, et al.,* No. 12–40421, USDC No. 4:07–CV-369, March, 2013.

172. Ibid., p. 882.

173. Ibid., p. 885.

174. Ibid., p. 897.

175. Ibid., p. 899.

176. Ibid., pp. 902–908.

177. Ibid., p. 935.

178. Ibid., p. 943.

179. This expert, like Dr. Kousser, had also testified in the previous Texas redistricting case in 2011.

180. Bench Trial Transcript, p. 945.

181. Ibid.

182. Ibid., p. 946.

183. Ibid.

184. Ibid., p. 947.

185. His design appears in his report to the court but was not directly discussed during his testimony but will be discussed in the next chapter.

186. An interview with a MALDEF official revealed that they had defeated more than eighty-five pieces of anti-immigrant legislation during the 2011 session.

187. Ibid., p. 947.

188. Ibid., p. 948.

189. Ibid., pp. 949–63.

190. Help America Vote Act, PL 157–252.

191. Bench Trial Transcript, pp. 1063–1067.

192. Ibid., pp. 1067–1069.

193. Ibid., p. 1070.

194. Ibid., pp. 1071–79.

195. Ibid., p. 1080.

196. Ibid.

197. Dr. Lichtman, like Kousser, Flores, and Ansolabehere, had also testified in the 2011 redistricting trial.

198. Bench Trial Transcript, pp. 1081–1104.

199. Ibid., p. 1104.

200. Ibid., p. 1111.

201. Ibid., pp. 1122–23.

202. Ibid., pp. 1137–64.

203. Ibid., p. 1324.

204. Ibid., p. 1326.

205. Ibid., p. 1407.

206. Ibid., p. 1418.

207. Ibid.

208. Ibid.

209. Ibid., pp. 1425–30.

210. Ibid., pp. 1443–48.

211. Shelly Kofler, "New Voter ID Law Forces Governor Candidate Wendy Davis To Sign Affidavit To Vote," *Kera News*, http://keranews.org/post/new-voter-id-law-forces-governor-candidate-wendy-davis-sign-affidavit-vote, October 28, 2013.

Chapter Six

There Is a Method to This Madness

WHY THE FACTORS?

This volume began as an inquiry into a methodological technique and it is on one level; on another it is a look into how a political system can shield a history of racial prejudice in the public policy process. The methodological technique developed here was dictated by the judicial system but refined by the requirements governing social science research. This unique arrangement is the result of the unusual circumstances that gave birth to the need for the technique, civil rights litigation. As a result of the birthing circumstances, the methodology must meet two standards for legitimacy and acceptance simultaneously; one legal, the other scholarly.

The legal requirements were laid down by the Supreme Court in *The Village of Arlington Heights v. Metropolitan Development Corporation* (1977) and have been modified slightly and referred to here as simply the *Arlington Heights* Factors *(AHFs)*. As demonstrated in an earlier chapter there are ten factors, each having a different number of variables that require operationalization in order to gather the data required to bring the factors to life. The number of variables and whether they require empirical or qualitative data depend on the particular situation under investigation. This will become evident as the factors are applied to the two case studies presented in the previous chapter. The principal reason for this is simply that every case is different, and each case may not require or have the data readily available to fit the variables under each factor.

What makes the *AHFs* acceptable to the court is that the court recommended them initially as areas where plaintiffs might seek the type of data that prove whether an actor or set of decision makers acted with racial purpose. Still, the courts are the final arbiters in legal matters and they determine what evidence is appropriate in these types of cases. The first requirement for the proof of racial purpose is that they pass legal scrutiny. However, what have yet to be explored here are the requirements from the world of social science research that make the *AHFs* as presented here acceptable to the world of scholarship. Here we look to the domain of research design for an answer to this query.

THE SCIENTIFIC METHOD AND *AHF*s

Generally, "good" social science requires that a research endeavor be organized in such a way that it follows a well-organized, commonsensical structure between the statement of the initial research question and achievement of the final answer. Oftentimes, in both the literature and nonscholarly circles, one will hear reference to the application of "the scientific method" as a way of ensuring that a research endeavor is well structured, disciplined, and controlled enough so that a clear answer to the posited question is derived. As a result within each step of the method, for instance in asking the initial question, certain controls or rules govern the process. What has come to be known as the scientific method is really a structured way in which to approach a research effort and is generally referred to as the standard governing acceptable research in both the natural and social sciences. [1]

The courts are also very cognizant of what is good science, having set down certain requirements for expert research under Rule 702 which were mentioned earlier but repeated here to refresh one's memory:[2]

1. the expert's scientific, technical, or other specialized knowledge will help the trier of fact to understand the evidence or to determine a fact in issue;
2. the testimony is based on sufficient facts or data;
3. the testimony is the product of reliable principles and methods; and
4. the expert has reliably applied the principles and methods to the facts of the case.

These rules were partially due to expert testimony submitted during the *Daubert v. Merrell Dow Pharmaceuticals*[3] trial and are sometimes referred to as the *Daubert Principles* or *Rules*. Generally, any testimony submitted by an expert witness that does not meet *Daubert* scrutiny may be excluded from the trial evidence and can jeopardize the plaintiff's or defendant's case. The expert must be cognizant that the report must assist the judges in understanding the evidence so they can reach an appropriate decision. Arguably the most important standard under Rule 702 is the first because it requires the witness to bring forth evidence that only an expert in the field is capable of generating that can "help the trier of fact to understand the evidence or to determine a fact in issue." This rule substantiates the presence of the expert and her report in the trial.

The Rule 702 specifications appear to be a declaration that any expert witness testimony must follow the principles of scientific investigation. The *Daubert* decision itself is insightful because the court is very specific and explains in great detail each of the principles. Suffice it to say there are references throughout the court's opinion speaking to scientific principles, appropriate methodologies, and so forth that closely resemble the language describing what the academy and scholars refer to as the scientific method.

The method[4] itself has a long history beginning with Aristotle through what has come to be known as the "Scientific Revolution"[5] in Western civilization. Contemporaneously, what is referred to as the scientific method varies from discipline to discipline yet still is centered on several core principles. Essentially, the following elements would fit the characteristics that define the scientific method and must be present in every research design or process:

- The formulation of a research question,
- The construction of a hypothesis,
- The identification of variables to be studied,
- Testing of the hypothesis,
- Evaluation of results,
- Suggestions for further research.

The above characteristics are derived from various lists from both the natural and social sciences, but they appear to include the core principles of the characteristics required for a research model or effort to be considered "good science." Besides the above steps and structure, the method allows for the research to be replicated, subject to external review, and data recorded and shared with other researchers. The next step is to determine how the *Arlington Heights* Factors measure up to the Scientific Method principles. One approach is to treat all of the factors as a research model and evaluate the entire model weighing the various parts against the principles set forth in the Method.

Formulation of a Question

The formulation of the question is important because the question itself will guide the research endeavor determining both the variables to be identified and the method of analysis. Most important, if the question is not structured correctly, one may not be able to provide an appropriate response even after all the data are gathered and analyzed. The research questions in both cases discussed in this volume are fundamentally the same: "Was there racial purpose or intent underlying the manner in which the Texas House of Representatives and Congressional districts were determined and drawn?" And, "Was there racial purpose or intent underlying the construction and passage of Senate Bill 14, the Voter Identification and Verification Bill in Texas?"

Both questions meet the criteria of a research question. They are simple, direct, and identify what variables need to be operationalized in order to answer the question. The explanatory variable is the same in both questions "Is there the existence of racial purpose" in both the redistricting and voter identification legislative processes. The question's structure does not presuppose the answer but clearly identifies what is being sought, whether a specific focus is embedded in the decisional process that gave birth to both pieces of legislation.

Constructing the Hypotheses

The most important aspect of hypothesis construction is ensuring that the hypothesis is testable. The testability of any hypothesis depends on the nature of the research strategy, whether one is utilizing a quantitative or qualitative approach. In this case, the data have determined that a mixed-methods research approach was the most appropriate. As a result, rather than constructing a hypothesis in the traditional sense where one determines whether to accept or reject the hypothesis depending upon the outcomes of a statistical test, we rely on a more generalized hypothesis construction.

The first step in constructing a hypothesis is to determine the theoretical foundation of the hypothesis. In the two cases here, developing an understanding of the theoretical foundation requires delving into the world of racial studies, principally the work of Ian Hardy-López, Eduardo Bonilla-Silva, Joel Olson, and Richard Delgado. The work of each of these scholars has contributed to the development of a clear understanding of what the relationship is between racial purpose and the Texas legislative process that gave birth to the congressional and state house redistricting plans and the construction and passage of Senate Bill 14. A thorough reading of what these scholars contributed to this discussion allows one to conclude that the research question is viable and that a research hypothesis can be constructed to answer the question.

Synthesizing the scholarship in this area is difficult because each scholar's work is complex, containing many layers of analysis. Nevertheless, their combined research leads to the theory underlying the analysis in this volume. Essentially, racial purpose was the driving force behind the manner in which redistricting was pursued in the determination of some of the congressional and state house districts and racial purpose was the motivation behind the creation and passage of the voter identification law in Texas. The reason this is a reasonable assumption is based on the notion that race plays a unique role in the history of Texas politics and is an essential element in the policy process under certain circumstances. The manner in which race is used in the political process is not designed to necessarily demean or hurt anyone; rather, race is used as a political weapon to gain and maintain political power in Texas by political parties. The victims of this action, which has been labeled *strategic racism*, are Latinos, African Americans, and Asian Americans. Images of these racial minority groups have been used to marshal voters to a political party's standard and to organize legislators to pass legislation that is designed to ensure that the political party maintains its position of dominance in the state and its political institutions.

Based upon this theory then, the research questions here are straightforward. "Was there racial purpose in the manner in which congressional and state house redistricting was pursued in the Texas legislature during the 82nd Session held in 2011?" The second question is similar to the first. "Was there racial purpose in the design and passage of Senate Bill 14 during the 82nd Texas Legislative Session of 2011?" From these research questions come the research hypotheses. Hypotheses 1 is "Racial purpose influenced the manner in which certain congressional and state house districts were designed during the 2011 Texas Legislative Session." Hypothesis 2 is "Racial purpose influenced the submission, design and passage of Senate Bill 14—The Voter Identification and Verification Act of 2011." A thorough review of the data will allow the expert to accept or reject either hypothesis.

Identification of Variables to be Studied

Both questions identify the explanatory variable, racial purpose or intent, and the variable to be affected, both pieces of legislation. Although the variables have been identified, they still require operationalization. The unique nature of these variables does not make operationalization easy. Each of these variables is not susceptible to simple definition where a single or simple value can be assigned for statistical analysis. For instance, "racial purpose or intent" cannot be operationalized as a simple variable having dichotomous variables or values that can be constructed into an index or scale. "Racial purpose" is a variable that must be a composite of other variables, some of which are quantifiable; others are not and must be measured qualitatively. It goes without saying that in the future some enterprising scholar may construct a statistical index or measure quantifying a concept that may be labeled "racial purpose" but to date one does not exist. From a legal perspective, this situation makes the determination of "racial purpose" or other similar variables subject to the "totality of circumstances test." In other words, one must gather a great deal of information from sources that contribute to an understanding of a concept such as racial purpose in order to define it substantively. This is why it is essential to construct chronologies, historiographies, discourse analyses, ethnographies, and other types of qualitative data in order to bring definition and understanding to concepts such as "racial purpose." Three of the four *Arlington Heights* Factors are designed to encourage the use of qualitative research techniques in cases where there is no direct evidence of "racial purpose." Finally, the unique circumstances of each case require that the questions be treated separately.

RACIAL POLARIZATION

In the redistricting case, operationalizing the requisite variables includes providing evidence of a history of racially polarized voting. Although racial polarization data indicate how differently racial groups vote from each other, they also indicate that there is a deeper division between races. This is particularly true if there are long-standing patterns of racial polarization. These data do not reveal what the differences are or what they are; racial polarization simply reveals that divisions exist. Racial polarization as defined in both the social science literature and by the Court in *Thornburg v. Gingles* is understood as existing where there is "a consistent relationship between [the] race of the voter and the way in which the voter votes." Racial polarization can also be understood as where "black [Latino] voters and white voters vote differently."[6] Reiterating, the race of the candidate is irrelevant only the preference of the voters is what is important when measuring racial polarization. Here evidence of racially polarized voting is generally provided through the development of statistical analyses of elections that go back to the previous redistricting lawsuits in 2003 and 2006. There were 169 elections analyzed that included both general and primary elections in the jurisdictions challenged. Racial polarization was indicated through the results of the statistical analyses that, in turn, were the results of the application of various types of statistical regression techniques. In this case, the court approved and accepted techniques that included EI (Ecological Inference) and multiple regression.

The 169 elections analyzed sought to discover if there was evidence that indicated if Latinos voted as a group significantly different from Anglos and whether African Americans and Latinos together voted significantly different from Anglos. The analyses were divided into two parts. Ecological Inference regression was conducted on 104 elections that looked at the voting patterns of Latino versus Anglo voters for the same candidates. Of the 104 elections, 95 or 91.3 percent of the elections were discovered to be extremely racially polarized. There were fifty two counties covered in the analyses that included six general elections, five Democratic Party, and two Republican Party primary elections. The elections were selected from the 2008 and 2010 rounds of partisan elections and featured a Latino candidate versus an Anglo. For demonstration purposes, these types of elections produce a clear picture of whether elections are generally polarized since the assumption is that voters will vote for candidates of their own racial groups in areas or regions that have a history of racial tensions or strained race relations between the groups under scrutiny.

The remaining sixty-five elections were subjected to multiple regression analysis where Latino, African American, and Anglo voters were included in the equation. Of the sixty-five elections, fifty-nine were determined to be significantly racially polarized with Latinos and African Americans voting substantially differently than Anglo voters. These elections were the identical ones that were subjected to EI analyses and covered the same counties. Essentially, the analyses discovered that Latinos and African American voters cast their ballots in substantially larger percentages for different candidates in the thirteen elections studied than did Anglos. Anglos did not vote for Latino candidates except in the Democratic Primary in Travis County. This last situation can be considered as an exception or anomaly, because Travis County is considered the most liberal Democratic area of Texas.[7] The reason that elections from only 2008 and 2010 were selected was that the 2002, 2004, and 2006 election results had been presented in the previous trial in 2006–2007; nevertheless, the racial polarization patterns remained relatively the same from expert reports submitted in previous voting rights litigation covering the 1990 and 2000 redistricting lawsuits.

It is also important to speak to the intensity or degree of polarization in all of the elections. Dr. Engstrom's research indicated that in the bivariate analyses all regions showed that upward of 82 percent of Latinos preferred Latino candidates; only Harris County showed a lower percentage. Still Latino support for Latino candidates stood at 75 percent. Generally, Anglo support for Latino candidates ranged between 17 percent and 24 percent in most regions except for Travis County, which showed a high of 48 percent of Anglo support for Latino candidates. Only in the most liberal of all Texas counties did Anglos vote in high numbers for Latino candidates; nevertheless, the support level did not rise above 50 percent.[8]

As the information indicates, operationalizing a variable such as racial polarization is a unique process. One cannot simply aggregate all of the information into one meaningful index unless the polarization is as severe as it appears in Dr. Engstrom's Expert Report and conclude whether a community is racially polarized or not. Generally a variable such as racial polarization, although given a specific definition and operationalized easily, must be reported in narrative form rather than as an aggregated statistic because the variable must be presented as one that depicts the behavior of voters over several election cycles. Additionally, it is important to discuss any outlying elections such as the three Democratic Primary elections in Travis County that indicated no racial polarization.

One may argue that the voters appear to prefer candidates of one particular party over another and this may have some credence, but the extreme intensity of the polarization as evidenced by the percentages of support among the different groups for Latino candidates can lead one to suspect that race and not party is driving voter preferences. The race/partisanship quandary is at the heart of this debate; as a result, the regression analysis of elections is not and cannot be the only data relied upon in determining racial purpose. Regression analysis by itself cannot parse the question as to whether a voter is casting a ballot because they are driven to do so as an ethnic or racial voter or whether the individual is casting their vote as a partisan. Consistent patterns of racially polarized elections, however, do give an indication of the racial divide within a community or jurisdiction. Qualitative data, historical information, patterns of disparate treatment, and so forth must be combined with the regression statistics in order to obtain a deeper understanding of the cause for patterns of racially polarized elections. The answer to Judge Tatel's concern as to whether racially polarized elections reflect partisan or racial preferences may be found in the depth the qualitative data provide to the patterns of racial polarization. That Latinos or African Americans consistently prefer candidates of one party to another may be a reflection of disparate treatment at the hands of individuals identified with one of the parties. In other words elections that appear polarized along both partisan and racial lines may not be simply either/or but both given whether minority group voters are pushed or pulled from one party to the other. The qualitative data may reveal the "push or pull factors" driving Latinos or African Americans from one party to another. These factors may include information derived by obtaining data over the variables identified by the *Arlington Heights* Factors. The next question is to determine what other factors affect the intensity of the racial voting patterns.

The attorney for the Latino Redistricting Task Force submitted the racial polarization data discussed here and prepared by Dr. Richard Engstrom as part of the *Arlington Heights* Factors data for both the redistricting and the voter identification cases. The reason for using the same data for both cases is simply that both cases involved proving that the State of Texas was in violation of the provisions of the VRA's retrogression standards. An essential element of the proof is that the courts must consider the extent to which elections are racially polarized when making their decision. Racial polarization is an important concept because by itself it is a strong indication that a given jurisdiction or society is racially separated politically. Severe polarization such as that existing in Texas is a reflection of the racism and racist antagonism that has existed between Anglos, Latinos, and African Americans throughout the history of the state.

HISTORICAL BACKGROUND OF THE DECISION

Redistricting

Another variable that requires sophistication to operationalize is the Historical Background of the Decision. These data, which have already been presented in this volume in an earlier chapter, are impossible to quantify so are generally presented in a qualitative format. The historical record of the nineteenth and twentieth centuries highlighting the various race-specific policies of the State of Texas toward Latinos is clear. Some of the policies designed to control the social standing of Latinos in the state include poll taxes, the maintenance of a separate educational system, racial covenants in real estate transactions, and the creation of separate social institutions. In the world of electoral politics Texas, besides the poll taxes[9] that were levied for many years before being ruled unconstitutional in the 1960s, continued to create barriers to the political participation of Latinos in the redistricting processes since the inception of the "one person, one vote" constitutional principle adopted in *Reynolds v. Simms.*

The history of racial discrimination in the redistricting process begins with the landmark *White v. Regester* lawsuit that was brought by Mexican Americans and African Americans in Texas in 1973 that challenged the multimember state house representational system that was used in Bexar and Dallas Counties.[10] The Court, with Justice Byron White delivering the opinion, ruled that the at-large system was structured in such a way as to not allow both groups to have an opportunity to elect candidates of their choice. The decision noted that the State of Texas had not been particularly responsible during the redistricting process because it created single-member districts in the large urban county of Harris while limiting Bexar and Dallas to multimember districts. Additionally, the Court noted that the state had deviated from the 10 percent population deviation rule established in *Mahan v. Howell*[11] in establishing the multimember districts. The Court also noted that the majority vote and "place" system of election coupled with a past history in both counties of severe voter registration requirements and discrimination in many areas including housing, education, and employment created a situation that mitigated against Latinos and African Americans from fully participating in the political life of the counties.[12]

The dispersion of minority voters among various districts to ensure incumbent protection and the maintenance of control of all the state legislative bodies by the ruling party has been a recurring theme since the inception of single-member districts in the 1970s. During the 1971 congressional redistricting, for instance, the legislature created a congressional district "with enough African American voters to elect an African American to Congress," in Harris County.[13] State Senator Barbara Jordan (D-Harris) left her seat and ran successfully in the new congressional district. Her departure, however, had dire circumstances for her African American constituents. Instead of preserving Jordan's old senate district that would have created the possibility that African American voters could have elected another African American to the state senate, the legislature divided up her district, dispersing the African American voters into other districts to preserve Democratic senatorial incumbents.[14]

The 1981 redistricting round emerged as a struggle between Governor Bill Clements, a Republican, and the state legislature dominated by Democrats. The Democrats wanted to protect and fortify districts for incumbents in Harris and Dallas Counties. The governor wanted a new majority-minority district in Dallas. The governor's motives were not altogether altruistic or his actions made in the spirit of civil rights. Governor Clements wanted to concentrate African American voters into one district in order to weaken the constituency base of Democratic incumbents in the Dallas–Fort Worth metroplex. The state legislature passed a plan protecting their incumbents in the Dallas–Fort Worth region, which Governor Clements vetoed. The deadlock threw the plan into the hands of the state's Legislative Redistricting Board, which drew a plan with minority opportunity districts in both Harris and Dallas counties. Litigation ensued that saw the plan reach all the way to the U.S. Supreme Court, who ordered the legislature to draw a new plan which included an opportunity district in Harris but not Dallas County; the plan was signed into law by a new Democratic Governor, Mark White.[15]

In 1991 the State of Texas was sued once again over the redistricting of the state House, Senate, State Board of Education, and Congressional districts by LULAC (League of United Latin American Citizens). This redistricting process was interesting on several levels, but it revealed a new strategy in the partisan struggle over control of the state government apparatus. From Reconstruction through the 1980s Texas had been a one-party state dominated by the Democratic Party. In the meantime, the Texas Republican Party, since the election of John Tower to the United States Senate succeeding Lyndon Johnson in 1961, joined Latinos and African Americans in the suits. The Republican Party attorneys argued that Latinos were being denied their share of districts in each of the four representative chambers. The political strategy was to pack many Latino voters into districts that would elect more Latinos. This strategy would also yield more Anglo districts, allowing Republicans to be more competitive with the Anglo Democrats in these latter districts. Republican Party operatives understood that the racially polarized electorate could be used to their advantage and began winning elections in the Anglo majority districts away from the Anglo Democrats. The redistricting strategy employed by Republican operatives was seen as part of an overall strategy to wrest control of the Texas State governmental apparatus from the Democratic Party.[16]

By the time the 2001 redistricting process arrived, the Republican Party was in firm control of the state senate and governorship, and plans were created for all four chambers that favored their reelection chances once more. As in the previous redistricting rounds, representatives of both the African American and Latino communities once again sued the State of Texas. The circumstances in 2001, however, were different than before. Redistricting was not discussed during the regular legislative session. In fact, the session expired without issuing a new redistricting plan. Additionally, Governor Perry refused to call a special session to redistrict. Various groups sued and forced the courts to create a plan that stood for the 2002 general election. The legislature decided to keep the court-imposed plan and was subsequently sued over the congressional plan that appeared to be one designed to allow the Republican Party to take control of the Texas delegation. The court ruled that CD23 was drawn to impede the ability of Latinos to elect a candidate of their choice. Additionally, the state had drawn CD23 with the express understanding that the demographics of the district were changing and voting increasingly more for Democratic candidates.[17] As an aside, this redistricting process featured the much-publicized intervention by then Representative Tom DeLay to ensure that the process favored Republican Party candidates.[18] The court forced the redrawing of CD23 which, in the subsequent election, elected a Democrat to Congress. The suit by LULAC argued that the district had been configured to ensure the election of a Republican by removing Latino voters from the district and replacing them with Anglo voters from areas that normally voted Republican. Prior to the final reconfiguration of CD23, a Republican Latino, Henry Bonilla, had held the office, but it was demonstrated by an expert witness that he had been losing the support of Latino voters in every election.

The 2010 redistricting process opened with expectations high on the side of Republicans and Latinos because reapportionment had assigned four new congressional seats to Texas. The Republicans clearly had their eyes on obtaining minimally three of the four seats with one being allocated as a "minority-majority VRA district."[19] Latinos expected the exact opposite hoping for minimally three of the four seats given that the population of Latinos had grown dramatically between 2000 and 2010. However, after the redistricting process was completed, it was difficult to discern how many Latino opportunity districts had been drawn. It was clear, though, that at least three of the new congressional districts had been drawn allowing Republicans to prevail and extend their control over the Texas delegation. Once the plans were passed by the legislature and signed into law by Governor Perry, lawsuits were filed by ten plaintiffs including the Latino Redistricting Task Force, LULAC, NAACP, the Democratic Party, and various individuals including several congresspersons.[20] In her opening arguments in the redistricting lawsuit, Ms. Nina Perales, the lawyer representing the Latino Redistricting Task Force, pointed out that between 1990 and 2000 Latinos had been responsible for 60 percent of the state's growth and had only been rewarded with one new congressional seat. Between 2000 and 2010, Texas Latinos again had been responsible for 60 percent of the state's population growth and again were rewarded with one congressional seat. She felt that the Texas legislature had been racially discriminatory in the manner in which congressional and state house districts had been allocated and the districts drawn.

During the trial, evidence was brought forth indicating that there had been racial intent in the drawing of several of the congressional and house districts. The evidence was not simply the empirical data indicating how voters from various racial groups were split or moved about in the various districts under scrutiny, but it was also qualitative and substantive. Essentially, a smoking gun e-mail was uncovered during the discovery phase that was of a communication between two Republican Party operatives. The two operatives were attorneys who worked for the Speaker of the Texas House and the Chair of the House Redistricting Committee. The memo discusses the construction of a "metric" that would allow redistricters to identify Latino majority precincts with low turnout rates that could be interchanged with high-performance Latino-majority precincts in two congressional districts, 23 and 27. The e-mail continues stating that if the "metric" is implemented properly then the result will be a congressional district that is a majority Latino district but will elect a Republican to office. The Federal District court saw this as the redistricters acting with a racial purpose to ensure Republican victory. The construction and use of the "metric" would act as a dilutive element and result in the construction of districts where Latinos would not have the ability to elect a candidate of their choice in violation of the precepts of the VRA.

The historical background variable, then, must be constructed as a narrative because it reflects a long history, fifty years, of efforts on the part of the Texas legislature to draw districts in all four of the representational bodies that would keep Latinos and African Americans from electing politicians of their choice. Each decade saw the redistricting process take on a different level of sophistication from the initial round in 1970 through the most recent edition in 2010. In the early decades, 1970 and 1980, the legislature, then dominated by Democrats, simply drew districts the way they saw fit to ensure incumbent reelection. The 1990 round marked an interesting political moment because it saw the Republican Party joining with Latinos in an effort at undercutting the strength of the Democrat Party by assisting Latinos in their quest for additional minority-majority seats.[21] The Republican Party used the redistricting round and the VRA as a crucial step in their effort of taking control of the Texas State governmental structure. Once in power, the Republicans behaved just like Democrats except in a more sophisticated manner culminating with their construction of the "metric" in an effort to ensure compliance with VRA provisions while allowing them to keep electoral control of the representational delegations.

Beginning with the 1990 redistricting process, the Republicans clearly took advantage of the racially polarized electorate to manipulate the redistricting process to their advantage. This continuous pattern of the Texas state legislature manipulating the Latino vote guaranteeing incumbency protection is sufficient to describe the entire process as one based on racial intent. The historical record suggests neither party could or can maintain control of the various representational bodies without manipulating the populations of Latino and African American voters.

Voter Identification

The legislative history behind Senate Bill 14 is not as clear as to whether there was historically racial intent behind earlier versions of the 2011 legislation. There were efforts in the legislative sessions of 2005, 2007, and 2009 to pass voter identification legislation. It should be noted at the outset that much of the following discussion on the history of voter identification legislation in Texas is drawn from the expert reports written by Drs. Morgan Kousser and Henry Flores, who testified on behalf of the United States and the Rodriguez Defendant Interveners in the 2012 *Texas v. USA Section* hearing in Washington, D.C.

There were three attempts at passing a voter identification bill prior to the 2011 session. Republican Party members of either the state House or Senate initiated the efforts in the previous sessions, beginning in 2005. All three attempts failed for various reasons, but the most telling was that the Democratic Party delegation in both state chambers possessed the requisite numbers to be able to defeat all three efforts. The Republican sponsors argued every session that the principal reason for the voter identification bill was to deter in-person voter fraud. In every session, Democrats, mostly Senators Rodney

Ellis (Houston), John Whitmire (Houston), and Leticia Van de Putte (San Antonio) and Representative Rafael Anchia (Dallas), argued that voter identification was simply a blatant attempt on the part of Republican legislators to construct another voting barrier against the participation of voters who would most likely support Democratic candidates. The Democratic spokespersons argued that the circumstances of the bill would weigh more heavily on older, younger, and poorer voters and those of racial minority groups.

House Bill 1706, sponsored by Representative Mary Denny (R-Denton) in the 2005 session, represented the first of the three attempts at passing a voter identification law in Texas. The bill could not obtain a favorable vote in the House, so Ms. Denny attached her bill to SB 89, a bill governing the behavior of election clerks that had already passed the senate. This was accomplished in order to bypass a Senate vote making the bill subject to the two-thirds rule and suffering an ignominious defeat at the hands of Democratic senators who had sworn to defeat the bill. Attaching HB 1706 to a previously passed bill, which was unusual in and of itself, allowed the voter identification bill to go to the conference committee, where it died without a hearing as the legislative session ended.

In the 2007 legislative session, Representative Betty Brown (R-Henderson) sponsored HB 218 that was a duplicate of HB 1706 from the previous session though with more identification card restrictions. Ms. Brown advertised her bill as "designed to keep illegal aliens, noncitizens and other people otherwise not qualified" from casting fraudulent ballots. Again, Democrats argued that the bill was designed to suppress the votes of the poor, elderly, and minorities, or the voters who did not support Republicans. Lieutenant Governor David Dewhurst, a Republican with gubernatorial ambitions, attempted to call a vote on HB 218 after it arrived in the Senate. Still, the Democrats threatened that they were willing to use the provisions of the two-thirds rule to block a vote on the bill. Mr. Dewhurst's tactics were poorly timed in that two Democratic senators were ill, one severely, and were forced to return to the senate floor to cast a vote prohibiting HB 218 from coming to the floor for a vote. One senator had the flu and immediately after casting his vote, left the chambers and vomited in an outer office. The other was in a hospital in Houston, Texas, being treated for the rejection of a liver from a transplant operation. He left the hospital against his doctor's wishes, went to Austin, and cast his vote. A Republican colleague who was a physician moved to have a hospital bed placed in the sergeant-at-arms office so that the ill senator, Mario Gallegos, could receive the requisite medical attention while monitoring the proceedings in the event he had to return for another vote. The Lieutenant Governor finally relented in his attempts at forcing a vote, and HB 218 died in the senate for lack of a vote.[22]

At the beginning of the 2009 session, Mr. Dewhurst pushed through a repeal of the Senate's two-thirds rule which had been in operation for more than fifty years.[23] The new version of the voter identification bill was sponsored by Senator Troy Fraser (R-Horseshoe Bay) and ended up dying ignobly due to infighting among the Republicans. The line was drawn when the new Speaker of the House, Joe Straus from San Antonio, a moderate Republican, whose ascension was supported by the Democrats principally organized and engineered by the leadership of the Mexican American Legislative Caucus, appointed another moderate Republican as chair of the House Elections Committee. The new Speaker's election was designed to heal the tense relations that had arisen between representatives of both parties in the previous legislative session. The Speaker appointed Mr. Todd Smith (R-Fort Worth) as the new Elections Committee Chair who immediately announced that he "wasn't put on this committee to rig elections in my party's favor" promising "to do everything in my power to accommodate [Democrats'] concerns about disenfranchising any legal voters, including constituencies that may traditionally support Democrats more than Republicans."[24] This position appeared to upset his conservative colleagues, particularly Representative Betty Brown, who had harbored ambitions to chair the same committee; his position on the voter identification bill appeared to be the proverbial "straw that broke the camel's back." He pointed out that one of his goals was to put forth a photo voter identification bill that was not as stringent as Indiana's and would allow "voters without one to present two other forms of identification."[25] This incensed Ms. Brown, who threatened to amend SB 362 to make it stricter. Nevertheless, Representative Lamar Smith submitted a new bill that featured a "photo identification or two other documents" together with $7.5 million to encourage voter education and registration. Eric Opiela, the Executive Director of the Texas State Republican Party,[26] organized House Republicans, obtaining signatures from seventy-one of the seventy-six on a pledge that they would not support the new identification bill unless it took effect in 2010, allocated no money for voter registration, and required voters at the polls to present photo identification without alternatives. Those provisions foreshadowed what would become known as SB 14 in the 2011 legislative session. The essentials of the pledge eventually led to debates, delays, and negotiations that resulted in the death of SB 362 because no resolution was reached before the session ended. Democrats argued, as they did in the previous two sessions, that no in-person voter fraud existed and that voter identification was simply an attempt by Republicans to place constraints on minority voters making it difficult to politically participate.[27]

The 2011 legislative session opened with Republicans in firm control of both chambers. This session was most unusual because it featured not just the voter identification card issue but redistricting as well. Intensifying the atmosphere of the legislative session, more than one hundred pieces of legislation focusing on immigration-related issues were filed. Additionally, there were either three or five bills, depending upon how one classifies the bill, attempting to stipulate English as the official language of Texas.[28]

In-person voting fraud was still a concern among Republicans supporting voter identification bills except this time the early conversation centered on the need to create a voter identification bill that would prevent undocumented aliens from coming across the border to vote.[29] Former Texas Republican state director Royal Masset was quoted as saying that supporters of voter identification were "basically using sheer racism to pump their own political points. They're trying to exploit the public fear of illegal aliens."[30] Going further, Masset stated that the notion that illegal immigrants voted was "one of those urban myths that just has caught on and everyone assumes is true."[31]

In the State House Representative Todd Smith was replaced as chair of the Elections Committee by Patricia Harless (R-Spring), from a community just outside of Houston, who was considered more conservative. At the beginning of this legislative session, nine other voter identification bills besides SB 14 were filed. Additionally, as described by Dr. Kousser, four extraordinary measures to ensure passage of SB 14 were instituted at the beginning of the session:

—SB 14 was designated "emergency legislation" allowing for debate and passage within the first sixty days of the session.
—SB 14 was exempted from the two-thirds rule.
—Republicans persuaded two Democratic House members to switch party affiliation, thus ensuring them of a supermajority even if all the Democrats were not present for a vote.
—Passed a rule disallowing "chubbing" in the House.[32]

"Chubbing" is the act of contesting, questioning, or continuing debate on a bill from the Local and Consent Calendar endlessly and is tantamount to a filibuster except it is conducted by a group of legislators in the party executing the "chubb." This process slows the legislation in queue preventing consideration of bills behind the bill being "chubbed." Prior to Mr. Dewhurst's motion there had been no time limit on the "chubb." Democrats had used this tactic to prevent another identification bill in another session from reaching the floor for consideration. This time, Lt. Gov. Dewhurst had a resolution passed that did not allow "chubbing" after midnight of any given day.

The most important day in the House session was March 23, 2011, when SB 14 was debated on the floor. Democratic members, mostly the Latinos and African Americans, although two Anglo Democrats joined in the debate as well, raised questions concerning the existence of voter fraud, budgetary constraints, and possible violations of the VRA. They brought forth research from the previous legislative sessions that there was no evidence of in-person voter fraud even after the state Attorney General launched an investigation that cost $700,000. Representative Rafael Anchia (D-Dallas) was particularly articulate in his objections, first obtaining admissions from the bill's sponsor, Patricia Harless that in-person voter fraud is almost impossible. In order to commit in person fraud, one is required to obtain information and identify a registered voter who has no intention of voting, obtain an identification or registration card of that person, and then vote. Mr. Anchia noted that the public record indicated that the only evidence of voter fraud that existed was where individuals had mailed in ballots for other voters, an aspect of the election process that was not even addressed in SB 14. When confronted with information of the lack of evidence that in-person voting fraud had been committed during the 2009 session, Senator Fraser noted that the lack of evidence was a good reason for adopting a voter identification bill, stating, "The problem in Texas is, we don't have the ability to identify when some-body is doing this."[33] Apparently Senator Fraser concluded that the lack of evidence was the result of not having a policy in place to catch the offend-ers. In Senator Fraser's perception in-person voter fraud was occurring, the election judges simply were not equipped to catch the perpetrators, thus the lack of evidence. Presumably, SB 14 would provide election judges with the weapons necessary to combat and defeat voter fraud in the state.

During the House Committee Hearing on SB 14 on March 1, 2011, Mr. Da-vid Carter, who had served as an election judge in Temple, Texas, presented his testimony concerning the danger of illegal aliens voting. He pointed out:

> The danger of voter fraud is the illegals that come into this country, fraudulently commit perjury, commit—say they're citizens, and they get automatically on the voter list. That's a problem. And the photo ID kills that problem. It solves it with no changes to registration or anything else. Voter ID IS the only thing that can fix the problem.[34]

Representative Mark Veasey, an African American representative Democrat from Fort Worth, then asked Mr. Carter, "Why would people that are in the shadows, why would they want to risk a jail sentence by casting a vote as an illegal alien?" Mr. Carter said the state didn't have the resources to inves-tigate that question. Mr. Veasey then asked, "So, it's your contention that there's hordes of illegal immigrants coming to vote in Texas?" Mr. Carter's response, although lengthy, is worth quoting in its entirety because it reveals the racial intent driving the voter identification bill:

> Yes. . . . I think the problem of voter impersonation is a miniscule problem, and it's very hard to do, and I think that having—getting three fake IDs would be a real problem. *I don't worry about that. I worry about a 20 percent increase in the state population of illegal aliens coming across in McAllen and Mission*

and points further west, Laredo, and not being caught by Border Patrol and not
being detected in the interior—and they're registering to vote. They are being
registered. (italics added for emphasis) [35]

Mr. Carter's response reveals another urban myth but one that has been around for a long time in Texas—a fear of invasion by Mexicans to reclaim their historic lands. This xenophobia, first chronicled by Carey McWilliams in his seminal work *North from Mexico*[36] and subsequently by others,[37] is tantamount to the fear southern whites expressed of freed slaves slaughtering them in their sleep and raping white women. Mr. Carter's statement reflects a fear of losing the privilege he and Anglos enjoy because they are white and a fear that they will lose their place of privilege due to the dramatic demographic changes in the population, principally to Latinos. Mr. Veasey's argument, that it is not rational for noncitizens who are in the country illegally to risk their freedom to cast a vote in an election, is a reasonable statement. All research has indicated that illegal immigrants are in the United States for economic opportunity. The United States Bureau of the Census and Pew Hispanic Research Center have concluded that more than 90 percent of those in the United States illegally are employed. As complaints from Alabama, Georgia, and Texas farmers have indicated throughout recent debates over immigration policy, without illegal aliens, their industries would collapse. Entire sectors of the building and construction industries in the Southwest would also collapse without undocumented workers. So, why would these individuals who are struggling to make a living risk their freedom by violating a federal law and casting a fraudulent ballot in any election? Mr. Carter's response is one reflecting fear of large numbers of individuals crossing the border with Mexico—the cities of Mission, McAllen, and Laredo are directly on the Mexican border—just to disrupt American elections. Mr. Carter's response also reflects an understanding that whoever these fraudulent voters may be, they will not support candidates of his party, thus his need to stop them from voting. One can reasonably conclude that Carter is afraid of the growing population of Latinos who are eligible to vote and who will most likely vote for Democratic Party candidates; consequently he wants the Voter ID law to stop them from exercising their franchise. Mr. Carter is using the veil of a fear of illegal aliens to reflect his fear of Latinos. For him, and those who think like him, the term illegal alien represents all Latinos. He is shifting his rhetoric from one of blatant racism to one of "nonracist" racism.[38]

The debate shifted, as did the rhetoric, because of the lack of evidence that any undocumented individuals had crossed the border to participate in the American electoral process. The supporters of SB 14 then insisted that regardless of the lack of any in-person voter fraud, something still had to be done to protect the sanctity of the ballot ensuring confidence and integrity in the electoral system. Additionally, supporters argued that SB 14 would increase participation rates particularly in the minority communities because citizens would have increased confidence in the process.[39] Supporters used data from the states of Indiana and Georgia to bolster their contention of increased voter participation, but, as Dr. Kousser pointed out in his report, they had failed to note that both states had become hotly contested battleground states where elections in 2006 and 2008 became important to both parties.[40] Essentially, Dr. Kousser intimated that the competitiveness of the elections in those years was the principal cause for the increased turnout. Dr. Kousser identifies three weaknesses with the confidence argument. In the first place, supporters never produced one witness, expert or lay, to corroborate their argument. Second,

> the fact that the political party that was overwhelmingly dominant—was winning every statewide election and, since the DeLay (former congressman) fostered victories in the 2002 legislative elections and his subsequent mid-term redistricting (2006), a majority of legislative and congressional seats, as well— was the one complaining about fraud in elections.[41]

Finally, supporters argued that the reason minority turnout was so low was that these voters had lost confidence in the electoral process because of ongoing voter fraud, and SB 14 would reinstate that confidence and lead to increased turnout of minorities.[42]

As chronicled in chapter 2 on that day, sixty-three amendments to SB 14 were submitted by legislators of both political parties, four by Republicans and fifty-nine by Democrats. All four of the Republican submissions passed. Of the fifty-nine amendments submitted by Democrats, ten were adopted, three failed on a floor vote, and thirty-eight were tabled. Of the thirty-eight tabled, five were specific references to the VRA all sponsored by either Latino, four, or African American members, one. Minority members of the legislature, all Democrats, sponsored forty-three of the fifty-nine amendments. Of the forty-three amendments sponsored by minority members, thirty-four were tabled, one failed, and eight adopted. All five references to the VRA were tabled even though there were passionate, sometimes almost comical discussions in each instance. All of the adopted amendments were not controversial; several were grammatical or syntactical changes, while the remainder were re-stipulations of various requirements that already existed under current law, such as no fees for requesting duplicate voter identification cards, ensuring that provisional ballots were available in polling places, or stating that if any parts of SB 14 were to be legally struck down, the other parts would remain legal.[43]

In the final analysis, it was clear that the House leadership did not want to discuss any possibility that some aspect of SB 14 violated or could be in violation of the VRA. In each of the five instances when a VRA-related amendment was sponsored, there was no conversation, simply a motion to table followed by a voice vote on the motion. Each amendment was over-whelmingly voted down along partisan lines (see Table 3-9). At other times either a Latino representative or an African American member, when making the motion to amend SB 14, would engage in a debate with Representative Harless (R-Spring), she declared that she "was not so advised" or claimed no knowledge of the topic such as when a member asked her if she thought discrimination still existed in Texas. The substance of these amendments and the arguments surrounding their demise have been chronicled in an earlier chapter; nevertheless, the overwhelming manner in which SB 14 was "pushed through" both bodies of the legislature simply lends more substantiation to the contention that there was racial purpose behind the creation and enact-ment of SB 14.[44] The passage of SB14 lacking substantive evidence for the bill's need while simultaneously vehemently refusing to discuss the role race played in the construction of the bill only lends more suspicion that racial intent was the principal reason for SB 14's substance and passage.

SPECIAL SEQUENCE OF EVENTS
LEADING UP TO CHALLENGE

Another *Arlington Heights* Factor requiring operationalization is that which speaks to irregularities in the way a piece of legislation is designed, structured, or passed. For instance, was the process rushed? Were unusual parliamentary procedures taken in order to pass the bill? Were there unusual political machi-nations surrounding the passage of the bill that directly affected its passage? The operative term here is "unusual," did the process or did the procedures that are normally followed in the passage of legislation change dramatically in order to pass the item under consideration. "Unusual" certainly described the circumstances surrounding the passage of both the redistricting and voter identification bills.

Redistricting

The most unusual of the unusual circumstances surrounding redistricting occurred during the 1990 round of redistricting during the trial phase. Evi-dence surfaced that there were confidential communications between lawyers for the Texas Republican Party and the presiding judge, James Nowlin, to manipulate the boundaries of one of the congressional districts ensuring a favorable election situation for a specific Republican State Senator's congres-sional ambitions. Judge Nowlin's machinations were uncovered by the Texas

Attorney General, who asked, after the redistricting trial's conclusion, for the reprimand of Judge Nowlin. The investigation uncovered evidence of secret phone calls from Republican lawyers to fund-raisers to the Federal judge. Witnesses working in the Texas Legislative Counsel's office later reported seeing the judge and Republican operatives working on maps on Legislative Council computers at the end of the day during the trial and before testimony had concluded. Essentially, the judge was drawing the map before the trial had even concluded. Subsequent to an investigation, Judge Nowlin was formally reprimanded.[45] This round featured the Republican Party supporting the efforts of Latino civil rights organizations in bringing voting rights lawsuits against the state as part of an overall effort at gaining control over both state assemblies as well as the congressional delegation. The strategy focused on creating more minority districts that were packed and centered in inner cities, isolating Anglo voters in suburban districts.[46] This strategy was intended to weaken the hold of Anglo Democrats over congressional districts, making them vulnerable through the removal of minority voters from their districts. This left Anglo congressmen running in Anglo majority districts dominated by conservative rural and suburban voters. This restructuring of districts is interesting on several levels. First, it served to create more minority-majority districts where Latinos and African Americans were able to win seats in Congress and both state chambers. At the same time, however, it created a favorable electoral situation for Republicans to win control over the congressional delegation and both state chambers that had been in the hands of Democrats for decades. Still the newly created majority-minority districts proved to be the foundation for the *packing* and *cracking* of growing Latino communities in future redistricting efforts.

The 2001 round of redistricting was unique because there were several trials, appeals, and retrials culminating with a mid-decade redistricting session called by Governor Perry. He insisted that the population had changed enough that Texas could proceed with a mid-decade redistricting which was not prohibited by any state or federal law. This redistricting round was overshadowed not just by Governor Perry's mid-decade redistricting but also by the scandal that ended the congressional career of Tom DeLay. Mr. DeLay was accused, although found innocent almost a decade later, of channeling corporate monies into a campaign to influence the redistricting process.[47] Eventually, the Court ordered that six congressional districts be redrawn with the most substantial redesign occurring to CD23 in southwest Texas. However, the award for "Best Drama by Any Legislative Body," if there ever was an award given for this category, had to have gone to the state legislature during the 2003 legislative session. The initial redistricting effort began during the 2001 session that closed with no plans being drawn and redistricting performed by the

Legislative Redistricting Board when Governor Perry refused to call a special session. Texas finally finished the 2001 redistricting at the end of 2006. In between 2001 and 2006, there were five United State Supreme Court decisions, six United States District Court decisions, three DOJ pre-clearance opinions including one objection, three State District Court, and three State Supreme Court decisions before the process ended. In all there were twenty legal decisions of some sort issued governing whether Texas had violated provisions of the VRA during this redistricting round. This many legal actions speak to the intransigence of Texas attempting to ensure that the redistricting process remains closed to racial minorities while protecting incumbents.

Although the 2001–2006 round of redistricting featured a great deal of legal maneuvering the featured attraction during this episode centered on the state legislature's redistricting machinations. The first chapter in this drama featured a "walkout" by fifty-one state house Democratic Party members to prevent a quorum from occurring, blocking a vote on the redistricting plan. This resulted in the regular session ending without a plan being approved. Governor Perry called a special session to consider another plan, but it ended when eleven State Democratic Senators fled the state to prevent a quorum in that body, preventing the use of the two-thirds rule by Republicans. The House members fled the state to a motel in Ardmore, Oklahoma, and did not return for two weeks even though Governor Perry requested that the federal government have them arrested by the FBI and the U.S. Marshal Service and returned to Austin. The senators later fled to a motel in Albuquerque, New Mexico, and stayed for almost two months, requiring the governor to call a third special session. They eventually returned and a congressional redistricting plan was passed in the third special session toward the latter half of 2003. In both instances, minority legislators pointed out that the congressional redistricting had been performed with racial intent in violation of the VRA.[48] This plan was sued by various civil rights organizations and found to partially violate the VRA, specifically CD23. An interesting highlight of the Supreme Court's decision in *LULAC v. Perry*[49] was that they ruled that retrogression in one district couldn't be addressed by the addition of another minority district in another part of the state. In other words, when a state attempts addressing a retrogression claim in the entire state, it must correct the retrogression where it occurs, in the specific district. The state may not pretend to address the claim by making an adjustment in another part of the state; making changes to a district removed a great distance from where the retrogression occurred. This last issue would also be a matter of contention in the 2011 round of redistricting. That Texas continued to violate the requirements of the VRA, in the same way and manner, from one redistricting cycle to another, speaks to a complete disregard for the VRA among the legislative leadership. Most important, however, this repetitive behavior speaks a great deal to the historic role race plays in the redistricting processes of Texas. The use of race in redistricting simply demonstrates how intensely race is part of the political culture of Texas.

The use of a multifaceted strategic approach on the part of Republican Party activists and legislators featured the redistricting process in 2011. The principal impetus was the drive to ensure a supermajority in both chambers and the state's congressional delegation allowing for the easy passage of legislation during the decade. Most important, however, was the certainty facing Republicans that fast-changing demographics would threaten their hold over the state political and governmental apparatus if they were not successful in creating ideologically conservative legislative bodies. One of the most important ways to ensure political control was establishing control over the state's legislative bodies. This session was characterized as the most racially inflammatory that had occurred over the last thirty years.[50] As pointed out earlier, the session featured more than one hundred anti-immigrant items of legislation, between three and five pieces of legislation demanding English as the official language of the state, racially inflammatory behavior on the part of legislators in committee hearings and on the floor of both chambers during the session, and demonstrations on the steps of the state capitol excoriating Hispanic legislators. Compounding the acidic atmosphere was the fact that the legislature was not only attempting to pass redistricting plans, it was also trying to pass a Voter Identification Bill, SB 14, that opponents claimed was designed to disenfranchise minorities, the young, elderly, and women. Essentially, Republicans were utilizing a tactic which Haney-López has christened as "strategic racism" to push through their redistricting plans and SB 14.[51]

Senate Bill 14

The passage of a voter identification law in Texas has been characterized by parliamentary machinations that have, on occasion, bordered on the sadly humorous. They are humorous because of the extent to which the minority party, in this case it has been the Democrats, has gone to evade casting votes required to pass a voter identification bill. The actions, on the other hand, reflect the extent to which the Texas legislature has become dysfunctional. Prior to 2007 the membership of the Texas legislature held their body up as an example of how both parties could come together in the tradition of a family and work their way through difficult legislation unlike the national Congress. The intense partisanship that inundated the national legislature appears, however, to have infected the Texas state legislature as well and was particularly obvious during the debates surrounding passage of the voter identification bills.

The 2005 session appeared to proceed along a normal trajectory with HB 1706 being formally introduced by a Republican member and chair of the House Elections Committee. The bill was referred to a subcommittee for hearings, passed out of the Elections Committee, passed out of the entire House but failed to obtain the two-thirds vote in the Senate in order to obtain a hearing. Essentially, the legislative process was followed and voter identification died in the same way any other piece of legislation normally would during a regular session. In other words, there appeared, at least to the average political observer, that there were no attempts to circumvent normal legislative processes to pass voter identification during the 2005 session. This would not last long, however, because politics took a dramatic turn during the 2007 session.

The 2007 legislative session began with Republican Representative Betty Brown introducing HB 218. The bill was passed out of the subcommittee and House Elections Committee, and passed out of the Senate's State Affairs Committee. An attempt was made to suspend the rules in order to take HB 218 out of turn in the Senate because it was fairly far down in the queue, but this required a two-thirds vote. Nevertheless, the drama that was created in attempting to seek this vote by Lt. Gov. Dewhurst[52] surpassed that seen in many television soap operas. The Lieutenant Governor called the vote on a date when he knew that two senators would be absent. Senator Carlos Uresti (D-San Antonio) was sick with stomach flu and Senator Mario Gallegos (D-Houston), had checked himself into a hospital because he began suffering the effects of liver transplant rejection. Minus these two crucial votes, the Democrats could not have blocked a vote on voter identification because they would have been short of the one-third required to do so. Nevertheless, a very ill Senator Uresti staggered into the Senate to cast his vote, his appearance described as Lazarus-like.[53] His appearance prevented HB 218 from getting to the floor for a vote. After this incident, Senator Mario Gallegos checked into a Houston hospital because he was suffering from the effects of a liver transplant rejection. Again, Dewhurst called for a vote on HB 218. Against his doctor's orders, Senator Gallegos left the hospital and returned to Austin to cast his vote. One Republican Senator, Bob Deuell (R-Greenville) a physician, felt so bad about this situation that he ordered a hospital bed placed in the Sergeant-at-Arms office to allow Senator Gallegos to continue receiving the medical attention he so badly needed.[54] Again, Democrats voted as a bloc and blocked the passage of HB 218, so it never received a vote of the entire Senate and died as the session expired.

In 2009, the voter identification bill, SB 362, began its journey in the Senate, introduced by Senator Troy Fraser. This time the Presiding Officer and Senate President, Lieutenant Governor David Dewhurst eyeing a potential

U.S. Senatorial campaign, decided that he was going to push the passage of the voter identification bill as hard as he could. Lt. Gov. Dewhurst declared the Senate as the committee of the whole in order to bypass the committee process and ensure a quicker path to passage. SB 362 was passed by the Senate, sent to House Elections Committee, where it was passed then referred to the Major State Calendar committee that, again, was designed to expedite consideration of SB 362. Except this time, as opposed to 2007, the Democratic House members took the action that eventually killed voter identification for this session. The Democratic House members engaged in a "chubbing" action which is similar to a filibuster except this is performed by all members asking questions, requesting information, engaging in discussions, debates and so forth until the session's clock eventually ran out of time and SB 362 died, having been said that it died being "chubbed" to death.

By the time the 2011 legislative session arrived the Republican Party leadership was armed and ready for a full-blown offensive to ensure the passage of a voter identification law. This time the bill was numbered SB 14 and it was sponsored by Senator Fraser who had sponsored SB 362 in the previous session. Right from the beginning of the legislative session it was clear that the Republican Party elected leadership wanted to have a voter identification bill passed when Governor Perry declared it an emergency bill again. This meant that the rule not allowing for the deliberation or voting of any bill within the first sixty days of the session was lifted. This also allowed SB 14 to bypass the committee process. A rule disallowing "chubbing" was passed in the House. Two Democratic House members were convinced to change parties, giving Republicans a supermajority in the chamber. This mitigated against the Democratic membership leaving the state. If they did, it would make no difference because being in the superminority meant that without any crossover votes from sympathetic Republicans the House Democrats were powerless to stop legislation. SB 14 sailed through both chambers and was signed into law by Governor Perry. Although the state House members made an effort at amending the bill, as discussed above, to no avail, voter identification became the law in Texas.

SPECIAL CIRCUMSTANCES
SURROUNDING LEGISLATIVE SESSION

Policies motivated by a racially discriminatory purpose are often disguised in color-blind language through the use of race-neutral terms or, in some cases, the intentional avoidance of topics pertaining to the legal protection of groups covered under federal law.[55] This is a schema that Haney López has labeled *strategic racism.*[56] Strategic racism is defined as "purposeful efforts to use racial animus as leverage to gain material wealth, political power, or heightened social standing."[57] Essentially, strategic racism requires the conscious manipulation of a political or policy process to one's strategic advantage through the manipulation of race or race consciousness. Strategic racism must be seen not as a single action by an individual political actor or group of actors to necessarily harm a particular group, in this instance Texas Latinos; instead it is a process that has an overall intention to use race to influence the substance of policy. In the context of redistricting and voter identification politics, strategic racism is played out as a process understood as the totality of circumstantial actions based on the use of race or racial shields to gain and maintain the political control over the governing levers of the state government.

The language and rhetoric used by the supporters of voter identification and those in control of the redistricting process reveal a need to control the political access of Latinos, not to disadvantage Latinos but to keep the political advantage they already enjoy. The problematic is simple. One cannot disadvantage a particular group, in this instance Democrats, without disadvantaging another group, Latinos, and doing them political harm. The manipulation of the Latino population simply to ensure the political advantage of a political party will do irreparable harm to the disadvantaged group. Disadvantaging a group that has already been subject to almost two hundred years of disadvantages merely buries that group deeper in the quagmire of subordination. This makes achieving full political participation even more difficult and may possibly lead to alienation from the political process for the disadvantaged group in the long term. The low political participation levels of Latinos may be partially attributed to the continuous efforts by political decision makers and elected leaders to construct barriers to inhibit participation and voting. When race is the variable with which the disadvantaged group is identified, then there is a clear case of strategic racism underlying the actions of the advantaged group. The most insidious form of strategic racism occurs when racial shields are utilized during the execution of the strategy. This is what happened during the redistricting process of 2011 and the passage of SB 14 during the same session. Racial shields will be defined and discussed thoroughly in the next chapter.

The 2011 Texas state legislative session was replete with examples of racial animus particularly toward Latinos. Throughout the session, code words were used in place of reference to Latinos in order to avoid charges of racism or having civil rights lawsuits brought against the actors or the state. An essential aspect of the strategy was to avoid being accused of passing legislation that had a racial purpose. During the congressional and house redistricting process, various individuals involved in redistricting, including various heads of the Texas Republican Congressional delegation, the chairs of the redistricting committees of both chambers together with their legal counsel, used the term "VRA districts"[58] to refer to majority-Latino or majority-minority districts. The conversations where these references were made occurred during the deliberations where the four new congressional districts would be distributed geographically. In one e-mail from Congressman Lamar Smith (R-CD21, San Antonio) to one of the redistricters, the congressman indicated that three Republican districts could be drawn and "one VRA" district. In another e-mail the same congressman changed his observation, writing to the same individual, that two of the new districts could be Republican, one "toss up" and one VRA. The congressman did not refer to the districts that were not designed for Republicans as "Democratic," Latino, or minority-majority districts, he referred to them as "VRA districts." He suggested that this district be reserved for designation under the Voting Rights Act. The congressman used VRA as a racial shield, hiding a reference to Latinos in order to avoid any semblance of racial intent. At the time, Texas was covered in its entirety by the VRA; as such all four of the new districts and how they were drawn were covered by the VRA.[59] In reality, all four districts were VRA districts because the law covered the entire state.

Beginning in November 2010, before the legislative session during which redistricting and voter identification were considered, communications between legal counsels of the State Speaker of the House and the Chair of the House Redistricting Committee revealed a conscious effort to manipulate the population of Latino voters during the process. This has been discussed at length earlier here; nevertheless, it reveals the racial intent of the Republican Party operatives. They clearly and consciously manipulated the Latino voter populations in CDs 23 and 27 to create districts that were majority Latino but would elect Republican candidates to Congress. The reason was to dilute the vote of Latinos because Latinos would not vote for the Republican candidates and the fear was these seats would be lost to Democrats. By splitting up various counties and precincts containing Latino voters, the redistricters diluted the voting power of Latinos and denied them an opportunity to elect a candidate of their choice. This is a clear example of strategic racism in the election process.

Two circumstances drove strategic racism during the redistricting and the consideration of voter identification: the rapid growth of the Latino population and the fact that Latino voters are supporting Democratic candidates at ever more increasing rates. The 2010 Census count for Texas indicated that the population of the state increased by 4,293,741 individuals—from 20,851,818 in 2000 to 25,145,561 in 2010. Sixty percent of the total increase was comprised of Latinos. In 2010, persons of Hispanic or Latino origin comprised

37.6 percent of the Texas population. While the total population of Texas increased by 20.6 percent, the Latino population increased by 41.85 percent with the Anglo population increasing only 4 percent.[60] It is not foreseen that this change is abating because according to the Census in 2010, 49 percent of babies born in Texas were Hispanic and by 2011 the Latino share of births in Texas had risen to 51 percent.[61] The logical projection then is that Latinos will be the plurality of the Texas population by 2020 and the majority by 2030.[62] If this trend continues and Latinos continue voting Democratic, it will be only a matter of time before political control of all legislative bodies in the state may experience another dramatic partisan, and this time racial, shift.

In addition to the change in total population, there are significant demographic changes in the voting-age population of Texas. From 2000 to 2010, the growth rate for the Hispanic voting-age population (HVAP) in Texas was approximately 43 percent. In 2010, 45 percent of all persons in Texas turning age eighteen (the age of eligibility to vote) were Latino.[63] There was also a steady increase in the Hispanic citizen voting age population of Texas. From 2005 through 2009, the Hispanic citizen voting-age population increased from 24.6 percent of the state's total citizen voting-age population to 25 percent. In each year from 2005 to 2009, inclusively, the number and proportion of the Latino citizen voting-age population increased.

Particularly interesting is that as of 2011 the following seventeen counties contained 77 percent of Texas's Latino population: Bexar, Brazoria, Cameron, Collin, Dallas, Denton, El Paso, Fort Bend, Harris, Hidalgo, Lubbock, Montgomery, Nueces, Tarrant, Travis, Webb and Williamson. Bexar, Cameron, Dallas, Harris, Hidalgo, Nueces, Tarrant, and Travis counties, which already contained significant Latino-origin populations in 2000, saw substantial growth in their Latino-origin populations in 2010. For instance, Latino intercensal growth amounted to nearly 78 percent of the total growth in Bexar County from 2000 to 2010. In Cameron, Dallas, and Nueces counties, the Latino growth from 2000 to 2010 in each county exceeded the total growth for their respective counties, suggesting that these counties saw substantial growth in their Latino communities accompanied by a reduction in their non-Latino populations.

Contrasting the growth of Latinos was a corresponding decrease in the Anglo population. The Latino growth from 2000 to 2010 is likely to continue given the young age structure of the Latino population relative to its Anglo counterpart and the birthrates indicating that Latino infants are now the majority of births in the state. Interestingly, several counties in Texas would have lost population during the intercensal period had it not been for the growth in the Latino population alone.

The data presented earlier here concerning the intense levels of racial polarization are another indication that Latinos vote in very large percentages differently than Anglos. Another layer in understanding strategic racism is the degree of racial polarization reflected in the data as also a reflection of the partisan polarization in the state. Haney López, as do other authors but he is the most recent to chronicle this particular phenomenon, points out that the racial polarization is really an artifact and direct outcome of the Republican Party's Southern Strategy that began during the presidential campaign of Barry Goldwater, experimented with by George Wallace during his presidential campaigns, and refined by the campaign of Richard Nixon. The principal strategy was to abandon all attempts to win the votes of African Americans and concentrate on solidifying the votes of white voters. In order to secure the white vote Republican politicians had to appeal to the racial animus that was alive and well in that historical period. However, rather than using vulgar racial descriptors to appeal to white voters, politicians used code language for terms of public policy that became associated with African Americans. As a result Republican politicians ran on campaigns that featured excoriations of "welfare queens," "compulsory busing," "food stamp cheats," and so forth.[64]

In Texas this same strategy was resurrected and used against Latinos in the form of campaigns against "school equalization," "bilingual education," and for policies that secured the borders against the invasions of illegal aliens and requiring English as the official language of the state. Where the Southern Strategy was designed to attract white voters, it was also designed to repel African American and Latino voters. The Southern Strategy is a clear example of strategic racism in action. The campaigns were designed to win and maintain control of political offices, not necessarily to denigrate African Americans or Latinos, but the effect was the opposite. Simultaneously, strategic racism drove Latinos and African Americans more and more into the ranks of the only other choice of political parties, the Democrats. As a result, one artifact is the racial polarization of voters in the South generally and Texas specifically. In general elections racial polarization is simultaneously partisan polarization. Nevertheless, partisan polarization as it exists in Texas could not occur without the execution of strategic racism on the part of Republicans.

At the beginning of the 2011 legislative session in which SB 14 was enacted, Texas newspapers and television outlets reported widely that the state's Latino population was booming and promised increased political strength for the Latino community.[65] In 2008, the Texas Comptroller issued a report stating that by 2020, "the Texas Hispanic population is expected to outnumber the White population. Between 2000 and 2040 the Hispanic population will triple in Texas' urban areas, from 5.9 million to 17.2 million. In rural areas, the Hispanic population is expected to double, from 777,000 to 1.6 million.[66]

In Texas, 80 percent of immigrants who are not U.S. citizens are Latinos.[67] Public discussions about non-U.S. citizens often expand to include reference to Spanish speakers and Latinos in general, regardless of their citizenship status. See, e.g., Tr. Exh. 202, *Texas v. United States*, No. 11-CV-01303 (D.D.C), filed at Dkt. 320-1. Legislative debates in Texas, including during the 2005, 2007, 2009, and 2011 sessions, often included statements in which the terms *immigrants* or *illegal immigrants* were used to refer to Latinos or Spanish speakers. For example, in the 2011 legislative session, State Representative Leo Berman introduced a bill requiring that all driver's license tests be conducted in the English language, claiming, "if you can't read English, you shouldn't be able to drive in Texas."[68]

During the 2005–2011 periods in which successive Texas legislatures took up a series of Voter ID bills, legislators introduced a number of so-called immigration bills whose effects would be felt most strongly by Texas Latinos, regardless of citizenship status. For example, in 2011, at least three bills sought to make English the official language (HB 176 by Jim Jackson; HB 301 by Leo Berman; and HB 81 by Flynn). Also in 2011, Representative Debby Riddle introduced a bill that would require public schools to identify to the Texas Comptroller all students in bilingual education classes. In 2011, Ms. Riddle created a makeshift campsite and slept for two nights at the Texas House of Representatives to make sure she was the first in line when the Chief Clerk's office opened for early filing of legislative bills. Ms. Riddle filed her Voter ID bill (HB 16) along with her immigration bills on that day.[69]

The debate in the 2005, 2007, and 2009 sessions around Voter ID often turned on claims that Voter ID was needed to stop voter fraud by non-U.S. citizens. The superficial or public rationale for SB 14 was to prevent voter fraud by noncitizens and even persons inside the United States illegally. In each of these legislative sessions where a voter identification bill was considered, references to "illegal aliens voting" appeared in speeches and written documents as the underlying reason for the proposed law.

On February 16, 2005, during a hearing on her bill to require documentary proof of U.S. citizenship for voter registration, Representative Betty Brown specifically referred to changing demographics in Texas as the reason for her bill. Following questioning by Representative Rafael Anchia, she responded by saying,

> Representative Anchia, I hope I said it right, has brought up some things about population trends and I think that just reinforces the need for it to happen now and not later because our population is growing very rapidly and we need to put these safeguards into place while this is happening.[70]

In December 2006, the Texas Conservative Coalition Research Institute discussed the need for a stricter law requiring photo voter identification at the polls in its report "Porous Borders, Porous Elections: The Imperative to

Verify Voters' Citizenship." The report concluded: "With over 1.6 million il-legal immigrants in the state, Texas cannot afford to leave its election system susceptible to their fraudulent votes. Voting is the most paramount right of our representative democracy, and must be reserved strictly for citizens of the United States. Whatever efforts are made to prevent illegal aliens from penetrating our borders, the state should amend its election law and practices so that illegal aliens are prevented from registering to vote or entering the vot-ing booth."[71] Voter identification was perceived primarily as a law that could control immigration from Mexico and not as a policy ensuring ballot security.

Two months earlier, the same organization released a report titled "State Approaches to Illegal Immigration," in which it urged the adoption of a policy requiring "Voters to Present a Driver's License or Texas Identification Card at their Polling Place."[72] The report explained that the recommendations were the "result of many months of research and discussion on the part of the task force members, their legislative staffs, and the TCCRI" and specifically credited the task force Chairman, State Representative Linda Harper-Brown, as well as the other members of the task force, State Representatives Brian Hughes, Bill Keffer, Debbie Riddle, Larry Taylor, and Corbin VanArsdale, all Republicans, for their work in creating the recommendations.

In the 2006 "interim" (during which the Legislature holds hearings but does not meet in official session), in a hearing held by the Senate State Affairs Committee, Senator Robert Duncan explicitly tied the need for Voter ID to the specter of noncitizen voting, stating:

The issue here today in this country today is how do we control illegal immigra-tion into this state. Certainly there are those out there who would claim that one reason we need to be tighter on voter identification for voter fraud is the fact that we do have a lot of folks coming into this country from other countries. . . . Could [undocumented immigrants] be manipulated to go vote? . . . If you're here without any authority to be here, how would you ever be caught? . . . What you're saying is that the individual person's incentive to vote—the person who is an immigrant to this country that's undocumented—that person's incentive to commit such a crime is very diminished. What if somebody says: Here's the way we're going to do this. Joe has access to 1,500 undocumented workers and we need some bodies to go vote. We've got these registration cards, so we're going to hire him to go do that. It's not the individual that I'm worried about. It would be the persons who, like back in the LBJ days, would have the ability to organize a fraudulent turnout. . . . Where I see a potential for fraud is in those people who are already breaking the law by organizing and being agents for per-sons who are over here illegally and providing identification and also as a point of contact for organization of illegal voting. . . . Is there any evidence that that is occurring? . . . I'm just talking in hypotheticals, because those are the issues surrounding the reasons for voter ID, right?[73]

Although there has never been any evidence in Texas that anyone was organizing undocumented immigrants to vote, and Senator Duncan admits as much in his statement, he nevertheless claims that Voter ID is necessary to prevent fraudulent voting by noncitizens.

In the 2007 legislative session, Lieutenant Governor Dewhurst issued a public statement following the defeat of the Voter ID bill in the Senate:

> Yesterday Republican Senator Troy Fraser brought up in the Senate for consideration House Bill 218 by Representative Betty Brown, which simply requires voters to present a driver's license or some other common form of identification at the election polls to prove they are who they say they are: U.S. citizens. . . . Yesterday all 11 Democrat members of the Texas Senate voted against the bill and blocked it from going forward. I think this is an outrage against all Americans. With eight to 12 million illegal aliens currently living in the U.S., the basic American principle of one person, one vote, is in danger.[74]

In discussing the need for HB 218 (Voter ID) in the same 2007 legislative session, Lt. Gov. Dewhurst stated, "Why isn't it necessary to prove that you're a U.S. citizen to vote in U.S. elections?"[75] Also during the 2007 session State Representative Betty Brown indicated that her voter identification proposal, approved by the House on April 23, 2007, was "designed to keep illegal aliens, noncitizens and people otherwise not qualified" from voting.[76]

On June 21, 2007, State Representative Dennis Bonnen (R-Angleton), who later served as the Chair of the State House Select Committee on Voter Identification and Voter Fraud in the 2011 session, wrote to a constituent regarding the bills to require voter identification (HB 218) and proof of citizenship for voter registration (HB626), both of which were defeated in the 2007 session: "I am just as frustrated as you are at the outcome of these bills" and went on to describe his efforts to secure passage of immigration-related bills.[77]

The Immigration Reform Coalition of Texas (IRCOT), a vocal and active participant in recent legislative sessions, repeatedly connected Voter ID to the need for state-level immigration laws. IRCOT consistently encouraged the passage of strict photo ID legislation as a way to control undocumented immigration, and even singled out for special recognition certain Texas state legislators as "Texas Defenders" based in part on their support for voter ID bills.[78] Bonnen proudly announced in his newsletter to constituents "In recognition of my work, the Immigration Reform Coalition of Texas bestowed upon me the 'Strongest Texas Defender' award in 2009, noting that I am one of ten Representatives who authored, co-authored, demonstrated consistent and/or early support of several vital immigration related bills."[79]

On April 9, 2009, in a hearing of the House Elections Committee, Rep. Betty Brown spoke in response to testimony by an Asian American advocate that people of Chinese, Japanese, and Korean descent often have problems voting with their identification because they may have a legal transliterated name and then a common English name that is used on their driver's license. Rep. Brown stated: "Rather than everyone here having to learn Chinese—I understand it's a rather difficult language—do you think that it would behoove you and your citizens to adopt a name that we could deal with more readily here?"[80]

In February, 2009, State Representative Patricia Harless, who later carried SB 14 in the House, responded to an e-mail from a member of the public which stated: "Letting these illegals come into our country and register under several names and then vote is not doing your job." In response, Harless wrote: "Securing integrity in the election system is very important to me, and this session I will support legislation establishing honest and secure voter I.D."[81] Representative Charles Perry (R-Lubbock), a cosponsor of SB 14 in the 2011 Session, wrote regarding the bill: "Currently, you don't have to show an ID to vote. This means our elections are not secure and are left open to fraud. It also means illegal immigrants and non-citizens can vote, and there are even incidences of legal citizens voting multiple times."[82] Combining of references to fraudulent voting by illegal immigrants and citizens in the same sentence is a subtle and insidious attempt at besmirching Latinos. Latinos are often referred to as illegal immigrants by racists regardless of their status. Governor Perry's statement blurs the difference between illegal immigrants and citizens, social categories that, to Texas Anglos, may both be filled by Latinos. Latinos, to racial thinkers, may be perceived as both or either illegal immigrants or citizens.

In 2009, State Rep. Leo Berman filed a bill imposing a state tax on money wired abroad, but limited the tax to money wired to Mexico, Central America and South America for personal, family, or household purposes. During that same session a number of legislators collaborated to cosponsor an English-only House Joint Resolution (HJR 32). In 2007, Rep. Linda Harper-Brown (R-Irving) filed a bill to eliminate bilingual education (HB 933). In 2011, State Rep. Leo Berman introduced a so-called immigration bill that would make English the official language of Texas. Berman explained, "That will shut off the state printing anything in any language but English and that's going to save millions of dollars right there." When asked whether recent bills focused on immigration would alienate Latino voters in general, Rep. Berman implicitly agreed, responding: "Most Hispanics right now do vote Democrat; there's no question about it. So what vote are we going after? We're going after a vote that doesn't vote Republican anyway."[83]

During the 2011 legislative session, State Representative Aaron Peña (R-Hidalgo County) publicly expressed concern that the tone of the immigration

debate was aimed at Latinos. He explained: "The tone of the debate is basically saying, 'We don't want you. . . . This is a war over our culture. These
people bring diseases into our country.'" He further described his efforts
behind the scenes as a Latino Republican to reduce the racial nature of the
debate.[84]

On February 8, 2011, Lt. Governor Dewhurst wrote to a constituent regarding photo identification, stating "Voter ID will help stamp out voter fraud and
increase public confidence in our election process by ensuring that only U.S
citizens—who are legally eligible—vote in Texas elections." The Lt. Governor continued, "As Lieutenant Governor, I have a responsibility to protect
and defend our Constitution and the laws of our state and nation, and I'm
proud to stand with the vast majority of Texans and Members of the Texas
Senate and uphold the sanctity of one person, one vote."[85]

During his U.S. Senatorial campaign David Dewhurst's website listed his
support of Voter ID legislation under the heading: "David Dewhurst Opposes
Illegal Immigration." Under this topic of illegal immigration, which includes
news articles on strengthening the U.S. border and increasing the size of the
Border Patrol, Lt. Gov. Dewhurst posted news articles describing his "push
for the voter ID law for two sessions" and quotes him as saying: "At the end
of the day, there's nothing more important than protecting the sanctity of everyone's right to vote."[86] In her testimony in *Texas v. Holder* (voter identification) case, State Representative Riddle, when asked about specific incidents
of voter fraud, described one incident in which a Hispanic, Spanish-speaking
woman appeared at the polling place to vote but needed assistance because
she was unable to communicate in English and was unfamiliar with the process. Representative Riddle offered this incident as an example of voter fraud
despite the fact that she also testified that she had no knowledge whether the
voter was a citizen or not.[87]

The Legislature was well aware, based on criticism from within the Republican Party, that the expressed purpose for the Voter ID law was racially
inflammatory and that it would likely have a disparate racial impact. Royal
Masset, former political director of the Texas Republican Party and a well-
known GOP consultant and political commentator, stated in a 2007 article in
the Quorum Report, a news service read by most legislators and staff:

> Under HB 218 my mother, who is a registered voter in Austin, cannot vote in
> Texas. Anyone who says all legal voters under this bill can vote doesn't know
> what he is talking about. And anyone who says that a lack of IDs won't dis-
> criminate against otherwise legal minority voters is lying. . . . HB 218 will lower
> voter turnout. There is no evidence on the record that non-American citizens
> have voted in past Texas elections in a manner that would have been stopped
> by HB 218.[88]

Mr. Masset concluded, "HB 218 is a direct descendent of poll taxes, and of allowing only white male property owners to vote. In its effect it is racist, barbaric, and antidemocratic and contrary to everything that made America great."[89] Masset also criticized the racially charged justifications for Voter ID in comments to the press stating, "They're just basically using sheer racism to pump their own political points. They're trying to exploit the public fear of illegal aliens."[90] Masset continued that voter ID bills are an "extremely popular vote on the grassroots level." But the idea that illegal immigrants vote "is one of those urban myths that just has caught on and everyone assumes is true."[91]

Other leading Republicans frankly admitted that there was no evidence of noncitizen voting to justify additional laws. In the same 2007 session, even Representative Phil King (R-Weatherford), who sponsored a proof of citizenship voter registration bill, acknowledged that "there is no evidence of extensive fraud in Texas elections or of multiple voting," still he claimed noncitizen voting could occur.[92] Similarly, John Colyandro, executive director of the Texas Conservative Coalition Research Institute, stated, "We have no idea of the magnitude of the problem, and until measures are put in place to verify the integrity of the voter rolls, we can't begin to put a figure as to how many people have illegally registered or illegally voted."[93]

State Representative Tommy Merritt (R-Longview) voted against the voter ID bill in the 2007 session, stated in 2009 that past Voter ID bills were more about energizing conservative Republicans than combating fraud and opined that the "The party is not focused on what's important to the people."[94] Also, in 2009, Royal Masset further commented that Voter ID would be "another last straw" for Latinos, who would be forced to spend time and money obtaining additional IDs because of an alleged threat of fraudulent voting. He explained, "One way to get Latinos upset is to start criminalizing them, to imply they are criminals . . . And Hispanics should take this personally, because it is aimed at them."[95]

In May 2008, the Texas Attorney General released his report on voter fraud prosecutions in the state. Despite creating a special vote fraud unit in his office and using a $1.4 million federal grant, the Attorney General prosecuted a total of twenty-six cases, most of which were related to ballot mishandling as opposed to impersonation fraud. Only one case dealt with noncitizen voter registration and resulted in the conviction of a local candidate who lied to noncitizens about their eligibility to register to vote. The only voter impersonation cases involved a woman who voted for her dead mother and a man who voted twice.[96] Since then, fewer than five illegal voting complaints involving voter impersonations were filed with the Texas Attorney General's Office from the 2008 and 2010 general elections in which more than 13 million voters participated.[97] The same holds true for noncitizens who are discovered to have cast a ballot in an election.[98] Despite evidence from the Texas Attorney General himself that noncitizen voting was rare, the drumbeat continued from legislators that Voter ID was necessary to stop voting by noncitizens. At the same time, however, the Voter ID bills being crafted in the legislature revolved around limited and difficult-to-obtain photo identification, as opposed to documents that require U.S. citizenship. Representative Dennis Bonnen, who served as the Chairman of the Select House Committee on Voter Identification and Voter Fraud in the 2011 session, testified in deposition that he did not know whether non-U.S. citizens could obtain a Texas driver's license, a concealed handgun license, or a military identification card—all forms of ID required by SB 14.[99] Representative Todd Smith, who chaired the House Elections Committee in the 2009 session, testified similarly that he did not know whether non-U.S. citizens could obtain a Texas driver's license, a concealed handgun license, or a military identification card.[100]

In the 2011 legislative session, the rhetoric that illegal aliens and non-citizens were the reason for the need for Voter ID had morphed into complete silence on the issue of race. The legislators supporting SB 14 even went so far as to completely avoid considering whether their actions met standards of existing federal law and whether the provisions of SB 14 would affect the voting power of minorities covered under the law. This complete refusal to discuss the protection of Latinos under the VRA is significant in the light of the history and legacy of racism in Texas evidenced by more than four decades of voting litigation beginning with *Smith v. Allwright* (1944) through *White v. Regester* (1973) and culminating with *Texas v. U.S.,* No.1:11-CV-01303 (D.D.C.).

The Texas legislators who supported passage of SB 14, during the 2011 legislative session, took pains not to refer to Latinos in their deliberations. As discussed earlier in this volume, the legislative record indicates that there were at least three instances when Latino and African American legislators attempted to engage the Voter ID supporters to explain whether the Voter ID bill complied with the VRA. In every one of these instances the discussion was cut short and the particular amendment being considered at that moment was voted on. A similar attempt to engage the Senate Committee of the Whole in a discussion whether SB 14 would violate the Voting Rights Act was ignored.[101] Senators in charge of the bill simply refused to discuss the matter of whether the State was covered under Section 5 of the VRA.

In his deposition, Senator Fraser, SB 14's sponsor, invoked "privilege" in response to every question regarding the possible connection between Voter ID and noncitizen voting despite being confronted with multiple e-mails from constituents identifying Voter ID as legislation aimed at noncitizens:

Q. [By Ms. Westfall] Could you describe the message?

A. He says—he's congratulating me on a wonderful voter ID bill for all legal citizens of Texas.

Q. Do you know whether you responded to this e-mail?

A. No, I do not.

Q. Do you know why this constituent was saying it was helpful for legal citizens of Texas?

[objection by Mr. Sweeten]

Q. (BY MS. WESTFALL) Do you have any understanding about why this constituent would link voter ID and other immigration bills in his e-mail?

MR. SWEETEN: Same objection. Same instruction.

A. Privilege.

Q. (BY MS. WESTFALL) Can you answer it outside of any privileged information or testimony that you might have?

A. I don't know this person.

Q. So, is your answer you don't know why he linked voter ID with illegal immigration?

MR. SWEETEN: Same objection. Same instruction.

Q. (BY MS. WESTFALL) Do you not know?

A. Privilege.

Q. Do you know whether other constituents, advocacy groups or interest groups also saw that there was a connection between the voter ID bill and immigration bills?

MR. SWEETEN: Same objection. Instruct you not to answer the question on the basis of legislative privilege.

A. Privilege.[102]

The rich and long history of racism in Texas election laws leads one to conclude that the Texas Legislature is "anchored" in the context of race relations. This means that regardless of the type of electoral policy at hand, during the legislative process race is never far from legislators' minds; race is the anchoring concept and drives the decisional process. In each decade, Texas has enacted election laws (including redistricting plans) that were blocked by objections from the U.S. Department of Justice for discriminating against minority voters or that were defeated in court for the same reason.[103]

What has changed historically is that legislators have evolved in their rhetoric from using language directly identifying minority group persons, beginning with terms such as Latinos, Hispanics, and Spanish-surnamed individuals, into VRA, Section 5, illegal alien or persons speaking another language. The final evolutionary stage for the rhetoric appears to have been "silence" or complete avoidance of a discussion concerning race or the VRA provisions. The great English poet Thomas Carlyle, who coined the famous saying "silence is golden," explained that often silence is meant to hide the true intent of speech and action: "all the considerable men I have known, and the most undiplomatic and unstrategic of these, forbore to babble of what they were creating and projecting."[104] In short, silence in a political debate, in the face of repeated calls to address the issue, can tell us more than the actual spoken word because it can reveal intensity, biases, and the true purpose of the legislators. In this instance silence became the ultimate racial shield and an essential cog in the strategic racism being implemented by Republicans in the legislature. The legislative record of 2011, understood in the context of the heated debate that session around immigrants and Latinos, the contemporaneous effort to enact redistricting plans to limit Latino political strength, and the past discussion of Voter ID in the 2005–2009 legislative sessions, indicates that Texas legislators were conscious of issues of race in Voter ID and understood that Texas would have to comply with the Voting Rights Act. Legislative leaders' refusal in 2011 to discuss whether the provisions of SB 14 violated the Voting Rights Act or had a disparate impact on minority voters suggests that they were unwilling to publicly discuss the true purpose of the law. Again, this behavior of avoidance lends additional substantiation that SB 14 was designed to serve a "racial purpose." This conclusion is bolstered also by the types of identification required by SB 14 which include a state driver's license, concealed handgun identification card, or a military identification, all of which can be obtained by individuals whether U.S. citizens or not. As a result the conclusion reached from all of the above testimony is, simply, that SB 14 was passed and signed into law not to prevent voter fraud but for the purpose of disenfranchising Latino and other minority voters.

LEGISLATIVE AND ADMINISTRATIVE HISTORY

It has become evident throughout this work that the 2011 legislative session during which both the redistricting and voter identification legislation were deliberated was rife with examples of racially tinged, acerbic language and behavior. This particular session was the most racially acrimonious ever in the recent history of this legislative body. The acrimony was reported publicly in news outlets and related by the media directly to the redistricting process, immigration legislation, or SB 14. The event that signified the level of racial animosity was a rally that featured the following statement by the Texas President of the Tea Party. The rally took place on the steps of the state capitol and was sponsored by State House member Leo Berman, R-Tyler. The most vitriolic part of the speech was recorded and posted to YouTube and appears below:

> If you want to know why we can't pass legislation in Texas it's because we have thirty-seven, no thirty-six Hispanics in the Legislature. All of the states that have passed legislation have a handful and I mean literally, some of them have no Hispanic legislators, well, maybe three or five or something. So that's part of our problem and we need to change those numbers. We need to do something about that in fact, during the debate on "sanctuary cities," several Hispanic legislators testified that their grandparents and their parents were migrant workers who came over here to work and that THEY even worked in the fields. And some of them even admitted that they had been here illegally and that they came illegally. So the problem is these Hispanic legislators . . . is that it's too close to them and they . . . simply cannot vote their conscience correctly. So that's about all I have to say to you, please come to the hearing, and help us spread this message. Thank you.[105]

Ms. Forest, the individual making the comments and also a founder of IRCOT (Immigration Reform Coalition of Texas), earlier stated that Texas Hispanic elected officials were responsible for an educational policy that educates "people who are not supposed to be in the state or speak our language."[106] The text of this rather long quote is interesting because it is clearly aimed solely at Latinos and makes the assumption that the Hispanic legislators, through their inaction, are responsible for undocumented immigrants being in Texas and working in the agricultural industry. The notion that Hispanics are working in the fields connotes that Latinos are occupying jobs that could be available to others, which is a traditional complaint of those who argue against immigrants. Ms. Forest even "meshes" images of Hispanic legislators with being agricultural workers and undocumented immigrants. One complaint made during the voter identification trial, *Texas v. Holder,* by a Latino representative, Mr. Trey Martinez Fischer, D-San Antonio, was he felt that the supporters of SB 14 who spoke of illegal immigrants were speaking of "people like me." Ms. Forest's comment is designed to create an image depicting Latinos as both undocumented and manual laborers. Making public statements such as the one above borders on the inflammatory and, at that time, increased the racial animosity that already smoldered during that legislative session.

Another example of the racial animosity raging during the 2011 legislative session happened during a hearing of the Senate Transportation Committee that occurred during the special session of the legislature in June. Senator Chris Harris, who was a member of the redistricting committee as well, responded to a witness testifying in Spanish. "Did I understand him correctly, that he has been here since 1988? Why isn't he speaking in English, then?" "It is insulting to us, it is very insulting."[107] The witness had indicated that he could speak English but that since this was his first formal presentation and he was very nervous he wanted to present in his native language. He had an interpreter to translate his words into English for the benefit of those who could not understand Spanish. Senator Harris did not appear to care whether the presentation was being translated into English, only that the witness did not use English for his presentation.[108]

Besides the racial animosity, the legislative processes surrounding both the redistricting and voter identification bill were replete with legislative irregularities. The irregularities that plagued the redistricting process have already been chronicled here. An analysis of the legislative process leading to the passage of SB 14, on the other hand, revealed irregularities in the process itself. For example, the bill was referred to the Senate Committee of the Whole on January 24, 2011, a highly unusual action given that this occurred at the beginning of the session. The hearing of the bill was set for the very next day, January 25, leaving little time for interested citizens around the state to prepare testimony and travel to the state capitol in time to participate in the hearing. The Senate then suspended its rules to vote on the bill the very next day, January 26. In three days, the bill was introduced, heard, and passed by the Senate, leaving little room for any type of deliberative process. SB 14 was then sent to the House, where opponents successfully raised a procedural objection during floor debate resulting in the bill being sent to the House Elections Committee. That same day, the House Elections Committee approved the bill; the House Calendars Committee considered and sent the bill back to the House floor. The unusual speed with which the voter identification bill moved through the House and Senate represents a significant procedural departure as well as preventing meaningful input and consideration.

Previous sessions also saw irregularities in the process. Particularly disturbing was the 2007 session where Senator Gallegos was forced to leave the hospital under life-threatening circumstances to cast his vote against the voter identification bill. Nevertheless, the irregularities of the previous sessions were escalated during the 2011 session, such as Governor Perry declaring it emergency legislation and Lt. Governor Dewhurst reorganizing the Senate into a Committee of the Whole to prevent the use of the two-thirds rule. Both chambers voted down numerous amendments that would have established safeguards against minority disenfranchisement, including amendments permitting additional forms of identification, affidavits of voters regarding identity, and additional voter education efforts. In one instance, Rep. Veasey offered an amendment restoring the voter certificate as a form of voter identification if the Texas Secretary of State concluded that a majority of voters who lacked photo identification were members of a racial or ethnic minority. The amendment was defeated on a motion by SB 14's sponsor, Representative Patricia Harless.[109]

Significantly, the 2011 legislature defeated proposed amendments that had been included in past versions of the voter identification bill and had received support in both chambers. For example, state-issued student identification cards and employment identification cards were approved as voter identification in past sessions but were excluded from SB 14. SB 14 was not only stricter than its predecessors but the 2011 legislature rejected amendments based on provisions that had received support from a majority of its membership. One suspects that the supporters of SB 14 wished to restrict student and public employee access to the ballot.

Essentially, the parliamentary rules for the passage of SB 14 in the 82nd Legislative Session in 2011 were changed and the committee structures uniquely controlled to focus solely on SB 14 and speed the passage of the bill. Rather than following normal legislative procedures and submitting SB 14 through the traditional committee structure and eliciting broad public support through the normal committee hearing process, the process was tightly controlled to ensure passage. Even the traditional two-thirds rule in the Senate was suspended. The changed structures and rules lends additional substantiation to the suspicion that the design and passage of SB 14 was an essential element of the strategic racism driving voting legislation in Texas in 2011.

Supporters of SB 14 over all the various legislative sessions claimed that the bills were necessary to prevent voter fraud but produced little evidence of impersonation voter fraud. It was even pointed out during the legislative debate in 2011 that the provisions of SB 14 could not prevent the type of voting fraud it was supposed to prevent. Additionally, it was pointed out that the voting fraud that did exist in the mail-in process was not even addressed in SB 14. The supporters began the 2011 legislative session stating that the goal of SB 14 was to prevent voter fraud instigated by illegal immigrants but as this allegation was shown to have no factual basis they changed the goal to the protection of the ballot and protection of the integrity of the ballot. They changed the goal without changing the substance of the legislation, a mistake that should not be made under normal circumstances when considering the development of any public policy. The goals and objectives of any policy will determine the implementing mechanisms and policy outcomes. Frankly, if one changes the goals or objectives of a given policy one must change the implementing mechanisms or the policy will not achieve its fundamental intent. This fundamental rule of public policy was violated by the Texas legislature leaving one to conclude that their stated goals were not the "true intent" of the voter identification law. Rather, the policy makers wished only to restrict the vote of these constituencies of voters who would not support candidates and policies of their party. SB 14 was not designed to lend integrity or security to the ballot process; it was designed to diminish the power of Latino voters in Texas.

NOTES

1. Kenneth Hoover and Todd Donovan, *The Elements of Social Scientific Thinking, 8th ed.* (Belmont, CA: Thomson Wadsworth, 2004), pp. 15–43.

2. Federal Rules of Evidence. Article VII. Expert Opinions and Testimony. Rule 702. Testimony by Expert Witnesses. Pub. L. 93–595, §1, Jan. 2, 1975, 88 Stat. 1937; Apr. 17, 2000, eff. Dec. 1, 2000; Apr. 26, 2011, eff. Dec. 1, 2011.

3. 509 U.S. 579 (1993).

4. The scientific method will be referred to as the method on occasion to avoid redundancy.

5. Bernard I. Cohen, "The Eighteenth Century Origins of the Concept of Scientific Revolution," *Journal of the History of Ideas,* 37, no. 2 (Apr–June, 1976): 257–88.

6. Ibid., *Thornburg v. Gingles.*

7. Richard Engstrom, "Report on Racially Polarized Voting in Selected Areas of Texas," August 9, 2011.

8. Ibid.

9. The "racial purpose" behind poll taxes is discussed by Michael Phillips in "Texan By Color: The Racialization of the Lone Star State," in David O'Donald Cullen and Kyle G. Wilkison, eds., *The Texas Right: The Radical Roots of Lone Star Conservatism* (College Station: Texas A & M University Press, 2014).

10. Texas first began redistricting after the passage of the constitution in 1876. The history of redistricting lawsuits against the state began in 1964 when a suit was brought arguing that Senate districts based on geography violated the "one-man, one-vote" set forth in *Renolds, Kilgarlin, et al. v. Martin, et al.* 252 F. Supp. 404 (S.D. Tex 1966). This suit was followed by *Kilgarlin, et al. v. Hill, et al.* 386 US 120(1967) that invalidated "flotorial districts" (large multicounty districts with a representative who "floats" elected from among the counties, in turn). In 1971 the state was sued twice in state court. The first suit argued that the process used to redistrict the house "ignored the integrity of county lines." This was struck down *Smith v. Craddick* 471 S.W. 2d375 (1971). The second suit actually defined the role of the Legislative Redistricting Board, *Mauzy v. Legislative Redistricting Board* 471S.W.2d570 (1971). These lawsuits are not considered civil rights in the conventional sense although *Kilgarlin v. Martin* was credited for giving Barbara Jordan the district that allowed her to win her first senatorial election.

11. 410 U.S. 315 (1973).

12. *White v. Regester, supra.*

13. Steve Bickerstaff, *Lines in the Sand: Congressional Redistricting in Texas and the Downfall of Tom DeLay* (Austin: The University of Texas Press, 2007), p. 40.

14. Ibid., pp. 28 and 40.

15. Ibid., pp. 28–29, 40–42.

16. Chandler Davidson, *Race and Class.* Cullen and Wilkison, *The Texas Right,* pp. 1–9.

17. *LULAC, et al. v. Perry, et al.*, 548 U.S. 399 (2006).

18. Steve Bickerstaff, *Lines in the Sand,* chap. 18.

19. E-mail from Congressman Lamar Smith to Gerardo Interiano, Subject: FWD:FWD:, April 05, 2011.

20. *Perez, et al. v. Perry, et al.,* No. SA: 11-CV-360, September 6, 2011.

21. Steve Bickerstaff, *Lines in the Sand,* pp. 42–43.

22. This episode was chronicled extensively by Dr. Kousser in his report citing a large number of newspaper articles and blogs from the local *Austin American Statesman* and *San Antonio Express News*. For a sampling of these articles see Kelly Shannon, AP, "Senator returns, vows to block voter ID bill – For now, Senate Democrats have votes needed to block measure," *Austin American Statesman,* May 4, 2007. Gary Scharrer, "Flu-stricken Uresti rushes in to vote," *San Antonio Express News,* May 16, 2007, p. A10. *Austin American Statesman* blog, "Letter from Lt. Gov. on VoterIDbill," May 16, 2007 </blogs/content/sharedgen/blogs/austin/capitolpressreleases/entries/2007/05/16/letter_from_lt_gov_on_voter_id.html/>. Juan Castillo, "ID plan puts spotlight on voter fraud," *Austin American Statesman,* May 23, 2007. Mark Lisheron, "Senate, used to solidarity, repairs split," *Austin American Statesman,* May 18, 2007. Kristen Mack, "In trying to win, has Dewhurst lost a friend?" *Houston Chronicle,* May 17, 2007. Mark Lisheron, "Ill senator settles in for voter ID fight," *Austin American Statesman,* May 22, 2007. Editorial, "Hospital bed handy for Gallegos, Senate ill will," *Austin American Statesman,* May 23, 2007.

23. Kousser, "Declaration of J. Morgan Kousser," June 1, 2012, p. 31.

24. Dave Montgomery, "He's on the inside now—of a pressure cooker," *Fort Worth Star Telegram,* Feb., 23, 2009, B01. Cited in Kousser, "Declaration," p. 33.

25. Dave Montgomery, "Hot debate over voter ID hits Texas House this week," *Fort Worth Star Telegram,* April 6, 2009, p. B01. Cited in Kousser, "Declaration," p. 35.

26. Mr. Opiela would play a prominent role during the 2011 redistricting session as the author of the now infamous e-mail directing Mr. Gerardo Interiano on the intricacies of constructing the Hispanic "metric" that would be used to make CD23 a Hispanic majority district that would elect Republicans to office. Mr. Opiela's actions during the redistricting process would be one of the main reasons the court concluded that he had acted with "racial purpose" in developing the strategy to design CD23 in the way that it appeared in the final plan.

27. Kousser, "Declaration," pp. 37–40.

28. Henry Flores, "Supplemental Report of Henry Flores, PhD in *Texas v. USA, et al.*," June 18, 2012, p. 10.

29. Juan Castillo, "ID plan puts spotlight on voter fraud," *Austin American States-man,* May 23, 2007. One Republican representative, Leo Berman from Tyler in East Texas, even pointed out that "Everyone on the floor needs a vote on illegal aliens to take home and say we did a little something about it." Cited in Kousser, "Declaration," p. 48.

30. Ibid.

31. Ibid.

32. Kousser, "Declaration," pp. 43–44. Citing Jason Embry, "Senate taking up voter ID Monday," *Austin American Statesman,* blog, Jan. 20, 2011, <http:www .statesman.com/blogs/content/shared-en/Austin/politics/entries/2011/01/20/senate_ taking_up_voter_id_mond.html>. Dave Montgomery, "Governor give voter ID bill emergency status in legislative session," *Fort Worth Star Telegram,* Jan. 21, 2011. Peggy Fikac, "The power of the party switch," *HC Politics Blog,* Dec. 14, 2010. Jim Ventuno, "The Senate could be Texas Democrats," *San Antonio Express News,* Dec. 19, 2010. Andrew Weber, "Texplainer: What is Chubbing?" *Texas Tribune,* Feb. 2, 2011. Robert T. Garrett, "Republicans act to avert Dems' stalling," *Dallas Morning News,* Jan. 25, 2011, A03.

33. Senate Debate, 2nd Reading, 2009, p. 56, Bates # TX_00076059. Cited in Kousser, "Declaration," p. 51.

34. W. Gardner Selby, "Voter ID back in the spotlight," *Austin American States-man,* Mar. 9, 2009. Cited in Kousser, "Declaration," p. 51.

35. House Committee Hearing, Mar. 1, 2011, pp. 50–53, Bates # TX 00028157-60. Cited in Kousser, "Declaration," p. 52.

36. *North From Mexico: The Spanish-Speaking People of the United States,* New York: Greenwood Press, 1968.

37. Rodolfo Acuña, *Occupied America: The Chicano's Struggle Toward Libera-tion* (San Francisco: Harper & Row Publishers 1972); Marcelo M. Suárez-Orozco and Mariela M. Páez, *Latinos: Remaking America* (Berkeley University of California Press, 2002); Otto Santa Ana, *Brown Tide Rising: Metaphors of Latinos in Contem-porary American Public Discourse* (Austin: University of Texas Press, 2002).

38. Eduardo Bonilla-Silva, *Racism without Racists: Color-Blind Racism and the Persistence of Racial Inequality in America, 4th ed.* (New York: Rowman & Little-field, 2014).

39. Cited in Kousser, "Declaration," pp. 62–63.

40. Ibid.

41. Ibid., p. 63.

42. Ibid., pp. 63–64.

43. Henry Flores, "Invisible Racism in the Texas Voter ID Law," A Paper Pre-pared for Presentation at the 2013 Midwest Political Science Annual Meeting, Chi-cago, IL, April 10–13, 2013.

44. All of the data for the discussion of the March 23 debate over SB 14 was taken from the *House Journal* for that date and first cited in Flores, "Invisible Racism," Midwest Political Science Meeting, Chicago, IL, April 10–13, 2013.

45. Roberto Suro, "Texas remapping battle heats up, threatening to singe the Democrats," *New York Times,* Jan. 26, 1992.

46. Ibid.

47. AP, "DeLay trial to look at 2003 Texas redistricting," *KHOU.com,* Houston, TX, Nov. 16, 2010.

48. Author not stated, "Texas' 11 runaway senators holdout," *Washington Times,* Monday, August 4, 2003. AP, "Killer bees were last quorum-busters," *Amarillo Globe-News: Amarillo.com,* Tuesday, May 13, 2003.

49. Ibid., *LULAC v. Perry* (2006).

50. Henry Flores, "Expert Report" and "Testimony During Trial."

51. Ian Haney-Lopez, *Dog Whistle Politics,* pp. 46–50.

52. In Texas the Lieutenant Governor is both the Presiding Officer and President of the State Senate.

53. Jaime Castillo, "No rewind button for Dewhurst's attack on patriotism of Dems," *San Antonio Express-News,* May 18, 2007.

54. Gary Scharrar, "Mario is Back (Updated)," *Blog.chron.com,* May 21, 2007.

55. *Hunter v. Underwood,* 471 U.S. 222 (1985).

56. Ian Haney López, *Dog Whistle Politics.*

57. Ibid., p. 46.

58. Undated e-mail from Congressman Lamar Smith, D00000128. Also, e-mail dated April 05, 2011, Subject: Fwd:FWD:, Attachment: 20110405161822763.pdf, Please see attached. It is confidential from Lamar. From: Ashlee Vinyard To: Gerardo Interiano.

59. Henry Flores, PhD, "Supplemental Expert Report on Behalf of Rodriguez Defendant Intervenors," June 8, 2012, pp. 8–9. Flores Direct Testimony in *Texas v. Holder, et al., No. 11-CV-01303 (DDC).*

60. U.S. Bureau of the Census, *Race, Hispanic or Latino, and Age: 2000,* American Fact-Finder, http://factfinder2.census.gov/faces/tableservices/jsf/pages/product view.xhtml?pid=DEC_00_PL-QTPL&prodType=table; U.S. Bureau of the Census, *Race, Hispanic or Latino, Age, and Housing Occupany: 2010,* American Fact-Finder, http://factfinder2.census.gov/faces/tableservices/jsf/pages/productview .xhtml?pid=DEC_10_PL_QTPL&prodType=table.

61. *Births by Public Health Region, County and City of Residence: Texas,* Texas Department of State Health Services, http://www.dshs.state.tx.us/chs/vstat/vs10/t09b .shtm. http://www.dshs.state.tx.us/chs/vstat/vs11/t09B.shtm.

62. Sylvia Manzano, "Texas Report: America's Voice," *Latino Decisions,* February 2014.

63. Texas State Data Center, *Census 2010 Summary File 1,* http://txsdc.utsa.edu/ Data/Decennial/2010/Index.aspx.

64. Haney-López, *Dog Whistle Politics,* pp. 30–31.

65. See, e.g., Ana Campoy and Maurice Tamman, "Latino Numbers Soar in Texas, Promising More Political Clout," *Wall Street Journal,* February 18, 2011. http:// online.wsj.com/article/SB10001424052748703561604576150772005192358.htm.

66. Susan Combs, "Texas in Focus: A Statewide View of Opportunities, *Texas Comptroller of Public Accounts,* http://www.window.state.tx.us/specialrpt/tif/popula tion.html.

67. U.S. Bureau of the Census, *Selected Characteristics of the Native and Foreign-Born Populations, 2006–2010 American Community Survey 5-Year Estimates,*

American FactFinder, http://factfinder2.census.gov/faces/tableservices/jsf/pages/productview.xhtml?pid=ACS_10_5YR_S)501&prodType=table.

68. January 13, 2011 interview on KXAN Austin, available at http://www.youtube.com/watch?v=6IiQQzfsoUA.

69. *Press Release: Representative Riddle Files "Arizona Style" Legislation, Voter ID Bill,* Debbie Riddle: State Representative (May 23, 2012), http://debbieriddle.org/representative-riddle-files-arizona-style-legislation-voter-id-bill.

70. *Hearing on HB 516 Before the House Committee on Elections,* 2005 Legislature, 79th Session, 1:36-1:37 (Tex. 2005), http://www.house.state.tx.us/video-audio/committee-broadcasts/committee-archives/player/?session=79&committee=240&ram=50216p13 (Statement of Rep. Betty Brown, responding to Rep. Rafel Anchia's comments about Latino population trends).

71. Texas Conservative Coalition Research Institute, *Porous Borders, Porous Elections: The Imperative to Verify Voters' Citizenship* (December 2006).

72. Illegal Immigration Task Force, Texas Conservative Coalition Research Institute, *State Approaches to Illegal Immigration* (October 2006).

73. *Invited and Public Testimony Regarding Interim Charges 3 and 8 Which Involve Voter Identification and Lobbying Practices Respectively: Hearing Before the Senate Committee on State Affairs,* 2006 Interim Leg., 44:47-53-55 (Tex. 2006), http://www.senate.tx.us/avarchive/ramav.php?ram=00002793.

74. *The Week in the Rearview Mirror, Texas Tribune: Texas Weekly* (May 21, 2007) http://www.texastribune.org/texas-weekly/vol-23/no-46/rearview.

75. Clay Robinson, "Dewhurst backs voter ID bill, moving primary," *Houston Chronicle* (April 25, 2007.

76. *Exerpt of Hearing Regarding HB 1290, HB 266, HB 101, HB 218, and HB 626 Before the House Committee on Elections,* 2007 Leg., 80th Sess. 57-58 (Tex. 2007).

77. Letter from Dennis Bonnen to Mike Murphy, June 21, 2007, Texas Bates No. 5994-5995.

78. *82nd Texas Legislative Session: Legislative Update from the IRCOT Team,* Immigration Reform Coalition of Texas, http://www.ircot.com/pending_legislation.htm.

79. *Insider's Report: Bonnen files illegal immigration bill,* Dennis Bonnen: State Representative (Jan. 13, 2011). http://www.dennisbonnen.com/index.php?option=com_content&view=article&id=60:bonnen-files-illegal-immigration-bill&catid=1:news&Itemid=2.

80. *Excerpt of Hearing Before the House Committee on Elections,* 2009 Leg., 81st Sess. (Tex. 2009), http://www.youtube.com/watch?v=1LFITORcYYw.

81. Deposition of Rep. Patricia Harless, 335:14-338:13, June 13, 2012.

82. Charles Perry, "DOJ-Stand down on voter ID," *Amarillo Globe-News* (Mar. 31, 2012) http://amarillo.com/opinion/opinion-colmnist/guest-columnist/2012-03-31/doj-stand-down-voter-id.

83. Wade Goodwyn, *Texas Republicans Take Harder Line on Immigration,* National Public Radio (March 29, 2011), http://www.npr.org/2011/03/29/134956690/texas-republicans-take-harder-line-on-immigration.

84. Ibid.

85. Letter from David Dewhurst to John Beck, Todd Smith, Feb. 8, 2011, Deposition Exhibit US-88 in *Texas v. Holder.*

86. *David Dewhurst Opposes Illegal Immigration,* David Dewhurst: U.S. Senate, http://www.dewhurstfortexas.com/david-dewhurst-opposes-illegal-immigration, Jay Root, "Texas Voter ID Bill Passes Senate, Heads to House," AP (Jan. 27, 2011).

87. Debbie Riddle, *Deposition,* 45:14-52:15, May 31, 2012.

88. Peggy Fikac, "A Republican, his mother and Voter ID," *Chron.com* (Apr. 24, 2007, 5:16 pm).

89. Royal Masset, "The Voter ID Bill will kill my mother's right to vote," *Quorum Report* (Apr 23, 2007).

90. Juan Castillo, "Voter ID debate replete with drama, but is voter fraud an urgent problem?," *Austin American Statesman,* May 23, 2007.

91. Ibid.

92. Ibid.

93. Ibid.

94. W. Gardner Shelby, "Voter ID fight takes new shape at Capitol," *Austin American Statesman,* Mar. 9, 2009.

95. Christy Hoppe and Terence Stutz, "ID win could backfire for GOP: Many Latinos say bill targets them; experts see that costing votes," *Dallas Morning News,* Mar. 16, 2009.

96. Wayne Slater, "Texas attorney general's two-year effort fails to unravel large-scale voter-fraud schemes," *Dallas Morning News,* May 18, 2008.

97. Gary Scharrar, "Cheating rarely seen at polls," *San Antonio Express News,* March 25, 2012.

98. Ciara O'Rourke, "How likely are you to be struck by lightning?" *Austin American Statesman,* Apr. 11, 2011.

99. Dennis Bonnen, *Deposition,* 95:9–96:19, June 6, 2012.

100. Todd Smith, *Deposition,* 188:16–189:7, June 1, 2012.

101. Senate Journal, 82nd Legislature, Regular Session, pp. 1017–1019.

102. Troy Fraser, *Deposition,* pp. 92–94, June 13, 2012.

103. See, e.g., list of eighteen Justice Department objections to statewide election changes in Texas since 1975, http://www.justice.gov/crt/about/vot/sec5/tx_obj2.php.

104. Thomas Carlyle, *Sartor Resartus,* 1836. Reprint. New York: Oxford University Press, 2000.

105. Rebecca Frost, Statement at Capitol Rally, June 11, 2011. http://www.youtube.com/watch?v=QISLjdGGpWQ&feature=player_embedded#at=48.

106. *Hearing before Senate Committee on Transportation and Homeland Security,* 2011 Leg., 82nd Sess. (Tex. 2011), http://www.youtube.com/watch?v=hNKWISYPdZ4.

107. *Hearing before Senate Committee on Transportation & Homeland Security,* 2011 Leg., 82nd Sess. (Tex. 2011), http://www.youtube.com/watch?v=hNKWISYPdZ4.

108. Ibid.

109. *Texas House Journal,* Mar. 23, 2011. http://www.journal.house.state.tx.us/hjrnl/82r/pdf/82RDAY40FINAL.PDF#page=74.

Chapter Seven

Strategic Racism Uncovered

The next steps in evaluating the new *Arlington Heights* Factors as a scientifically accepted way in which to uncover whether racial purpose fueled a specific public policy initiative and/or process are to present the working hypotheses of the investigation together with a discussion of the findings. The chapter concludes with a presentation of what was learned from the exercise and what other issues require exploration. The explication of the findings will include an extended discussion of a way in which the data may be interpreted for the courts and conclusions reached through the application of the refined *Arlington Heights* Factors.

Recapitulating what we have discussed to this point results in two general conclusions. Restructuring the *Arlington Heights* Factors to discover whether racial purpose played the principal role in the redistricting process and in the construction and passage of SB 14 proved successful. In both cases, racial purpose was the guiding light the Texas legislative leaders and their staffs followed as they designed the congressional and house districts and the voter identification bill that were passed during the 2011 legislative session. Direct evidence was found in the redistricting case that proved beyond a doubt that racial purpose was the driving force behind the diminution of the Latino vote. In the case of SB 14, a plethora of circumstantial evidence derived from historiography, legislative records, and media sources provided the evidence supporting the contention that racial purpose laid at the heart of SB 14.

The second conclusion is that restructuring the *Arlington Heights* Factors from ten to four categories allows for the creation of a more efficient, if not elegant, research design that uncovered racial purpose in both cases. This same design may also be used in future litigation where it is contended that racial purpose is behind an alleged discriminatory action in the public sector.

DISCUSSION OF THE FINDINGS

Hypothesis 1—Racial purpose influenced the manner in which certain congressional and state house districts were designed during the 2011 Texas Legislative Session

The evidence is relatively straightforward for Hypothesis 1. The evidence trail begins with the e-mail communications between Messrs. Eric Opiela and Gerardo Interiano where they discuss the need for the creation of a metric that will allow for the creation of Hispanic-majority districts that will elect only Republican candidates while, simultaneously, inhibiting Latino voters from electing candidates of their choice. The evidence suggests that the main reasons these specific efforts were undertaken were to give the appearance that there was no violation of the VRA provisions on retrogression and to allow the Republican Party to retain at least two congressional seats. Second, Mr. Opiela, the Republican operative who appears to have started the conversation surrounding the creation and use of the metrics, understands that Latinos most likely would and will not support Republican candidates for office. The evidence for the second reason is produced by Dr. Engstrom's expert report on the racially polarized nature of elections in Texas over the previous decade. These data reveal that the racially polarized nature of elections, during the era covered in Professor Engstrom's report, is a continuation of a pattern that has existed for several decades unabated as shown in Dr. Flores's expert report.

Racially polarized voting is a reflection of the strained racial relations that have been in existence in the state since the first Anglos arrived in the 1820s. The combination of discriminatory treatment and the manipulation of racial images through the use of racial shields in the twenty-first century simply harden and institutionalize racial polarization. The argument that the data in Dr. Engstrom's and Dr. Flores's reports reflect partisan rather than racial polarization is only reflected in the general election results. Nevertheless, the patterns of racial polarization remain even when nonpartisan or primary elections are analyzed. In the end, race underlies the partisan separation because it is clear that the Republican Party, in Texas, has taken a particularly antagonistic attitude toward Latinos, as the Democrats did before 2000. This attitude is exemplified by the efforts of Republicans in the legislature in 2011 when more than one hundred pieces of legislation, including the Sanctuary City and English Only Laws, were passed over the objections of Democratic lawmakers.

The evidence trail leading from the Opiela e-mail moves to the tables produced in Dr. Flores's report indicating how election precincts having a majority of Latino voters and with records of high performance were moved out of Congressional District 23 and majority-Latino precincts, from adjacent congressional districts, having low-performance records were moved in to CD23. More than 600,000 individuals residing along the jurisdictional boundaries of CD23 were manipulated in order to achieve the desired outcome. This resulted in a congressional district that showed an increase in the Latino majority population but would turn out at a lower rate creating favorable electoral conditions for the Republican congressional candidate.

In the other congressional district under investigation, CD27, the data would not allow for the simple manipulation of precincts along the jurisdictional boundaries. Instead this district had to be redesigned completely. The counties to the south of Nueces County, which were overwhelmingly Latino, were completely removed and replaced with counties to the north of Nueces which were mostly Anglo. Again, Latinos were removed because it was believed by the redistricters that they would not support Republican Party candidates but that the Anglos would.

It is clear from just these actions that the Latino population was manipulated in order that an electorally favorable situation was created for Republican candidates ensuring the party's control over the state's congressional delegation. The goal in the manipulation of the Latino population in the state house districts was to ensure that the Republican Party gained and maintained a "supermajority" in that chamber to prevent the minority party from influencing any legislation. By far the most convincing evidence that racial purpose was the impetus for redistricting in Texas was the state did not even attempt to refute the racial purpose allegations during the redistricting trial.

Hypothesis 2—Racial purpose influenced the submission, design, and passage of Senate Bill 14-The Voter Identification and Verification Act of 2011. The evidence that racial purpose was the driving force behind the initiation, design, and passage of SB 14 lies initially in the manner in which the goals of the legislation were set forth. When SB 14 was first proposed it was advertised as a bill that was necessary to prevent illegal aliens or immigrants from crossing the border and casting fraudulent ballots in Texas elections. Even when initially confronted with research, in earlier legislative sessions that evidence was lacking of in-person voter fraud on the part of illegal immigrants, supporters of SB 14 refused to modify the legislation. In one important instance an African American legislator, during the debate in the house, pointed out that it didn't even make sense for individuals in the state illegally to reveal their presence by voting, to no avail. Another opposing legislator pointed out that voter fraud in Texas occurs with mail-in ballots and SB 14 did not address this issue. As the debate became heated and moved from the senate to the house, supporters dropped references to voting fraud of illegal immigrants. The goal of SB 14 now became to protect the ballot's integrity and security. Opponents then pointed out that the Republican Party had been dominant for a while so it didn't make any sense that they were pushing legislation to protect the integrity and security of the election system. Again, to no avail. There were five attempts to make amendments to SB 14 to ensure that it did not violate the tenets of the VRA; all were tabled. Every attempt to raise a discussion concerning the effects of SB 14 on minority communities was avoided. In the final analysis SB 14 was passed in both chambers along partisan lines over the objections of the minority senators and representatives. Most important to this discussion was that although the goal of SB 14 was changed, dropping the reference to illegal immigrants, the substance of the legislation remained unchanged.

The refusal to listen to any suggestion that the bill might have a deleterious effect on racial minority voters, the bill could not achieve its stated goals, and the lack of funds available to implement the bill all raise the suspicion that there was simply racial purpose underlying the bill. The bill was designed to make it more difficult for constituent groups who tend to vote in support of Democrats, specifically Latinos, African Americans, the young and elderly, from registering and casting a ballot.

JURISPRUDENTIAL LAYER

There are several layers of analysis to this investigation, therefore the findings are relative to specific layers. For instance, from a jurisprudential perspective the results were quite clear. The courts found against Texas in both cases. The Federal District Court in San Antonio found that Texas had acted with racial purpose in the drawing of the congressional and house districts and ordered the state to redraw the districts. The state appealed to the U.S. Supreme Court, which upheld that racial purpose part of the decision but pointed out that the district court had erred in neglecting to consider the parts of the redistricting plan that passed constitutional muster. Instead, the District Court in Texas had chosen to say that it was going to draw an "independent map" based on neutral principles. Regardless, the Supreme Court concurred with the lower court and Texas was forced to redraw parts of both redistricting plans.[1] In the end the state opted for allowing the Federal District Court to draw the plans that were used for the 2012 elections and during the subsequent legislative session, the state chose not to redraw plans but to continue using the court-drawn plans until the next round of redistricting in 2020. Some of the plaintiffs disagreed with the court-drawn plan and filed another suit that was heard in the summer of 2014 as a Section 3(c) petition.

Research Design Layer—Modifying the *Arlington Heights Factors*

For the community of expert witnesses, this research can be seen as a comprehensive starting point of how to apply the *Arlington Heights* Factors. The most important weakness of using the *Arlington Heights* Factors as an analytical tool or model is generally that working with a model having ten characteristics is unwieldy. Understandably when the court made their observations in *Arlington Heights* they were attempting to present comprehensive guidance for attorneys. The courts' astuteness notwithstanding, they created a methodological problematic for social scientists. Complicating the methodological landscape, the court even added an eleventh category intimating that other areas of investigation might exist beside the stated ten within which appropriate data might be uncovered.

One of the most important principles of social science research is to develop a research strategy that is as simple as possible yet elegant in its ability to address the complexity of a social research problem. The issue at hand and the available data and resources that may be brought to bear on the project also guide simplicity and elegance. One of the most important first steps in developing such a research strategy is to narrow the scope of the design as much as possible without affecting the design's elegance. One easy way in which this can be accomplished is by merging some of the characteristics, creating a smaller group that require discussion. This step is easy to accomplish when considering the *AHFs* because many of the original ten characteristics overlap with each other in the first place. In the first chapter of this volume the eleven *Arlington Heights* Factors are presented as initially identified by the court. However, the description of each of the factors indicates that many of the factors are actually either the same as or are embedded in others. The table below depicts the original eleven Factors compared to the four modified Factors.

As the information in the table displays original Factors 1 and 4, "Disproportionate Impact" and "Effect on Population," can be combined into one category labeled "Disparate Impact." Both are illustrated by many of the same variables and data used to demonstrate Disparate Impact in Voting Rights

Table 7.1. Modifying the *Arlington Heights* Factors

Old Factors	New Factors
1 and 4	Disparate Impact
2, 3, and 5	Historical Background of Decision
3, 6, and 7	Specific Sequence of Events Leading to Challenge
8, 9, and 10	Legal and Administrtive History

litigation such as comparative socioeconomic statistics. Here the beginning of the "sensitive inquiry" begins with a display of consistent patterns of racial polarization data. These statistics generally referred to by practitioners and professionals as "RPV" (Racial Polarization Voting), provide the core data indicating that two different racial groups perceive candidates and politics quite differently from each other. From here the other factors are brought into the analyses in an attempt to understand why racial polarization in the electorate exists.

Original Factors, 2, 3, and 5 may be grouped as one factor which can be named "The Historical Background of the Decision." Each of the original factors requires developing a chronology of what led up to the final passage of the policy in question. All of these factors allow the investigator to determine whether racial purpose exists as a motivating force in the development of the policy. Grouping original factors 3, 6, and 7 develops the third modified factor, "Specific Sequence of Events Leading to Challenge." Original Factor 3 is equally important in this modified category because it also speaks to the rationale as to why plaintiffs feel that they were wronged thus bringing the lawsuit initially. The final modified category, labeled "Legal and Administrative History," combines original factors 8, 9, and 10 and speaks to the manner in which the legislation was managed from its inception through final passage. This factor is where investigators attempt gathering data as to any unusual changes or modifications to traditional legislative policies or procedures. Essentially this factor is intended to uncover any irregularities in the normal or traditional legislative process surrounding the passage of the legislation in question. The data in this category discusses the history of the legislation's origins, the original rationale and goals for the legislation, evidence of public and legislative hearings and debates, and final debate and passage. The investigator is attempting to uncover any irregularities or departures from the normal way in which legislation is passed.

The principal difficulty in this type of research is that several of the factors require a great deal of depth in investigation as they entail developing historical behavioral patterns of jurisdictions. The most direct evidence, as pointed out by the court in *Arlington Heights,* where clear statements of discriminatory behavior on the part of the political actors involved, is often lacking. In the redistricting case, however, a "smoking gun" was found in the e-mail communication between the redistricters. "Smoking gun" memos are normally not available and attorneys will do all possible to prevent these from entering the record. Consequently, the depth of research under the court's "totality of circumstances" rule must be performed because racial purpose is generally determined using a "preponderance of evidence" test. This latter test is generally the guiding rule in most civil cases and simply requires obtaining as much evidence as possible within the given time frame in order to allow the court to reach a conclusion that racial purpose was the driving force behind the legislation being contested. There is no defined threshold or standard for the "preponderance of evidence test" so one must simply continue to build toward what the judge or judicial panel feels is an acceptable evidentiary threshold.

Methodological Layer

Much was learned from a scholarly perspective both from a methodological and a theoretical perspective. In the world of methodology it is evident that in research areas where there is a great deal of uncertainty, such as hidden behavioral activity or unspoken intentions, what can be called "gray data areas," the most fruitful research methodology is a mixed-methods research (MMR) approach. Quantitative methodologies are limited to discrete databases but are necessary in order to understand phenomena such as racially polarized voting, the voting behavior of various racial groups and so forth. Quantitative methods are of little assistance when attempting to detect the construction and use of "racial shields." In other words, quantitative methods are not suitable to the development of a chronology of the way racial rhetoric changes as society evolves. Historiography, social behavior, and understanding the construction of racism or the development of "strategic racism" require differing types of qualitative methodological approaches. These methods also have their limitations in that they cannot cross over and perform the same discovery as quantitative techniques. The recommended and preferred approach, then, in order to obtain a complete and thorough picture of the role racial purpose plays in voting rights litigation, is a judicious combination of both quantitative and qualitative approaches. As a result the *Arlington Heights* Factors modified from ten characteristics to four in order to make data gathering much easier, meet the scientific method's standards. A hypothesis (es) can be constructed that can be tested, variables can be identified and operationalized, data can be identified and analyzed in a systematic manner, and the data are of sufficient quality to address the hypothesis (es). Essentially, the modified *Arlington Heights* Factors allow for a facile merging of both qualitative and quantitative techniques that can be applied to determine whether racial purpose or intent is a central element, if not the principalmotivating force, behind a law or policy contested under the VRA.

Theoretical Layers

Defining Racial Shields

From a theoretical perspective the search for racial purpose in both of these cases provides a rich data source for exploring the work of academics who are performing "cutting edge" research in the fields of "whiteness studies,"[2] "abolition theory,"[3] "color-blind theory,"[4] and "strategic racism."[5] These areas overlap somewhat with "critical race theory" in legal studies but are markedly different methodologically. Nevertheless, they are the only fields of contemporary political theory that are attempting to decipher the evolving world of racism. As discussed throughout this work, racism and the concomitant use of racial epithets have evolved. What passed as common, albeit base, language and racial characterizations from the eighteenth through middle twentieth centuries are no longer socially acceptable.[6] The old terminology has changed with the times, but changed in a strategic fashion; today "racial shields" are used in the place of the old racist and racial vocabulary. Racial shields are words or language used to replace traditional references to a race or racial group. Where the original language is crude and vulgar, the racial shields tend to be unobtrusive, bureaucratic and objective appearing. Instead of referring to Latinos as "wetbacks" they are now referred to as "illegal immigrants." This particular reference sometimes used in concert with words such as "invasion from the south" conjures images of "hordes of Mexicans flooding across the border."[7] This language is used to generate political support for white candidates by appealing to the xenophobia of less knowledgeable or uneducated white voters. The shield, then, conceals the intended xenophobic appeal's intention to elicit a certain action triggered by that appeal. The language may not be intended to directly harm any particular group of individuals; rather, it provides the speaker with a strategic advantage by organizing his or her constituents around the racial connotations of the verbiage. In this instance, the anti-immigrant language becomes the racial shield for anti-Mexican sentiments. This imagery sends a signal to a certain group of voters having negative perceptions of Mexicans that this politician will view policies through racist lenses or, at least lenses compatible with those of their constituents. The verbiage surrounding a particular law, such as in the case of SB 14, was also anti-immigrant and designed to signal potential supporters that the legislation was designed to create a voter participation barrier against Latinos. The racial shield, in other words, is designed as a strategic weapon to gain a political advantage and shield racist opinions, attitudes, and actions from the public eye.[8]

RACIAL SHIELDS AND THE PERSISTENCE OF RACISM

Racial shields evolve because society's mores and attitudes change over time but a society's attitudes toward various racial groups do not. One of the most striking aspects of this work is the fact that race and racism play such persistent roles throughout the history of electoral politics, specifically redistricting politics, in Texas. Why this is the case requires attempting to understand why race and racism seem to have a prominent role in the historical development of Texan culture. As discussed earlier and by other authors, the relations between Anglos and Latinos since their first encounters have been fraught with racial tension. As Anglos subordinated Latinos economically, politically, and culturally they did so using race as the rationale. This treatment has led to a persistent "racialization" of Latinos to date.[9] As a result Latinos are seen and treated differently by Anglos in almost every walk of life on a daily basis. In other words, Latinos were and always have been treated differently by Anglos because of their race. No matter which assimilationist tactic Latinos pursue, whether it's insisting to identify as "white" or "American," the group as a whole are seen as different, as other and not part of what is normally accepted as essential contributors or members of the core American culture. This otherness coupled with separate treatment is exemplified in the creation of separate educational and social facilities, segregated residential patterns, and different treatment in the legal and political processes. The Supreme Court recognized this and directly stated as such in their opinion in *Hernandez v. Texas* (1954).

Perhaps one avenue to pursue in seeking the answer to the persistency of the race quandary can be found in the controversial work of Daniel Jonah Goldhagen.[10] Goldhagen published research attempting to determine why a large number of Germans willingly participated in the Holocaust that decimated European Jewry. His research was an attempt at countering the arguments of those who felt that the actions of German Nazis during World War II against Jews were the result of coercion by party officials, officials simply obeying orders from their superiors, or of decision makers falling prey to a "herd mentality." Regardless of the excuse, Dr. Goldhagen proposed, after extensive documentary and survey research, that the principal motivation for the extermination of the Jews was a deep-seated anti-semitism buried deep in the historical memory of German culture. So the extermination of the Jews was an outcome of this deep-seated hatred toward Jews. Although he was vilified by many historians, Goldhagen's work won several awards including the Gabriel A. Almond Award, in 1994, from the American Political Science Association for the best dissertation in comparative politics and the 1997 Democracy Prize from the *Journal for German and International Politics*. His work was criticized primarily because his conclusions appeared too absolutist, giving the impression of accusing all Germans of anti-Semitism or, at a minimum, possessed of anti-Semitic feelings. A close reading of Goldhagen's research, however, does not necessarily have to be interpreted so narrowly because his research also uncovered many exceptions to the horrific anti-Semitic actions of the Nazis. In his seminal work, Goldhagen describes many instances where Germans were aghast at discovering the savagery of the Holocaust and many instances where Germans tried to hide or assist in Jews escaping the clutches of their tormentors.

The importance of Dr. Goldhagen's work is that it provides an initiating point from which the question concerning the persistence of racism in Texas politics may be addressed. He identified eight elements that had to be demonstrated empirically that would allow one to conclude whether prejudice, in his case anti-Semitism, existed within a society or culture existed. If these characteristics existed within a society, then Goldhagen indicated that prejudice drove the extermination policies and processes. The discussion here is obviously quite different and is designed to address why long-term persistence of racism exists within the Texas public policy process. As a result, not all of Goldhagen's research is appropriate but some of it, some of the elements, may assist in discerning the depth and breadth of the racial prejudice that does exist in Texas today and provide the answer as to how racial purpose came to be infused in the redistricting process and the design and passage of SB 14 during the 2011 legislative session.

Borrowing from Dr. Goldhagen[11] suggests that the model adopted here must include at least the following variables. The variables also appear to address the Court's concerns in *Arlington Heights.*

1. A historical record of Latinos being referred to differently along racial lines in order to be identified as a distinctly separate racial group.
2. Evidence of disparate treatment of Latinos at the hands of various institutions in the state's history.
3. The disparate treatment of Latinos in various public policy settings is treated as part of the normal public policy process.
4. Finally, evidence that the dominant cultural race is treated differently than Latinos in comparative policy areas.

It goes without saying that each of the above variables must be presented within a historical context. If not, then one can argue that racism is not persistent but may simply be a coincidental occurrence as the State of Texas argued during both trials. It must be clear that this does not mean that if evidence exists that "anti-Latino" bias is an essential element in Texas' political culture that all Anglo-Texans who participate in the development or passage of legislation passed with racial purpose are racists. On the contrary, discovering deep-seated prejudices within anyone is impossible without thorough investigation by psychologists or sociologists. What is being proposed is that "anti-Latino" bias is an essential element in Texan culture and this bias may be brought to bear by some decision makers during the process. Other supporters may have been coerced, were following a herd mentality for various reasons, or may have negotiated some arrangement to trade a vote for future considerations.

Essentially, what is being proposed here is that an "anti-Latino" bias, a racist pall, overlaid the legislative and policy making deliberations that produced both the redistricting plans and SB 14. Moreover, this pall was the result of a long, historical evolution that began when Anglos and Latinos were first introduced to each other and continues to this day. Like many cultural attributes or socialization forces this bias does not infect necessarily all who are exposed to it. Some individuals outrightly and forcefully reject socialization pressures; others wholeheartedly embrace them. Nevertheless, the bias can be so deep-seated that it can find its way into the public policy process through the actions of a few influential and powerful legislators or political actors.

The data presented throughout this volume speaks directly to the four variables in the model presented above. As discussed at the beginning of this work, the relationship between Anglos and Latinos in Texas has remained filled with tension and racial animosity over the more than two hundred years these groups have interacted with each other. Discriminatory policies adopted by Anglos, after taking control of the government and economy of the state, placed Latinos in a subordinate social and political position. This subordinate position has not allowed Latinos to advance for more than a hundred years. This creates a "lag time" where Latinos fall further behind and deeper into the lower levels of society from which it is almost impossible to extricate themselves except on an individual basis. An essential element of the discrimination that Latinos have faced in Texas is the manner in which barriers to their political participation have been constructed in order to minimize their political influence. Beginning with the "white primaries" and poll taxes to the sophisticated redistricting and implementation of the most stringent voter identification card requirement in the United States, Latinos have had to struggle to have their vote fully count in almost all elections in the state. With their vote less valued than that of whites, Latinos are also less as citizens than Anglos. Where Anglos enjoy the gold standard of citizenship because their vote counts, Latinos don't enjoy the same level of citizenship because their vote is diluted and valued less.

The history of voting rights litigation in Texas reveals decades of efforts on the part of the state's leadership to inhibit minority voters from exercising their franchise fully. Beginning with the "White Primaries" of the 1920s and the poll taxes imposed in the 1930s through the recurring redistricting lawsuits of the 1970s, 1980s, 1990s, 2000s and now the current decade reveals the intense and obstinate refusal to allow Latinos and African Americans to be full citizens in the state's political culture. This history is both at the heart of the intense racial polarization afflicting the state but also an important reason for maintenance of the VRA, particularly a preclearance provision.

The state's persistence in violating the VRA is simply a reflection of the overall political culture of the state. On one level it speaks to the ideological orientation of the elected leadership because they have directed staff to write the discriminatory policies required to keep Latinos and African Americans in their subordinated political condition. This can be argued as simply a matter of libertarian politics where the state leadership struggles against the imposition of laws from the federal government. This theme is a recurring one in almost all state level elections with Governor Perry even supporting a state secessionist movement briefly until it became a political embarrassment.[12] This anti-government sentiment was found in both cases here. The state argued that times had changed and the discrimination that existed during the passage of the VRA in 1965 no longer existed. This was first trumpeted in the *Northwest Austin Municipal Utilities District, No. 1* opinion articulated by Chief Justice Roberts. Justice Roberts opined the same perception in the *Shelby County* decision, saying it was one of the main reasons for overturning Section 4 (b) of the VRA and gutting the pre-clearance provisions. This argument is a racial shield to conceal a frontal attack on voting rights in the United States by conservative ideologues. Both lawsuits discussed here found the State of Texas arguing not just that times had changed and racial tensions were not what they were but that the provisions of the VRA violated the Tenth Amendment of the Constitution. The state's attorneys even gave the Roberts Court added fuel by suggesting in their briefs that Sec 2 of the VRA, one of the permanent sections of the law, has passed its prime and is no longer needed because racial discrimination in electoral law has disappeared opening the door for Justice Roberts's team to do even more damage to voting rights.

IS IT POLITICS OR RACE?

One of the most important questions raised in both trials is a seeming conundrum raised by judges several times—Judge Tatel certainly raised it during the SB14 trial—was the distinction between whether racial polarization or the actions of the Texas State legislature are purely political and not racially oriented. One reason for this conundrum in voting rights cases may be found in the manner racial polarization is demonstrated in the litigation process, a demonstration confined by the parameters and rules governing quantitative analyses. Normally a database is constructed where the percentage of votes received by a particular candidate is regressed on the percentage of voters of a racial group, i.e., Latinos, African Americans, or Anglos, in a set of election precincts in and within a given jurisdiction. The most common elections used are general elections and feature a racial minority versus an Anglo candidate. General elections are the most commonly used in these analyses because they are the most abundant that feature candidates of different races competing against one another. The data are then subjected to an algorithm, such as EI, and regression analyses are performed yielding estimations of support for each candidate by race. Racial polarization is revealed when the estimates indicate that the racial groups support opposing candidates significantly.

Some observers of these results will point out that one cannot clearly determine whether the support levels are based upon support for the party or race of the candidate. This is settled partially through the derivation of additional estimates from nonpartisan and/or primary elections conducted within the same jurisdictional boundaries as the general election estimates. These latter efforts are attempts at controlling for the effects of partisanship. The final estimates are then compared to those derived from the regression analyses of the general elections.

Still the conundrum persists as it was in the redistricting and voter identification cases when various judges asked that regardless of the extent of racial polarization, it still remained that it was not clear that decision makers were making decisions either racially or politically motivated. The two experts to whom the question was addressed failed to answer the question to the satisfaction of Judge Tatel. Frankly, if Judge Tatel was not satisfied with the experts' responses, neither will be the Supreme Court.

The answer to the conundrum can be both simple and complex simultaneously. The complexity of the response is encountered as one attempts to untangle the mathematics of the regression analyses. The complexity is caused by at least three intricate, interwoven variables that defy unraveling. The first, and most simple to explain, is the nature of the operationalized variable used in the regression equation. The dependent variable in the simple equation is defined as the votes cast for the candidate. The candidate is defined two ways simultaneously, as a person of a particular race and as a candidate representing a particular party. The issue is that the voter can only cast one ballot, and it is difficult, if not impossible, to determine if voters are casting their ballots for the candidate because of their race or their partisan affiliation, at least without asking the voter and receiving a truthful response. The identification of the candidate then becomes part of the conundrum because they possess two qualities that are being measured: their race and their party affiliation. The problematic is one cannot separate one from the other methodologically without sophisticated subsequent questioning of each voter.

The second issue confounding the conundrum is the nature of regression analysis itself. As Gary King, the developer of EI, pointed out when he first offered his solution "the ecological inference problem is caused by the lack of individual-level information, no method of ecological inference, including that introduced in this book, will produce precisely accurate results in every instance."[13] Essentially, all data used in regression analyses are "group-level" data, so one can only obtain estimates of what the group prefers but one can never determine what individuals within the group are deciding for themselves.

The next issue is the nature of the group-level data used within the regression equation. Such data are based upon population estimates derived from Census Bureau aggregations that, in themselves, are fraught through with errors and are changing on any given day. This is particularly true for the Latino population where the identifiers for this group include race, self-identification as a Hispanic, and then identification by national origin. Several interesting social categories are emerging in relation to the counting of Latinos and those are the increasing number of Latinos identifying as "other" under racial and those identifying as "multiracial." The error estimations for the population data, which can be found in Bureau reports, are never considered in the calculations of the regression analyses. As a result, the regression estimates are, at best, a "point-in-time" estimate of a ballot cast by a group that may be improperly identified. This complexity of the conundrum may never be unraveled but these are the best and only data available for litigation researchers to use and the court has "blessed" the statistical techniques used in the reports supporting all sides in voting rights litigation.

As complex as the conundrum may appear it also possesses a simple response and the most important response that must be considered in voting rights litigation. Simply put, the decision of the voters, redistricters, and legislators may be political but it is driven by race and the effects fall heavily on the shoulders of a particular racial group covered by the VRA. Regardless of whether the decisions made by the individuals involved a political rationale, that decision was driven by racial considerations. As the e-mail evidence produced during the Section 5 hearing indicated together with the subsequent, detailed actions of the redistricters in redrawing CD23 race was the variable used to achieve the political end. Race preceded partisan considerations in the decisional redistricting equation. In this case racial purpose or the intention to manipulate Latino voters preceded the action to protect the incumbent. Protecting the incumbent could not be achieved without consciously manipulating Latino voters in the redistricting process.

In the voter identification case, racial purpose was uncovered through analysis of the changing rhetoric as SB 14 evolved from its initial incarnation to its final edition. The answer to Judge Tatel's question is that the actions of the decision makers were not solely based on racial or political considerations. In Texas, the political goal could not and cannot be achieved without the use of race, thus having a racial purpose. For Republicans, or for that matter if the tables were turned, the Democrats, to maintain political control, they must use race to energize their constituency and manipulate the political structure. The ends in each case were political but they were preceded by a racial concern. The end result was that it was the Latino community that bore the weight of the political ends. The social equation then reads that the political actions of voters, decision makers, and legislators were sandwiched between a racial purpose and intent and resulted in a racial effect. In the final analysis the answer to the conundrum is that the decisions in the redistricting and voter identification cases were both racially and politically motivated. One simply cannot have one without the other in the State of Texas.

HOW CAN THIS RESEARCH BE
HELPFUL TO THE COURTS?

This research makes several significant contributions to both the scholarly and legal canons; substantively, the contributions may be identical to both fields. These case studies provide detailed accounts of how racial purpose can evolve from ideological intention, through the development of public policy, to the creation of the final legislation. In the redistricting case the original intentions of the racial strategists are quite clearly stated in a series of e-mails exchanged among them setting forth the reasons for the use of race to achieve a political goal and the manner in which to carry out the strategy. The case study then proceeds to uncover how the redistricters, acting in their capacities as "racial strategists," drew the boundaries of both congressional and state house districts to accomplish their goal of ensuring that politicians of their political party have an electoral advantage. In the final analysis, Latino voters were manipulated in such a manner that any opportunity they could possibly have of electing a candidate of their choice was denied. In effect, the value or weight of Latino voters in these districts was lessened in comparison to the votes of their Anglo fellow citizens. Latino voters found themselves casting votes that were not substantively equal to those of Anglo voters; this defines Latino citizenship as lesser than Anglo citizenship. In the words of the late Professor Olson, this mitigates against the "color-blind" society the United States claims it is moving toward. All citizens are equal under the law when all citizens are valued equally and treated accordingly. In the world of electoral politics, this translates into all votes, regardless of who cast them, being given the same weight. Full citizenship, the "gold standard of citizenship," can only be achieved when all citizens are treated equally, including valuing equally each of their votes. The manner in which the Texas redistricters manipulated Latino voters denied Latinos access to that "gold standard." Latinos were considered citizens because they had a right to cast a vote but they were not "fully" citizens because the value of their vote was, through mathematical manipulation, diluted.

The case study reviewing the creation and passage of SB 14 provided a clear example of the evolution of racial shields and how they were changed as each was proven to be false. This case began with the use of a racial shield defined as undocumented immigrants crossing the border to cast fraudulent ballots, as a rationale for the legislation. The choice of acceptable documents allowing one to vote was an indication of the racial intent underlying the legislation. The only photo identification cards allowed by SB 14 were state-issued driver's licenses, a license to carry a handgun identification card, and an identification card issued by the state. Three forms of federal identification were allowed, including a passport, a military identification card, and a certificate of citizenship. Excluded from the list were any student identification cards or other state-issued cards such as employment identifications, even those issued by the state under certain circumstances. What is interesting about the list is that both the state-issued driver's license and state-issued identification cards are obtainable without photo identification and are also susceptible to forgery.[14] Citizenship and naturalization certificates come in a broad variety depending on the year of issuance and some come with photo identification while others do not. A noncitizen can obtain a military identification card because citizenship is not a requirement for entering military service. This inconsistency was also pointed out during the legislative debate to the supporters.

During the legislative debates surrounding voter identification, both during the 2009 and 2011 sessions, research was provided to the supporters indicating the lack of in-person voter identification fraud along with evidence that the weakness in the system was in the mail-in ballot system. When it was pointed out that the goal of preventing undocumented immigrants from casting fraudulent ballots was an issue lacking substance because illegal immigrants would not expose themselves simply to cast votes in elections they probably didn't understand, the racial shield was reconstituted. Instead of preventing illegal immigrants from casting ballots, the goal of SB 14 became to protect the integrity and security of the ballot. Even though the goal was changed, the substance and particulars of SB 14 remained the same. Also, no effort was made to address the insecurity surrounding the mail-in ballot process.

Several members of the state house raised the final objections that speak directly to the issue of the role of racial purpose in this process during debate concerning the legality of SB 14. In every instance the question as to whether SB 14 violated the federal Voting Rights Act was ignored. At one point, during a particularly frustrating moment, Representative Patricia Harless indicated that it was not the state's responsibility to follow the federal law, it was the court's responsibility to tell the state it had or had not. Why supporters did not even wish to perform the research as to the legality of SB 14 is not clear given the available data. Nevertheless, supporters refused to discuss this issue as well as any issue as to whether race played a role in the creation and passage of the voter identification bill. In the end, supporters not only refused to discuss the issues concerning race, they also did not address the questions raised concerning the integrity and security of the ballot and voted, along partisan lines, to pass SB 14.

Another contribution this research makes can be found in the realm of racial studies. The data generated from the two case studies adds substantiation to the theoretical frameworks of Olson's, Bonilla-Silva's, and Haney-López's works. Both cases speak to the notion that full citizenship is a function of race as described by Olson. The removal of Latino citizens from one congressional or state house district simply to ensure that they cannot influence the outcome of an election is equal to devaluing the citizenship of these voters. The provisions of SB 14 are much the same as forcing certain groups, among which Latinos are the most prominent, to doubly register to vote. This makes Latinos doubly prove their citizenship which, according to Olson's model, would make the citizenship of Latinos worth half that of Anglos. Olson argues that democratic society has created a hierarchy of citizenship based along racial lines with African Americans at the lowest levels of the hierarchy. He does not speak of Latinos in his research. It appears that Professor Olson was also trapped in the dual-race theoretical model. According to Professor Joel Olson, the various laws that were passed after the two Reconstructions, post–Civil War and era of civil rights, to reclaim the political privilege that "whites" had lost, caused the devaluation of the citizenship of African Americans. The reaction to the First Reconstruction saw the passage of Jim Crow laws throughout the South and in many parts of the remainder of the United States. After the Second Reconstruction, the civil rights period beginning with the creation of the Civil Rights Commission by President Truman and culminating with the election of Richard Nixon in 1968, various states beginning with Mississippi began passing laws to regain the ground they lost due to the integration of public accommodations. State-level laws passed against school integration, affirmative action in school admissions, and restrictions on welfare including food stamps and Medicaid exemplified this situation. These laws were fortified by conservative Supreme Court decisions that backtracked from the gains made in voting rights and public accommodations during the era of the Warren Court. This legal *retrenchement* was accentuated by the Roberts Court's *Shelby County* decision that practically "gutted" the Voting Rights Act of 1965.

Using Olson's framework, the *retrenchement* of the Second Reconstruction served to diminish the citizenship of African Americans and placed them in another category defined by their race that was less than the citizenship category of Anglos. The actions of the redistricters during the 2011 Texas redistricting process as well as the supporters of SB 14 were a significant part of the *retrenchement* of the Second Reconstruction. At the same time, however, the devaluation of Latino citizenship is a continuation and another evolutionary stage of the activities of strategic racists in Texas state history. The history of the white primaries, the creation of the poll taxes, establishment of single member representational districts, racial districting, and establishment of strict voter identification laws have all been attempts to minimize and dilute the Latino vote. This vote dilution is not just one isolated or single action on the part of a few individuals but rather part of the normal manner in which Texas Anglo politicians have always treated Latinos. The changing demographics have provided enough evidence to racist policy makers that the only way in which they will be able to maintain control of the Texas political apparatus is to minimize the political participation and power of Latinos. This minimization lessens the value of the citizenship of Latinos, devaluing their vote and relegating them to a lower level of citizenship.

The e-mail uncovered during the redistricting trial and all of the public documentation that was part of the record during the SB 14 trial revealed that there was a clear intent to manipulate Latino voters to the advantage of the Republican Party. There was no evidence in any of the documentation that any of the individuals in control of the legislative process intended to harm Latinos because they belonged to a racial or ethnic group. That purpose may have been in the hearts and on the minds of some individual political actors but there is no way possible to discern that sort of intention. What did come through in the documentation was the intention of using Latinos as a group to create a politically advantageous position for Republican Party candidates. In the redistricting process moving Latino voters into districts where their vote becomes ineffective, where they do not have the opportunity of electing a candidate of their choice, is a strategically political decision. In the legislative process that created SB 14 the limitation of the types of identification cards and the deliberate disregard for the cost of obtaining the correct identification clearly disadvantaged entire groups of voters among whom the majority were Latinos. This too was a strategic decision. Those in control of the public policy process in both instances had the intention of diminishing the value of the Latino vote in one instance and creating additional registration barriers in the other. The decision makers, political staffers, and legislators intended to disadvantage Latino citizens in order to win, maintain, and control the political representational institutions of the state. This is a perfect example of the "strategic racism" Haney-López speaks of in his work.

In the final analysis, the usefulness of this research to the courts is that by moving away from looking at racial intent or purpose through traditional lenses when racism was defined in terms of discriminatory practices from the first half of the twentieth century practices that conjure images of the Ku Klux Klan burning crosses and intimidating individuals to prevent them from voting, the courts must move to a more sophisticated level of analysis. As Bonilla-Silva, Olson, and Haney-López have pointed out and Justice Roberts clearly indicated in both the *Northwest Austin Municipal Utility District, No. 1* and *Shelby County* opinions, times have changed and the racism of old has also changed. The changing face of racism requires new methodologies in order to understand the changing face and the fields of "whiteness studies," "color-blind studies," and "strategic racism" can lend a depth of understanding that has been lacking. Racism still exists; it is just expressed differently, requiring different methodologies to understand its sophistication.

NOTES

1. *Perez, et al. v. Perry, et al.*, 565 U.S.____(2012), *Per Curiam.*

2. Joel Olson, *The Abolition of White Democracy* (Minneapolis: University of Minnesota Press, 2004).

3. Ibid.

4. Eduardo Bonilla-Silva, *Racism without Racists: Color-Blind Racism and the Persistence of Racial Inequality in America, 4th Ed.,* New York: Rowman & Littlefield Publishers, Inc., 2014.

5. Ian Haney-López, *Dog Whistle Politics.*

6. Olson, Bonilla-Silva, and Haney-López all discuss this evolution nationally. David O'Donnell Cullen, et al. in *The Texas Right: Radical Roots of Lone Star Conservatism,* College Station, TX: Texas A & M Press, 2014 present the most comprehensive and contemporary portrayal of the evolution of racism and "whiteness politics" in Texas history.

7. This language has been used by at least one of the Republican Lieutenant Governor candidates in the 2014 elections, Mr. Dan Patrick. His language and television campaign advertisements have drawn the ire of both Republican and Democratic Latinos. One prominent Republican Latino even declared that he would vote for the Democratic candidate if Mr. Patrick wins the Republican nomination because he found Mr. Patrick's rhetoric hurtful and distasteful. *Texas Tribune,* Feb. 8, 2014.

8. Haney-López, *Dog Whistle Politics,* p. 35.

9. See extensive discussion on this topic in Julie A. Dowling's *Mexican Americans and the Question of Race,* 2014, Austin, TX: University of Texas Press, particularly in chapter 1.

10. Particularly see his *Hitler's Willing Executioners: Ordinary Germans and the Holocaust,* 1996, New York: Alfred A. Knopf, Inc. Goldhagen was an associate professor at Harvard whose research drew heavy criticism from many ideological sec-

tors. Some accused his research of being overly biased against Germans, others saw his work as that of an angry Zionist. Nevertheless, his work won several prestigious awards for research in this field.

11. The complete model may be found between pages 375–461 of *Hitler's Willing Executioners.*

12. http://politicalticker.blogs.cnn.com/2009/04/16/texas-governor-says-secession-possible/

13. King, *A Solution to the Ecological Inference Problem,* p. xv.

14. This was an issue that was raised during the legislative debate in the House on March 23, 2011. A Texas driver's license may be obtained using several forms of identification that do not have photos, see http://www.dps.texas.gov/DriverLicense for a complete list of acceptable documents.

Bibliography

Acuña, Rodolfo. 1972. *Occupied America: The Chicano's Struggle Toward Liberation.* New York: Harper & Row Publishers.

Ahram, Ariel I. 2013. "Concepts and Measurement in Multimethod Research." *Political Science Quarterly.* 66: 280–91.

Allen, Ruth. 1941. *Chapters in the History of Organized Labor in Texas.* Austin: University Of Texas Publications.

Banfield, Edward. 1970. *The Unheavenly City.* Boston, MA: Little, Brown and Company.

———. 1974. *The Unheavenly City Revisited.* Boston, MA: Little, Brown and Company.

Barr, Alwyn. 1973. *Black Texans: A History of Negroes in Texas, 1528–1971.* Austin, TX: Jenkins Publishing Co., The Pemberton Press.

Beard, Charles. 1914. *An Economic Interpretation of the Constitution of the United States.* New York: The Macmillan Company. Dexter Edition, 2003. NY: Dover Publications, Inc.

Bickerstaff, Steve. 2007. *Lines in the Sand: Congressional Redistricting in Texas and the Downfall of Tom DeLay.* Austin, TX: University of Texas Press.

Blum, Edward. 2007. *The Unintended Consequences of Section 5 of the Voting Rights Act.* Washington, DC: The AEI Press.

Bonilla-Silva, Eduardo. 2001. *White Supremacy: Racism in the Post–Civil Rights Era.* Boulder, CO: Lynne Rienner Publishers, Inc.

———. 2014. *Racism without Racists: Color-Blind Inequality in America, 4th Ed.* New York: Rowman & Littlefield.

Brater, Jonathan. Feb. 7, 2012. "The Past Is Not Past: Why We Still Need Section 5 of the Voting Rights Act." *Boston Review.*

Brennen Center for Justice. 2013. "Voting Laws Roundup, 2013." New York: New York University School of Law.

Buffon, Georg L. Leclerc. 1791. *Natural History, General and Particular.* Translated by William Smellie, 3rd ed. (Toronto: University of Toronto Libraries, 2011).

Campbell, Stanley. 1970. *The Slave Catchers: Enforcement of the Fugitive Slave Laws, 1850–1860.* Chapel Hill, NC: University of North Carolina.

Cantrell, Gregg. 1999. *Stephen F. Austin: Empresario of Texas.* New Haven, CT: Yale University Press.

Carlyle, Thomas. 1836. 2000. *Sartor Resartus.* Edited by Kerry McSweeney and Peter Saber. New York: Oxford University Press, 2008.

Cohen, Bernard I. Apr–Jun, 1976. "The Eighteenth Century Origins of the Concept of Scientific Revolution." *Journal of the History of Ideas.* Vol. 37, No. 2: 257–88.

Cooke, Henry W. 1971. "Segregation of Mexican American School Children." In Wayne Moquin with Charles Van Doren, eds. *A Documentary History of Mexican Americans.* New York: Praeger.

Davenport, Charles. 1929. *Race Crossing in Jamaica.* Washington, D.C.: The Carnegie Institute.

Davidson, Chandler. 1990. *Race and Class in Texas Politics.* Princeton, NJ: Princeton University Press.

Davidson, Chandler. 1992. "The Voting Rights Act: A Brief History." In Bernard Grofman and Chandler Davidson, eds. *Controversies in Minority Voting.* Washington, D.C: The Brookings Institution.

—— and Bernard Grofman, Editors. 1994. "The Effect of Municipal Election Structure on Black Representation in Eight Southern States." In *Quiet Revolution in The South.*

Davis, Sue. 2008. *Corwin and Peltason's Understanding the Constitution, 17th ed.* Belmont, CA: Wadsworth CENGAGE Learning.

DeLeón, Arnoldo. 1987. *Gringo Justice.* Notre Dame, IN: University of Notre Dame Press.

Delgado, Ricardo. 2009. "The Law of the Noose: A History of Latino Lynching." *Harvard Civil Rights-Civil Liberties Law Review.* Vol. 4: 297–312.

——. 2012. *Critical Race Theory: An Introduction.* New York: NYU Press.

Epstein, Richard, et al., editors. 2006. *The Future of the Voting Rights Act.* New York: Russell Sage Foundation.

Feagin, Joe R., and Karyn D. McKinney. 2003. *The Many Costs of Racism.* New York: Rowman & Littlefield Publishers, Inc.

Fehrenbach, Theodore Reed (T.R.) 1968. *Lone Star: A History of Texas and Texans.* New York: Macmillan.

Fehrenbacher, Don E. 2001. Completed and Edited by Ward M. McAfee. *The Slaveholding Republic: An Account of the United States Government's Relations to Slavery.* New York: Oxford University Press.

Fernandez, Ricardo, and Judith T. Guskin. 1981. "Hispanic Students and School Desegregation." In Willis D. Hawley, ed. *Effective School Desegregation.* Beverly Hills, CA: Sage.

Flores, Henry. 2003. *The Evolution of the Liberal Democratic State with a Case Study of Latinos in San Antonio, Texas.* Lewiston, NY: The Edwin Mellen Press.

——. Apr. 10–13, 2013. "Invisible Racism in the Texas Voter ID Law." A paper Prepared for presentation at the 2013 Midwest Political Science Annual Meeting, Chicago, IL.

Foucault, Michel. 1979. *Discipline and Punish: The Birth of the Prison.* Translated by Alan Sheridan. New York: Vintage Books.

Garcia, Mario T. 1989. *Mexican Americans: Leadership, Ideology and Identity, 1930–1960.* New Haven, CT: Yale University Press.

Gobineau, Arthur de. 1853. "An Essay on the Inequality of the Human Races."

Goldberg, Robert A. 1983. "Racial Change on the Southern Periphery: The Case of San Antonio, Texas, 1960–1965," *Journal of Southern History.* 49: 349.

———. 2010. "The Challenge of Change: Social Movements as Non-State Actors." *Utah Law Review.* Vol. 1: 65–79.

Gomez, Laura E. 2006. "Off-White in an Age of Supremacy: Mexican Elites and the Rights Of Indians and Blacks in Nineteenth Century New Mexico." In Michael A. Olivas, ed. *"Colored Men" and "Hombres Aqui:" Hernandez v. Texas and the Emergence of Mexican-American Lawyering.* Houston, TX: Arte Público Press.

Gonzales, Manuel G. 1999. *Mexicanos: A History of Mexicans in the United States.* Bloomington, IN: University of Indiana Press.

Goode, Judith, and Edwin Eames. 1996. "An Anthropological Critique of the Culture of Poverty." In George Gmelch and Walter P. Zenner, eds. *Urban Life,* 2nd ed. Lone Grove, IL: Waveland Press.

Gossett, Thomas F. 1997. *Race: The History of an Idea in America.* New York: Oxford University Press.

Grant, Madison. 1916. *Passing of the Great Race.* New York: Scribner's.

Grebler, Leo, Joan Moore, and Ralph Guzman. 1970. *The Mexican-American People: The Nation's Second Largest Minority.* New York: The Free Press.

Grofman, Bernard, Michael Migalski and Nicholas Noviello. April, 1985. "The 'Totality of Circumstances Test' in Section 2 of the 1982 Extension of the Voting Rights Act: A Social Science Perspective." *Law and Policy.* Vol. 7, Issue 2, pp. 199–223.

Guinier, Lani, and Gerald Torres. 2002. *The Miner's Canary: Enlisting Race, Resisting Power, Transforming Democracy.* Cambridge, MA: Harvard University Press.

Hamilton, Alexander, James Madison, and John Jay. 2001. "Federalist 84." In *The Federalist, The Giddeon Edition.* Edited by George W. Carey and James McClellan. Indianapolis, IN: Liberty Fund.

Handman, Max S. January, 1930. "Economic Reasons for the Coming of the Mexican Immigrant." *American Journal of Sociology* 35, No. 4.

Haney-López, Ian F. 2003. *Racism on Trial: The Chicano Fight for Justice.* Cambridge, MA: Harvard University Press.

———. 2014. *Dog Whistle Politics: How Coded Racial Appeals Have Reinvented Racism and Wrecked the Middle Class.* New York: Oxford University Press.

Harrington, Michael. 1962. *The Other America: Poverty in the United States.* New York: Simon and Shuster.

Hasen, Richard L. 2013. "Shelby County and the Illusion of Minimalism." *Legal Studies Research Paper Studies Research Paper Series No. 2013–116.* Irvine, CA: University of California School of Law, Irvine.

Hoover, Kenneth, and Todd Donovan. 2004. *The Elements of Social Scientific Thinking,* 8th ed. Belmont, CA: Thompson Wadsworth.

Immigration Coalition of Texas. Jan. 13, 2011. "Legislative Update from the IRCOT Team." http://www.ircot.com/pending-legislation.htm.

———. May 4, 2011. "82d Texas Legislative Session: Legislative Update from the IRCOT Team." http://www.ircot.com/pending_legislation.htm.

Irons, Peter. 1999. *A People's History of the Supreme Court.* New York: Viking Press.

Jefferson, Thomas. 1899. "Notes on Virginia." *The Writings of Thomas Jefferson.* New York: G. P. Putnam's Sons.

Kahneman, Daniel, Paul Slovic, and Amos Tversky, eds. 2008. *Judgment Under Uncertainty: Heuristics and Biases.* New York: Cambridge University Press.

Kahneman, Daniel. 2011. *Thinking, Fast and Slow.* New York: Farrar, Straus and Giroux.

Key, V. O. 1949. *Southern Politics in State and Nation: A New Edition.* Knoxville, TN: University of Tennessee Press.

King, Gary. 1997. *A Solution to the Ecological Inference Problem: Reconstructing Individual Behavior from Aggregate Data.* Princeton, NJ: Princeton University Press.

Kousser, J. Morgan. 1999. *Colorblind Justice: Minority Voting Rights and the Undoing of the Second Reconstruction.* Chapel Hill and London: The University of North Carolina Press.

Leonard, William. Oct. 28, 1916. "Where Both Bullets and Ballots are Dangerous." *Survey.* 86–87.

Levitt, Justin. 2007. "The Truth About Voter Fraud." The Brennen Center. New York: New York University School of Law.

Lewis, Oscar. 1959. *Five Families: Mexican Case Studies in the Culture of Poverty.* New York: Mentor.

Lowerie, Samuel H. 1932. *Cultural Conflict in Texas, 1821–1835.* New York: Columbia University Press.

Lukens, Patrick. 2012. *A Quiet Victory for Latino Rights: FDR and the Controversy Over Whiteness.* Tucson, AZ: The University of Arizona Press.

Malik, Kenan. 1996. *The Meaning of Race: Race, History and Culture in Western Society.* New York: New York University Press.

Mann, Thomas E., and Norman J. Ornstein. 2012. *It's Even Worse Than It Looks: How the American Constitutional System Collided With the New Politics of Extremism.* New York: Basic Books.

Mirandé, Alfredo. 1987. *Gringo Justice.* Notre Dame, IN: Notre Dame University Press.

Montague, Ashley. 1997. *Man's Most Dangerous Myth: The Fallacy of Race,* 6th ed. Walnut Creek, CA: Alta Mira Press.

Montejano, David. 1987. *Anglos and Mexicans in the Making of Texas, 1836–1986.* Austin, TX: University of Texas Press.

Moynahan, Patrick. 1969. *On Understanding Poverty: Perspective on the Social Sciences.* New York: Basic Books.

McWilliams, Carey. 1968. *North From Mexico: The Spanish-Speaking People of the U.S.* New York: Greenwood Publishers.

Noel, Linda C. Aug., 2011. "I am an American: Anglos, Mexicans, Natives, and the National Debate over Arizona and New Mexico Statehood." *Pacific Historical Review.* Vol. 80, No. 3.

Offe, Claus. 1974. *Structural Problems of the Capitalist State: Class Rule and the Political System, On the Selectiveness of Political Institutions.* London: Sage Publications, Inc.

Olmstead, Frederick L. 1857. *A Journey Through Texas; or, a Saddle-Trip on the Southwestern Frontier.* New York: Dix, Edwards and Co. Reprint. Austin, TX: University of Texas Press, 1978.

Olson, Joel. 2006. *Abolition of White Democracy.* Minneapolis, MN: University of Minnesota Press.

Passel, Jeffery S., D'Vera Cohn, and Ana Gonzalez-Barrera. Apr. 23, 2012. "Net Migration From Mexico Falls to Zero—And Perhaps Less." Washington, D.C.: Pew Research Center.

Perales, Nina, Luis Figueroa, and Criselda G. Rivas. Spring, 2008. "Voting Rights in Texas, 1982–2006." *Southern California Review of Law and Social Justice.* Los Angeles, CA: University of Southern California, Gould School of Law.

Perry, Michael J. 1977. "The Disproportionate Impact Theory of Racial Discrimination." *University of Pennsylvania Law Review.* 125: 540 Philadelphia, PA: University of Pennsylvania Law School.

Persily, Nathaniel. 2007. "The Promise and Pitfalls of the New Voting Rights Act." *Yale Law Journal.* 117: 174. New Haven, CT: Yale Law Journal Company, Inc.

Phillips, Michael. 2014. "Texan By Color: The Racialization of the Lone Star State." In David O'Donald Cullen and Kyle G. Wilkison, eds. *The Texas Right: The Radical Right of Lone Star Conservatism.* College Station, TX: Texas A & M University Press.

Pinder, Sherrow O. *Whiteness and Racialized Ethnic Groups in the United States.* New York: Lexington Books.

Prewitt, Kenneth. 2013. *What is Your Race? The Census and Our Flawed Efforts to Classify Americans.* Princeton, NJ: Princeton University Press.

Razak, Sherene. 1998. *Looking White People in the Eye.* Toronto: University of Toronto Press.

Rice, Mitchell F. 1986. "The Discrimination Purpose Standard: A Problem for Minorities in Racial Discrimination Litigation?" *Boston College Third World Law Journal.* 1. Boston, MA: Boston College School of Law.

San Miguel, Guadalupe, Jr. 1987. *"Let Them Take Heed:" Mexican Americans and the Campaign for Educational Equality in Texas, 1910–1981."* First Edition. Mexican American Monograph Number 11. Austin, TX: University of Texas Press.

Segrest, Mab. 1994. *Memoir of a Race Traitor.* Boston, MA: South End Press.

Shipman, Pat. 1994. *The Evolution of Racism: Human Differences and the Use and Abuse of Science.* New York: Simon & Schuster.

Small, Mario Luis, David J. Harding, and Michèle. Lamont. 2010. "Reconsidering Culture and Poverty." *Annals of the American Academy of Political and Social Science.* 629 (1): 6–27.

Smolin, Lee. 2013. *Time Reborn: From the Crisis in Physics to the Future of the Universe.* New York: Houghton Mifflin Harcourt.

Taylor, Paul. 1930. "Mexican Labor in the United States: Dimmit County. Winter Garden District. South Texas." *University of California Publications in Economics.* 6, No. 5.

———. 1934. *An American-Mexican Frontier: Nueces County, Texas.* Chapel Hill, NC: University of North Carolina Press. Reprint. New York: Russell & Russell, 1971.

Tenayuca, Emma, and Homer Brooks. 1939. "The Mexican Question in the Southwest." *Political Affairs.*

Texas Conservative Coalition Research Institute. Oct., 2006. "State Approaches to Illegal Immigration."

———. Dec., 2006. "Porous Borders, Porous Elections: The Imperative to Verify Voters' Citizenship."

Tucker, William. 2007. *The Funding of Scientific Racism: Wickliffe Draper and the Pioneer Fund.* Champaign-Urbana, IL: University of Illinois Press.

Valencia, Reynaldo, Sonia R. Garcia, Henry Flores, and José Roberto Juárez. 2007. *Mexican Americans and the Law: ¡El pueblo unido jamás sera vencido!* Tucson, AZ: University of Arizona Press.

Wachtel, Paul L. 1999. *Race in the Mind of America: Breaking the Vicious Circle Between Blacks and Whites.* New York: Routledge Press.

Webb, William Prescott. 1935. *The Texas Rangers: A Century of Frontier Defense.* Boston and New York: Houghton Mifflin. Reprint. Austin, TX: University of Texas Press, 1965.

West, Cornel. 1993. *Race Matters.* Boston, MA: Beacon Press.

Wexler, Jay. 2011. *The Odd Clauses: Understanding the Constitution Through Ten of Its Most Curious Provisions.* Boston, MA: Beacon Press.

Zinn, Howard. 2003. *The People's History of the United States.* NY: Harper Collins.

Index

About the Author

Henry Flores is the Distinguished University Research Professor of political science and international relations in the Institute for Public Administration, Politics, and Public Policy at St. Mary's University. Since 1986, Dr. Flores has served as an expert witness in more than fifty federal voting and civil rights lawsuits including serving as the statistical testifying expert in *NAACP v. Harris,* which focused on the presidential challenge in Florida in 2000. Dr. Flores is the author of *The Evolution of the Liberal Democratic State With a Case Study of Latinos in San Antonio, Texas* (2003) and coauthor of *Mexican Americans and the Law* (2004) with three other colleagues. Dr. Flores was recently honored by the School of Law for his work in Chicano civil rights. He was presented with the Lifetime Achievement Award for his contribution and continued dedication to Latino voting rights issues.

Printed in the USA
CPSIA information can be obtained
at www.ICGtesting.com
LVHW041737280124
769859LV00015B/70